D0945007

Academe in Mystery and Detective Fiction

An Annotated Bibliography

John E. Kramer
with the assistance of
Ron Hamm and Von Pittman

The Scarecrow Press, Inc.
Lanham, Maryland, and London
2000

SCARECROW PRESS, INC.

Published in the United States of America
by Scarecrow Press, Inc.
4720 Boston Way, Lanham, Maryland 20706
http://www.scarecrowpress.com

4 Pleydell Gardens, Folkestone
Kent CT20 2DN, England

This book is adapted from *College Mystery Novels: An Annotated Bibliography*.
[New York]: Garland. 0-8240-9237-6. © 1983 by John Kramer

British Library Cataloguing in Publication Information Available

Library of Congress Cataloging-in-Publication Data

Kramer, John E., 1935-
Academe in mystery and detective fiction : an annotated bibliography / John E. Kramer.
p. cm.
Includes index.
ISBN 0-8108-3841-9 (cloth : alk. paper)
1. Detective and mystery stories, American—Bibliography. 2. Detective and mystery stories, English—Bibliography. 3. Education, Higher, in literature—Bibliography. 4. College teachers in literature—Bibliography. 5. College stories, American—Bibliography. 6. College stories, English—Bibliography. I. Title.

Z1231.F4 K73 2000
[PS374.D4]
016.813'087208—dc21

00-032230

∞™ The paper used in this publication meets the minimum requirements of American National Standard for Information Sciences—Permanence of Paper for Printed Library Materials, ANSI/NISO Z39.48-1992. Manufactured in the United States of America.

Contents

INTRODUCTION

This bibliography provides citations for and annotations of 486 "college-mystery" novels. A college mystery, as I have operationally defined it for this book, is a full-length work of mystery fiction that meets one of two criteria.[1] The novel is set, all or in significant part, at an institution of higher education, or it features characters from colleges or universities who act within their academic roles in off-campus locales.[2]

The bibliography is intended for three audiences. First, it is aimed at individuals who find leisure-time pleasure in reading mystery novels that have plots, settings, and characters drawn from the world of higher education. I hope that the bibliography will direct those devotees of college mysteries—many of whom probably have their own real-life connections with academe—to stories of academic murder, mayhem, and detection that they have not previously encountered. Second, the bibliography is designed for people who might want to conduct scholarly investigations of the college-mystery subgenre of mystery fiction. Third, it is offered as a resource for those students of popular culture who are interested in the images of higher education that are projected through fiction. I hope that the book will lead members of the latter two groups to mysteries that will serve their research needs.

Almost all of the college novels cited in the bibliography are set in North America or Great Britain.[3] The citations themselves refer, in most cases, to the novels' first American editions. Citations for first British publications are provided when a mystery was published only in England, when it was published initially in England, or when it was published in England under a different title. The 486 novels were published between 1910 and 1999.[4] The entries are presented chronologically, by date of the novels' initial publications. In the many instances where more than one novel was published in a particular year, the entries for that year are presented in alphabetical order by author. Author and title indices are included at the end of the volume. Two other indices are included as well. One is an index of the colleges and universities that serve as settings for the mysteries. The other is an index of the administrative positions and academic disciplines of the books' major characters.

As every aficionado of mystery fiction knows, the field lacks clearly demarked boundaries. When, for example, is a "thriller" or a "crime novel" a "mystery"? In constructing the bibliography I excluded science-fiction epics, horror tales that involve the supernatural, and mysteries intended expressly for juveniles. The bibliography is built around a core of conventionally structured detective novels. Thrillers and crime novels are included when they have academic protagonists (students, faculty members, or administrators at colleges and universities) who are clearly influenced by the opportunities, constraints, and experiences of academic life.

Each of the 486 annotations consists of two paragraphs. The first paragraph is the product of my reading of the mystery. It deals with the plot of the story and the characters who populate it. I have tried, in each case, to emphasize the academic content of the tale, paying special attention to academic disciplines, academic ranks, and the location and nature of the academic institution. I also have tried to keep the annotations interesting, so that they have a modicum of entertainment value even while they provide information. In many instances I have identified episodes or characters that may be of special interest to users of the bibliography. In the interests of readability I have refrained from the use of literary jargon, and in deference to those readers who might aspire to outguess the books' detectives, in no annotation have I "given away" the solution to a book's mystery.

Some college mysteries contain thinly disguised portraits, often unpleasant, of real-life inhabitants of the academic world. In several cases the actual identities of fictional characters have been suggested to me, but for fear of enshrining erroneous information in print I have not included those identifications in my annotations. Nor, except in the most clear-cut circumstances, have I attempted to identify those actual colleges or universities on which institutions with fictional names are modeled.

While compiling this bibliography I did not include or exclude books on the basis of literary quality; therefore, the bibliography contains references to what, in my view, are some of the best and some of the worst mysteries ever written. However, tastes in literature vary from person to person, and I have no wish to impose my standards on others. My annotations sometimes suggest the literary quality of the novels in question, especially in extreme instances, but for the most part I have left qualitative evaluations to the bibliography's users.

The primary purpose of the second annotation paragraph is to provide biographical material about the novel's author. The subgenre exhibits a wide range of authorship, and college mysteries have been written by well-known as well as by unknown writers. As might be expected, many of the authors of college mysteries have been college and university faculty members and their spouses. In writing the author-information portions of my annotations I have included, whenever the information was available, the authors' higher-education connections.[5] The second paragraph of the annotations also does double duty as a site for cross-listing. When an author has published more than one college mystery, I have provided in the second paragraph the title of the author's additional work or works, and by entry number I have identified the place in the bibliography where the citations and annotations of the additional novel or novels can be found.

Following the 486 annotations is a brief annotated bibliography of books, journal issues, and essays about college mysteries. I have limited the references in that section to writings in which several or more college mysteries are discussed. I have not included references to writings that dwell exclusively on a specific college mystery or on a specific college-mystery author.[6] My intent is to provide users of this book with a list of references that will prove helpful should they care to delve into what scholars have had to say, not about individual books or authors, but about the college-mystery subgenre as a whole.

The book is the product of a twenty-five-year personal interest in fiction about higher education.[7] Indeed, dedicated students of the subject may remember that in 1983 Garland Publishing Company issued an earlier bibliography, compiled by me and my son, that bore the unwieldy title *College Mystery Novels: An Annotated Bibliography, Including a Guide to Professorial Series-Character Sleuths*.[8] That bibliography began with one-or-two page essays about fifty-one fictional professors who detect in more than one mystery novel. Following each of the series-character essays, I listed the novels in which the detecting professor appears, regardless of whether the novels are set on college or university campuses. All told, the fifty-one series-characters appeared in 324 novels, most of which involved them in off-campus adventures and, hence, were not college mysteries. The second portion of the Garland bibliography cited and described 308 "freestanding" college mysteries—that is, college mysteries not graced by the appearance of series-character professor-detectives.

My retirement as a professor of sociology at the State University of New York College at Brockport in May of 1997 gave me the time to create this present bibliography. Originally, I hoped to update the material in the Garland bibliography and produce a second edition, but that effort was thwarted by an abundance of riches. The number of series-character professor-detectives has more than doubled since 1983, and as this present bibliography indicates, the number of college mysteries has exploded as well.[9] The first bibliography was 356 pages long. A comprehensive update would have run 700 pages or more! To keep the size of this volume manageable, I had to make and implement several editorial decisions. First, I decided not to carry the essays about series-character professor-detectives forward into this bibliography. I decided to make individual entries for those novels in which series-character professor-detectives sleuth on campus, thereby blending together the references to all college mysteries. Then, again in the interests of space, I decided to discard all of the freestanding entries in the Garland book that were anything less than full-fledged college mysteries.[10] Finally, I decided to include in this volume only those "new" mysteries—mysteries not cited in the Garland bibliography—that fully met my operational, college-mystery criteria.[11] Consequently, this bibliography makes reference only to novels that have enough "academic" content to qualify them as college mysteries as that term has been defined for this volume. This bibliography is a direct descendant of the Garland book, but it is not a second edition.

Of the 486 entries in this bibliography, 143 are carried forward (often with extensive editing) from the freestanding section of the Garland book. Another nineteen are on-campus mysteries that feature detection by series-character professor-detectives who have entries in the Garland bibliography. Those nineteen mysteries were cited in the Garland book. However, since no mysteries graced by the presence of series-character professor-detectives were annotated in the Garland bibliography, those nineteen novels are annotated for the first time in this volume. The remaining 324 novels cited and annotated in this bibliography are entirely "new." Fifty-eight of the 324 were published before work on the Garland bibliography stopped in 1982, but they were unknown to me and my son when the Garland book was being created. The other 266 "new" novels were published after the Garland bibliography was completed.[12]

As indicated in the bibliography of books and articles about college mysteries, I have written elsewhere about the college mystery's nature and meaning. Nonetheless, as an orientation to this bibliography it might be useful for me to offer some very brief comments about the college-mystery subgenre. Casual readers of mystery fiction sometimes fall prey to the false assumption that college mysteries are all the same. In fact, the subgenre displays considerable diversity. Writers of general works about mystery fiction often confine their discussions of college mysteries to the witty, "murder-can-be-fun" Oxbridge novels of the 1930s, 1940s, and 1950s that, in the main, featured amateur detectives. However, as this bibliography shows, college mysteries can be police procedurals or gritty private-detective stories, and even where amateurs do the sleuthing the novels may be deadly serious instead of playful. Most college mysteries have been (and continue to be) centered on the faculty and administrative side of academe, but users of this bibliography will find novels in which undergraduates and graduate students play crucial roles. The most often encountered type of college mystery is the "cozy," in which murders take place off stage, the "action" in the tale consists primarily of extended, sometime witty talk, and the detection is largely cerebral. While users of this bibliography will encounter an abundance of cozies, they also will find mysteries in which murders take place in full view of the books' readers and mysteries in which detectives and others engage in vigorous physical combat. Indeed, the common ground of college mysteries lies not in their form or in the academic role of their characters, but in their focus on the interplay between good and evil in the ritualized world of higher education. In that context it should be noted that the college mystery displays a diversity of settings as well as a diversity of literary structures. Any college mystery chosen at random is as likely to be set at a low-status or middling-status institution as at Oxford, Harvard, or some another high-prestige university. Thus, the college-mystery subgenre, taken in its entirety, seems to suggest that the good-versus-evil conflict is endemic to the higher-education process and not localized at any specific institutional status level.

If the college-mystery subgenre incorporates stylistic diversity, it also has exhibited change, especially in the roles of women as authors of and as characters in college-mystery novels. As this bibliography makes clear, women have been writing mysteries set at colleges and universities since the inception of the subgenre. Yet, early-day female college-mystery writers, like their male counterparts, almost always employed males as their faculty and administrative characters. The gender nature of the college mystery began to change dramatically in the 1960s, when a growing number of women began to write college mysteries and when college-mystery authors, men as well as women, began to place female characters in faculty and administrative roles. Since the early 1960s some college mysteries have incorporated strong feminist slants. Women, usually faculty members, have been portrayed as suffering under male-dominated academic regimes, and the novels often have featured female victims who are murdered by male villains. The victims in these feminist novels frequently are avenged (or, at least, their murderers are apprehended) by strong female detectives. More recently, still another gender-related change has begun to occur in college mysteries. In college mysteries written by women as well as by men, women faculty and administrative characters are now often treated as organizationally unremarkable, and women, while they are currently over represented in the ranks of modern-day faculty detectives, are as likely as men to be portrayed as villains. The gender-role changes in college mysteries obviously reflect the gender-role changes that have occurred in higher education itself. As the bibliography of writings about college mysteries suggests, relatively little scholarly research has been done on the subgenre. The identification of other changes in the college mystery, whether associated with changes in academe or with changes in the fashions of mystery fiction writ large, awaits the further research that this bibliography aims to stimulate.

To conclude this introduction, I want to express my appreciation to the people who, in many important ways, helped me with this project. Two individuals, Von Pittman and Ron Hamm, deserve special mention. Von Pittman is director of the Center for Distance and Independent Study at the University of Missouri-Columbia. A user of the Garland bibliography and a keen student of all fiction about higher education, Von provided me with several forms of help, including the screening of many possible college mysteries to see if those mysteries had sufficient "academic" content to be included in this volume. Of equal consequence, Von and his wife, Joyce, have become good friends to me and my wife, Joan. I also want to thank Lyn Ennis, Von's assistant, for her work. Ron Hamm, recently retired as executive director for external affairs at Texas A&M at Kingsville. He is another user of the Garland bibliography and another sedaloas scholar of fiction about academe. Between (and sometimes during) post-retirement trips to various corners of the world, Ron acted as an invaluable "consultant" on a variety of matters, and he and his wife, Peggy, also have become good friends.

Two other Garland users, Earl Rogers and Peter Nover, contributed significantly. Earl Rogers, certainly the world's most indefatigable student of literature about his home state is recently retired from the library at the University of Iowa, and he sent me a steady stream of recommendations about mysteries set in Iowa and elsewhere. My appreciation goes, as well, to Peter Nover of the University of Bonn in Germany. A young man whose knowledge of college mysteries is close to encyclopedic, Peter furnished me with leads to many of the college mysteries included in this bibliography. Furthermore, as a man of many languages, he also read Driss Chraibi's *L'Inspecteur Ali à Trinity College* (420), a work published only in French, and drafted the annotation. Since my only language is English, the Chraibi novel would never have made it into this bibliography had not Peter volunteered his contribution.

On the local Brockport scene special thanks go to Bob Gilliam and Diane Fair of the interlibrary-loan office at SUNY-Brockport's Drake Memorial Library. This bibliography could never have been started, let alone finished, without their willingness to search for and acquire mystery novels from the deepest corners of the library universe. Bob also worked with me on my two Garland bibliographies, and over the past twenty years he has become America's leading expert on the whereabouts of obscure works of fiction. Two other denizens of SUNY-Brockport who deserve thanks are Bob Rutzen and Gloria Condoluci. Bob, the longtime chairperson of the sociology department, has my efforts consistently encouraged. Gloria Condoluci, the even longer-time secretary to the sociology department, performed an abundance of important tasks as this book was being produced. Thanks go, too, to head librarian Mark Jaccarino and the staff of the Seymour Public Library in Brockport. I made extensive use of that facility during my labors, and the personnel was never less than helpful and full of good cheer.

Three people at Scarecrow Press merit appreciative citation. Amanda Irwin, Katie Regen, and Christine Ambrose all displayed immense patience as I worked (not always with maximum efficiency) to complete this book.

Finally, I want to thank Joan Andrews Kramer, my wife of forty-two years. My time-consuming activity while compiling this annotated bibliography was not part of her image of our ideal retirement, but she managed to remain patient for the many months it took to complete this book.

NOTES

1. The term "academic mystery" is employed frequently in the literature about mystery fiction to refer to the kinds of mysteries cited and annotated in this bibliography. However, the term is often used to encompass mysteries set in high schools and prep schools. The term "college mystery," which also is encountered frequently in the literature about mystery fiction, refers specifically to mysteries with settings and characters drawn from the world of higher education.

2. For example, mysteries in which professors attend academic conferences qualify for inclusion in the bibliography. On the other hand, mysteries in which professors detect in off-campus, nonacademic environments do not qualify for inclusion. For the most part, I also excluded "archaeological dig" mysteries and mysteries set in law schools and medical schools. All three forms of mystery exist in abundance, and each constitutes a small mystery-fiction subgenre of its own. Though academicians often appear on the pages of all three types of novels, the stories tend to focus on nonacademic issues. In law-school mysteries, for instance, faculty members often moonlight as practicing attorneys and the books' plots revolve

around the faculty-attorneys' extramural legal work. Only when the academic characters in archaeological dig, medical-school, or law-school mysteries concentrate on matters that are internal to their institutions of higher education are those novels are included in the bibliography.

3. My search for college mysteries centered on novels by British and North American authors, and most of those authors naturally set their tales at British and North American institutions of higher education. I make no claim to have systematically foraged for college mysteries that are set elsewhere. Yet, rather than discard the smattering of college mysteries I discovered that take place in Australia, Cyprus, China, Ireland, India, Israel, and Norway, I included them in this bibliography.

4. A few melodramatic novels in which crimes occur at colleges or universities were published both in Great Britain and the United States in the nineteenth century. However, the identities of the villains in those novels is seldom in doubt, and the tales lack any significant detection. My research suggests that *The Innocent Murderers*(1), set at "Graydon College" in New England and published in 1910, is the earliest American or British novel that modern-day readers would recognize as a college mystery.

5. Author information was drawn from a variety of sources, including biographical reference books, the covers of novels, and internet sites. In some cases I had direct correspondence with authors, agents, and publishers. Many of the author-information entries in this bibliography blend materials drawn from two or more sources. The most extensive source of author information was the multivolume *Contemporary Authors: A Bio-Bibliographical Guide to Current Writers in Fiction, General Nonfiction, Poetry, Journalism, Drama, Motion Pictures, Television, and Other Fields* (Detroit: Gale, 1962–1999). Other especially useful references were Jacques Barzun and Wendell H. Taylor, *A Catalogue of Crime,* 2d ed. (New York: Harper & Row, 1989); Willetta L. Heising, *Detecting Men: A Reader's Guide and Checklist for Mystery Series Written by Men* (Dearborn, Mich.: Purple Moon Press, 1998); Willetta L. Heising, *Detecting Women 2: A Reader's Guide and Checklist for Mystery Series Written by Women* (Dearborn, Mich.: Purple Moon Press, 1996); Lesley Henderson, ed., *Twentieth-Century Crime and Mystery Writers,* 3d ed. (Chicago: St. James Press, 1991); and Bill Pronzini and Marcia Muller, eds., *1001 Midnights; The Aficionado's Guide to Mystery and Detective Fiction* (New York: Arbor House, 1986). Some author information also was drawn from Allen J. Hubin, *Crime Fiction II: A Comprehensive Bibliography, 1749–1990* (New York: Garland, 1994), but the massive Hubin bibliography was more useful for determining publishers, dates of publication, and the placement of novels within authors' writing careers and within series of mysteries with the same detectives. Despite my best efforts, the author information in this bibliography is uneven in its depth. Where I have been unable to locate any biographical data about an author, the second paragraph of the annotation is limited to information about the career and (when relevant) the series placement of the mystery.

6. A few authors of college mysteries, most notably Dorothy L. Sayers, John Innes Mackintosh Stewart and Caroline Heilbrun, have been the subject of consid-

erable scholarly attention, although the many books and articles about them have not always focused directly on their authorship of college mysteries. A comprehensive annotated bibliography covering the scholarly writing about all college-mystery authors, and/or about all college mysteries, would have been far too large to be accommodated in this volume.

7. For an annotated bibliography of American "mainstream" college novels, see John E. Kramer Jr., *The American College Novel: An Annotated Bibliography* (New York: Garland, 1981).

8. John E. Kramer Jr. and John E. Kramer III, *College Mystery Novels: An Annotated Bibliography, Including a Guide to Professorial Series-Character Sleuths* (New York: Garland, 1983). While that book was being prepared John E. Kramer III was a high-school student and later a student at Dartmouth College. His role was principally that of researcher; he scoured reviews in back runs of magazines and newspapers searching for probable college mysteries, and he screened many of the leads to see if they qualified for inclusion in the Garland book. Armed with the extensive familiarity with fictional crime that was afforded him by his contributions to *College Mystery Novels*, John III has gone on to become an attorney, and he was far too busy in that role to play any part in the preparation of this present book.

9. The number of series-character professor-detectives now exceeds 130, and it is entirely possible that those sleuthing pedants might eventually find themselves in an annotated bibliography (compiled by me or by someone else) devoted exclusively to them and their exploits. In this present bibliography, I make note, in the appropriate annotations, whenever the detection in a college mystery is conducted by a series-character professor-detective.

10. When we began work on the Garland bibliography my son and I had no idea how many college mysteries we would find. To ensure ourselves an ample supply of novels to cite and annotate we employed a very elastic definition of the college mystery. We included in the freestanding section of the Garland book 165 mysteries—most of them featuring professors in off-campus adventures—that would not qualify as college mysteries as the term is defined for this present volume.

11. The procedures my son and I used to located college mysteries while we were preparing the Garland bibliography are described in detail in that book's introduction. Those procedures were exhausting but not exhaustive. In general, they involved reading through decades-long back runs of newspapers and magazines (British as well as American) that reviewed mystery novels. Between the completion of the Garland bibliography, in mid 1982, and the start of work on this bibliography in May of 1997, I compiled a steadily accumulating list of novels that seemed, on the basis of the information I had available, to have a reasonable liklihood of being college mysteries. In part those leads were drawn from advertisements and reviews in a variety of current newspapers, magazines, and booksellers' circulars, but during that time I also received identifications of prospective college mysteries from many users of the Garland bibliography. The Garland users sometimes pointed me to post-1982 mysteries but more often took delight in informing me of pre-1982 college mysteries that my son and I had missed. When work on this

present bibliography began in May of 1997 I had identified approximately five hundred mystery novels (not included in the Garland bibliography) that had the possibility of qualifying as college mysteries. Every effort was then made to locate copies of those five hundred novels, screen them for admissibility into this bibliography, and read and annotate them if they proved to be admissible. I would like to claim that the 486 college mysteries cited and annotated in this volume constitute all college mysteries ever published. Alas, I cannot do so. Out there, in the land of long-forgotten mysteries, there doubtless exist college mysteries that have escaped my attention and, in the case of pre-1982 mysteries, the attentions of the Garland bibliography's users as well. Furthermore, despite the best efforts of SUNY-Brockport's interlibrary loan office I was never able to obtain copies of approximately forty of the five hundred or so novels I identified as possible college mysteries. From reviews I am certain that at least several of those not-to-be-found novels would have qualified for inclusion in this bibliography had I been able to examine and annotate them. Thus, with regard to this bibliography's comprehensiveness, I can claim only that it includes all those college mysteries of which I am aware and could examine and annotate.

12. Of the college mysteries cited in this bibliography, 218 bear publication dates during the seventy-one years between 1910 and 1981, while 268 were published in the seventeen years between 1982 and 1999! The production of college mysteries certainly has accelerated dramatically in the past few decades, but one must use caution when trying to employ the entries in this bibliography to state that acceleration in statistical terms. My methods of identifying possible college mysteries published after 1982 were considerably more efficacious than the methods my son and I employed to find college mysteries issued before that date. Thus, the number of pre-1982 college mysteries that I failed to identify may significantly exceed the number of post-1982 college mysteries that are missing from this bibliography.

Annotations

1. JOHNSTON, WILLIAM (1871–1929), AND PAUL WEST (1871–1918). *THE INNOCENT MURDERERS.* NEW YORK: DUFFIELD, 1910.

Precisely at 8:41 A.M. on May 18, 1908, Professor Josiah Hopkins leaves his home for another day in the chemistry department at Graydon College. Graydon is a small, coeducational institution in upper New England. When the professor does not come home that evening, Mrs. Hopkins engages the services of Philip Sullivan, a noted private detective from Boston, to determine her husband's whereabouts. Upon arriving at the college, Sullivan quickly learns that the professor's research assistant, a comely young lady named Ernesta Frost, also is missing. Then, as he conducts a late-night reconnaissance of the Graydon campus, Sullivan catches sight of four of Professor Hopkins's faculty colleagues furtively walking from the direction of the local cemetery. With a wheelbarrow, several shovels, and dirt-soiled boots, they seem to be returning from a burial. Armed with this intelligence, Sullivan sets out to earn his $100 fee, but as he discovers after some arduous sleuthing, cases on college campuses can be considerably more complex than the run-of-the-mill Boston missing-persons investigations to which he is accustomed. By the end of the novel Sullivan has become familiar with the new science of radiology, and he has learned something about how bumbling professors, even when they mean no harm, can create labrynthian mysteries.

William Johnston was born in Pittsburgh and graduated from Western University of Pittsburgh. He spent much of his early adult life as a journalist with *The New York World.* While working as a newspaperman he wrote eight mystery novels, of which *The Innocent Murderers* was his first. Johnston then became a vice president for public relations at the Celotex Company, and at the time of his death he was a member of the Celotex board of directors. The identity of Paul West is unknown.

2. WELLS, CAROLYN (1869–1942). *THE MYSTERY GIRL.* PHILADELPHIA: LIPPINCOTT, 1922.

John Waring, the bachelor president-elect of the "University of Corinth" in New England, dies in his locked study after his jugular vein is pierced by a stiletto-like instrument. The death-dealing weapon cannot be found (and no one can determine how the killer left the scene without unlatching the door or windows), but suspects are not in short supply. Emily Bates, a widow who was scheduled to become Waring's bride, stands to inherit oodles of money from her betrothed's estate. Gordon Lockwood, Waring's private secretary, was known to have been in the president-elect's residence during the night of his employer's demise. And then there is Anita Austen, a beautiful young lady from New York City, who was once seen kissing Waring's photograph. Miss Austin, "the mystery girl" referred to in the book's title, claims to have come to Corinth to paint pictures of the school's environs in winter, but none of the other characters in the novel believes that story for a minute. The local police are thoroughly baffled, and Maurice Trask, a headstrong lawyer who wants to clear Miss Austin of suspicion so that he might marry her, hires Fleming Stone to bring matters to a speedy and satisfactory conclusion. Stone is a scholarly Carolyn Wells series-character private detective. Accompanied by Terrence "Fibsy" McGuire, his ever-present factotum, Stone arrives at the university on page 272. By the time the book ends, a mere seventy-seven pages later, the whole matter has, indeed, been resolved. The crucial clue in the case is literary in nature, but the emphasis of *The Mystery Girl* is on the social rather than the academic life at Corinth.

Carolyn Wells was one of the pioneers of American mystery fiction. Born in Rahway, New Jersey, she lived most of her life in New York City. Wells wrote more than eighty mystery novels during her career. Sixty-one of her mysteries featured Fleming Stone as sleuth. *The Mystery Girl* was Stone's thirteenth published exploit.

3. CONVERSE, FLORENCE (B. 1871). *INTO THE VOID: A BOOKSHOP MYSTERY.* BOSTON: LITTLE, BROWN, 1926.

The night after he reads some of his work at a bookshop in the New England town of "Hawthorne," the noted poet Paul Slocombe disappears. Also missing is attractive Patience Farwell, the bookshop's manager. The shop is community owned, and several members of its board of directors are associated with "Dickinson College," a nearby school for women. The board raises $4,500 as a reward for locating Slocombe and Farwell, and in hopes of collecting the money many of the board's members quickly turn detective. Included among the aspiring sleuths are Miss Armitage, Dickinson's president, and Isabel Carter, Dickinson College's Masefield Professor of Poetry. Those two worthies, along with Officer Murphy, Hawthorne's traffic policeman, eventually solve the mystery. There are no corpses in the story, but there are many literary clues about the whereabouts of the two missing persons, and there is an abundance of clever, satirical writing, much of it directed at social, literary, and academic pretentiousness. Several of the principal characters are devoted readers of mystery fiction, and modern-day mystery buffs will be interested to learn that President Armitage cannot publicly admit to having read G. D. H. Cole's latest whodunit because Cole's socialism renders him a forbidden author on the Dickinson campus.

Into the Void was the first of two mysteries by Florence Converse.

4. STRANGE, MARK [PSEUD.]. *MIDNIGHT.* LONDON: FABER & GWYER, 1927.

Midnight is set at the "Moreton Training College," a two-year institution in England that educates female elementary-school teachers. Angela Pyke, the secretary to Miss St. Clair, the college principal, is discovered stabbed dead in her office. Superintendent Briggs of the local police finds the case too baffling, and he quickly calls upon Scotland Yard for help. The Yard sends Assistant Detective-Inspector Foster, a young man who is "fair, clean-shaven, [and] showing signs of becoming stout in later life." Foster is assisted in his efforts by Norah Parkinson, Moreton's attractive assistant principal. Miss Parkinson apparently discounts the corpulence in Foster's future because during the course of the story the two sleuths develop a romantic relationship, and by the end of the tale they are engaged to be married. As for the suspects, the most likely one is Dr. Paul, the college physician, who seems to show too much interest in the murder, but the school teems with others who might have had the opportunity, if not an obvious motive, to commit the crime. Competent, but not a brilliant detective, Inspector Foster makes one gaff that many real-life members of modern-day college communities will appreciate, even though this novel was published in 1927. Unfamiliar with the low salaries paid to the staff members and faculty in teacher-training colleges, Inspector Foster thinks he has hit upon the reason for Miss Pyke's killing when he finds twenty-four pounds missing from the school's strongbox. All he needs to do to find the guilty party, so he reasons, is to find someone badly in need of money. He abandons this tactic when he learns that all of the faculty and staff at Moreton live a hand-to-mouth existence.

Mark Strange is the pseudonym for four anonymous writers. In an author's note at the front of the book, those four individuals identify themselves only as M., A., R., and K. As the note explains it, M., A., and K. "discussed the plot and then wrote alternate chapters until the book was complete in outline. R. was then called upon and inserted 10,000 additional words distributed evenly among the different parts." In any event, with a murder, academic suspects, and on-campus detection, *Midnight* seems to have been the first British novel that modern readers would recognize as a college mystery.

5. BROOME, ADAM [GODFREY WARDEN JAMES (B. 1888)]. *THE OXFORD MURDERS.* LONDON: BLES, 1929.

"St. Anthony's College," Oxford, is thrown into something of an uproar when Athanasius Septimus Konti arrives to begin his undergraduate studies. A black prince from West Africa, "Septic" (as he quickly comes to be known) brings with him a large ceremonial drum, a great quantity of expensive wearing apparel, and two wives. Since women are not allowed to reside in St. Anthony's, the wives are dispatched with great fanfare to a hotel. For a time, Septic is the major topic of discussion in the Oxford community, but the attention of the locals soon turns to other matters—the murders of three dons and an unsuccessful attempt on the life of another. In each killing the victim is beaten unconscious and a hole is drilled through his skull into his brain. Various representatives from the British police become involved in the case. However, the crucial sleuthing is provided by Reggie Crofts, who is depicted first as a St. Anthony's student and then as a junior colonial administrator in West Africa, and by Barbara Playfair, Reggie's girlfriend and the niece of an Oxford faculty member. Few regular consumers of mysteries will be surprised at the identity of Oxford's assassin-by-drill. But since the killer sucked out the brains of his victims in order to improve his own intellect, most professorial readers will want to stop and ponder the threatening implications of the crimes.

The Oxford Murders was the second of twelve mystery novels that Godfrey Warden James published during his career. All of James's mysteries were issued under the Adam Broome pseudonym. A later James/Broome mystery novel, titled *The Cambridge Murders* (32), appears in this bibliography.

6. COHEN, OCTAVIUS ROY (1891–1959). *THE MAY DAY MYSTERY.* NEW YORK: APPLETON, 1929.

The murder of Pat Thayer, a senior at coeducational "Marland College," brings fat, cheroot-smoking Jim Hanvey onto the campus for some slow-paced sleuthing. Hanvey is in the employ of the "Banker's Protective Association," and he happens to be in the vicinity doing detective work on a bank heist. The late Mr. Thayer, who was stabbed in his room in the Psi Tau Theta House, was a card cheat, a bootlegger, and a notorious love-'em-and-leave-'em womanizer, and his death proves to be connected with the bank robbery that is the reason for Hanvey's presence in the Marland area. As the title of the book indicates, Pat Thayer was killed on May Day. Marland College is a picturesque institution in the American South. Along with Jim Hanvey's sometimes infuriatingly sluggish detection, the book offers many, many passages about the beauty of Marland's campus in the spring.

Octavius Roy Cohen was born in Charleston, South Carolina, and graduated from Clemson College in 1911. Admitted to the South Carolina bar in 1913, he abandoned the practice of law two years later to write fiction. Known primarily for his African American dialect stories and for his detective novels, Cohen also wrote stage dramas. *The May Day Mystery* was the second of four Cohen mysteries to feature Jim Hanvey.

7. DAVIDSON, T. L. [DAVID LANDSBOROUGH THOMPSON (1901–1964)]. *THE MURDER IN THE LABORATORY.* NEW YORK: DUTTON, 1929.

Set at an unidentified British university, this competently crafted story begins with the death of Walter Sheppary, a research fellow in toxicology. Sheppary expires in his laboratory after consuming cyanide. His body is found by Dr. Martin Blythe, one of the university's most distinguished junior scientists, and by George Wroxham, a medical student. Dr. Blythe quickly calls the police, and Detective Inspector Mellison of Scotland Yard is soon on the scene. Dr. Blythe, George Wroxham, and Mellison then engage in sleuthing. They first determine that Sheppary was murdered; then, and after establishing that dismal fact, they set out to rid the university of his killer. One of the trio's prime suspects is sinister Professor Franklin, the head of the toxicology department. A laconic man, with an inexplicable aversion to smoking his pipe in public, Franklin is indeed a suspicious character. It is not until the three detectives probe the details of Walter Sheppary's private life, however, that the case can be closed. In contrast to some university-laboratory mysteries, this occasionally satirical novel does not dwell on the chemical properties of exotic poisons. The stress, instead, is on alibis, motives, and deep, dark family secrets.

David Landsborough Thompson was born in Aberdeen, Scotland, and educated at Grenoble and Cambridge Universities. A longtime professor of biochemistry at McGill University in Montreal, he wrote several well-regarded scientific textbooks. *The Murder in the Laboratory* was his only mystery novel.

8. LILLY, JEAN. *FALSE FACE*. NEW YORK: DUTTON, 1929.

Natica Crane is in love with Granville Perkins, but Granville is infatuated with Poppy Brown. Poppy hopes to marry K. C. Gildersleeve, but K. C. yearns for Natica. All of the participants in this unhappy, lovelorn circle are students at an American institution of emotional suffering known as "Jefferson University." Two of the group are the children of faculty members and one—K. C. Gildersleeve—is the son of Jefferson's president. The only nonacademic offspring, Granville Perkins, compensates for his inferior lineage by being the son of a millionaire, and it is Granville who becomes the victim in the story. He is shot dead in his car late one night outside his fraternity house. Natica Crane is the prime suspect because she is the last person known to have seen young Mr. Perkins alive. Her plight naturally discomforts her father, William Rutherford Crane, Jefferson's stellar Shakespearean scholar, and he undertakes some sleuthing in order to save his daughter from arrest. Also functioning as detectives in the saga are Chief Simmons and Inspector Mannie of the local police and Bruce Perkins, who is Granville's older brother and an attorney. Meanwhile, the other faculty father in the affair, Harrison Brown, stays at home cramming calories into his corpulent body and preparing lectures on Teutonic literature, even though his own daughter could well have ended Granville's life. As for President Gildersleeve, he tries to put the best face on things by claiming that no one connected with his university could possibly be a murderer. Brimming over with clues, the book is short on action but long on talk since the major characters spend most of their time interrogating each other. Modern-day academics may not find *False Face* to be the most exciting mystery in this bibliography, but they will appreciate the now-extinct lifestyles of the Jefferson faculty. The Cranes employ a live-in black maid named Melissa, and the Browns' needs are attended to by Keno, a Japanese houseboy.

The identity of Jean Lilly is not revealed by any extant bibliographic resource. *False Face* was the second of four mysteries that she published. Attorney Bruce Perkins, who debuts in *False Face*, sleuths again in Lilly's third and fourth novels.

9. ORR, CLIFFORD (1899–1951). *THE DARTMOUTH MURDERS*. NEW YORK: FARRAR & RINEHART, 1929.

Three Dartmouth students are killed. Two die as the result of steel needles that are mysteriously fired into their skulls. The third is shot accidentally-on-purpose as a posse of Dartmouth vigilantes searches for the killer of the first two victims. Fortunately for what remains of the Dartmouth student body, Joseph Harris happens to be in Hanover. The father of the undergraduate-narrator of the story, a Big Green alumnus, and a lawyer who writes mystery novels as a hobby, Harris is asked by Dartmouth's president to become the school's temporary detective-in-residence. With the help of his son—whose own sleuthing actually breaks the case—Harris resolves matters by the end of the book, but not before some members of the Dartmouth community become tired of his officious behavior. Included in the story's large collection of characters is a rustic-but-sagacious local sheriff, a host of undergraduates (many of them exceedingly wealthy), and Professor "Bossy" Bostwick, an ingratiating professor of English who makes his bachelor digs the command post for the investigation. Although some of the idiomatic language in the novel is now badly dated, modern-day readers will not complain about a lack of real and false clues. Nor will devotees of action mysteries be disappointed, as the story's participants engage in chases through the picturesque New England countryside that borders the beautiful Dartmouth campus.

Clifford Orr was born in Portland, Maine, and graduated from Dartmouth. Most of his career was spent as an editor for *The New Yorker*. A sometimes song lyricist, as well as a sometimes mystery writer, Orr wrote the words to the 1929 hit "I May Be Wrong, But I Think You're Beautiful." *The Dartmouth Murders* was adapted for a 1935 motion picture. The Chesterfield Productions film was directed by Charles LaMont and starred Robert Warwick as Joseph Harris. Although Orr made his home in New York City, he returned to the Dartmouth environs in June of 1951, after learning he had a terminal illness. He died, four months later, in a Hanover, New Hampshire, nursing home.

10. VAN DINE, S. S. [WILLARD HUNTINGTON WRIGHT (1888–1939)]. *THE BISHOP MURDER CASE.* NEW YORK: SCRIBNER'S, 1929.

Professor Bertrand Dillard, one of the world's greatest mathematical physicists, lives in semiretirement in a large house on West 75th Street in New York City. Sharing his abode are Belle Dillard, his attractive young niece, and Sigurd Arnesson, his adopted son. Arnesson, nearing forty, is an associate professor of mathematics at Columbia. The story begins with the murder (by bow and arrow) of Joseph Robin, a young playboy and one of Belle's acquaintances. Called in on the case is the effete Philo Vance, an illustrious S. S. Van Dine series-character detective who was one of Professor Dillard's students. Vance unmasks the killer. As the clues pile up, readers learn a great deal about the dark secrets that underlie the seemingly placid professorial lives of Dillard and Arnesson. It will not give too much of the plot away, perhaps, to note that two years after the culprit in the case is brought to justice, one of the two professors wins a Nobel Prize.

Willard Huntington Wright was born in Charlottesville, Virginia. He did his undergraduate work at St. Vincent and Pomona Colleges in California and took graduate work in English at Harvard. He also studied art in Munich and Paris. From 1907 until 1923 he held a variety of editing positions with American newspapers and magazines. He also attempted, without great success, to become a best-selling novelist. Wright did not begin his mystery-writing career until after he suffered a mental breakdown in 1923. During his two-year convalescence he read over two thousand detective novels and determined to try his own hand at the craft. Wright's extremely popular Philo Vance series, aimed primarily at educated readers, earned him the immense royalties that had eluded him during his earlier, abortive career as a writer of mainstream fiction. *The Bishop Murder Case* was the fourth of twelve Philo Vance novels.

11. FITZSIMMONS, CORTLAND (1893–1949). *70,000 WITNESSES.* NEW YORK: MCBRIDE, 1931.

"State College" is an American football powerhouse, and Walter Demuth is its star halfback. When State College plays its big home game of the season against "University," 70,000 spectators pack the stadium in hopes of watching Demuth lead his team to victory. Demuth performs in his usual stellar fashion until, late in the contest, he falls dead while scoring a touchdown. Was his sudden collapse the result of a heart attack, or was it murder? An autopsy is inconclusive, and Jack Kethridge, a local police detective, has the State College team reenact the sequence of plays that led up to Walter's fatal run. At the end of the mock scrimmage Rudolpho Cannero, Walter Demuth's stand-in, falls dead as he strides into the end zone. *70,000 Witnesses* is a how-did-he-do-it as well as a whodunit, and not until the very end of the story does Detective Kethridge discover the method by which Walter Demuth and Rudolpho Cannero were killed. Meanwhile, he interrogates a host of suspects. The possible murderers include Ranny Buchan (Walter Demuth's roommate), Dorothy Demuth (Walter's sister), the whole of the State College football squad, and even referee Harry Collins (who, as a Harvard graduate, is naturally a suspicious character).

Cortland Fitzsimmons was born in Richmond Hills, Queens, New York. He attended New York University and City College of New York. Early in his working career he was employed as a salesman in several industries, and from 1929 until 1938 he served as sales manager for the Viking Press. During the last fifteen years of his life he operated a bookstore in Los Angeles. A well-respected writer, Fitzsimmons was better known for his inventive plots than for his characterizations. *70,000 Witnesses* was the third of seventeen mystery novels he wrote during his lifetime. It was adapted for a 1932 Paramount Pictures film that starred Phillips Hulmes, Dorothy Jordan, Charles Ruggles, Johnny Mack Brown, and "Big Boy" Williams. Fitzsimmons also created a series-character professor-detective named Percy Peacock. A psychologist, Professor Peacock sleuths in two nonacademic mysteries. Those mysteries are *Death Rings a Bell* (Philadelphia: Lippincott, 1942) and *Tied for Murder* (Philadelphia: Lippincott, 1943).

12. STRANGE, JOHN STEPHEN [DOROTHY STOCKBRIDGE TILLETT (B. 1891)]. *MURDER ON THE TEN-YARD LINE.* DOUBLEDAY, DORAN & CO., 1931. PUBLISHED IN ENGLAND AS *THE MURDER GAME.* LONDON: WILLIAM COLLINS AND SONS, 1931.

The "Yorke University" versus "Winslow" game is always one of America's outstanding football spectacles. This particular year there is an extra-added attraction. Coach Diederich of Yorke is shot and killed just as the first half is ending. Jim Gaynor, a sports reporter for *The New York Sphere*, asks his friend Van Dusen Ormsberry to investigate. Ormsberry, a John Stephen Strange series-character detective, finds that Coach Diederich had many enemies and that most of them were in the grandstands, within easy shooting distance, when the fatal bullet was fired. By the conclusion of this book, the murderer has been brought to justice, and, one assumes, the Yorke University athletic department has recruited a new football coach so that the games may go on.

Dorothy Stockbridge Tillett was the author of more than twenty mystery novels published between 1928 and 1961. All of her works were issued under the John Stephen Strange pseudonym. *Murder on the Ten-Yard Line* was the last of three Van Dusen Ormsberry sagas. Tillett is best remembered by mystery buffs for eight novels that featured photographer Barney Gantt as sleuth.

13. WEES, FRANCES SHELLY (1902–1982). *THE MYSTERY OF THE CREEPING MAN.* PHILADELPHIA: MACRAE-SMITH, 1931.

Professor Edgar Murchison disappears. The head of the physiology department at an unidentified American university, Murchison drops from sight on the last day of the spring semester. Ordinarily, the disappearance of a prominent professor in a mystery novel brings out a small army of professional and amateur sleuths, but in this instance no one seems overly concerned. A man of unusual habits, Murchison has been known to disappear before. Furthermore, the antivivisectionists in the local community are glad to see him go, because it is well known that he has been conducting painful research on animals. Murchison lived in a university-owned house, and some weeks after he vanishes the school rents the home to Michael Forrester and his wife Tuck. Michael is an attorney and Tuck runs a stenography service. The Forresters become interested in Murchison's whereabouts because they experience a series of break-ins, and because they suspect that the uninvited intruder may be their home's previous occupant. The Forrester's detection eventually leads them to a nearby cave, in which they come dangerously close to dying as unwilling guinea pigs in a psychological experiment. Real-life academic scientists often complain about the inadequacy of their laboratory facilities. After reading about the Forresters' subterranean adventures, they are likely to be thankful that their own laboratories are above ground.

Frances Shelly Wees was born in Gresham, Oregon. She received a teacher's certificate from the Saskatoon (Canada) Normal School in

1923. During her varied career Wees was director of the Canadian Chautauquas, an account executive for a Toronto public relations firm, a director of the United Nations Relief and Rehabilitation Agency in Ottawa, and a public relations consultant to the Toronto Art Gallery. Her publishing credits include many books for children, as well as ten mystery novels.

14. FORD, LESLIE [ZENITH JONES BROWN (1898–1983)]. *BY THE WATCHMAN'S CLOCK.* NEW YORK: FARRAR & RINEHART, 1932.

"Landover College," a private, all-male institution in Maryland, forms the backdrop for this sometimes wordy but sometimes fast-paced mystery of manners. The victim in the story is Daniel Sutton, a wealthy businessman who resides near the college and who, through his donations, is the school's chief benefactor. Sutton bullies unmercifully all of those around him, and when he is shot dead in his study one night, there is a long list of people who had ample motive for the crime. The story is narrated by Martha Niles, the wife of Ben Niles, a Landover professor of anthropology. Professor Niles is a suspect in the case, because the truculent Mr. Sutton had threatened to withdraw his support for the anthropology department, but the finger of suspicion also points toward several of Sutton's house guests, his two adult offspring, and several members of Landover's impoverished black community. Martha Niles does some of the sleuthing, but the detection is shared by a number of other characters as well, including courtly Dr. Knox, Landover's president. Academic readers may feel ambivalent about the novel's conclusion. Daniel Sutton's killer seems to escape justice, but under the terms of Sutton's will Landover College receives 250,000 acres of oil-rich land in New Mexico.

Zenith Jones Brown was born in Smith River, California. She attended the University of Washington, where, from 1921 through 1923, she taught English as a teaching assistant and later as an instructor. In 1921 she married Ford K. Brown, who was to become a professor of English at St. John's College, Annapolis, Maryland. During the 1920s the Browns spent time in Oxford, where Ford Brown was conducting research under a Guggenheim Fellowship, and Mrs. Brown began her writing career with a series of mysteries (under the pseudonym David Frome) with British settings. By the early 1930s, Mrs. Brown began to write mysteries set in and around her Annapolis home, and thereafter some of her works were set in England and some in the United States.

She employed the pseudonyms Leslie Ford and Brenda Conrad on her later mysteries. *By the Watchman's Clock* was her second Leslie Ford novel. One of Mrs. Brown's David Frome mysteries, *Mr Pinkerton Finds a Body* (25), also is included in this bibliography.

15. HUGHES, BABETTE PLECHNER (B. 1906). *MURDER IN THE ZOO.* NEW YORK: APPLETON-CENTURY, 1932.

The "zoo" in the title of this novel is an animal laboratory maintained by the psychology department of an American institution of higher learning called "Earl College." The victim is Courtney Brown, an unpopular professor, who is shot dead in the lab. Handling the detection is Ian Craig, a world-famous Earl College professor of Oriental philosophy, who takes time out from his many prestigious lecture engagements to engage in sleuthing. A tall, blonde bachelor, Craig is both erudite and loquacious, and while operating in his detection mode he is prone to draw ideas from a variety of sources ranging from Oscar Wilde to Li-Po. *Murder in the Zoo* incorporates a large cast of Earl College characters, and it contains considerable sly humor directed at faculty manners and non-manners. It also directs some sharp literary jabs at behavioralistic psychology. In a prologue one of Professor Craig's faculty colleagues explains that the text of the book is really a journal kept by Professor Craig as he was bringing Professor Brown's murderer to justice.

Babette Plechner Hughes was born in Seattle, Washington. While a sophomore at the University of Washington she married Glenn Hughes, then her instructor of playwriting and later a professor of English and director of the division of drama at the university. Mrs. Hughes wrote two mysteries that starred Professor Ian Craig. The second was *Murder in the Church* (26). In addition to her two Ian Craig mysteries, Mrs. Hughes wrote *Last Night When We Were Young* (New York: Rinehart, 1947), an autobiographical account of her tempestuous days as a University of Washington student. Most of Babette Hughes's later life was spent in the business world. During the 1940s and 1950s, she was the president of Benn Hall Associates, a public relations firm.

16. PROPPER, MILTON (MORRIS) (1906–1962). *THE STUDENT FRATERNITY MURDER.* INDIANAPOLIS: BOBBS-MERRILL, 1932. PUBLISHED IN ENGLAND AS *MURDER OF AN INITIATE*. LONDON: FABER & FABER, 1933.

Stuart Jordon, a student at the "University of Philadelphia," is murdered by poison while being initiated into a fraternity. Tommy Rankin, a Philadelphia police detective and an experienced Milton Propper series-character sleuth, handles the investigation. Rankin finds that the late Mr. Jordan had mortal enemies off as well as on the Philadelphia campus, and to apprehend the killer he must probe deeply into Stuart's unusual life history. *The Student Fraternity Murder* is noteworthy as an early-day American police procedural. It also offers considerable insight into fraternity life in the 1930s. Moreover, as an extra added attraction it provides a how-to-do-it course for young ladies who might want to pass as men and live undetected in all-male dormitories.

Milton Propper was born in Philadelphia and received an LL.B. from the University of Pennsylvania Law School in 1929. An aspiring writer, he did not apply for admission to the Pennsylvania bar. Instead, he wrote mystery novels and short stories and, early in his career, experienced significant critical and financial success. By the mid-1930s, however, Propper's literary popularity faded, and he took a position with the Social Security Administration, serving first in Philadelphia and then in Atlanta. During the 1950s Propper suffered from bouts of depression and was placed under psychiatric care. In 1962 he committed suicide.

17. WHITE, T(ERENCE) H(ANBURY) (1906–1964). *DARKNESS AT PEMBERLEY*. LONDON: GOLLANCZ, 1932; NEW YORK: CENTURY, 1933.

Who shot Mr. Frazer, a first-year student at the University of Cambridge, as he sat in his small flat at 23 Copper Street? Who, within a few minutes of the first murder, shot Mr. Breedon, a history don, in his locked rooms at "St. Bernard's College"? And who, a few days later, decapitated Rudd, a university porter? The man in charge of finding the answers to these questions is Inspector Buller of the Cambridge police. A sensitive and perspicacious sleuth, Buller is perhaps the only detective in college-mystery fiction who enjoys flute playing as a hobby. A third of the way through this tale Buller does, indeed, identify the guilty party. However, he lacks sufficient proof to place the evildoer under arrest, and he resigns from the force in frustration. At this point the story changes from a whodunit to an unusual action tale in which the villain stalks the detective. Now a private citizen, Buller travels to Derbyshire, to a country house called Pemberley, where he visits an acquaintance named Sir Charles Darcy. Buller's real reason for going to Pemberley is to see Elizabeth Darcy, Sir Charles's comely sister, a woman with whom he has fallen in love. Buller tells Sir Charles about his "unsolved" murder case, and Sir Charles, as frustrated as Buller that a diabolical killer may get away with murder, makes the mistake of going to Cambridge and threatening to kill the murderer. In short order, the murderer travels to Pemberley and concocts a sadistic plan to kill Sir Charles, Elizabeth, and Buller. Before the book concludes Buller must draw upon all of his police skills to prevent the miscreant from carrying out his wicked scheme. In the first third of this novel, which takes place entirely in Cambridge, readers are introduced to several denizens of the university. In addition to the murder victims, the Cambridge characters include the aged, cocaine-addicted master of St. Bernard's and a brilliant lecturer in chemistry who hopes to become master after the incumbent dies. Because the portraits of the Cambridge personages in the novel are generally unflattering, the publisher insisted that the author tell his readers that *Darkness at Pemberley* is a work of fiction. In a disclaimer placed at the front of the book, the author states that the characters in the novel are "figments of the detective story convention," and he claims that no one should associate St. Bernard's College with a real Cambridge college it might resemble. Furthermore, argues the author, "No person in the real college would be in the least likely to write incriminating letters, or take drugs, or to commit blackmail or murder."

Terence Hanbury White was born in Bombay, India. He received a B.A. from Queens' College, Cambridge in 1928. After Cambridge he served for a short time as a schoolteacher before resigning at age thirty to devote his full attention to writing. *Darkness at Pemberley* was written during White's brief schoolmaster career. Before his death in 1964 White produced a large and varied oeuvre of fiction and nonfiction for both children and adults. One of his works of fiction, *The Once and Future King* (New York: Putnam, 1939), was the basis for the Lerner and Loewe musical play *Camelot.*

18. WHITECHURCH, VICTOR L(ORENZO) (1868–1933). *MURDER AT THE COLLEGE*. LONDON: WILLIAM COLLINS AND SONS, 1932. PUBLISHED IN THE UNITED STATES AS *MURDER AT EXBRIDGE*. NEW YORK: DODD, MEAD & CO., 1932.

"St. Oswald's College," of "Exbridge University" in England has a reputation for the scholarly attainments of its fellows. The college's image takes a bit of a beating, however, when a visitor is stabbed dead in the rooms of one of its more illustrious dons. Detective-Sergeant Ambrose handles the investigation. An intelligent, pipe-smoking man of about thirty, Ambrose refuses to be awed by a large pool of accomplished but eccentric academic suspects. One of those upon whom Ambrose focuses his attentions is Mr. Hewitt, a man so dedicated to the intellectual life that he seldom leaves his quarters. Another is Dr. Blake, a professor of theology who fancies himself a master of disguise. Though Ambrose discovers the killer's identity, the culprit escapes capture. Instead of the usual detective-explains-to-all denouement, the last chapter of this book consists of a long, revelatory letter from the murderer. Written from hiding to a former colleague at the college, the letter explains the killer's motives and methods for the crime.

Victor Lorenzo Whitechurch was born in Norham, England. An Anglican clergyman, he served in several Midlands parishes before becoming, in retirement, honorary canon of Christ Church, Oxford. Whitechurch's extensive literary oeuvre includes romantic novels, books on theology, and eight works of mystery fiction. Written while he was convalescing after a long illness, *Murder at the College* was Whitechurch's last book.

19. MASTERMAN, J(OHN) C(ECIL) (1891–1977). *AN OXFORD TRAGEDY.* LONDON: GOLLANCZ, 1933; NEW YORK: DOVER, 1981.

The dons of "St. Thomas's College," Oxford, gather in the common room after an especially amusing dinner with Ernst Brendel, a visiting lawyer-criminologist from Vienna. One by one, the dons drift away until only Brendel and Francis Winn, vice president of St. Thomas's, are left chatting over cigars. Then Dean Maurice Hargreaves bursts in, almost beside himself with agitation. "My God!" he exclaims. "Come up quickly. Someone's shot Shirley—in my room." Hargreaves' announcement thus plunges St. Thomas's into what eventually becomes a murder-suicide, and it thrusts Brendel and Winn (who narrates the tale) into one of the most carefully written and purely academic mysteries to appear in this bibliography. Shirley, as Winn informs us, was an unpopular fellow in classics who had a sizable list of enemies. Eight dons emerge as suspects, as do Callendar (the college butler) and several of the college's undergraduates. In the end, it is Brendel who deduces the truth about the matter, but the killer avoids arrest by consuming a fatal dose of prussic acid. Jacques Barzun and Wendell H. Taylor in *A Catalogue of Crime* call *An Oxford Tragedy* "a masterpiece," and it would be difficult to quarrel with that evaluation. The book is rich with Oxford atmosphere, and it incorporates enough real and false clues to satisfy even the most demanding readers. Moreover, the actions and reactions of its participants are entirely in keeping with real-life academic behavior. As the novel concludes, the surviving St. Thomas's dons seem to have quickly forgotten the deaths of their two colleagues. They are, instead, bickering over the redecorations of the college rooms left vacant by the unfortunate affair.

John Cecil Masterman was born in Kingston Hill, Surrey. He received a B.A. in 1913 and an M.A. in 1914 from Worcester College, Oxford. A lecturer and tutor at Christ Church, Oxford, from 1913 until 1947, Masterman then became provost of Worcester College and vice chancellor of the university. At the beginning of World War I Masterman was studying in Germany and was interned as a civilian prisoner for the duration of the conflict. During World War II he was a director of British counterintelligence and was one of the officials responsible for leading the Germans to believe that the 1944 D-Day landings would come at Calais. See Masterman's *The Double-Cross System in the War of 1939 to 1945* (New Haven: Yale University Press, 1972). A second Masterman novel, a nonacademic tale titled *The Case of the Four Friends* (London: Hodder & Stoughton, 1956), also features Ernst Brendel and many of the people from St. Thomas's College who figure prominently in *An Oxford Tragedy*. In *The Case of the Four Friends* Brendel returns to St. Thomas's after an absence of twenty years and, during the small hours of the morning in the college's senior common room, tells a story about corruption, rivalry, and retribution in a London law firm.

20. MORRAH, DERMOT (MICHAEL MACGREGOR) (1896–1974). *THE MUMMY CASE.* LONDON: FABER & FABER, 1933. PUBLISHED IN THE UNITED STATES AS *THE MUMMY CASE MYSTERY*. NEW YORK: HARPER & ROW, 1933.

After a fire destroys most of the bursary at "Beaufort College," Oxford, the charred remains of a body are found in the rooms of Professor Peter Benchley. Is the body that of Benchley or is it that of a mummy that the professor was seen examining in his bedroom only hours before the conflagration? In a burst of pure academic democracy, the fellows of Beaufort vote to declare that the body is Benchley's, but Denys Sargent and Humphrey Carver, two of the college's junior members, decide to conduct further inquiries. Their exploits, and their many discoveries during their investigation, provide the ingredients for as witty a story as can be found in all of college-mystery fiction. A bitter feud among world-famous Egyptologists, a faked drowning, a (off-stage) sword duel between professors, the loss of a favorite Meerschaum pipe, and a scenic, fact-finding trip to the Isle of Wight are only a few of the many elements that are worked into the plot of this highly civilized, sometimes-satirical, and always entertaining story.

Dermot Michael MacGregor Morrah received an M.A. (first-class honours) from New College, Oxford, in 1921. From 1921 until 1928 he was a fellow of All Souls College, Oxford. In 1928 he began a long career as a leader writer and editor for various London newspapers. Morrah's oeuvre includes historical works and many studies of the British royal family. Something of a joiner, at different points in his life Morrah was a fellow of the Society of Antiquaries, chairman of the Press Freedom Committee of the Commonwealth Press Union, director of the British Wine Society, and a councillor of honour of the Monarchist League. *The Mummy Case* was his only mystery novel.

21. PATRICK, Q. [RICHARD WILSON WEBB (B. 1901)]. *MURDER AT CAMBRIDGE*. NEW YORK: FARRAR & RINEHART, 1933. PUBLISHED IN ENGLAND AS *MURDER AT THE VARSITY*. LONDON: LONGMANS, GREEN & CO., 1933.

The protagonist of this lively, atmospheric mystery is Hilary Fenton, an American graduate studying English at "All Saints College," Cambridge. Hilary has a B.A. from Harvard, a father who is a justice of the United States Supreme Court, and an effervescent personality. Even the murder by shooting of Julius Baumann, a South African fellow student, and the stabbing of Hankins, an All Saints College gyp, cannot depress him for long. Nor is Hilary subdued by his failure to impress Dorothy Dupuis, a Newnham College undergraduate whose wondrous physiognomy has earned her the nickname "The Profile." The murders are investigated by Inspector Horrocks of the Cambridge Police, but Hilary manages to lend an enthusiastic hand. Who is the killer loose in All Saints? It is not Stuart Somerville, the loudmouthed aristocratic oarsman whom Hilary first suspects. But it is someone who is present at All Saints on a daily basis. And what is a gyp? A gyp is a male servant at Cambridge (at Oxford he is called a scout). The term is defined, along with a host of other Cambridge colloquialisms, in a four-page glossary following the text of the story.

Richard Wilson Webb was born in England but spent most of his adult life in the United States. He employed the Q. Patrick pseudonym both on mystery novels that he wrote by himself and on novels that he wrote with various collaborators. Webb's most lengthy collaboration was with Hugh Callingham Wheeler. Another Q. Patrick college mystery, *Death and the Maiden* (47), appears in this bibliography. *Death and the Maiden* is a work by Webb and Wheeler.

22. SPROUL, KATHLEEN. *DEATH AND THE PROFESSORS.* NEW YORK: DUTTON, 1933. PUBLISHED IN ENGLAND AS *DEATH AMONG THE PROFESSORS.* LONDON: EYRE & SPOTTISWOODE, 1934.

There's trouble in the physics department at "Dunster College," an exclusive institution for men in New England. Old Professor Clarence Shearer and upstart Professor Peter Storm don't get along. Part of the problem is that Storm is having an affair with Shearer's young wife. Storm collapses and dies after a dinner party at which Shearer is also a guest, and then the next evening Shearer is found dead in his home with his throat cut from ear to ear. Richard Van Ryn Wilson, a Kathleen Sproul series-character sleuth, happens to be spending the semester at Dunster giving lectures on criminal psychology, and he leaps into action. A wealthy New York City consulting detective when he is out of his academic guise, Wilson is assisted by Manners, his butler, and by his longtime friend Dr. Eric Dieterlee, a New York physician. Dr. Dieterlee, by yet another happy coincidence, is paying Wilson a visit. The sleuths' attentions first center on Professor Shearer's widow, Lillian, but since the author sees fit to parade before her readers virtually the entire Dunster faculty and student body, and several townspeople as well, new suspects emerge right up until the end of the story. Among the possible killers are Timothy Bates (a mathematics professor with a terrible temper), Leavitt Walz (a brilliant student who was expelled from the college for having an affair with Ruth Storm, Peter's teenage sister), Alicia McSorley (an attractive laboratory assistant in the physics department), and Gracien Lowell (a dotty old lady who wanders the campus at night getting mysterious scratches on her face). Even prim and proper Dr. Parmer, Dunster's president, is thought capable of the crime, and he certainly had a motive since the deaths of Storm and Shearer restore peace to the physics department. Richard Wilson finally sorts through all of the suspicious characters, and along with identifying the guilty party, he finds that Storm's demise was brought about by a highly ingenious method that is not employed by any other villain in college-mystery fiction. The book is ideal reading for those who like a plethora of clues and characters. Nostalgia buffs will enjoy the scene in which one of Leavitt Walz's former fraternity associates tells sleuth Wilson how the brothers angrily stripped Walz of his membership when they found that he was engaging in sexual relations without benefit of marriage.

The identity of Kathleen Sproul remains in the realm of research opportunities for the biographically curious. *Death and the Professors* was the second of five mystery novels she published between 1932 and 1946, and it was the second of four Richard Van Ryn Wilson adventures.

23. WALLIS, J(AMES) H(AROLD). *THE MYSTERY OF VAUCLUSE*. NEW YORK: DUTTON, 1933.

This imaginative mystery takes place at Yale. The time is 1937 (five years after the book's publication). Thanks to the benefaction of Professor Lycett Dart, a chemist who has grown wealthy through his scientific discoveries, Yale has opened one of the world's first centers for adult education, and it has constructed a complex of buildings, known as "Vaucluse," in which approximately two hundred adult students can live and learn. The centerpiece of the complex is an ancient abbey, brought to New Haven from the Orkney Islands. Though the exterior of the abbey retains its original form, the inside has been altered to provide an office for Professor Dart and residential suites for ten students. One night Professor Dart is stabbed dead in his office, shortly after he announces that he has discovered a way to convert sugar into gasoline, and the ten adult students living in the abbey become immediate suspects. The detective on the scene is Captain Kevin Devaney of the New Haven police. To investigate systematically, Devaney immediately forbids the ten student-residents of the abbey to leave the windowless building, and confined to the small, enclosed space they begin to bicker and accuse one another of murder. There is some anti-Semitism directed at Dr. Israel Westberg, a Jewish surgeon who has enrolled as a student at Vaucluse in order to work with Professor Dart on a possible substitute for sleep, and as Devaney's detection moves forward another of the adult students, 112-year-old Herman Denzler, becomes the book's second stabbing victim. The novel includes detailed floor plans of Vaucluse and of the abbey, and it is prefaced by a roster of thirty of the tale's major characters. On page 267 the publishers insert a notice that all the clues have been presented, and they challenge readers to guess the identity of the killer before they proceed to the end of the book.

James Harold Wallis was born in Dubuque, Iowa. He received a B.A. from Yale in 1906. After a career in the newspaper business he moved to Scarsdale, New York, in the late 1920s to pursue a second career as a creative writer. Though Wallis wrote poetry and mainstream novels, he achieved his greatest commercial success with mysteries. *The Mystery of Vaucluse* was the third of ten mysteries he published during his lifetime.

24. BOYD, MARION [MARION MARGARET BOYD HAVINGHURST (D. 1974)]. *MURDER IN THE STACKS*. BOSTON: LOTHRUP, LEE, & SHEPARD CO., 1934.

"Kingsley University," in the American Midwest, is an untroubled institution to which evil is almost a complete stranger. When Donald Crawford, the school's reclusive assistant librarian, is found dead of a fractured skull in the library stacks, everyone assumes that his demise was the result of an unfortunate fall. Everyone, that is, except Tom Allen, a young member of the English department. Tom brings his dark suspicions to the attention of President Mittoff, who authorizes him to do some unofficial sleuthing. Although Tom bungles the job rather badly at times, he is able to show by the book's conclusion that Crawford was murdered. And, from the dozen or so faculty and librarian suspects who come to his attention, he is able to pick out Crawford's killer. As his reward, Tom wins the heart of Carla Robinson, a pretty instructor of French who occupies an office on the library's second floor. Furthermore, President Mittoff, apparently unconstrained by any rules about following departmental recommendations for salary increases, gives Tom an on-the-spot raise for restoring Kingsley University to its former state of languid academic bliss.

Marion Margaret Boyd Havinghurst received an A.B. from Smith College in 1916 and an M.A. from Yale in 1926. Married to a professor of English at Miami University of Ohio, she held teaching positions in the Miami English department at various times throughout her adult life. A well-respected poet and mainstream novelist, she began and ended her mystery-writing career with *Murder in the Stacks*. The reason her foray into the detective-story field was so brief may be suggested by a notation on the book's dust jacket. The blurb tells us that

Marion Boyd started the story in a library, "but the surroundings became so fearsome to her that she finished the book elsewhere. . . . It is a good writer who can scare herself with her own thoughts."

25. FROME, DAVID [ZENITH JONES BROWN (1898–1983)]. *MR. PINKERTON FINDS A BODY.* NEW YORK: FARRAR & RINEHART, 1934. PUBLISHED IN ENGLAND AS *THE BODY IN THE TURL*. LONDON: LONGMANS, 1935.

Sir William Brame, a millionaire clothing manufacturer, is shot dead one evening on Trul Street, just outside the gates of "St. Jude's College," Oxford. The case is investigated by blustery Inspector J. Humphrey Bull of Scotland Yard and by his unofficial assistant, Evan Pinkerton, a timid little man with an extraordinary talent for sleuthing. Before these two David Frome series-character detectives crack the case, two more murders occur. The additional victims are Ronald Brame, Sir William's St. Jude's-student son, and Beulah, Ronald's secret wife. Before marrying Ronald, Beulah was the commoner granddaughter of Higson, an aged college servant. Whimsical in tone, *Mr. Pinkerton Finds a Body* is exceedingly rich with Oxford atmosphere. Careful descriptions are provided both of the university and of the commercial portions of the city. The most likely suspects are old Higson (who, at one point, makes a false confession), an Oxford senior tutor named Kewly-Smith, and Ronald's sister, Natalie. As it happens, however, the murderer turns out to be a most unlikely individual, and the motive for the crimes, while nonacademic in nature, is very, very British.

Mr. Pinkerton Finds a Body was the tenth of sixteen mystery novels that Zenith Jones Brown published under the pseudonym David Frome. Another mystery by Zenith Jones Brown, *By the Watchman's Clock* (14), appears earlier in this bibliography. *By the Watchman's Clock* was published under the pseudonym Leslie Ford.

26. HUGHES, BABETTE PLECHNER (B. 1906). *MURDER IN THE CHURCH*. NEW YORK: APPLETON-CENTURY, 1934.

Arthur Quinn, a distinguished British astrophysicist, is visiting "Western Institute of Technology" in California. While attending services in a Catholic church he collapses and dies after sucking on poisoned throat lozenges. Western's harried President Radford asks Ian Craig to investigate Quinn's murder. Craig, a professor of Oriental philosophy at Stanford, is a Babette Hughes series-character sleuth, and he has acquired a reputation in academic circles as a peerless detective. Professor Craig finds this case a serious challenge. For one thing, Quinn was engaged in a bitter scientific competition having to do with the development of light-rays, and several of his rival physicists are on the Western faculty. For another, Quinn was known as a philanderer, and any number of women, including his wife, might have wanted him dead. And finally, there is the matter of how and why Quinn was in church. Not a practicing Catholic, Quinn was, instead, a staunch enemy of all organized religion, and he considered all clergy to be charlatans. A man who has trained his mind to register clues "as a seismograph registers earthquakes," Professor Craig almost suffers from clue overload in this story, as well as from an excess of suspects, before he identifies the book's murderer.

An earlier Professor Ian Craig mystery by Babette Hughes, *Murder in the Zoo* (15), appears in this bibliography. In the time between that adventure and *Murder in the Church,* Professor Craig apparently experienced upward academic mobility. During *Murder in the Zoo* he was a professor at "Earl College." In *Murder in the Church* he is a professor at Stanford.

27. DANE, JOEL Y. [JOSEPH FRANCIS DELANEY (B. 1905)]. *MURDER CUM LAUDE*. NEW YORK: SMITH & HAAS, 1935. PUBLISHED IN ENGLAND AS *MURDER IN COLLEGE*. LONDON: GEORGE BELL & SONS, 1935.

This novel is set at "Cardaff University," an institution located in the New York City suburbs. When a male undergraduate is shot dead on the campus, the case is assigned to Sergeant Cass Harty of the local police. A World War I veteran, Harty is a tough cop with little sympathy for collegiate fripperies. As he begins his investigation, another male student is murdered. The second victim is stabbed, and his body is discovered among the cadavers being readied for dissection in the university's medical school. After some determined detection Harty roots out the murderer, but not before he learns more than he cares to know about student pranks, left-wing political protest, and secret societies. Faculty members and administrators are limited to token performances. However, one administrator is at least accorded a good description. Dr. Averill P. Coife, Cardaff's pompous dean, is portrayed as resembling "a Shakespearian actor of the old school who [has] gone badly to seed."

Joseph Francis Delaney published four detective novels in the 1930s. All of them featured Sergeant Cass Harty as sleuth, and all were issued under the Joel Y. Dane pseudonym. *Murder Cum Laude* was the first work in the Cass Harty series.

28. EBERHARD, FREDERICK G(EORGE) (B. 1889). *THE MICROBE MURDERS.* NEW YORK: MACAULEY, 1935.

The body of Professor Larkin, an Egyptologist at an American university, is found disemboweled and mummified in his home. Fortunately, ex-inspector O'Hare of Scotland Yard happens to be in the United States, and the baffled local police call upon him for assistance. The title of the book gives away the method of the murderer, but not until the end of the novel is the motive revealed and the culprit unmasked. Suspects in the tale include "Smooth" Larkin, the professor's confidence-man brother, and a host of the professor's male and female scientific colleagues. Reviewing the book in *The New York Times* (March 31, 1935), Isaac Anderson noted that *The Microbe Murders* "is a wild tale, and the telling of it is marred by some exceedingly bad writing."

Frederick George Eberhard was born in South Whitley, Indiana. After an undergraduate education at the University of Chicago, he received an M.D. from Northwestern in 1912. *The Microbe Murders* was the last of five mystery novels Eberhard published during his literary career.

29. FAIRWAY, SIDNEY [SIDNEY HERBERT DAUKES (1879–1947)]. *THE LONG TUNNEL.* LONDON: STANLEY PAUL, 1935; GARDEN CITY, N.Y.: DOUBLEDAY, DORAN & CO., 1936.

Seton Holbrook, a research scientist at "St. Botolph's Medical College" in London, dies after ingesting poison. Richard Carford, a young, bachelor professor of bacteriology at the college, is arrested as Holbrook's murderer. Carford stands trial and is acquitted, but his colleagues at St. Botolph's still believe him guilty of the crime. Ostracized by his former friends, Carford sets out to find Holbrook's real killer and, in the process, to clear his own name. He eventually succeeds in accomplishing both tasks. The motive for the crime, as Carford discovers, is rooted in the race for a cure for cancer, and the book is replete with detail about medical research in Britain in the 1930s. The book also includes a heavy dose of romance since the busy Carford takes time from his sleuthing to court Ruth Jessel, the daughter of a country parson. Academic readers will find the unflattering portraits of Carford's fellow St. Botolph's faculty members of more than passing interest, and they will appreciate, too, the book's ending. After the guilty party commits suicide, and after Carford's workmates are finally convinced of his innocence, our professorial protagonist relocates with his wife Ruth to the idyllic isle of Jersey, where he takes charge of a marine biology research station.

Sidney Herbert Daukes was a prominent London medical practitioner who wrote fiction as an avocation. He published nine mystery novels during his lifetime. Most of his mysteries centered on the medical profession.

30. SAYERS, DOROTHY L(EIGH) (1893–1957). *GAUDY NIGHT*. LONDON: GOLLANCZ, 1935; NEW YORK: HARCOURT, BRACE & CO., 1936.

Mystery writer Harriet Vane has recently been acquitted of a murder. Her nerves jangled from the experience, she is therefore responsive to an invitation to attend a presumably pleasant reunion at "Shrewsbury College," the Oxford women's college that is her alma mater. During her stay in Oxford, Vane receives several threatening notes. When she returns to London, she is contacted by the administration of Shrewsbury and asked to return to Oxford in order to investigate various other ominous happenings that have been taking place at the college. Putting her literary skills at sleuthing to work, Vane succeeds in developing a long list of Shrewsbury faculty and staff who could be disrupting the college's scholarly tranquility. She succeeds, too, in finding herself in physical danger. The love of her life, Lord Peter Wimsey, has been observing Vane's labors from afar. When the danger to Vane reaches crisis proportions, Lord Peter enters the case, and in as long and as intricate a denouement as can be found in any college mystery, he identifies the perpetrator of Shrewsbury's reign of evil deeds. Some critics have found the murderless *Gaudy Night* too long (483 pages in the original Gollancz edition), too wordy, and/or too prone to digress from detection in order to concentrate upon Harriet Vane's blossoming romance with Lord Peter. Nonetheless, the book is filled with engaging academic characters, overflowing with between-the-wars Oxford atmosphere, and it provides a series of penetrating portraits of women academicians at Shrewsbury College who want their scholarship to be taken seriously.

Dorothy Leigh Sayers was born in Oxford. The only child of the headmaster of Christchurch Cathedral Choir School, she was one of the first women to obtain an Oxford degree (first honours in medieval literature from Somerville College in 1915). Sayers taught modern languages at a girls' high school in Yorkshire from 1915 to 1917, was a reader for Blackwell Publishers in Oxford for one year during World War I, and then spent ten years as an advertising copywriter in London. In 1926 she married journalist Oswald Atherton Fleming, and in 1931 she retired from the advertising business to pursue her own writing on a full-time basis. A poet, playwright, editor, screen and radio writer, translator of Dante, expert on medieval culture, historian of mystery fiction, and feminist long before feminism was a popular or even acceptable orientation, Dorothy Sayers is best remembered by modern-day mystery buffs for her series of elegant detective novels and short stories featuring suave and urbane Lord Peter Wimsey. *Gaudy Night* is the twelfth novel in the Wimsey canon. Unlike most of the other books in the series, *Gaudy Night* pays less attention to Wimsey's exploits than it does to the adventures of Harriet Vane. And, unlike any of the other books in the Wimsey series, *Gaudy Night* takes place in an academic setting.

31. SIMMONS, ADDISON (B. 1902). *DEATH ON THE CAMPUS*. NEW YORK: CROWELL, 1935.

Death on the Campus is 293 pages long, considerably longer than the usual academic mystery. And, no wonder! Twenty people meet violent deaths; five sleuths work more or less independently of each other; and there are ten major suspects in the case. The tale is set at an unidentified American university. The first victim is Philip Yerkes, a professor of English, who is shot dead in his office. An amateur detective, Yerkes was investigating the apparent suicide of a faculty colleague. Professor Ben Ingram, yet another member of the school's English department, discovers Yerkes' body. He then calls President Meade, and even before they telephone the police, Ingram and Meade begin to interrogate individuals who were near Yerkes' office at the time of his death. Only after Ingram and Meade fail to identify Yerkes' killer do they ask for official assistance, and in response to their belated call District Attorney Kent Bloomingdale and Captain Packer of the local homicide squad arrive on the scene. At this point the carnage begins in earnest. Most of the likely suspects in the affair are killed by unknown assailants and another, Professor John Hardwick Bailey, tries unsuccessfully to commit suicide. As the story develops, it becomes evident that an underworld "mob" is at the bottom of all the evil. Professorial readers will revel in the scene toward the end of the book in which the aging Thaddeus Davis, still another professor of English, opens fire with his hair-triggered submachine gun on a gaggle of gangsters. Because the book incorporates so many plotting elements, and because it has such a large list of characters, it cannot be summarized adequately. Indeed, the author finds it necessary to use fifteen pages of text to provide the denouement. It can be noted with reasonable dispatch, however, that by the finale of this saga the university's English department has many, many faculty vacancies.

In *Crime Fiction II: A Comprehensive Bibliography, 1749–1990,* Allen J. Hubin identifies Addison Simmons as the possessor of undergraduate and law degrees from Harvard. *Death on the Campus* was the first of two mystery novels Simmons published during his lifetime.

32. BROOME, ADAM [GODFREY WARDEN JAMES (B. 1888)]. *THE CAMBRIDGE MURDERS.* LONDON: BLES, 1936.

Two black students from Africa are shot dead in Cambridge, and the leading suspect is Sir Wedgwood Camberley, a crotchety professor of anthropology. Sir Wedgwood is known to dislike blacks in general, and he is known, too, to have harbored a particular dislike for one of the deceased. That unfortunate chap aroused Sir Wedgwood's enmity by arriving late to one of the professor's lectures. When Inspector Worpledon of the Cambridge police learns that Sir Wedgwood owns an unregistered pistol of the same caliber used in the shootings, it seems only a matter of time until the professor will be arrested. But then another police official, Chief Constable Deepcut, is shot dead with a larger-caliber handgun, and Sir Wedgwood himself is shot and wounded while he is in Africa conducting research. Matters are finally resolved by Inspector Bramley of Scotland Yard, who gets help from the Cambridge Amateur Detective Society (CADS), a collection of Cambridge undergraduates that includes Molly Camberley, Sir Wedgwood's attractive daughter. Most of the story takes place in Cambridge, but there are several chapters in which Sir Wedgwood is depicted on his African travels. Like *The Oxford Murders* (5), an earlier college mystery by Adam Broome, *The Cambridge Murders* includes several white characters who proudly display racially bigoted attitudes. Yet by the end of *The Cambridge Murders* it is clear that racism can sow the seeds of self-destruction.

33. FULLER, TIMOTHY (1914–1971). *HARVARD HAS A HOMICIDE.* BOSTON: LITTLE, BROWN & CO., 1936. PUBLISHED IN ENGLAND AS *J FOR JUNIPER.* LONDON: COLLINS, 1937.

Professor Singer, an art historian, is stabbed dead in his room at Hallowell House at Harvard, and the person who finds his body is

"Juniper" Jones, one of his graduate students. The authorities are called, but stolid Sergeant Rankin of the Cambridge police seems unable to cope with the brilliance of the Harvard witnesses and suspects he must interview. Thus, Jones, who breezed through four undergraduate years at Harvard without studying, and whose graduate career has also been a study-free experience, embarks on his own detection. Before bringing the case to a conclusion, Jones finds that Professor Singer's murder is linked to art theft and plagiarism. Quick-witted and insouciant, Jones drinks too much and chain-smokes Camel cigarettes. His crime fighting is facilitated by Sylvester, his black valet. Sylvester polishes Jones's shoes, runs errands, and lends him money in moments of temporary financial distress. By the end of this light but cleverly constructed story, Sergeant Rankin has come to appreciate Jones's unique personal qualities, and he tells him that if there is ever another murder at Harvard he will allow him to be in charge of the investigation.

Timothy Fuller was born in Norwell, Massachusetts. He entered Harvard in 1932 but did not graduate. *Harvard Has a Homicide* was written while Fuller was still a Harvard student. Much of his post-college life was spent as a copywriter with the Boston advertising firm of Harold Cabot and Co. Fuller continued to write mysteries, using Juniper Jones as his detective in four further novels. After graduate school Jones becomes a member of the Harvard fine arts faculty, but in none of his subsequent exploits does his sleuthing take place at Harvard. However, in *Reunion with Murder* (Boston: Little, Brown & Co., 1941) Jones attends a Harvard class reunion at a country club and apprehends the killer of a classmate who is murdered on the golf course.

34. INNES, MICHAEL [JOHN INNES MACKINTOSH STEWART (1906–1994)]. *DEATH AT THE PRESIDENT'S LODGING*. LONDON: GOLLANCZ, 1936. PUBLISHED IN THE UNITED STATES AS *SEVEN SUSPECTS*. NEW YORK: DODD, MEAD & CO., 1936.

Death at the President's Lodging is set at "St. Anthony's College," Oxbridge, and the crime in the story is the late-night murder of Josiah Umpleby, St. Anthony's president. Dressed in a dinner jacket, and with his head wrapped in an academic robe, Umpleby is found shot dead in his locked college rooms. Oxford-educated Inspector John Appleby arrives from London to investigate, and he discovers that several of St. Anthony's dons had sufficient motive, as well as the opportunities, for ending President Umpleby's life. The clues in the affair have to do with the physical locations of the suspects' own rooms in the college, the dons' access to keys to various college doors, and the professional jealousies that pervade St. Anthony's. The book contains many literary allusions, a steady stream of witty donnish dialogue, and cunning puzzle development. One of the St. Anthony's characters is Giles Gott, a young literary scholar and junior proctor. Gott also writes murder mysteries, and in *Death at the President's Lodging* he renders valuable assistance to Inspector Appleby. Gott makes appearances in several subsequent Stewart mysteries, and many literary critics have seen him as Stewart's fictionalized version of himself. Scholars of mystery fiction generally rate *Death at the President's Lodging* one of the most engaging of all college mysteries, and after its publication the book stimulated many other academicians, both in the United States and Great Britain, to compose droll college mysteries of their own.

John Innes Mackintosh Stewart was born in Edinburgh, Scotland, and received a B. A. (honors) from Oriel College, Oxford, in 1928. He began a long and distinguished academic career in 1930 as a lecturer in English at the University of Leeds. He then took a post as lecturer in English at the University of Adelaide, Australia, where he served from 1935 until 1945. He was a lecturer at Queen's University, Belfast, from 1946 to 1948, and a fellow of Christ Church, Oxford, from 1949 until his retirement in 1973. Under his own name Stewart published many mainstream novels, and he wrote book-length studies of Shakespeare, Kipling, and Thomas Hardy. Under the pseudonym Michael Innes, Stewart published more than forty mystery novels, many of which featured Inspector Appleby. *Death at the President's Lodging* was Stewart's first mystery, and it was begun when he was traveling by ship to take up his lectureship in Australia. Three other Stewart/Innes mysteries appear in this bibliography. They are *The Weight of the Evidence* (57), *Operation Pax*(91), and *Old Hall, New Hall* (106). Three more Stewart/Innes mysteries, none of which is sufficiently "academic" to warrant inclusion in this bibliography, might nonetheless be of interest to readers of college mysteries. They are *Stop Press* (London: Gollancz, 1939), *Appleby Plays Chicken* (London: Gollancz, 1957), and *A Family Affair* (London: Gollancz, 1969). Published in the United States as *The Spider Strikes* (New York: Dodd, Mead, & Co., 1969), *Stop Press* is a countryhouse mystery in which several Oxford dons and students play important roles. *Appleby Plays Chicken* was published in the United States as *Death on a Quiet Day* (New York: Dodd, Mead & Co., 1957). It deals with the adventures of a "reading party" of Oxford students on a visit to Dartmoor. *A Family Affair* was published in the United States as *Picture of Guilt* (New York: Dodd, Mead, & Co., 1969). The detective in the story is

John Appleby, who resolves the puzzling matter of art thefts that have occurred at the highest levels of the British art world. The book offers several scenes at Oxford, at which Appleby's son Bobby is an undergraduate, and a central character is a professor of art from Cambridge.

35. POST, MORTIMER [WALTER BLAIR (1900–1992)]. *CANDIDATE FOR MURDER.* GARDEN CITY, N.Y.: DOUBLEDAY, DORAN & CO., 1936.

"Chatham University," somewhere in the United States, is thrown into disarray by four murders. The first victim is Carl Schact, a young, anti-Nazi chemist from Germany. Carl dies after eating nicotine-laden peppermint candies. The second victim is Geoffrey Nye, the chairperson of the political science department. Nye is stabbed with an ice pick in a dark corner of the Chatham Faculty Club. Next to go is Babette Whipple, Nye's young and attractive niece. Miss Whipple, too, is the recipient of ice pick hospitality at the faculty watering hole. Finally, Henry Winston joins the ranks of the deceased. Henry is a foundation executive and the executor of Geoffrey Nye's estate. He is killed when he opens the door of his hotel room, trips off a booby-trapped shotgun, and literally loses his head in the excitement. The local police enter the affair, but the real sleuthing is done by four professors who band together to pool their amateur talents. Lowell Gaylord, the sixty-year-old, portly chairperson of Chatham's English department, is the leader of the group. His assistants are Angus McDermott (a professor emeritus of medicine), Lens Penga (chairman of the biology department), and Arthur Churchill (a professor of law). Likely suspects include Karl Stein (a visiting Nazi academic from Germany), Avery Cox (a physician), Lynn Hazlitt (a chemist), and John Cannon (the desk clerk at the faculty club). Using logic, processes of elimination, and some personally perilous entrapment schemes, the four professorial detectives eventually get their man. Written with some light touches, despite an unremitting buildup of real and false clues, the book offers several unusual academic situations. At one point Professor Gaylord becomes so engrossed in the murder that he loses his customarily cheerful and pacifying disposition. As a result, the department over which he presides explodes with long-simmering jealousies and animosities. Toward the end of the story, the four professorial gumshoes dress in costumes and attempt to snare their quarry at a gala masked ball at the Faculty Club. And both the police and the professor-detectives spend a great deal of time interrogating the late Professor Nye's retinue of servants. The resident of a large, imposing house near the Chatham campus, Nye employed a maid, a housekeeper, a chauffeur, and a gardener.

Walter Blair was born in Spokane, Washington. He received his undergraduate education at Yale and then obtained an M.A. and a Ph.D. from the University of Chicago. From 1929 until his retirement in 1968, he was a member of Chicago's English department, and from 1951 until 1960 he served as department chairman. A critic, a biographer, a student of humor and folklore, and an authority on Mark Twain, Blair published extensively, but *Candidate for Murder*, which he wrote under the pseudonym Mortimer Post, was his only mystery novel.

36. RANKEN, J. L., JANE CLUNIES ROSS, ET AL. *MURDER PIE.* SYDNEY, AUSTRALIA: ANGUS & ROBERTSON, 1936.

After attending a psychology class one evening at an unidentified Australian university, Hugh Decker is found drowned in a lake near the campus. An adult student by night and a communist agitator by day, Hugh had both friends and enemies among his classmates. Urquhart Sterne, the young lecturer who instructs the class that Decker attended shortly before his death, is asked by the police for information about his students because all of his pupils come under immediate suspicion. For his part, Sterne sees the murder as a chance to test some of his pet psychological theories, and he begins to engage in some independent sleuthing. Two more adult students are killed, and Sterne almost loses his own life when he is waylaid, knocked unconscious, and dropped into a deep, snake-filled tunnel through which water is carried from the countryside into the city. While the motive for murder in this story proves to be nonacademic, the book includes many classroom scenes and some unique campus characters. Among the latter is Solomon Banks, a small, portly gentleman who "purveys frogs, fish, guinea pigs, and other small animals" to the university's zoology department. Indeed, as he is scouring the lake for frogs to sell to his zoologist customers, it is Banks who discovers Hugh Decker's body.

Murder Pie was written by committee. In an operation coordinated by J. L. Ranken and Jane Clunies Ross, two Australian academicians, sixteen members of university faculties in Australia each contributed a chapter. The names of all the authors, and the chapters that each wrote, are listed in the book's table of contents. As Rankin and Ross admit in a preface, the result of the mass collaboration reflects a shared enthusiasm for mysteries but not consistency of style. Some chapters are satirical; others are more serious in nature. And though Rankin and

Ross removed flagrant inconsistencies of plot in their editing, each contributor apparently was allowed to add one or more fillips to what emerges as a story brimming over with clues and suspects.

37. STEEL, KURT [RUDOLPH HORNADAY KAGEY (1904–1946)]. *MURDER GOES TO COLLEGE.* INDIANAPOLIS: BOBBS-MERRILL, 1936.

The institution of higher learning referred to in the title of this character-crammed novel is "Chelsea College," a high-prestige, private school in New York City. The murder is the shooting of Thomas Kelly, a Chelsea professor of mathematics. Kelly was using his skills in addition and subtraction to moonlight as a financial consultant to Strike Fusil, a notorious Harlem racketeer. Fusil is a suspect in the case, but so, too, are at least a dozen other principals in the story. Among the academic suspects are Chancellor Walter MacShean, Dean Everitt James, Paul Broderick (a black-bearded professor of English who writes mysteries of his own as a sideline), and Howard Sayfort (a professor of psychology). The sleuthing is done by Henry Hyer, a Kurt Steel series-character private detective. Hyer is appropriately tough talking and cynical, and he finds that Chelsea's genteel veneer covers not only Kelly's involvement with the underworld, but embezzlement and widespread faculty wife swapping as well. Real-life college teachers will savor the portrait of Dean James. A small, "ferret-eyed" man, James is systematically looting Chelsea's treasury, and when caught in the act by Hyer (who calls him "Weasel Face"), he collapses in tears and begs for mercy. And serious students of college mysteries will be interested in the depiction of Decker, Chelsea's black elevator operator. Whereas college porters are the sources of crucial information in many British mysteries, Decker serves in that capacity in *Murder Goes to College*. The faculty and staff of Chelsea are housed in a high-rise building, and Decker monitors all of the conversations between his passengers.

Rudolph Hornaday Kagey was born in Tuscola, Illinois, and was educated at the University of Illinois and Columbia University. From 1928 until his death in 1946, he was a member of the philosophy department at Washington Square College of New York University. At the time of his death he was acting director of the university's evening division. Kagey wrote ten mystery novels during his lifetime, nine of which starred private eye Hank Hyer. *Murder Goes to College* was the third book in the Hank Hyer series. All of Kagey's mysteries were published under the pseudonym Kurt Steel.

38. BOUCHER, ANTHONY [WILLIAM ANTHONY PARKER WHITE (1911–1968)]. *THE CASE OF THE SEVEN OF CALVARY*. NEW YORK: SIMON & SCHUSTER, 1937.

The sleuth in this riddle-filled story is John Ashwin, a professor of Sanskrit at the University of California at Berkeley. Assisted by Martin Lamb, a research fellow in German, Ashwin gets to the bottom of two related murders. The first is the apparently motiveless stabbing of the "unofficial" ambassador from the Swiss Republic. The second is the poisoning of a young instructor of history named Paul Lennox. An amateur actor, Lennox brings a new sense of reality to the Berkeley stage by actually expiring while acting out a death scene in a university production of *Don Juan Returns*. Professor Ashwin and Martin Lamb are both avid readers of mystery fiction, and the book incorporates many references to classic works of the genre. Due, no doubt, to their familiarity with the tactics of other fictional sleuths, Ashwin and Lamb are ever alert for red herrings. Furthermore, they are sufficiently sophisticated to realize that two murders need not be the work of one murderer. Most of the suspects in the case are residents of Berkeley's International House, where Martin Lamb is one of the few American lodgers. Professor Ashwin, who never ventures out of his study during the story, utters one line that can serve as useful advice for all sleuths in genteel, academic detective stories. At the end of the tale Ashwin gathers together the book's surviving characters and announces which of them murdered the Swiss diplomat. Immediately thereafter he offers the killer a glass of scotch. "A mere accusation of murder," declares Ashwin, "should never stand in the way of hospitality."

William Anthony Parker White was born in Oakland, California. He received a B.A. from the University of Southern California in 1932 and an M.A. from the University of California at Berkeley in 1939. *The Case of the Seven of Calvary* was the first of four mystery novels that White published during his lifetime. White employed the pseudonym Anthony Boucher throughout his career, and it is under that alias that he is remembered (and often revered) for the penetrating reviews of mystery fiction he offered to readers of *The New York Times* from 1951 until his death in 1968.

39. MACDUFF, DAVID (B. 1905). *MURDER STRIKES THREE*. NEW YORK: MODERN AGE BOOKS, 1937.

It is commencement day at an unidentified liberal arts college in the eastern United States. Professor Russell Stearne Finley, a distinguished archaeologist, is scheduled to read the names of the graduates as they step forward to receive their diplomas. But Professor Finley does not appear. He is found shot dead in his office at the college's Swann Museum. And, what's more, the professor's prize mummy, "Benny," is missing from the museum's exhibits. That same afternoon George Goeckler of the Latin department is stabbed dead in an automobile. A few days later Professor Otto Goeckler (an archaeologist, and no relation to George) turns up drowned in a nearby river, his face apparently eaten away by extremely hungry fish. The sleuthing in the story is done by Reuben Mallock, the chief of detectives of Buckhill County, and by Geoffrey Fowler, a young instructor at the college. Fowler is an early suspect in the case, but Anne Faulconer, Professor Finley's attractive secretary, and Andrew Finley, the professor's hunchbacked, dwarfish son, emerge as more-likely culprits as the mystery deepens. *Murder Strikes Three* offers relatively little of the civilized dialogue usually associated with college mysteries, but it contains many interesting on-campus scenes. Professorial readers will appreciate the vignette, early in the book, in which Geoffrey Fowler and several of his junior faculty cronies fortify themselves with gin rickeys before heading reluctantly to what they expect will be a long and tedious graduation ceremony.

According to Allen J. Hubin in *Crime Fiction II: A Comprehensive Bibliography, 1749–1990*, David MacDuff was born in Scotland, attended the University of California, and was a press agent and newspaperman. *Murder Strikes Three* was MacDuff's only mystery novel. The tale was issued as part of an early-day experiment, by Modern Age Books, in the publication and mass marketing of paperback novels. Presumably worried that the book's sales would be hurt if prospective readers thought the saga was a conventional, slow-moving college mystery yarn, Modern Age took pains to promote the story as a hard-hitting detective epic. The blurb on the cover of the book reads, in part: "Tough, fast, terse, this story of a campus murder has no academic flavor to it."

40. MILLER, JOHN [JOSEPH SAMACHSON (1906–1980)]. *MURDER OF A PROFESSOR*. NEW YORK: PUTNAMS, 1937.

The professorial victim referred to in the title of this novel is Ellsworth Owen, a member of the chemistry department of a large, unidentified American university. After years of suffering from slowly spreading cancer, Professor Owen apparently takes his own life with an overdose of painkiller. Sergeant Fogerty of the Homicide Squad is not content to rule out foul play, however, and Fogerty's investigation not only establishes that the professor was murdered, but it also leads to the identification of his killer. The story is told from the perspective of Philip Waring, one of Professor Owen's junior colleagues. Along with several other university chemists, Waring becomes a suspect in the case, and he must engage in some sleuthing of his own to avoid arrest. Although *Murder of a Professor* is not one of the more inspired examples of mystery fiction in this bibliography, it does keep its readers guessing until the end. Moreover, for those who are interested in chemical analysis, the book offers some fine examples of in-the-laboratory detective work.

Joseph Samachson was born in Trenton, New Jersey. He received a B.S. from Rutgers in 1926 and a Ph.D. from Yale in 1930. Samachson's primary career was as a chemist. After holding a variety of posts with commercial firms and hospitals, he became a clinical associate professor of biochemistry at Loyola University of Chicago in 1968. As a writer, Samachson collaborated with his wife, Dorothy, on several books about music and the theater. He also published many science-fiction novels. *Murder of a Professor* was Samachson's only conventional mystery. Much of Samachson's fiction was published under the pseudonyms John Miller, William Morrison, and Brett Sterling.

41. OWENS, HANS C. *WAYS OF DEATH*. NEW YORK: GREEN CIRCLE BOOKS, 1937.

It is "Tap Day" at an American university that very much resembles Yale. Bob Somers, a junior, confidently expects to be offered membership in one of the institution's most prestigious secret societies, and his father, Judge Albert Somers, has come from New York City to witness the great event. Bob gets his cherished invitation, but even as the selection ceremonies are taking place outside in the quadrangle, Judge Somers is shot dead in Bob's dormitory room. The local police quickly identify Johnny Redfield, a campus security guard, as the judge's probable killer. However, when Redfield is murdered the police admit their bewilderment, and President Davenport asks Percival Trout, dean of the university's school of psychology, to pick up the threads of the case. Trout, a major in army intelligence during World War I, possesses an M.D., a Ph.D., and an LL.D. He also possesses an imperious manner and is given to such endearing outbursts as, "Shut up. . . . If you had my brains, even you might amount to something." Playing no favorites, the deanly detective treats everyone (including President Davenport) as a suspect before announcing the name of the guilty party. Neither the murderer nor his motive turn out to have university connections, but in addition to the depiction of Dean Trout, the book contains some arresting academic portraits. Of special interest to president watchers will be the characterization of courtly President Davenport. A gentleman of the old school, Davenport buys all of his black derby hats from a shop on Ludgate Hill, London, and for male guests in his home he keeps on hand a supply of the finest Havana cigars.

42. COLE, G(EORGE) D(OUGLAS) H(OWARD) (1889–1959), AND MARGARET (ISABEL POSTGATE) COLE (1893–1980). *OFF WITH HER HEAD!* LONDON: COLLINS, 1938; NEW YORK: MACMILLAN, 1939.

The severed head of a woman is delivered in a biscuit tin to the room of an Oxford undergraduate. When it rested atop its body, the head was the property of a shady lady-of-the-town whose charms had been shared with many members of the Oxford academic community. Called in to assist the local police with their inquiries is Tom Fairford, a young, bachelor Scotland Yard inspector. Fairford has no shortage of suspects. Some are undergraduates. Some are unsavory London types who have taken up temporary residence in Oxford. And one is Dr. John Holland, an accomplished surgeon and a temporary member of the Oxford faculty. Fairford solves the case with the assistance of Ann Maitland, the niece of Dr. George Milligan, the master of "St. Simon's College." Fairford and Ann also fall in love, much to the master's distress. Dr. Milligan, a paragon of stuffiness whose idea of an opening conversational gambit is to offer an opinion on the arts of primitive Africa, does not relish the thought of a policeman in the family. Written with a light touch and replete with satirical references to Oxford personages and folkways, the book is a classic British college mystery.

George Douglas Howard Cole was educated at St. Paul's School and at Balliol College, Oxford. A fixture on the British intellectual scene until his death in 1959, George Cole was a socialist economist, a fellow of the Fabian Society, and a prolific writer of professional books, political tracts, and (with his wife, Margaret) mystery novels. Margaret Isabel Postgate Cole received her education at Roedean School and Girton College, Cambridge. The sister of mystery writer Raymond Postgate, Mrs. Cole combined writing with political activism as a longtime socialist member of the London County Council. Critics generally applauded the Coles' mysteries as intelligent, well crafted, and entertaining. Another mystery by the Coles, *A Knife in the Dark* (49), also appears in this bibliography.

43. AUGUST, JOHN [BERNARD AUGUSTINE DEVOTO (1897–1955)]. *TROUBLED STAR*. BOSTON: LITTLE, BROWN & CO., 1939.

These are difficult times at "Morrison University," a state institution in the Midwest. Henry Zimmerman, a newspaper mogul, wants to run for the U.S. Senate, and to gain notoriety he has launched an assault on Stephen Bradford, Morrison's noble president. President Bradford, so Zimmerman would like the readers of his papers to believe, is guilty of running a sin-filled campus. Zimmerman sends Bill Snelling, an unprincipled reporter, to Morrison to sniff out scandal. In fact, there are two related scandals at Morrison just waiting to be discovered. Ann Bradford, the president's daughter, was once secretly married to Alec Cornish, a government geologist who, as fate would have it, has just arrived on the campus to conduct federally financed research. And Carl Gibson, an obnoxious, young professor of sociology, has had clandestine affairs with many Morrison ladies, including Ann Bradford. As Snelling begins his journalistic inquiries, Carl Gibson is found shot dead in his home, and Ann Bradford, Alec Cornish, and the school's wise-but-weary dean, Oliver Hannah, quickly become suspects. So, too, does Frank Mason, the chairperson of Morrison's sociology department, with whom the late Professor Gibson had often quarreled. In self-defense, Cornish and Dean Hannah try their hands at detection, but the most energetic sleuthing is done by Emery Smith, the undergraduate editor of the daily student newspaper. At 310 pages, the book is considerably longer than most mystery novels, and the extra pages allow the author to stuff the story with a running description of the Zimmerman-Bradford controversy, several romantic subplots, and considerable material about Morrison's physical and social environment. Readers are even treated to an excursion to the Tetlow Inn, a near-the-campus watering hole owned by Maxie Blotz, a racketeer with ties to the New York mob, and a man to whom Carl Gibson owed large gambling debts.

Bernard Devoto was born in Ogden, Utah. He attended the University of Utah before military service as an infantry lieutenant in World War I. After the war Devoto enrolled at Harvard, and he graduated in 1920. He was an instructor of English at Northwestern University from 1922 until 1927, and from 1927 until 1929 he was an instructor at Harvard. Following his brief stint in academe Devoto went on to hold editorial positions with *Harpers* and *The Saturday Evening Post* and to become one of America's most prominent men of letters. He wrote novels, mysteries, short stories, literary criticism, and works of history. One of his historical works, *Across the Wide Missouri* (Boston: Houghton Mifflin, 1944), won him a Pulitzer Prize in 1948. John August was a pseudonym that Devoto employed on some of his works of fiction. *Troubled Star* was the first of four Devoto mysteries that bear the August pen name.

44. BAGBY, GEORGE [AARON MARC STEIN (1906–1985). *THE CORPSE WITH PURPLE THIGHS.* GARDEN CITY, N.Y.: DOUBLEDAY, DORAN & CO, 1939.

George "Baggy" Bagby, the author-narrator of this tale, attends his class reunion at a college that very much resembles Princeton. He finds a dead body outside the firehouse that serves as reunion headquarters, but when he goes into the building to summon help, the body mysteriously disappears. Understandably both perplexed and embarrassed, Bagby calls his old friend, Inspector Schmidt, to come and help him investigate. Inspector Schmidt is a Bagby series-character detective. *The Corpse with Purple Thighs* takes its readers to many parts of the college campus, and it features several individuals who are connected with the college even as the reunion is taking place. One is Bob Larraby, an undergraduate, who is still in town awaiting the results of his final exams. Another is Harry Stedman, an alumnus who is now a professor of economics. The thighs referred to in the book's title became purple from a poorly dyed pair of pants worn as part of a reunion costume. Real-life professors, especially those teaching in nonelite colleges, may find the novel interesting for the information it contains about the postcollege careers of graduates of high-status institutions. For the most part, the reunioners in the story, many of whom eventually make the Bagby-Schmidt suspect list, are wealthy men, but some have become affluent through shady business practices and many others have spent their time after college simply clipping coupons. As one character in the book describes the latter group, "The firehouse is full of guys who were born with silver spoons in their mouths and who developed lockjaw early enough to hang onto the precious hardware."

Aaron Marc Stein was born in New York City. He received an A.B. from Princeton in 1927. After graduating Stein held journalist positions with *The Saturday Evening Post* and *Time* before embarking on a career as a full-time writer of fiction. A prolific mystery writer, Stein wrote more than one hundred detective novels, some of them under the pseudonyms George Bagby and Hampton Stone. Three other Aaron Marc Stein mysteries, all of them published under his real name, appear in this bibliography. Those mysteries are *The Case of the Absent-Minded Professor* (60), *The Cradle and the Grave* (84), and *A Body for a Buddy* (217).

45. BAYNE, SPENCER [FLOYD ALBERT SPENCER (1899–1978), AND PAULA TERESA BAYNE SPENCER (B. 1907)]. *MURDER RECALLS VAN KILL.* NEW YORK: HARPER & BROTHERS, 1939.

Independently wealthy Dr. Cameron, a professor of biblical literature and language at "Brampton University" in upstate New York, has a brilliant adolescent son named Edward. The lad requires an enriched education in order to realize his full potential, so Professor Cameron hires Hendrick "Hal" Van Kill, an erudite but unemployed archaeologist, to serve as Edward's live-in tutor. The professor resides in a secluded mansion near the Brampton campus, and his household includes four attractive female student-boarders with whom he has more than the usual landlord-renter relationship. One of the young ladies is found dead in the mansion's garden, her abdomen sliced open, and then Professor Cameron is seriously injured when he apparently falls down a long flight of stairs. Fearful of negative publicity, the university authorities work with the local coroner to have the young woman's death ruled a suicide and the professor's fall an accident. However, Hal Van Kill knows better, and he launches his own investigation that ultimately leads to the identification of a killer. Most of this literate and often-satirical novel takes place on the grounds of the Cameron mansion, but readers are provided with many opportunities to observe oily Dean Ormont, the power behind the throne at Brampton University and a man who aspires to the school's presidency. At one point in the story Ormont tries to motivate Hal Van Kill to stop his detection by offering him a full professorship, but having observed the immorality of one Brampton professor and the sliminess of the institution's probable next president, Van Kill declines the invitation.

Spencer Bayne was the joint pseudonym of Floyd Albert Spencer and Paula Teresa Bayne Spencer. Floyd Albert Spencer received a Ph.D. from the University of Chicago and was a professor of Greek and classics. During his career he taught at Ohio Wesleyan University, the University of Illinois, New York University, and Queens College. *Murder Recalls Van Kill* was the first of three Hendrick Van Kill mysteries by Spencer Bayne.

46. LONG, AMELIA REYNOLDS (1904–1976). *THE SHAKESPEARE MURDERS.* NEW YORK: PHOENIX, 1939.

One of the highlights of the academic year at a world-class university in Philadelphia is to be a Shakespeare seminar taught by Professor Godfrey Shelley of Oxford. So impressive are Professor Shelley's credentials that several faculty members sign up to take the course along with many of the English department's graduate students. Not long after the seminar commences Dr. Duncan King, one of the faculty participants, is stabbed dead. Dr. King meets his end shortly before he is to give a class presentation on Macbeth. Then four other murders occur (three of the subsequent victims are seminar attendees), and in each instance the method of killing mimics a lethal technique employed in one or another of Shakespeare's works. The detective in the case is Edward Trelawney, a criminal psychologist, who happens to be at the university taking advanced courses in his chosen field of endeavor. Fortunately, Trelawney also knows a good deal about the intricacies of Shakespeare's plots, and he is able to bring the guilty party to justice. While no college mystery surpasses *The Shakespeare Murders* in its extensive layering on of literary allusions, the book can nonetheless be read with interest by those whose familiarity with Shakespeare is minimal. Real-life academics should certainly take inspiration from Professor Shelley's dedication to teaching. Shelley doggedly insists on holding his weekly seminar, even as the number of dropouts-by-murder keeps increasing.

Amelia Reynolds Long was born in Harrisburg, Pennsylvania. She received a B.S. degree from the University of Pennsylvania in 1931 and an M.A. in English from the same institution in 1932. Most of Long's early adult life was spent as a college textbook editor for Stackpole & Co., a Harrisburg publishing firm. In 1958 she became curator of the William Penn Museum in Harrisburg, and she served in that position until her retirement in 1976. Using her own name as well as various pseudonyms, Long published more than thirty mystery novels between 1936 and 1953. She also produced over three hundred short stories, a book-length dictionary of terms used in the examination and observation of the natural environment, and several books of poetry. Five other mysteries by Amelia Reynolds Long appear in this bibliography. *Death Looks Down* (62) was written under Long's own name. *Murder Most Foul* (70) was published under the name Kathleen Buddington Coxe. *Stone Dead* (67), *Murder from the Mind* (76), and *The Lady Is Dead*

(92) were written under the pseudonym Patrick Laing. Using the pen name Adrian Reynolds, Long also wrote a three-novel series featuring a professor-detective named Dennis Barrie. Professor Barrie, who teaches English at an American college that is never identified, appears in *Formula for Murder* (New York: Phoenix, 1947), *The Leprechaun Murders* (New York: Phoenix, 1950), and *The Round Table Murders* (New York: Phoenix, 1952). All three Professor Barrie novels are off-campus tales, hence none of them is accorded an entry in this bibliography.

47. PATRICK, Q. [RICHARD WILSON WEBB (B. 1901) AND HUGH CALLINGHAM WHEELER (1912–1987)]. *DEATH AND THE MAIDEN*. NEW YORK: SIMON & SCHUSTER, 1939.

This intricate, clue-crammed story is set at "Wentworth College," an institution in the New York City area. When Grace Hough, a Wentworth undergraduate, is found dead after a "severe blow" to the back of her head, Lieutenant Timothy Trant of the New York Homicide Squad is put in charge of the case. Miss Hough was blackmailing her professor of French, but as Trant learns after considerable sleuthing, the professor was not the only person on the Wentworth campus who wanted to extinguish her life. The story is narrated by Lee Lovering, Grace's roommate. Everyone's friend, Miss Lovering deliberately deceives Lieutenant Trant on a number of occasions in order to protect persons who, in her view, could not possibly be capable of murder. However, Lieutenant Trant is a Princeton graduate as well as an experienced Q. Patrick series-character detective. Knowing that evil may lurk where it is least suspected, he eventually sees through Miss Lovering's deceptions. College-mystery buffs will have to be alert when reading this novel; the book contains more red herrings than most of the other works in this bibliography.

An earlier Q. Patrick academic mystery, *Murder at Cambridge* (21), also appears in this bibliography. *Murder at Cambridge*, published in 1933, was written by Richard Wilson Webb. *Death and the Maiden* was the result of a subsequent collaboration between Webb and Hugh Callingham Wheeler. Born in Northwood, a London suburb, Wheeler took an honours degree in English at the University of London in 1932. After a chance meeting, Webb invited Wheeler to write with him under the Q. Patrick alias and, in 1933, Wheeler emigrated to Philadelphia, where Webb was employed with a pharmaceutical firm. The Webb-Wheeler collaboration endured for nearly two decades, until Webb's health forced him into retirement. Wheeler then utilized a new pseudonym, Patrick Quentin, on some of his works. One of Wheeler's solo mysteries, published under is own name, is *The Crippled Muse* (New York: Rinehart, 1952). Although the book is not a college mystery, it may be of interest to some of the users of this bibliography. The protagonist is Horace Beddoes, a middle-aged professor of English at "Wentworth College" in Ohio, who has a series of life-threatening adventures on the isle of Capri.

48. MERSEREAU, JOHN (B. 1898). *MURDER LOVES COMPANY*. PHILADELPHIA: LIPPINCOTT, 1940.

James Yates Biddle is a professor of horticulture at the University of California at Berkeley. In addition to his teaching duties, he oversees an experimental forest near the campus. When two men are found dead of cyanide poisoning in his "garden," Professor Biddle turns sleuth. He is assisted by Kay Ritchie, a sprightly female reporter for a San Francisco newspaper, and impeded by Police Inspector Angus Drift, a dour minion of the law who holds professor-detectives in low regard. A vigorous man in his mid-thirties, Biddle steals time from his many responsibilities to romance Miss Ritchie. Some of his courting is done to the melodious strains of "Davy Doolittle's Dizzy Drudges," the house band at the "Raleigh Rainbow Room" in Oakland. Captivated by Biddle's intellect and charm, Ritchie is willing to overlook most of his many eccentricities. The good professor drives a sports car that he has christened Xantrippe. He awakes each morning to his "happy chimes" alarm clock. And he refuses to read any books that contain split infinitives.

John Mersereau was born in northern Michigan but moved with his family to California when he was eight years old. He attended the University of California at Berkeley. At the time *Murder Loves Company* was published, Mersereau was a Hollywood screenwriter. Although his characterization of James Yates Biddle includes many of the qualities that contribute to a successful professorial series-character detective, Mersereau began and ended Professor Biddle's literary life with this single adventure.

49. COLE, G(EORGE) D(OUGLAS) H(OWARD) (1889–1959), AND MARGARET (ISABEL POSTGATE) COLE (1893–1980). *A KNIFE IN THE DARK*. LONDON: COLLINS, 1941; NEW YORK: MACMILLAN, 1942.

A Knife in the Dark is set at "Stamford University," a two-hour train ride to the north of London. In a foreword to the book the Coles call

Stamford a "dream university," but the place takes on nightmarish qualities when Kitty Lake, the wife of a Stamford reader in organic chemistry, is stabbed through the heart with a Maori dagger. Mrs. Lake, so it seems, was something of a one-woman hospitality squad, and various of her academic and nonacademic lovers come under suspicion for her murder. Several individuals share the detection in this story. Colonel Grieg, Superintendent Codd, and Inspectors Johnson and Jackson, all of the Stamford police force, have a hand in the investigations, but the case is finally resolved by Mrs. Elizabeth Warrender, a distant relative of the Lakes and an infrequently employed G. D. H. and Margaret Cole series-character sleuth. The time is 1940. Refugees from continental Europe have relocated in the town of Stamford, and though the story incorporates many references to university matters, it also deals with the fears of wartime Britons that Nazi spies have entered their midst.

Leaders in the socialist movement in England for nearly forty years, George and Margaret Cole collaborated to produce many literate, well-constructed mysteries. Another mystery by the Coles, *Off with Her Head!* (42), appears earlier in this bibliography.

50. KENT, DAVID [HERMAN HOFFMAN BIRNEY (1891–1958)]. *JASON BURR'S FIRST CASE.* NEW YORK: RANDOM HOUSE, 1941.

The narrator of this story is Paul Craig, head of the anthropology department at "Markham University" in "Steelbury," Pennsylvania. George Armitage, multimillionaire founder of the Armitage Museum of American Archaeology on the Markham campus, is stabbed dead in his museum office, and Professor Craig discovers his body. The weapon was a dart from the museum's extensive collection of Native American weapons. At first, the police suspect Craig of the crime, and they take him to the local stationhouse where they subject him to a third-degree interrogation, but the incompetent local medical examiner soon rules that Armitage died of a sudden heart attack and simply fell on the dart as he was expiring. Happy to be exonerated, but unhappy with the medical examiner's facile natural-death pronouncement, Professor Craig asks Jason Burr to help him look for George Armitage's real killer. A former newspaper reporter in Philadelphia and New York, but now a man of leisure thanks to an inheritance, Burr has established residence in Steelbury, where he has taken occasional courses at the university and has impressed all who have met him as a man of almost superhuman intelligence. Burr also is eccentric. When he wants to attract the attention of his deaf servant, he fires a pistol into a gong that stands in his study. Throughout the main portion of the book Burr and Craig hunt down the real murderer, and, in the process, they move on and off the Markham campus. Although several members of the Markham University community, as well as a visiting dean from "Southwestern University," play likely suspect roles, the nature of this tale is not entirely university related. Some of the plot has to do with members of the Armitage family fighting over the deceased's estate. Nevertheless, readers who remain with the story until its end will be rewarded when the solution to the mystery proves to be thoroughly academic, and they will be compensated, as well, by information about how to fabricate rare Native American artifacts.

Jason Burr's First Case was Herman Hoffman Birney's first mystery novel. He clearly intended Jason Burr as a series-character detective. *Jason Burr's First Case* was followed by another, nonacademic Jason Burr exploit, titled *A Knife Is Silent* (New York: Random House, 1947), in which Burr sleuths in Haiti. Alas, *A Knife Is Silent* marked the end of Birney's brief Jason Burr series as well as the end of his mystery-writing career. In *Crime Ficton II: A Comprehensive Bibliography, 1749–1990,* Allen J. Hubin notes that Herman Hoffman Birney was born in Colorado and was an amateur archaeologist.

51. MCCLOY, HELEN (1904–1993). *THE MAN IN THE MOONLIGHT*. NEW YORK: WILLIAM MORROW, 1941.

"Yorkville University" in New York City is in a state of turmoil. Professional jealousies and domestic difficulties are tearing apart its faculty. Nazi spies are skulking between its buildings. Evil capitalists are trying to usurp for themselves the profits from scientific breakthroughs made in the school's laboratories. And the institution's finances are in such poor condition that faculty salaries have just been reduced! No wonder that Yorkville's president (whose own paycheck, presumably, has not been cut) is off on an extended lecture tour of South America. During (but not because of) the president's absence, corpses of murdered faculty members and their spouses begin to turn up on and near the campus. Dr. Basil Willing, a prominent New York psychiatrist who happens to be a Yorkville graduate as well as a Helen McCloy series-character detective, is asked to help investigate the killings. Though he cannot hope to deal with all of his alma mater's problems, Dr. Willing does at least end the spate of murders. Overstuffed with academic and international intrigues, *The*

Man in the Moonlight features a large and generally unpleasant cast of academic characters.

Helen McCloy was born in New York City. After attending the Sorbonne in 1923-1924, she served as a correspondent for various American and British newspapers in Paris and London, and in 1930 she began a two-year stint as the London correspondent for the fine arts section of the *Sunday New York Times*. She began to publish detective fiction in 1938. McCloy's Dr. Basil Willing series is generally held in high esteem by mystery buffs. *The Man in the Moonlight* was the second of thirteen Basil Willing novels.

52. HOLMAN, (CLARENCE) HUGH (1914–1981). *DEATH LIKE THUNDER*. NEW YORK: PHOENIX, 1942.

Mike Leiter, a radio scriptwriter from New York City, accepts a position at "Abecton College" in rural South Carolina. Mike's job is to organize a "department of radio." He makes little progress, however, because shortly after his arrival in the steamy heart of Dixie he finds himself in jail after being falsely arrested for the murder of an Abecton history professor. Only Norman Travis, a local boy who has recently established a law practice in Abecton after ten years with a prestigious New York law firm, stands between Yankee Leiter and the full force of southern justice. With the help of Juanita Dickens, his sharp-tongued, attractive secretary, and Ruth Dessauseux, Leiter's impulsive girlfriend, Travis is able to identify the professor's actual killer. The unmasking of the murderer comes during Leiter's trial, but much of the action preceding the courtroom scenes is set on the Abecton campus, and most of the suspects in the case are Abecton faculty members and administrators. Dr. Arnold Jarvis Taine (an instructor of history), Dr. Isaac Hews (an aged psychologist), Dean William Andrew Thomas, and President Yates Thorndyke Bell are all crucial figures in the story. Real-life professors may enjoy the vignette in which the stuffy Dean Thomas breaks down and cries on the witness stand, and flesh-and-blood presidents will appreciate Yates Thorndyke Bell's description of his presidential duties. When asked to summarize his role at Abecton, Bell says that he is a "combination of circus barker, press agent, and professional beggar." The book incorporates an abundance of clues, several subplots, and a few explanations (offered by Norman Travis) of the prejudices that small-town southerners harbor against carpetbaggers from the North.

Clarence Hugh Holman was born in Cross Anchor, South Carolina. He received a B.A. from Presbyterian College in Clinton, South Carolina, in 1938 and a Ph.D. from the University of North Carolina in 1949. At the time *Death Like Thunder* was published, Holman was serving as director of radio and instructor of English at Presbyterian College. In 1946 Holman moved to the University of North Carolina as a graduate student and instructor in French. He eventually became Keene Professor of English at North Carolina, provost of the university, and chairman of the board of governors of the University of North Carolina Press. *Death Like Thunder* was the first of five mystery novels that Holman published during his lifetime. One of his subsequent mysteries, *Up This Crooked Way* (73), appears later in the bibliography.

53. JOHNSON, W. BOLINGBROKE [MORRIS GILBERT BISHOP (1893–1973)]. *THE WIDENING STAIN*. NEW YORK: KNOPF, 1942.

The Wildmerding Library, on the campus of a high-status but unidentified university in the eastern United States, is known far and wide for its great collections of rare manuscripts. But when Mademoiselle Coindreau, an assistant professor of French, is found dead of a broken neck after a suspicious fall from one of the building's galleries, the Wildmerding Library begins to acquire a new, less-edifying reputation. Gilda Gorham, the library's chief cataloger, looks into Mademoiselle Coindreau's demise. However, just as Gorham pinpoints old Professor Hyett of the classics department as the most likely murderer, Hyett becomes the second library patron to expire on the premises. More sleuthing is required, and Gilda Gorham, with help from Lieutenant Kennedy of the local police, is equal to the task. Laced with limericks and peppered with false as well as real clues, *The Widening Stain* is one of the brightest and wittiest of all American college mysteries. Many, many professors appear in the story, and each pedant has his or her unique set of eccentricities. The surprising motive for the killings, which is revealed in the book's last chapter, may give modern-day academic feminists additional ammunition for their arguments.

Morris Bishop was born in Willard, New York. He received an A.B. and a Ph.D. from Cornell. A longtime professor of romance languages at Cornell, Bishop wrote in a variety of fields. His oeuvre includes textbooks, biographies, poetry, and a history of Cornell. *The Widening Stain* was his only mystery novel.

54. LEWIS, LANGE [JANE LEWIS BRANDT (B. 1915)]. *MURDER AMONG FRIENDS*. INDIANAPOLIS: BOBBS-MERRILL, 1942.

Kate Farr takes a job as secretary to Ulysses Calder, the wise and humane dean of a university medical school in Los Angeles. Miss Farr's predecessor, Garnet Dillon, was a beautiful young woman who was efficient as a typist but, as Dean Calder puts it, was "not necessarily good" when it came to sexual conduct. Miss Garnet has mysteriously disappeared, and Kate Farr, taking an introductory tour of the medical school's facilities, finds her body laid out in the embalming room. Detective Richard Tuck of the local police enters the case at this point. An autopsy shows that Miss Garnet was both poisoned and pregnant, and Tuck's sights fall upon various male medical students, all of whom were known to have been smitten by Miss Garnet's charms. Kate Farr, meanwhile, falls in love with Johnny Greenwood, one of the student-suspects, but this does not prevent her from providing sleuth Tuck with some amateur assistance. The ending of the story is unusual, and readers may find it difficult to distinguish between the good guys and the bad ones.

Jane Lewis Brandt was born in Oakland, California, and received an A.B. from the University of Southern California in 1939. *Murder among Friends* was her first mystery novel. Another mystery by Jane Lewis Brandt, writing again under the pseudonym Lange Lewis, is included in this bibliography. That novel, which also features the detection of Lieutenant Tuck, is *Juliet Dies Twice* (58).

55. MITCHELL, GLADYS (MAUDE WINIFRED) (1901–1983). *LAURELS ARE POISON*. LONDON: MICHAEL JOSEPH, 1942.

Miss Murchan, the warden of Athelstan Hall at "Cataret Training College," disappears during a school dance. Miss duMagne, the principal of the teacher-training institution, sends for Mrs. Beatrice Bradley. A Gladys Mitchell series-character detective, Mrs. Bradley is a distinquished psychologist and criminologist who acts as a consultant to the British Home Office. Installed as Athelstan's temporary warden, Mrs. Bradley gets to the bottom of the affair. The story, written with Gladys Mitchell's usual blend of neofantasy, semisatire, and genteel dialogue, includes the murder of Athelstan Hall's cook, many college "rags," and a discussion of the "fetishism" involved in the preparation of vegetables. The staff, faculty, and students of Cataret College (all of them female) display various eccentricities. As for Mrs.

Bradley, who is required to teach in the story as well as to act as detective, real-life academicians will marvel at the ease with which she delivers off-the-cuff lectures on a dizzying array of arcane topics.

Gladys Mitchell was born in Cowley, Oxfordshire, England. She was a student at Goldsmith College from 1919 until 1921 and received a diploma in history from the University of London in 1926. Miss Mitchell taught English and history and coached track and field sports at several British girls' schools until her retirement in 1961. Her first Beatrice Bradley mystery novel, *Speedy Death*, was published by Gollancz in 1929. *Laurels Are Poison* was the fourteenth book in what was to become a very popular fifty-novel Bradley series. In addition to *Laurels Are Poison*, a later Beatrice Bradley exploit, *Spotted Hemlock* (115), also appears in this bibliography.

56. CAMPBELL, MARY ELIZABETH (1903–1984). *SCANDAL HAS TWO FACES*. GARDEN CITY, N.Y.: DOUBLEDAY, DORAN & CO., 1943.

It is June of 1939 and at a large state university in Ohio the English department is about to give final examinations. Trouble arises when the questions to one of the tests turn up in a fraternity house. Then the widely disliked director of the freshman English program, a man who is also the university's dean of liberal arts, is found murdered in his office. Matthew Craig, the local prosecuting attorney, takes personal charge of the murder case. In the process of discovering the identity of the dean's killer, he also plugs the leaks in the English department's security system. A great many faculty members, most of them teachers of freshman English, pass across the pages of this story, and more than one of them proves to have a suspicion-provoking secret life. Moreover, several of the faculty spouses in the story are something other than happy, loving helpmates. *Scandal Has Two Faces* is on-campus detective fiction in undiluted form. Readers who enjoy excavating for dirt beneath the clean surface veneers of academe will find that this book more than meets their requirements.

Mary Elizabeth Campbell was born in Cambridge, Ohio. She received A.B. and A.M. degrees from Radcliffe and a Ph.D. from Yale. At the time *Scandal Has Two Faces* was published, Campbell was a member of the English department at Indiana University. *Scandal Has Two Faces* was the second of two mystery novels that Campbell published during her literary lifetime.

57. INNES, MICHAEL [JOHN INNES MACKINTOSH STEWART (1906–1994)]. *THE WEIGHT OF THE EVIDENCE.* NEW YORK: DODD, MEAD & CO., 1943.

Detective Inspector John Appleby, who made his debut as a Michael Innes series-character sleuth in *Death at the President's Lodging* (34), ventures onto academic turf once again in *The Weight of the Evidence.* This time the scene is not Oxbridge. Instead, it is "Nesfield University," a seedy provincial institution somewhere in the north of England, where the members of the faculty mask their professorial shortcomings with pretense and pomposity. The crime that brings Appleby to Nesfield is the murder of Professor Pluckrose, a biochemist, who is crushed by a meteorite. The object does not fall from the sky. Rather, it is pushed onto Pluckrose from atop a university building while he sits taking the sun in a deck chair. The major suspects in the bizarre affair are all Nesfield teachers and administrators, and while few of those worthies have convincing alibis to offer, most are quite willing to provide Appleby with preposterous, self-serving explanations for Pluckrose's death. *The Weight of the Evidence* is one of the more ingeniously constructed tales in college-mystery fiction. Garnished with sharp satire, the book offers innumerable references to obscure and not-so-obscure literary figures, to pioneers of modern science, and to heroes of ancient myths.

In addition to *Death at the President's Lodging*, Michael Innes's *Operation Pax* (91) and *Old Hall, New Hall* (106) also have entries in this bibliography.

58. LEWIS, LANGE [JANE LEWIS BRANDT (B. 1915)]. *JULIET DIES TWICE*. INDIANAPOLIS: BOBBS-MERRILL, 1943.

Everyone stays awake in Professor Edwin Brewer's psychology class at "Southwest University" in Los Angeles. They keep alert because the professor likes to have his students learn by doing. When he teaches about homicidal behavior, for example, he pours ketchup over one student, hides his "murder victim," and then instructs other members of the class to go through the classroom building in search of the bogus corpse. On the occasion chronicled in *Juliet Dies Twice*, the student-searchers find a real corpse, that of Ann Laird, a young lady who was about to star in Southwest's production of *Romeo and Juliet*. Laird is discovered, with her head bashed in, lying on the floor of the prop room used by the drama department. One prime suspect, of course, is the innovative Professor Brewer, but several other faculty members, as well as a host of students and townspeople, could have put an end to poor Miss Laird's acting career. The only nonsuspects in the story are Lieutenant Richard Tuck of the Los Angeles Homicide Squad, who does the sleuthing in the case, and Dr. Trinklehaus, Southwest's president. The tall, lean Lieutenant Tuck is not the culprit because he is a Lange Lewis series-character detective. And Dr. Trinklehaus, who wanders the campus muttering, "This is a terrible thing," is clearly too intellectually challenged to have committed what seems, on initial appearances, to be a murder without clues.

Jane Lewis Brandt's *Murder among Friends* (54) appears earlier in this bibliography.

59. MAGOON, CAREY [ELIZABETH CAREY AND MARION AUSTIN WAITE MAGOON (B. 1885)]. *I SMELL THE DEVIL*. NEW YORK: FARRAR & RINEHART, 1943.

Miss Christopherson, the custodian of the rare books room at "Cowabet College" in Michigan, is a "tiresome" protector of her literary treasures, but no one has an apparent reason for murdering her. Yet murdered she is, stabbed in the back in her office. Since there are no immediate suspects in the case, all of the regular users of the rare books room are interrogated by State Police Sergeant Robert Morningstar. Those individuals include Adelaide Stone and Henrietta Fellows, two spinster teachers of English at "Kenneth State Teachers College," who are spending a year doing graduate work at Cowabet. The story is narrated by Miss Stone, who writes with considerable self-deprecating humor, especially about her weight (187 pounds), and whose amateur sleuthing eventually brings Miss Christopherson's killer to his just reward. Much of the plot revolves around the value of a rare collection of Cyprian's sermons that Adelaide is examining as part of her dissertation research. Though she certainly is no fool, Stone mixes serious detection with frequent flights of mental fancy. The title of the novel refers to her conviction, based on laborious readings of medieval texts, that she can detect evil by its legendary odor ("a combination of fresh-blood, moldy leather, and a dead rat in a trap for a week").

60. STEIN, AARON MARC (1906–1985). *THE CASE OF THE ABSENT-MINDED PROFESSOR*. NEW YORK: DOUBLEDAY, DORAN & CO., 1943.

The absent-minded professor in the title of this classic college mystery is Alpheus Chambers, a world-famous anthropologist at a small college in the American Midwest. Chambers finds the corpse of a gangland hoodlum in the manuscript room of the college library. Since he claims not to remember his actions before his discovery, everyone in the school's indigenous community is prepared to believe that he is the gangster's murderer. Only Tim Mulligan and Elsie Mae Hunt, a pair of Aaron Marc Stein series-character sleuths, doubt that Chambers committed the crime. Mulligan and Hunt are itinerant archaeologists who happen to be on campus cataloging the "Horton Collection" of rare gold pieces. Quickly familiarizing themselves with the college's internal politics, they identify the guilty party and, while doing so, blow open a host of smoldering college scandals. The large roster of suspects includes faculty members, students, and the college's belligerent football coach. Readers who enjoy president watching will be particularly interested in the portrait of President Webster and his vacuous, "birdlike" wife, Sarah. When informed of the murder, Dr. Webster utters those time-honored administrative words, "This is profoundly disturbing." When Tim Mulligan suggests to Sarah Webster that the school's football players are dull-normal louts, she counters by proclaiming, "All our football men are fine, clean-living youths."

The Case of the Absent-Minded Professor was the fourth of a sixteen-book Tim Mulligan-Elsie Mae Hunt series. Another Tim Mulligan-Elsie Mae Hunt mystery, *The Cradle and the Grave* (84), appears in this bibliography. Two other novels by Aaron Marc Stein also have entries. They are *The Corpse with Purple Thighs* (44) and *A Body for a Buddy* (217). *The Corpse with Purple Thighs* was published under the pseudonym George Bagby.

61. LA ROCHE, K. ALISON. *DEAR DEAD PROFESSOR*. NEW YORK: PHOENIX, 1944.

This book is set at "Roseview College," an exclusive women's college in the eastern United States, and the eponymous "dear dead professor" is Walter Morton, chairperson of the Roseview chemistry department. Morton is stabbed dead in his laboratory. One of the more dedicated faculty philanderers in academic mystery fiction, Morton had two student girlfriends (one of them pregnant) and a female laboratory assistant with whom he shared more than an interest in the poison gas research he was conducting for the United States government. All three of Morton's extramarital lady friends are suspects in the case, although one of them (nonpregnant student Gloria Knight) quickly exits from the story when she becomes the second corpse on the Roseview scene. And then there is Althea, the professor's long-suffering wife. A woman of action, Althea has compensated for Morton's wanderings by taking up with Albert Townes, a Roseview professor of astronomy. The task of sifting through the list of Morton's many possible killers falls to Rufus Albert Jones, the Gary Cooperish local police chief, and to Barbara Crew, a perky Roseview student enlisted as Rufus's temporary, on-campus stenographer. Jones and Crew find the double-murderer, though not before Crew almost becomes yet another fatality. Furthermore, in what appears to be an inevitable consequence of any male-female interaction at the Roseview campus, Jones and Crew fall in love. At the end of the story they are preparing to elope to Florida. Competently written and laden with both clues and cliches, *Dear Dead Professor* offers the clear message that women's colleges are pervaded with sexual frustrations. Neither handsome nor nice, Walter Morton is uncharitably described by Barbara Crew as "a Latin type with oily black hair and lips too red for a man." And yet, in the Roseview hothouse atmosphere, he is able to pick and choose among the nubile young ladies who populate the school.

The identity of K. Alison La Roche continues to elude literary biographers. It is evident, however, that he or she had more than a passing familiarity with the extracurricular customs at institutions such as Roseview College. In any event, *Dear Dead Professor* was La Roche's only mystery novel.

62. LONG, AMELIA REYNOLDS (1904–1976). *DEATH LOOKS DOWN.* CHICAGO & NEW YORK: ZIFF-DAVIS, 1944.

Professor Rourke of the "University of Philadelphia" begins a graduate seminar on Edgar Allen Poe, but three of his students are soon murdered by strangulation. At this point the seminar comes to a halt, but the clue-sifting is just beginning. The sleuth in the tale is criminal psychologist Edward Trelawney, the Amelia Reynolds long series-character who displayed a vast knowledge of Shakespeare while solving the mystery in Long's earlier college novel, *The Shakespeare Murders* (46). In *Death Looks Down* Trelawney exhibits an impressive familiarity with Poe's works as well, as he and Katherine "Peter" Piper, a surviving seminar participant, bring the killer to justice. The participants in *Death Looks Down* engage in several protracted discussions of Poe and his stories, but the book also features some intricate detection, a large number of academic suspects, and more than a few attention-getting happenings. For example, the body of yet another murder victim in the novel, a wealthy collector of Poe artifacts, is substituted for an effigy of an unpopular professor that is to be burned at a basketball pep rally, and the collector's carcass is consumed by fire as hundreds watch. The denouement takes place in the university library's dark and forbidding "American Literature Room," and because a raging thunderstorm has severed the campus's electric power, Edward Trelawney must expose the killer under flickering gaslight. To add to the drama, the killer is tricked into a confession when Trelawney has a student masquerade as a victim and appear as an apparition while the denouement is unfolding.

Death Looks Down is one of six mysteries by Amelia Reynolds Long that have entries in this bibliography. Like *Death Looks Down, The Shakespeare Murders* (46) was published under Long's real name. *Murder Most Foul* (70) was published under the pseudonym Kathleen Buddington Coxe. *Stone Dead* (67), *Murder from the Mind* (76), and *The Lady Is Dead* (92) were published under the name of the books' series-character professor-detective, Patrick Laing.

63. MILLAR, KENNETH (1915–1983). *THE DARK TUNNEL*. NEW YORK: DODD, MEAD & CO., 1944. ALSO PUBLISHED AS *I DIE SLOWLY*. NEW YORK: LION BOOKS, 1945.

Set during World War II at "Midwestern University," this lively novel includes murder, espionage, detection, and suspense. The protagonist and narrator is Robert Branch, a professor of English. Alarmed over security leaks at Midwestern, Branch conducts an unofficial investigation that ultimately requires him to employ his brawn as well as his brains. As he detects, Branch encounters Nazi agents, alluring ladies with mysterious pasts, the body of a murdered professor of German, and a psychotic homosexual. Fortunately for the Allied cause in World War II, by the end of the story Professor Branch has thwarted Nazi attempts to infiltrate one of America's leading academic centers for the development of technology. An unconvincing disclaimer at the end of the book announces that although Midwestern University "bears a certain physical resemblance to the University of Michigan," the institution is in fact "a figment of the author's imagination."

Kenneth Millar was born in Los Gatos, California. Raised in Canada, he attended the University of Western Ontario as an undergraduate and then received a Ph.D. in English literature from the University of Michigan. *The Dark Tunnel* was Millar's first novel. Millar is known to mystery readers primarily for his twenty-four-novel Lew Archer series published under the pseudonym Ross Macdonald. One of Millar's Lew Archer novels, *The Chill* (132) is included in this bibliography. *The Dark Tunnel* was originally published under Millar's real name, but in reprint editions it sometimes appears under the Ross Macdonald pseudonym.

64. ROGERS, SAMUEL (B. 1894). *DON'T LOOK BEHIND YOU!* NEW YORK: HARPER & BROTHERS, 1944.

This novel is set at "Woodside University" somewhere in Midwestern America. Daphne Gray, the lovely young fiancée of a psychology instructor, is being stalked by someone who follows her everywhere but never reveals himself. Since several murders already have taken place in the Woodside community, Miss Gray fears she will be the next victim. Professor Paul Hatfield offers Miss Gray his assistance. Hatfield is a middle-aged chemist who sometimes acts as a consultant to Inspector Waters of the local police. As the tale progresses Hatfield must deal with several abrasive Woodside faculty members, and one of them proves to be a demented sadist. The book was marketed as a "spine-tingling thriller," and in one attempt to provoke terror there is a scene, toward the end of the tale, in the dissecting room of the university's medical school. Modern-day readers may find themselves as engaged by Professor Hatfield as by the story itself. Hatfield has little by way of a sense of humor, but he speaks in a voice "both inspired and intimate," and he has the ability to gain the immediate confidence of others. Well-read in fields beyond his own academic discipline, Hatfield has a working familiarity with psychological theory, and he uses this knowledge in his personal life as well as in his detection. For example, he stays happily married by spending most of his weekends alone in a hilltop cabin. He travels to the cabin on a bicycle that he leaves parked at the bottom of the hill in an old piano box. Then, once ensconced in his weekend abode, he engages in his principal form of recreation, watching birds and owls.

Samuel Rogers was born in Newport, Rhode Island. He received a B.A. from Brown University in 1915 and then did graduate work at the University of Chicago. A mainstream novelist as well as a writer of mysteries, Rogers was a professor of French at the University of Wisconsin when *Don't Look Behind You!* was published. Professor Hatfield went on to serve as detective in two more Rogers mysteries. Those mysteries are *You'll Be Sorry!* (New York: Harper & Brothers, 1945; published in England as *Murder Is Grim* [London: Hammond, 1955]) and *You Leave Me Cold!* (New York: Harper & Brothers, 1946). Both of Rogers's two subsequent Professor Hatfield stories take place near

Woodside University. Both contain some university characters, but neither is sufficiently "academic" to warrant an entry in this bibliography.

65. THAYER, (EMMA REDDINGTON) LEE (1874–1973). *FIVE BULLETS.* NEW YORK: DODD, MEAD & CO., 1944.

It is February of 1942 and Professor Jean Liebling, an impoverished refugee from Hitler's Germany, has found employment at "Sweetwater College." Sweetwater is an academic backwater in the central Florida town of "Highlands." A world-famous psychologist, Liebling likes to give practical demonstrations of stimulus-response, and one morning he tries to shock his students by having a male student fire a pistol, presumably loaded with blanks, without warning in his classroom. Unfortunately, real bullets fill the air and another male student is killed. At first the local police assume that the shooter substituted actual bullets for the fakes, and knowing that the two young men were rivals for the affection of the same Sweetwater coed, they treat the case as a homicide. By happenstance, long-running Lee Thayer series-character private investigator Peter Clancy and his proper British factotum Wiggar are in town doing hush-hush government work having to do with Nazi spies. In town by chance, as well, is Zinnia Zingara, a middle-aged, urbane newspaperwoman who is forging a second career writing books about Peter Clancy's exploits. A recent victim of the flu, Zinnia has come to the deepest South to recuperate for a few weeks at a boarding house run by a former college classmate. Zingara narrates the story, as she, Clancy, and Wiggar learn that there may be more than one gun in a classroom at Sweetwater College, and that the tentacles of the Third Reich can reach even into one of the sleepiest American outposts of higher education. Modern-day academics, many of whom may believe that firearms have no place on a college campus, even in the hands of campus-security forces, will be interested to learn that at Sweetwater in the early 1940s the school keeps a "college pistol" in the administration building and lends it freely to faculty members who plan to discharge it in their classes. Contemporary readers may be interested, too, in the author's depictions of several of Sweetwater College's "Negro" servants. All speak in servile ("Yes, suh, Mistah Clancy") dialect, but toward end of the story, when their loyalties are tested, all of them prove to be valuable workers in the fight against Nazi Germany.

Lee Thayer studied at Cooper Union and the Pratt Institute. Her early working years were spent as a designer of book covers. She began to write mysteries in mid-life and published her first novel in 1919. She continued to publish into her nineties, and at her death, at age ninety-nine, she had produced over sixty-five mysteries. Peter Clancy and his valet Wiggar were Lee Thayer series characters and appeared in all but one of her novels. *Five Bullets* was the thirty-sixth novel in the Clancy/Wiggar series.

66. CAMPBELL, R. T. [RUTHVEN TODD (1914–1974)]. *UNHOLY DYING*. LONDON: JOHN WESTHOUSE, 1945; NEW YORK: DOVER, 1985.

A conference on genetics draws scientists from all over the world to the "University of Gowerburgh" in Scotland. One of the attendees, Professor Ian Farquhar Porter from Canada, has a reputation as a man who steals the ideas of others. As the meeting proceeds Porter further alienates his fellow conference-goers by his obnoxious personal behavior, and when he is found dead of cyanide poisoning Inspector Hargrave of the local police has a multiplicity of suspects from whom to choose. Unhappily, Hargrave is something of a bumbler, and the task of serious sleuthing in the story falls to the most eminent participant at the conference, Professor John Stubbs. A man of extreme brilliance, with the bluster and ego to match, Stubbs is a botanist, but he seems to have no fixed academic address. Instead, he lectures regularly at Oxford and Cambridge, and as a "national treasure" he serves Great Britain in a variety of consulting capacities. Before Professor Stubbs can identify Porter's killer, an American professor, Herman Swartz, also is murdered. The device used to dispatch Professor Swartz is too ingenious to be revealed in this bibliography. Some of this witty tale is narrated by Professor Stubbs's nephew, Andrew Blake, a newspaper reporter who is covering the conference. Stubbs, whose beard is stained yellow with nicotine from his pipe, spends as much time as possible drinking in pubs. His favorite reading is detective fiction. While pursuing the killer of the two North American professors, he employs some unorthodox detection methods, and by the end of the book the villain has been brought to a macabre form of justice.

A poet, a biographer, an art historian, a writer of fantasy novels, and an author of children's books, Ruthven Todd was born in Edinburgh, Scotland. He attended Fettes College and the Edinburgh College of Art. Todd immigrated to the United States in 1948 and became a naturalized citizen in 1959. He taught creative writing at Iowa State University during the 1950s. *Unholy Dying* was the first of seven Professor John

Stubbs mysteries that were published in England in 1945 and 1946 by the publishing house of John Westhouse. Todd wrote the Stubbs series while serving as a civil defense officer in London during World War II. The Stubbs series was his only foray into mystery fiction.

67. LAING, PATRICK [AMELIA REYNOLDS LONG (1904–1976)]. *STONE DEAD*. NEW YORK: PHOENIX, 1945.

The deaths of two undergraduates in quick succession upset the usual routines of a university in the eastern United States. The first to die is Bob Curtis, an earnest young man who had recently given his fraternity pin to Corinne Douglas. Curtis commits suicide in his dormitory room. The second corpse is that of Miss Douglas. A promiscuous young woman who is described by one character in the novel as having "a face like an angel and a mind like a sewer," Douglas is found naked, wedged between two stone nymphs just under the edge of a campus fountain. Since no wounds are found on Douglas's body, many members of the university community are willing to write off the two deaths as some sort of bizarre joint suicide. Not willing to do so is Patrick "Paddy" Laing, the university's eminent blind criminal psychologist who serves as the book's narrator. With the help of Lieutenant McDermott of the local police, and with the special assistance of Diedre "Derry" O'Hara, a perky graduate student who acts as his eyes, Professor Laing quickly finds that Corinne Douglas was murdered, and through his subsequent detection he eventually learns that a member of the university community did the evil deed. To compensate for his blindness, Laing has developed keen hearing and smelling capacities, and it is an olfactory clue that leads him to the solution of the mystery. The novel includes students, faculty members, and administrators as characters, and all of them perform their roles in perfect college-mystery fashion. The university's superscholarly dean of arts and sciences, for example, cannot find it in his heart to lament the death of Corinne Douglas, who has caused him no end of administrative troubles during her undergraduate career. However, he has no idea how to deal with either the internal or external consequences of a murder in his domain, and he laments that Corinne's exit from the ranks of his undergraduate charges was in so public a manner.

Series-character professor-detective Patrick Laing appeared in six mysteries by Amelia Reynolds Long. Three of the six Laing mysteries, *Murder from the Mind* (76) and *The Lady Is Dead* (92), are college mysteries, set at the institution at which Laing teaches, and those mysteries are included in this bibliography. In addition to the three Patrick Laing college mysteries, three other novels by Amelia Reynolds Long have entries in the bibliography. They are *The Shakespeare Murders* (46), *Death Looks Down* (62), and *Murder Most Foul* (70). *Murder Most Foul* was published under the pseudonym Kathleen Buddington Coxe.

68. LESLIE, JEAN. *ONE CRIED MURDER*. GARDEN CITY, N.Y: DOUBLEDAY, DORAN & CO., 1945.

This sometimes-whimsical novel is set at an unidentified university near Los Angeles during the closing days of World War II. A visiting professor of psychiatry, a man named Wagner, is found shot dead in his office in the psychology department. A pistol lies near the body. The discoverer of the corpse is Peter Ponsonby, a professor of English. Ponsonby, whose area of professional expertise is Shakespeare, writes best-selling mysteries as an avocation. He notifies the chairman of psychology, "Fitz" Fitzgerald, that there is a corpse on the premises, but Fitzgerald, who prefers to assume that Wagner committed suicide, refuses to call the police. Instead, he notifies Dean Robert Turner, who, after examining the death scene, telephones President Van Beuren. Despite Ponsonby's continuous protestations, neither Turner nor Van Beuren will notify the law, and eventually they call a mortician instead. Only after Professor Ponsonby tells Van Beuren that the mortician will inevitably notify the county coroner, who may not appreciate a hasty movement of the body, does the president finally relent and telephone the authorities. The man in charge of the responding police contingent turns out to be Webster Holbrook, a 1934 graduate of the university. Now a detective-lieutenant, Holbrook is remembered as one of the university's most obnoxious students. Almost the whole of the subsequent story takes place at the university and it includes an enormous number of academic characters. Often by asking himself what Georges Bouchet, his own detective creation, would do, Peter Ponsonby matches sleuthing wits with the unlikeable Detective Holbrook. By the end of the novel a murderer been identified and, as an unusual bonus for readers of college-mystery fiction, a group of Nazi sympathizers also has been purged from the university.

Peter Ponsonby, a series-character professor-detective, served in three mysteries by Jean Leslie. The second Ponsonby novel, *Two-Faced Murder* (77), also appears in this bibliography. The third Ponsonby adventure is a nonacademic tale titled *Three Cornered Murder* (Garden City, N.Y.: Doubleday, 1948). Jean Leslie was born in

Omaha, Nebraska, but was raised in California. She was a California resident when her Peter Ponsonby series was being written. She published nine mysteries during her literary lifetime. Her character of Peter Ponsonby was inspired by professors she encountered while a graduate student in psychology.

69. REES, DILWYN [GLYN EDMUND DANIEL (1914–1986)]. *THE CAMBRIDGE MURDERS.* LONDON: GOLLANCZ, 1945.

The detective-protagonist of this leisurely and elegant Cambridge mystery is Sir Richard Cherrington, the vice president of "Fisher College" and professor of prehistory at the university. Sir Richard is a reader of detective novels, and his familiarity with sleuthing is called into play when, in quick succession, two persons associated with Fisher College are murdered. The first victim is Sam Gostin, a porter. Gostin is shot, and his body is found on a path between two college buildings. The second victim is Bill Landon, the college's unpopular dean. Dean Landon is shot with the same gun that dispatched Gostin. His corpse travels far from Cambridge, to the town of "Twyford Junction," where it is discovered in the trunk of an undergraduate who has just come home from the university at the conclusion of the Lent term. Fortunately for Sir Richard, Fisher is one of the smaller colleges of Cambridge, and thus the number of suspects is kept to a workable number. Those who might have committed the murders include Giles Farnaby (the student-owner of the body-bearing trunk), Kilmartin (a college butler), and Dr. Quibel (Fisher College's aged president). Thanks to the interest he displays in the case, for a brief time even Sir Richard makes the list of suspects maintained by Inspector Robertson-MacDonald of New Scotland Yard. At the conclusion of the story Sir Richard tracks the murderer to Paris, where, over a dinner of fine food and wine, he obtains a confession. Students of mystery fiction usually consider *The Cambridge Murders* one of the best Oxbridge whodunits, and Sir Richard Cherrington, a bachelor who sometimes reflects with dread on the possibility of dying old and alone in his college rooms, is often regarded as one of mystery fiction's more engaging professor-detectives.

Glyn Edmund Daniel was born in Lampeter in southern Wales. He received a B.A. from Cambridge in 1935 and a Ph.D. from Cambridge in 1938. After service in the Royal Air Force in World War II, he returned to Cambridge in 1945 as a lecturer in archaeology. In addition to his academic duties, Daniel became a television personality in Great Britain thanks to his popular BBC program "Animal, Vegetable, Mineral." In 1974 he became Disney Professor of Archaeology at Cambridge. *The Cambridge Murders* was the first of two mysteries Professor Daniel published during his lifetime. The second, *Welcome Death* (New York: Dodd, Mead & Co., 1955), also features the detection of Sir Richard Cherrington. In *Welcome Death* Sir Richard solves a murder mystery in a small Welsh village. Although Daniel used a pseudonym on *The Cambridge Murders,* he published *Welcome Death* under his real name.

70. COXE, KATHLEEN BUDDINGTON [AMELIA REYNOLDS LONG (1904–1976)]. *MURDER MOST FOUL.* NEW YORK: PHOENIX, 1946.

The gossip network at "Mercer College," a small coeducational school in the eastern region of the United States, is activated when pretty Annie Clay, an unmarried telephone operator in the men's dormitory, is forced to leave her job because her pregnancy is beginning to show. Dorothy Lane, the wife of the college dean, can't wait to tell her cronies of poor Annie's condition, and she has some ideas of the father's identity as well. When Annie is run over by an automobile, Dorothy and her lady friends are virtually aglow with suspicion that Annie's death was not a simple case of hit-and-run. The matter soon becomes more than a mere subject for chatter when Dean George Lane is shot dead in his office, when two of the other women gossipers' husbands are found murdered, and when Tom Blackburn, Mercer's football coach, is discovered dead of a broken neck at the bottom of a rubbish chute in the apartment house were the unfortunate Annie Clay lived. The detectives in this fast-paced story are Kathleen "Buddie" Coxe, an energetic Mercer student who narrates the story, and Professor Francis Thrush, a youngish, bachelor member of the school's psychology department. Suspects in the affair include all of the female gossipers, as well as Leslie Spencer, a new professor of chemistry who, thanks to a football injury incurred in his Mercer undergraduate days, now suffers mental blackouts after which he cannot remember his whereabouts. The motive for the killings turns out to be one that is common on college campuses, and *Murder Most Foul* is a pure-type entry in that large segment of the college-mystery subgenre in which male professors and female students develop romantic relationships while solving crimes.

Murder Most Foul is one of six mysteries by Amelia Reynolds Long to appear in this bibliography. The others are *The Shakespeare Murders*

(46), *Death Looks Down* (62), *Stone Dead* (67), *Murder from the Mind* (76), and *The Lady Is Dead* (92). The latter three mysteries were written under the pseudonym Patrick Laing.

71. DAVIS, NORBERT (1909–1949). *OH, MURDERER MINE*. KINGSTON, N.Y.: QUINN, 1946.

Melissa Gregory, a young instructor of anthropology at "Breckinbridge University" in Los Angeles, goes to her office one morning only to find it occupied by Eric Trent, a handsome new instructor of meteorology. Miss Gregory, it seems, has been moved into a nearby cubicle on the orders of T. Ballard Bestwyck, Breckinbridge's autocratic president. To make matters worse, Gregory recognizes Trent as a model for cold cream advertisements run by "Heloise of Hollywood," a woman who is Eric Trent's wife. A few nights later Gregory's boyfriend, Assistant Professor of English Frank Ames, has his throat slit outside Gregory's apartment. Then Beulah Cowys, another of Gregory's faculty colleagues, is strangled dead while taking a beauty treatment in Heloise's storefront salon on Sunset Boulevard. Although intimidated by the above events, Gregory tries her hand at detection. She is assisted by Norbert Davis's series-character sleuths Doan and Carstairs. Doan is a stocky, wisecracking private detective whom Heloise has employed to keep female students away from her husband, and Carstairs is a huge Great Dane that Doan won in a craps game. After some death-defying derring-do Gregory, Doan, and Carstairs manage to capture the murderer, but not before Heloise becomes the third victim in the story when she is killed in her mansion. The motive in this story is not academic, but the novel contains many campus scenes, many Breckinbridge University characters, and some irreverent looks at higher education. For example, one character in the story masquerades as a professor of biochemistry after killing the real professor in Mexico. A one-time barker in a medicine show, the imposter manages to avoid student complaints by "drawing on the lingo of drugs" and by practicing the oratorical techniques he learned in his former occupation.

Norbert Davis is best known to historians of mystery fiction as a frequent contributor of short stories to pulp magazines such as *Black Mask* and *Dime Detective.* He also wrote three novels with Doan and Carstairs as detectives. *Oh, Murderer Mine* was the last of his Doan and Carstairs mysteries.

72. EUSTIS, HELEN (B. 1916). *THE HORIZONTAL MAN*. NEW YORK: HARPER & BROTHERS, 1946.

Almost all serious students of mystery fiction consider *The Horizontal Man* to be one of the best college-mystery novels. Set at "Hollymount College," an exclusive women's college in New England, this brooding, psychological story centers on the murder of Kevin Boyle, a twenty-nine-year-old bachelor member of the Hollymount English department. Boyle's skull is crushed by a blunt instrument. He is discovered dead in his apartment one evening, and by the next morning several Hollymount students, faculty members, and administrators find that their lives will never be the same. Particularly aggrieved by Boyle's murder are Leonard Marks and George Hungerford, two of the deceased's faculty colleagues. Marks, a junior member of the English department, feels guilty because he and Boyle carried on a continuing rivalry. Hungerford, a burnt-out hulk of a man, experiences emotional torment because he feels as though he has lost a son. Some of the detection in the story is by the timid and self-tortured Marks, and some is by Jack Donnelly, a local newspaper reporter. Donnelly is helped in his investigations by Kate Innes, the editor of the Hollymount student paper, and the generally lighthearted banter between Donnelly and Innes acts to offset the serious and weighty dialogue offered by most of the book's other characters. Mention should be made of Hollymount's President Baimbridge, a man who wishes the whole affair had never occurred. In the interests of his school, Baimbridge makes some inquiries of his own. All of the sleuthing proves to be unnecessary, however. At the climax of the tale, in one of the most effectives scenes in all of college-mystery fiction, the villain gives himself away.

Helen Eustis was born in Cincinnati. She received a B.A. from Smith College in 1938. *The Horizontal Man* won an Edgar from the Mystery Writers of America for the best first mystery novel of 1946. Eustis's only other full-length mystery, *The Fool Killer* (New York: Doubleday, 1954), is not a college mystery and was given only modest praise by reviewers.

73. HOLMAN, (CLARENCE) HUGH (1914–1981). *UP THIS CROOKED WAY.* NEW YORK: MILLS, 1946.

Up This Crooked Way is set at "Abecton College" in South Carolina. It begins with the shooting of Walter Perkins, the unpleasant, miserly owner of a lodging house occupied by unmarried members of the college's faculty and staff. The most likely suspect-tenant is Philip Kent, an associate professor of English. Kent already has been acquitted of another murder, and most members of the Abecton community are ready to believe that he is a pathological killer. Happily for Professor Kent, Sheriff "Mac" Macready is not willing to leap to conclusions based on Kent's lurid past. Macready finds that Perkins's wife, Olga, had reason to kill her husband, and he learns, as well, that Steel Carlise (an Abecton physicist), Jackie Dean (a nubile young college librarian), and Robert Herbert (an instructor of history) all had motives for exterminating their landlord. Crisply written and crammed with real and false clues, *Up This Crooked Way* incorporates some sly humor. For example, Sheriff Macready is an elected official who feels it necessary to pretend he is illiterate in order to get votes from the noncollege portions of his constituency. But Macready is, in fact, a closet Chaucer buff. When he attends one of Philip Kent's classes as part of his detection, he cannot prevent himself from rising and offering a long, off-the-cuff quotation from *The Canterbury Tales.*

Death Like Thunder (52), an earlier mystery by Clarence Hugh Holman, appears in this bibliography. Like *Up This Crooked Way*, *Death Like Thunder* is set at Abecton College. However, none of the principal characters in either story appears in both books. Yates Thorndyke Bell, the forthright president of Abecton College in *Death Like Thunder*, has been replaced by Dr. Bruce F. Walsh by the time *Up This Crooked Way* opens. Dr. Walsh is a more usual fictional college president. A man who revels in the status of his office, Dr. Walsh takes particular delight "in the thick nap of the carpet of his long, austere office."

74. IRVING, ALEXANDER [RUTH FOX HUME (1922–1980) AND ANNE FAHRENKOPF]. *BITTER ENDING.* NEW YORK: DODD, MEAD & CO., 1946.

Dr. Claude G. Madison is found dead in an office at an American university. Brilliant but unlikeable, Madison held an appointment at the university medical school. An autopsy shows that he died of strychnine poisoning. The office in which Dr. Madison expired belongs to Dr. Anthony Post, a glib, wisecracking member of the medical school's anatomy department. Because Dr. Post has carried on a well-known relationship with Dr. Madison's attractive wife, he immediately comes under suspicion. He is taken to the local police station and questioned overnight, but even as the questioning proceeds Ellen Denine, the anatomy department's secretary, is bludgeoned dead in her home, and the police must look for other suspects. Thanks to Dr. Madison's propensity for making enemies, there are other suspects aplenty. They include Joseph Kruger (the anatomy department's harried and indecisive chairperson), J. T. Bedford (the medical school's properly pompous president), and Christine Arnold (a stunning blonde medical student who has displayed a rare enthusiasm for dissecting dead bodies in her anatomy classes). The detection in the story is shared by Lieutenant Gillon of the local police and the irrepressible Dr. Post, whose knowledge of medicine eventually leads to the mystery's solution. There are many laboratory scenes in the novel, and much of the plot revolves around academic activities at the medical school. Those who consider smoking an antisocial activity may recoil at a scene, toward the beginning of the book, in which Dr. Post lights a cigarette while demonstrating how to cut a cadaver. On the other hand, academic administrators may empathize with Dr. Kruger's frantic efforts to reschedule his department's classes after the police shut down the anatomy lab for two days while conducting their investigations.

Bitter Ending was the first of three mysteries by Ruth Fox Hume and Anne Fahrenkopf. All three were written under the pseudonym Alexander Irving. No biographic information is available about Anne Fahrenkopf. Ruth Fox Hume was born in New York City. A one-time medical student, she taught chemistry at Dumbarton College and Latin at Catholic University before becoming a mystery writer. She was the wife of Paul Hume, the *Washington Post* music critic whose negative appraisal of Margaret Truman's singing talents brought about a famous fatherly rebuke from the White House.

75. KYD, THOMAS [ALFRED BENNETT HARBAGE (1901–1976)]. *BLOOD IS A BEGGAR*. PHILADELPHIA: LIPPINCOTT, 1946.

Professor Oscar Biddler, the chairperson of the English department at a large university in the eastern United States, is showing a film to his drama class, and Anne Ridgeway, his young, attractive secretary, is operating the projection equipment. Biddler is shot dead as the film unreels, and when the lights are turned on, Miss Ridgeway is hunched over the professor's corpse. Although Ridgeway is not holding the fateful pistol (it has been thrown into a far corner), the thirty students in the classroom are convinced that she committed the murder. Sam Phelan, the local police detective assigned to the case, is not so certain. Captivated by Ridgeway's good looks, Phelan insists upon developing a long list of other suspects, most of whom are members of the university's faculty. Phelan's eye falls in particular upon Professor "Clockworks" Partridge, the English department's director of graduate studies, with whom the late Professor Biddler once had a bitter quarrel over the worthiness of a Ph.D. dissertation. He looks hard, too, at Professor Twines, an extremely popular teacher of English whom Biddler was trying to get fired on the ground of grade inflation. A thoroughly academic mystery, *Blood Is a Beggar* introduces its readers to a host of university characters and situations, and it incorporates considerable not-so-veiled satire directed both at academe and at college-mystery novels. Moreover, some clever literary irony is built into the book's structure. Casual consumers of mystery fiction may have little difficulty guessing Professor Biddler's killer. However, serious students of the genre, who have been conditioned to discount the obvious in detective yarns, may have to work their ways through to the book's denouement in order to discover the identity of the guilty party.

Alfed Bennett Harbage was born in Philadelphia. He received an A.B. from the University of Pennsylvania in 1924 and a Ph.D. from the same institution in 1929. After teaching at his alma mater and at Columbia University, in 1952 Harbage became a professor of English and comparative literature at Harvard. A Shakespearean scholar of international renown, Harbage was named Cabot Professor of English Literature at Harvard in 1960. *Blood Is a Beggar* was the first of four mystery novels Harbage published during his lifetime. Harbage's second and third mysteries both star Sam Phelan in their sleuthing roles, but neither is concerned with academic matters. Harbage's final mystery, *Cover His Face* (Philadelphia: Lippincott, 1949), has an academic protagonist, but since the book is not set in academe it does not have an entry in this bibliography. The featured performer in *Cover His Face* is Gilbert E. Weldon, an impoverished instructor of English at the "University of Allegheny," who travels to England in search of a cache of unpublished writings by Samuel Johnson.

76. LAING, PATRICK [AMELIA REYNOLDS LONG (1904–1976)]. *MURDER FROM THE MIND*. NEW YORK: PHOENIX, 1946.

Henry Bishop, the junior member of a six-person psychology department at a university in the eastern United States, is bludgeoned to death in his office. Fortunately for the cause of academic law and order, one of Bishop's departmental colleagues is Professor Patrick Laing, an Amelia Reynolds Long series-character detective who already has solved a campus mystery at this institution in *Stone Dead* (67). In his customary no-nonsense manner, Laing, who happens to be blind, immediately begins a quest to find the killer. *Murder from the Mind* centers squarely on rivalries within the university's psychology department. As the case unwinds, all of the department's surviving faculty, save Patrick Laing himself, become suspects. So, too, does Peter Milton, a former department member who now has a mysterious case of amnesia and has resigned from the university to regain his memory. Central to the story is Professor Mona Mason, a beautiful widow whose late husband was department chairman at the time of his death in an automobile accident. Given to wearing a perfume that "mingle(s) grotesquely" with the formaldehyde used in the department's brain-anatomy laboratory, the pulchritudinous professor nonetheless attracts the romantic interests of several of her workmates and thereby generates bitter animosities between them.

In addition to *Murder from the Mind* and *Stone Dead*, still another Professor Patrick Laing mystery by Amelia Reynolds Long, titled *The Lady Is Dead* (92), appears in this bibliography. Three other, non-Laing mysteries by Amelia Reynolds Long also have entries. They are *The Shakespeare Murders* (46), *Death Looks Down* (62), and *Murder Most Foul* (70). *Murder Most Foul* was published under the pseudonym Kathleen Buddington Coxe.

77. LESLIE, JEAN. *TWO-FACED MURDER*. GARDEN CITY, N.Y.: DOUBLEDAY, 1946.

Series-character detective and whodunit-author Peter Ponsonby, a professor of English at a university somewhere in California, visits his friend Ken Grayson, a professor of English at a university deep in the desert southwest. Upon his arrival, Ponsonby finds that everyone is out looking for Jane Titus, who has disappeared. Jane is the young wife of a biochemist and the daughter of Jim York, the chairperson of the English department. Eventually, Mrs. Titus is found dead in a field. Ponsonby's reputation both as a detective and as a writer of mysteries has preceded him. Local Police Chief Amos Schroeder, who feels that the university faculty do not respect him, asks Ponsonby to look for clues to Mrs. Titus's killing at the university while he detects in friendlier off-campus locales. By attending several faculty parties, during which he acquires important information, and by deliberately accusing an innocent person so that the real killer is tricked into an incriminating reaction, Professor Ponsonby eventually brings the culprit in the case to justice. Many members of the southwest university faculty, as well as their spouses, appear in the book, and the story revolves around several romantic entanglements within the faculty community. Readers interested in the unexpected consequences of surveys might find *Two-Faced Murder* of special interest. Peggy Ann Allison, the wife of a badly wounded war veteran, earns extra money by on-campus polling for a toothpaste company. As she administers her questionnaires, Mrs. Allison hears and then passes on gossip throughout the university.

One Cried Murder (68), another Professor Peter Ponsonby adventure by Jean Leslie, appears earlier in this bibliography.

78. THOMAS, CAROLYN [ACTEA CAROLINE DUNCAN (B. 1913)]. *PROMINENT AMONG THE MOURNERS*. PHILADELPHIA: LIPPINCOTT, 1946.

John Herron, the president of "Larkin College," is stabbed dead during a faculty reception in his home. An anomaly among fictional academic presidents, Herron was a kindly man without dedicated enemies, and thus the only immediate suspects are a few neurotic professors who had trivial grievances against him. The sleuthing in the case is provided by Sheriff Townsend, a perceptive local policeman, and by Susan Eyerly, Larkin College's newly hired director of publicity. Sheriff Townsend and his attractive assistant eventually bring Herron's murderer to justice, but not until two more killings occur. Larkin College is a venerable coeducational institution in the American Midwest, and the roots of the president's murder lie in the school's past. Herron was writing a history of Larkin, and the moral of this story seems to be that college presidents should concentrate on their schools' present-day problems and allow long-forgotten scandals to remain dormant. In addition to President Herron and Susan Eyerly, the book contains a great many other academic characters, some of whom are drawn with venom-laced ink. Social scientists may want to take special note of the portrait of Scott Gerald Ball, a boorish young sociologist. Scott Gerald Ball insists on being addressed by his full name, and, though he is not quite capable of physical murder, he verbally assassinates anyone who doubts his interpretations of "the significance of rural-urban curve variations."

Prominent among the Mourners was the first of four mysteries written by Actea Caroline Duncan during her literary lifetime. It was the only one of the four with a college setting.

79. ADLER, TERRY. *ON MURDER'S SKIRTS*. NEW YORK: PHOENIX, 1947.

Jasper B. Hubbard is one of college-mystery fiction's nastier academics. The chairman of the biology department at "Landon University" in Indiana, Professor Hubbard plagiarizes his graduate students' brightest ideas and researches his faculty members' backgrounds so he can blackmail them. Moreover, he is trying to give up cigarettes and the resulting stress, which reinforces his naturally bullying personality, makes his secretary Ellen Carter's life so unbearable that she is about to resign her position. Little wonder, then, that when Hubbard is found dead in his office, the apparent victim of a coronary occlusion, the news receives "polite attention" rather than sympathetic hand-wringing from those who knew him. The eventual results of Professor Hubbard's autopsy generate more interest, however, because the procedure shows that Hubbard actually was poisoned. Then, when Professor Donald Bray, the biology department's long-suffering second-in-command, is also murdered by poison, and when Ellen Carter narrowly escapes an attempt to poison her, the biologists at Landon fear that someone may be out to annihilate the entire department. The sleuth in this story is Dr. Dennis Rafferty, an intern in surgery at the university's medical school. Rafferty becomes involved primarily because he has romantic designs on Ellen Carter. By the end of the novel Rafferty and Miss Carter are engaged, and the biology department, with all of its dirty secrets fully exposed to public view, is in a shambles.

At the time *On Murder's Skirts* was published Terry Adler was a resident of California. *On Murder's Skirts* was Adler's only mystery novel.

80. FREEMAN, KATHLEEN (1897–1959). *GOWN AND SHROUD*. LONDON: MACDONALD, 1947.

Augustus Spencer, a professor of archaeology at a new (but unidentified) British university, has an affair with Miss March, his resident housekeeper. When he decides to end the liaison, in order to marry his cousin, Miss March is no longer content to clean his abode and cook his meals. She threatens to provoke a campus scandal, and, shortly thereafter, she is found dead in her quarters, her skull smashed by a series of blows delivered from behind. Professor Spencer seems to be the prime suspect, but as the story unfolds into a series of subplots, other murders are committed and other potential villains are introduced. Police Inspector Poole successfully sorts through all of the complications to produce a denouement that requires seventeen pages of the book's text. In addition to Professor Spencer's tangled home life, Inspector Poole must cope with the disputed ownership of archaeological treasures brought back from the island of Xanthos, undergraduate rivalries over a university scholarship, and the problem of whether Sir Thomas Hyde, the wealthy squire of Viccam Court, will continue to provide the university with sizable financial contributions.

Kathleen Freeman was born in Birmingham, England, and educated at the University of Cardiff. A longtime lecturer in Greek at University College, Cardiff, she was a prolific writer of mystery fiction. Most of her more-than-thirty detective novels were issued under the pseudonym Mary Fitt. *Gown and Shroud* was the only book-length mystery that she published under her real name.

81. GRAY, JONATHAN [JACK TAYLOR (1874–1958)]. *UNTIMELY SLAIN*. LONDON: HUTCHINSON, 1947.

Set in the days just before World War II, this novel begins as a conventional British detective mystery and turns into a spy thriller. Humphrey Wayne, a tutor in medieval history at "St. Michael's College," Oxford, is found murdered in the college library. It turns out that Wayne, a one-time British undercover operative, was killed by Nazi agents because he was in possession of crucial information about Germany's ambitions toward Poland. Sir Harker Mulready, the head of British Intelligence, recruits Geoffrey Tarleton, a junior research fellow in history at St. Michael's, to travel to Poland in order to foil the German plans. Since Sir Harker's last words to Tarleton are "God rest the souls of the gallant men who have gone before," Britain's newest espionage agent knows that the road ahead will be fraught with peril. Indeed, during the second part of the book, Tarleton surmounts a vast array of obstacles before completing his mission. Although the second half of the story digresses into almost pure derring-do, the initial chapters contain especially well-drawn portraits of St. Michael's characters, heavy doses of academic atmosphere, and interesting on-campus sleuthing.

Jacques Barzun and Wendell H. Taylor, in *A Catalogue of Crime* report that Jack Taylor was an economist at the University of Rochester (New York) who possessed an M.A. from Oxford. *Untimely Slain* was Taylor's only venture into the field of mystery fiction.

82. WALLIS, RUTH (OTIS) SAWTELL (1895–1978). *COLD BED IN THE CLAY*. NEW YORK: DODD, MEAD & CO., 1947.

Cold Bed in the Clay is set at a state university in the American Midwest. Don Adriance, an instructor of freshman English who has just arrived at the school, is found dead in a roadside ditch. Adriance is the apparent victim of a hit-and-run accident. Eric Lund, an ex-FBI agent, happens to be at the university as a guest lecturer in criminology. Lund suspects that Adriance's death may have been murder, and his eye falls first on Adriance's widow, Audrey, a young lady with a shocking secret in her past. By the end of the tale Lund's attentions have turned to several other faculty wives and their husbands. Written in a rich, sometimes-obscure style more often encountered in avant-garde mainstream novels than in detective stories, *Cold Bed in the Clay* takes its readers deep inside a troubled faculty milieu. Furthermore, through Cadwallader, an inquisitive dog-about-campus, the book opens to public view the contents of the garbage cans into which faculty families toss the flotsam from their lives.

Ruth Sawtell Wallis was born in Springfield, Massachusetts. She received an A.B. from Radcliffe in 1919, an M.A. from Radcliffe in 1923, and a Ph.D. from Columbia in 1929. During most of her professional career she was a professor of sociology at Annhurst College in Putnam, Connecticut. *Cold Bed in the Clay* was one of five mystery novels she published during her lifetime.

83. LOCKRIDGE, FRANCES LOUISE (1896–1963), AND RICHARD LOCKRIDGE (1898–1982). *MURDER IS SERVED*. PHILADELPHIA: LIPPINCOTT, 1948.

It is final examination time at "Dyckman University" in New York City, and John Leonard, an associate professor of psychology, is grading the blue books turned in by the students in his experimental psychology course. The exam of Peggy Mott, an aspiring Broadway actress, is titled "Hatred" and contains so much bitter prose that Leonard is convinced that Mott is about to commit a murder. Looking for guidance, Leonard telephones Jerry North, his publisher. Jerry, one-half of Frances and Richard Lockridge's celebrated amateur detective team of Mr. and Mrs. North, is at first inclined to dismiss Leonard's call as the ranting of an eccentric intellectual. But when John Mott, Peggy's husband, is stabbed dead in a restaurant by an unknown assailant, Jerry and his amazingly intuitive wife, Pam, drop all of their other responsibilities to engage in sleuthing. Helped by Lieutenant Bill Wiegand and Sergeant Aloyius Mullins of the New York Police, the Norths find the villain. For his part, poor Professor Leonard is quickly tabbed by the Norths as a likely suspect; then he barely survives an attack by the book's mysterious, knife-wielding assassin. Much of *Murder Is Served* takes place in central Manhattan. Nonetheless, the book has considerable "academic" content, and the first chapter, in which John Leonard is depicted ruminating in his classroom about the frustrations of college teaching, contains some of the most insightful professorial introspection in college-mystery fiction.

Frances Louise Lockridge was born in Kansas City, Missouri. She attended the University of Kansas. Richard Lockridge was born in St. Joseph, Missouri, and attended Kansas City Junior College and the University of Missouri. At the time the Lockridges were married, in 1922, Richard was a reporter for the *Kansas City Star*. The couple moved to New York City shortly after their wedding and Richard joined the staff of the *New York Sun.* The Lockridges published their first mystery novel in 1940—a Mr. and Mrs. North adventure—and until Frances's death in 1963 they collaborated on nearly sixty more detective novels. In addition to the Norths, the Lockridges created a number of other series-character sleuths. Those include New York City Police Captain Bill Wiegand, New York Homicide Detective Nathan Shapiro, New York City Assistant District Attorney Bernie Simmons, and New York State Police Captain Merton Heimrich. Many of the Lockridges' novels feature more than one of their series-characters. Another product of the Lockridges' collaboration, *The Drill Is Death* (124), appears in this bibliography. Richard Lockridge continued to write mysteries after Frances's death, and a mystery by Richard Lockridge, *Twice Retired* (157), also has an entry.

84. STEIN, AARON MARC (1906–1985). *THE CRADLE AND THE GRAVE.* GARDEN CITY, N.Y.: DOUBLEDAY, 1948.

Several World War II Marine veterans enroll at "Newton College," an undistinguished institution in New England, where their former captain, Tommy Milton, is now a professor of archaeology. Unhappily, the wives of the ex-marines do not get along with each other, in part because of real and rumored wife swapping in the veterans' housing complex, and the animosity between them reaches a crescendo when one of the wives is killed and her infant child is kidnapped. Tim Mulligan and Elsie Mae Hunt, two itinerant archaeologists who also serve as Aaron

Marc Stein series-character detectives, happen to be visiting their friend Professor Milton, and they dig into the veterans' domestic turmoil and unearth the villain. As Mulligan and Hunt conduct their investigation, they also learn who killed Clark Howard, a wealthy playboy, whose body is found near the Newton campus. In addition to Professor Milton, several Newton faculty members play important roles in the story, but because the focus of the book is on the ex-marines' romantic entanglements, readers are offered little direct information about the lack of rigor in the Newton College academic program. Nonetheless, as the blurb inside the book's front cover tells us, for the ex-marines "getting an education was going to be tougher than getting the Japs."

The Case of the Absent-Minded Professor (60), another Tim Mulligan-Elsie Mae Hunt mystery by Aaron Marc Stein, appears earlier in this bibliography. *The Corpse with Purple Thighs* (44) and *A Body for a Buddy* (217), two other Stein mysteries, also have entries. *The Corpse with Purple Thighs* was published under the pseudonym George Bagby.

85. BRAMHALL, MARION. *MURDER IS CONTAGIOUS*. GARDEN CITY, N.Y.: DOUBLEDAY, 1949.

When Bert Johnson, the star football player and top scholar at "Midwestern University," begins to fall behind in his studies, Kit Acton, the wife of economics professor Dick Acton takes it upon herself to investigate. A married veteran, Johnson lives with his wife and infant daughter in "Quonset Village." Mrs. Acton's initial inquiries suggest that Johnson's problems are related to his daughter's case of measles, but the plot soon thickens. Jim Smythe, a wounded vet confined to a wheelchair, is found dead with a kitchen knife protruding from his back, and Sally Blair, the hard-drinking wife of yet another student-veteran, is beaten to death. There are many, many suspects since, as Mrs. Acton discovers, Quonset Village contains more romantic entanglements and disentanglements than any dozen soap operas. Most of the likely murderers, like Bert Johnson and his spouse, are students or their wives, but one faculty member makes the suspect list as well. He is Amos Fielder, a professor of English, whose daughter is romantically involved with Ken Kimberly, one of Quonset Village's rare bachelors. Professor Fielder comes under suspicion-by-ancestor because, among other matters, Mrs. Acton learns that his aunt was a brilliant academic physicist who once poisoned a colleague who was promoted over her head because he was a man. Not under suspicion, but noteworthy nonetheless, is "old" Dr. Miller, the university's president. Described as an individual to whom "no one pay(s) any attention," President Miller laments Jim Smythe's killing because it occurs inopportunely on the first day of the annual alumni fund drive. A Marion Bramhall series-character detective, Kit Acton narrates this tale. Dick, her professorial husband, twirls his Phi Beta Kappa key at stressful moments and makes salient suggestions as Kit proceeds with her sleuthing. As for Amos Fielder, he resigns from Midwestern at the end of the story. With various family secrets revealed to the entire university community, he leaves the school to write romantic historical novels.

In *Crime Fiction II: A Comprehensive Bibliography, 1749–1990*, Allen J. Hubin reports that Marion Bramhall was the daughter of a minister and resided in Massachusetts. *Murder Is Contagious* was the last of five Marion Bramhall mysteries in which Kit Acton serves as detective.

86. BRONSON, F(RANCIS) W(OOLSEY) (1901–1966). *THE BULLDOG HAS THE KEY.* NEW YORK: FARRAR & STRAUS, 1949.

The sleuth in this uniquely premised novel is Ed Brakely, a United States government intelligence agent and a member of the Yale class of 1922. It is June of 1947, and Brakely is sent to New Haven under the guise of attending his twenty-fifth reunion. His real mission is to investigate an international jewel-smuggling operation. One government agent already has been killed on the case, and Ed Brakely almost meets his own death several times before the novel reaches its conclusion. On his way to the resolution of the affair, Brakely comes into contact with several Yale professors and administrators, with a beautiful and mysterious blond, and with a host of his reunioning classmates. He also revisits many of his old haunts, including the Taft Hotel, Woolsey Hall, and Yale baseball field. In one compelling scene, he is forced to kill an antagonist in a Yale dormitory room. Although the motives behind the mayhem in *The Bulldog Has the Key* are not academic in nature, Yale is an integral part of the story. The book will have special appeal for Yalies, but it can be read with enjoyment by anyone who appreciates solid, on-campus mysteries.

Francis Woolsey Bronson was born in Minneapolis and, like Ed Brakely, was a 1922 graduate of Yale. Known to generations of Yale men as "Bus," Bronson was from 1937 until shortly before his death the editor of the *Yale Alumni Magazine.* The following note is placed at the beginning of *The Bulldog Has the Key*. "This is the only official account of our Twenty-fifth Reunion. Members of the Class who appear in the narrative are real people copied faithfully from life. The author therefore disclaims responsibility if at times their behavior falls short of what it might have been." *The Bulldog Has the Key* was the last of three mystery novels that Bronson published during his lifetime.

87. HODGKIN, M(ARION) R(OUS) (B. 1917). *STUDENT BODY.* NEW YORK: SCRIBNER'S, 1949.

"Carodac College" is a coeducational American institution at which the students pay considerably less attention to their studies than to their sex lives. In fact, the most hated man on campus is the night watchman. Known to everyone but his immediate family as "The Goon," that meanie sneaks around the school's cloisters surprising unsuspecting couples with a flashlight. Carodac's relentless pursuit of academic mediocrity is temporarily forgotten, however, when three of its undergraduates meet mysterious deaths. One of the victims, a young woman named Candy, was the roommate of Nora Pickham, a senior who majors in English literature between gossip sessions. Pickham turns amateur detective and her suspects include fellow students, The Goon, several Carodac administrators, some faculty wives, almost the entire staff of the college library, and even bombastic old Professor Beacon. At one point, the latter incriminates himself, at least in the eyes of anyone who appreciates succinctness, by admonishing Pickham: "Young woman . . . does it occur to you that a murder has been done, that the murderer is still at large, that it might very well be myself, and that you have by sheer ignorance, stumbled upon a situation in which I, for one, have little interest, but which is of quite stupendous importance to others?" Slow paced, and not among the most suspense-filled mysteries in this bibliography, the book is nonetheless noteworthy for the views it presents of Carodac's intellectually empty environment.

Born in New York City, Marion Rous Hodgkin received a B.A. from Swarthmore College in 1939. *Student Body* was the first of two whodunits she wrote during a brief excursion into the field of mystery fiction.

88. SABER, ROBERT O. [MILTON K. OZAKI (B. 1913)]. *THE BLACK DARK MURDERS.* KINGSTON, N.Y.: QUINN, 1949.

Helen Sweeney, a student at "Royce College" in Chicago, is suddenly attacked and stabbed dead one pitch-black night while strolling the campus with her boyfriend. A few nights later another female student, Marilyn Ledmon, takes a nocturnal campus stroll with her young man and meets the same fate. The Chicago police are baffled. It was so dark on both occasions that neither boyfriend caught even a glimpse of the murderer. Phil Keene and Hal Cooper, two private detectives hired by Marilyn Ledmon's wealthy father, try their hands at solving the mysteries. Keene, who is an avid reader of the detective tales of Professor Caldwell, a Milton K. Ozaki series-character detective, masquerades as a student. Cooper, in turn, bones up on the science of optics and stages an in-the-dark trap through which the identity of the murderer is revealed. Narrated in the first person by faux-student Keene, the story is fast paced and delves into both the student and faculty sides of life at Royce. Professors who suffer from cataracts will find the tale of special interest, and college-president watchers will appreciate the author's depiction of Dr. Yates, Royce's superloquacious, white-haired chief executive. Refusing to believe that the murderer will strike again, Dr. Yates goes against the advice of his trustees and refuses to shut down the college until the villain is apprehended. Then, when Hal Cooper lays his trap, everything depends on Dr. Yates, who is not in on the plan, talking for fifteen minutes at the start of a faculty meeting. Dr. Yates does not disappoint and, in fact, uses the occasion to offer his long-suffering listeners, as well as the book's readers, a detailed summation of the case thus far.

The identity of Milton K. Ozaki has eluded those who compile the standard biographic reference works; however, Jacques Barzun and Wendell H. Taylor, in *A Catalogue of Crime*, identify him as a graduate of Ripon College, a Chicago tax accountant, and the owner of a beauty salon. Between 1946 and 1961 Ozaki published twenty-seven mystery novels, thirteen of them under the name Robert O. Saber. Professor Caldwell, whose novels are avidly read by Phil Keene in *The Black Dark Murders*, starred in three off-campus mysteries written under Ozaki's real name. A brilliant professor of psychology at "North University" in the American Midwest, Professor Caldwell's most noteworthy characteristics are an encyclopedic knowledge of poisons, a fondness for pipe smoking, and a dislike of women. During the course of his three-novel series the professor is writing a book titled *A Syllabus of Wifery,* which will be the definitive work about the perils of marriage. The three novels in the Professor Caldwell series are *The Cuckoo Clock* (Chicago: Ziff-Davis, 1946), *A Fiend in Need* (Chicago: Ziff-Davis, 1947), and *The Dummy Murder Case* (Hasbrouck Heights, N.J.: Graphic Publishing, 1951).

89. HUBBARD, MARGARET ANN [MARGARET PRILEY (B. 1909)]. *MURDER TAKES THE VEIL*. MILWAUKEE: BRUCE PUBLISHING, 1950.

"The College of St. Aurelian," a Catholic institution for young women, is located deep in the bayous of Louisiana. Mother Theodore, the superior of the college, hires three men as new lay instructors. One of the new recruits has committed an off-campus murder, and he sets out to eliminate the only person who can implicate him, a St. Aurelian student named Trillium Pierce. Thanks to his efforts, Miss Pierce suffers far more than her fair share of terror-filled moments during the story. Once they become aware of what is happening, Mother Theodore and the other nuns at St. Aurelian attempt to discover which of their new recruits is making poor Miss Pierce's life so miserable. With the help of a wise local sheriff, the troublemaker is eventually identified and hauled off to pay for his misdeeds. Casual readers of mysteries may have difficulty identifying the culprit before the end of the story. On the other hand, dedicated devotees of college-mystery novels will have no such problems. For those fortunate individuals, the author provides a clear onomastic clue on page four.

Margaret Priley was born in Souris, North Dakota. She received a B.S. in 1932 from the University of Minnesota and then began a successful career as a writer of adventure books for juveniles. *Murder Takes the Veil* was the first of four mystery novels that Priley wrote for adult consumption.

90. WESTBROOK, PERCY D(ICKIE). (B. 1916). *INFRA BLOOD*. NEW YORK: PHOENIX, 1950.

Benjamin Henry, a young Shakespearean scholar at Harvard, decides to spend his Christmas vacation studying a rare Shakespeare folio recently acquired by "Banks College" in Maine. The Banks library is nearly empty, but he finds that two other experts in Shakespeare have had the same idea. One of these individuals, Ira MacDonald, soon dies of a throat slashing in the library's stacks. Then, almost before MacDonald's blood can be mopped up, Miss Sauerman, the library's keeper of rare books, dies after her throat is cut near the very spot in the stacks where MacDonald met his demise. Professor Samuel Cutting, Banks College's stellar professor of criminal psychology, is deputized by the local police to look into the killings, and after first establishing Benjamin Henry's probable noninvolvement in the murders he enlists the Harvard visitor as his assistant. The attention of the detective duo quickly falls on Jonathan Tierney, the third user of the Shakespeare folio. A gaunt, secretive man whose academic connections are unclear, Tierney is often seen wandering the nearby snow-covered countryside after midnight. Cutting and Henry look, too, at several Banks College faculty members and at Dr. Hoffman-Walter, the library's bombastic director. The motive for the murders turns out to be perfectly academic, and the book contains several riveting late-night scenes in which Cutting and Henry try to trap the book's villain in the Banks library stacks after closing time.

Percy Dickie Westbrook was born in Brooklyn, New York. He received an A.B. from Columbia in 1937 and a Ph.D. from the same institution in 1951. At the time *Infra Blood* was published Westbrook was a professor of English at the State University of New York at Albany. Widely published in the field of English literature, Westbrook employed Professor Samuel Cutting as a detective in two earlier mysteries, neither of which is set in the world of higher education. The earlier books in the three-novel Cutting series are *Happy Deathday* (New York: Phoenix, 1947) and *The Red Herring Murder* (New York: Phoenix, 1949).

91. INNES, MICHAEL [JOHN INNES MACKINTOSH STEWART (1906–1994)]. *OPERATION PAX*. LONDON: GOLLANCZ, 1951. PUBLISHED IN THE UNITED STATES AS *THE PAPER THUNDERBOLT.* NEW YORK: DODD, MEAD & CO., 1951.

A group of scientists, operating from a sanitarium outside of Oxford, plots to develop a drug that will bring it power over the world. The drug, known as Formula Ten, destroys its victims' capacity for aggressiveness. This sinister band is foiled, however, by John Appleby of New Scotland Yard, Michael Innes's tireless series-character sleuth, and by Oxford undergraduate Jane Appleby, John Appleby's twenty-one-year-old sister. In the process, the two Applebys also find the truth behind the disappearance of Oxford undergraduate Geoffrey Ourglass, the young man to whom Jane Appleby is engaged. *Operation Pax* is a dizzying tale that intermixes life-and-death action sequences, droll dialogue, literary allusions, and quiet detection, and its plot defies easy summation. The book offers many scenes in Oxford, inside and outside of the university's colleges, and several of its primary characters have university connections. One of the more interesting academic players is Dr. Ourglass, young Geoffrey's uncle, an Oxford don whom the author describes as "an obscure man from an obscure college."

Another is Mark Bultitude, a rotund university tutor whose idea of humor is to disquiet acquaintances by informing them that they look "wretched." The book is especially noteworthy for two episodes in the Bodleian Library. In one, a small-time confidence man named Routh is pursued by a villain through the Upper Reading Room. In the other, Jane Appleby faces death during an eerie chase in the dark, vast book-storage area underneath the library. In a prefatory note at the beginning of the tale Innes tells his readers that he has never visited the "subterranean region" of the Bodleian and has drawn it, for purposes of his story, from the reports of "reliable persons."

Three other Michael Innes mysteries have entries in this bibliography. Those books are *Death at the President's Lodging* (34), *The Weight of the Evidence* (57), and *Old Hall, New Hall* (106).

92. LAING, PATRICK [AMELIA REYNOLDS LONG (1904–1976)]. *THE LADY IS DEAD.* NEW YORK: PHOENIX, 1951.

Dr. Eric Fordyce is a visiting member of the chemistry department at a university in the eastern United States. He is at the university to work on a government-sponsored research project. Dr. Fordyce's son, Mark, is an undergraduate at the university. An aspiring actor, Mark acquires the lead in *Dr. Faustus,* a play being staged by Professor Antonio Barto of the theater department. Mark's achievement would make most parents proud, but Dr. Fordyce storms into the play's dress rehearsal and loudly insists that his son leave the cast. A few nights later the Fordyce home burns and a body, thought to be that of Dr. Fordyce, is found in the ashes. Immediately thereafter Professor Barto disappears. Patrick Laing, a blind professor of psychology who serves as narrator of the story, suspects foul play. Using his heightened senses of smell and hearing, and with his wife, Diedre, acting as his eyes, he launches an investigation. Along with Mark Fordyce, several university faculty members and administrators emerge as suspects after Professor Laing discovers peccadilloes in their pasts. By the conclusion of the tale Professor Laing, an Amelia Reynolds Long series-character professor-detective, has solved the third multimurder mystery on his home campus. The "lady" in the book's title is the late Helena Stedman, an aging actress, whose natural death (before the start of the story), prompts several of the book's principal participants to remember the parts they played in her scandal-ridden life.

Stone Dead (67) and *Murder from the Mind* (76), two earlier Professor Patrick Laing mysteries, appear in this bibliography. In Laing's earlier adventures, Diedre O'Hara is the professor's student girlfriend. She has become his wife in *The Lady Is Dead.* Three other Amelia Reynolds Long mysteries, without the detection of Patrick Laing, also can be found in the bibliography. Those mysteries are *The Shakespeare Murders* (46), *Death Looks Down* (62), and *Murder Most Foul* (70). *Murder Most Foul* was published under the pseudonym Kathleen Buddington Coxe.

93. VARNAM, JOHN. *TRAVELLING DEADMAN.* LONDON: HODDER & STOUGHTON, 1951.

Two people disappear from "Kirminster University" in central England. One is Mary Kennion, the wife of an engineering student. The other is Professor of Industrial Engineering Fortescue Cranch. Investigating both of the missing-persons cases is Detective-Inspector Richard Semlake of the Kirminster police. Professor Cranch is soon found beaten dead in a coal wagon in the Kirminster railroad yards. The next day Mrs. Amelia Mendling, the bachelor professor's housekeeper, is beaten dead in the professor's home. Meantime, David Kennion, Mary Kennion's husband, is found badly battered (but still alive) on a riverbank, and nearby lies the suffocated corpse of the Kennions' infant son. Inspector Semlake initially assumes that he has at least two separate crime sequences to investigate, but he eventually finds that all of the events are linked. Although the book provides only a few scenes on the Kirminster campus, most of the primary characters have university connections, and as the inspector trolls for clues there are many episodes at Professor Cranch's home, a gloomy, late-Victorian structure that lies just beyond the university's boundaries. Among Semlake's suspects are Larissa Pfeffer (a hard-drinking university psychologist whose dislike of policemen prompts her to tamper with evidence), Edward Lampard (a lecturer who has spent many years acting as Professor Cranch's research assistant), and Anthony Frayne (a graduate student who happens to be Mary Kennion's half-brother). Also on the suspect list is Homer P. Quellen, a flamboyant professional conjurer and sometimes firearms broker, who is appearing in Kirminster and who has a long-standing relationship with the ill-fated Mrs. Mendling. Although it is by no means a comedy, *Travelling Deadman* is written with dollops of dry wit, and devotees of college mysteries will be pleased to learn that the murders in the tale were perpetrated by a villain with a solid academic motive.

Travelling Deadman was the second of three mysteries that John Varnam published during his literary career.

94. ELLIS, VIRGINIA. *DEATH COMES LIKE A THIEF.* NEW YORK: ARCADIA HOUSE, 1952.

Why would anyone want to shoot Professor of Geology Alex Heath dead in his "Lane University" office on a beautiful evening in June? Certainly Ann Cambridge doesn't know, and as the geology department's secretary she is privy to all of the dirt about the faculty. To be sure, Professor Heath was considered aloof by some of his students because he usually kept his office door closed, and some of his junior faculty members were jealous of the $75,000 in research funds he had just received from the estate of the late Leah Gardner. But neither of those phenomena would seem to have been motivation for murder. Peter Wylie, the chief of the local San Marcos, California, police department, suspects Bill O'Halloran, a graduate assistant, who had been heard arguing with Professor Heath shortly before the killing. Ann Cambridge is not convinced of O'Halloran's guilt, and with the help of Bill Dana, her graduate-student boyfriend, she seeks to find the truth. On Cambridge's list of possible killers are Sylvia Heath, the professor's seemingly befuddled wife, and several Lane administrators and attorneys who took part in processing the Gardner bequest through the university bureaucracy. Professor Heath had voiced suspicions to Cambridge that he had not gotten all of the monies due him from the Gardner will, and on the evening of his death he was composing a letter detailing his concerns. In view of what Cambridge eventually learns about the ways in which various high-placed worthies skimmed funds from the Gardner bequest into their own pockets, *Death Comes Like a Thief* can be read as an argument for the zealous auditing of university financial records.

The identity of Virginia Ellis is not revealed by any of the ordinary bibliographic reference sources, but *Death Comes Like a Thief* appears to have been her only mystery novel.

95. FARRER, KATHERINE (B. 1911). *THE MISSING LINK*. LONDON: COLLINS, 1952.

Perdita Link, the infant daughter of John and Perpetual Link, is kidnapped. John Link is an Oxford don. Inspector Richard Ringwood of Scotland Yard, an Oxford graduate himself, is assigned to the case, and his inquiries take him among John Link's university colleagues, to a band of gypsies camped outside of Oxford, and even to the ape cages at the "Bestiarick Gardens," a small zoo run by the university. Located just off High Street, the gardens are entered by a "noble" gateway that, according to the author, "just missed being designed by Sir Christopher

Wren." *The Missing Link* is a playful tale that deals, at root, with the antagonisms between humanists and behavioralistic psychologists. All of the story's characters, save the apes in the zoo, possess high-powered vocabularies and significant measures of sardonic wit. There are several intriguing on-campus scenes, including a faculty meeting at John Link's college and a dinner at the college that Inspector Ringwood attends in order to learn more about humanist Link's academic enemies.

Born Katherine Newton, Katherine Farrer read literature at St. Anne's College, Oxford. In 1937 she married the Rev. A. M. Farrer, a fellow of Trinity College, Oxford. She began writing detective fiction when her only child, a daughter, went away to school, and eventually she published three novels. *The Missing Link* was the first of her detective tales, all of which feature Inspector Richard Ringwood. The third of Katherine Farrer's mysteries, *Gownsman's Gallows* (108), also is included in this bibliography.

96. OLSEN, D. B. [DOLORES HITCHENS (1907–1973)]. *ENROLLMENT CANCELLED.* GARDEN CITY, N.Y.: DOUBLEDAY, 1952. ALSO PUBLISHED AS *DEAD BABES IN THE WOOD.* NEW YORK: DELL, 1954.

A knife-wielding killer murders two female undergraduates of little virtue at "Clarendon College," a small, high-quality institution in Southern California. The first to die is Sandra Norris, whose sexual exploits with members of the faculty were well-known on the Clarendon campus. Her body is found in a eucalyptus grove. Her shoes are missing, and a note attached to her corpse reads "Enrollment Cancelled." Next to go is Audrey Long, another young woman of shaky morals, and a similar note is pinned to her. The sleuth in the story is Professor A. Pennyfeather, a D. B. Olsen series-character detective who teaches English at Clarendon. A bachelor in his late fifties, Pennyfeather has never revealed his first name to anyone at Clarendon. Nor, though he is often called "Doc" by his students, did he ever finish his doctorate. A specialist in Chaucer and Milton, in this novel he displays a surprising knowledge of psychosexual deviation as he labors to identify Clarendon College's version of Jack the Ripper. The case involves a campus shoe fetishist, a faculty wife who has a tendency to imbibe too much alcohol, an assistant professor of history who feels that colleges and universities should be bastions of moral purity, and a female librarian who experiments with different shades of lipstick even while she spends much of her time placing mothballs on the library's shelves.

Dolores Hitchens was born in Texas and attended the University of Southern California. She specialized in light, sometimes-whimsical murder mysteries. Professor A. Pennyfeather was only one of several series-characters she created. Her most popular series-sleuths were Rachel and Jennifer Murdock—two elderly spinsters who appear as a detection team in nine Hitchens novels. Using the pseudonym D. B. Olsen, Hitchens wrote six Professor Pennyfeather mysteries. *Enrollment Cancelled* was the last novel in the Pennyfeather series and the only one with a campus setting.

97. VULLIAMY, C(OLWYN) E(DWARD) (1886–1971). *DON AMONG THE DEAD MEN*. LONDON: MICHAEL JOSEPH, 1952; BALTIMORE: PENGUIN, 1955.

Kerris Bowles-Ottery, a professor of chemistry at the "University of Ockham" in England, discovers a traceless compound that, when mixed with food or drink, produces in its recipients heightened feelings of well-being and amusement. Those who ingest the concoction laugh, sing, dance, and otherwise display the symptoms of advanced euphoria. They also fall dead in a matter of hours, but, as Bowles-Ottery rationalizes, they expire happily. With this lethal but humane compound at his disposal, Bowles-Ottery sets out to rid the university of his enemies. The first to go merrily to his maker is Professor Gasson-Brown, the institution's faculty bully and a man who "thunderously occupied" the chair of Greek literature. Then a host of other victims follow. Since the author intersperses his narrative with excerpts from Bowles-Ottery's diary, readers have no doubts about the professor's guilt. The question, instead, is whether he will get away with his crimes. Written as satire, the book includes little serious detection but offers some of the wittiest prose in academic mystery fiction. Set in 1928, the book also provides many sardonic insights into the behavioral and intellectual foibles of genteel academic folk in England between the wars.

One of England's more diverse twentieth-century writers, Colwyn Edward Vulliamy did not attend a university. He received a private education at home before embarking on a long and illustrious literary career. Best remembered for his biographies of such historic personages as Voltaire, Boswell, and William Penn, Vulliamy turned in his later years to social satires and to mysteries. *Don among the Dead Men*, which combines both of his late-in-life interests, was the fifth of ten mystery novels that he published before his death in 1971.

98. WALLACE, FRANCIS (1894–1977). *FRONT MAN*. NEW YORK: RINEHART, 1952.

When head football coach Pop Tierney dies of a heart attack, Chancellor Paxton of "State University" hires Johnny Stone as Pop's replacement. Stone, a former star halfback at State, wants to continue Pop's winning tradition, but powerful gambling interests have other plans for the team. As the season begins, a dedicated booster named Benny Bomas is murdered, and Stone himself is kidnapped. Most of the investigatory work in the story is handled by Stone, who feels that his responsibilities as coach extend to off-the-field concerns. But when Stone is held against his will in a shack far out in the countryside, the detective chores fall to Ruth Dee, the athletic department's attractive secretary. Miss Dee, who is described early in the book as an "excellent specimen of female on the hoof," is a resourceful woman. However, neither she nor Stone can compete with Nip, the football team's canine mascot, for real sleuthing skill. It is Nip who captures the principal villain of the piece, even as State is in the process of defeating its archrival, "Prairie," by a score of 24 to 23. As for Chancellor Paxton, he becomes a born-again athletic purist. Realizing toward the end of the book that he has allowed intercollegiate football to become his institution's main reason for being, Dr. Paxton quotes from the Bible and asks God to forgive him for his administrative sins.

A graduate of Notre Dame University, Francis Wallace spent most of his working life as a New York City sportswriter. From 1937 until 1948, he wrote "Pigskin Review" for the *Saturday Evening Post*, and he continued that column for *Colliers* from 1949 until 1956. Wallace also wrote many fiction and nonfiction books about sports. *Front Man* was the second of two mysteries that he wrote during his career.

99. WAUGH, HILLARY (BALDWIN) (B. 1920). *LAST SEEN WEARING*. GARDEN CITY, N.Y.: DOUBLEDAY, 1952.

A classic police procedural, *Last Seen Wearing* begins with the mysterious disappearance from "Parker College" of Marilyn Lowell Mitchell, an eighteen-year-old freshman. Parker College, a fashionable institution for women, is located in the town of "Bristol," Massachusetts, and the case is handled by Chief Ford and Sergeant Cameron of the local police. Through diligent sleuthing the two law officers find

Miss Mitchell's body in a nearby river, determine that she was murdered, and then apprehend her killer. Among the possible culprits in the case are male students at nearby "Carlton College," a Parker College security guard, and several members of the Parker College faculty. Though Ford and Cameron are clearly adept at policework, academic readers may find one flaw in their reasoning processes. Early in their investigation they discover that Miss Mitchell was two months pregnant, and they decide that her death was most probably the work of the man who impregnated her. Going through the roster of men on the Parker campus, they come to the school's president, an individual named Howland. After reviewing Dr. Howland's long list of degrees (from Yale, Harvard, and Columbia) and after noting that he is, after all, a college president, the two detectives immediately dismiss him from their list of suspects.

Hillary Baldwin Waugh was born in New Haven, Connecticut, and received a B.A. from Yale in 1942. After service as a naval aviation officer in World War II, he began what proved to be a highly successful career as a mystery writer. *Last Seen Wearing* was his fourth mystery novel. Some of Waugh's books have been published under the pseudonyms H. Baldwin Taylor and Harry Walker.

100. LEVIN, IRA. (B. 1929). *A KISS BEFORE DYING*. NEW YORK: SIMON & SCHUSTER, 1953.

Two sisters, the daughters of a millionaire copper magnate, are murdered. At the time of their deaths the young women are students at two different institutions of higher education in Wisconsin. Then the third surviving sister—a Columbia University graduate living in New York City—finds herself in jeopardy. The villain in all three instances is a mentally unbalanced young man who romances the heiresses in hopes of gaining access to the family fortune. Written as a psychological thriller, the book has little classical detection, but it incorporates many sudden, spine-chilling discoveries by its characters. Much of the story takes place at "Stoddard University," the school attended by the first victim. Stoddard is graced by one of the more zealous administrators in college-mystery fiction. Almost before the first sister's body is cold, Dean Welch has the presence of mind to suggest that her family might like to make a sizable cash contribution to the university in her memory.

Ira Levin was born in New York City and graduated from New York University in 1950. *A Kiss before Dying* was his first novel. The book won the Mystery Writers' of America Edgar Allan Poe Award for best first mystery novel of 1953. In 1956 *A Kiss before Dying* was transformed into a United Artists motion picture starring Jeffrey Hunter, Joanne Woodward, and Robert Wagner. Levin followed *A Kiss before Dying* with such horror-mystery blockbusters as *Rosemary's Baby* (New York: Random House, 1967) and *The Stepford Wives* (New York: Random House, 1972).

101. MAINWARING, MARION. *MURDER AT MIDYEARS*. NEW YORK: MACMILLAN, 1953.

A quintessential college mystery, *Murder at Midyears* is set at "Collins College," a New England institution for high-status young women. The book begins with a short history of Collins and then moves quickly to a meeting of the school's department of English literature. Presiding over the gathering is Gabriel Mersey, the dictatorial and corrupt head of the department. Gabriel is so loathsome that neither his colleagues nor the book's readers are surprised when, three chapters later, someone slips the evil old autocrat a lethal dose of cyanide. The sleuth in the story is Toby Sampson, a local assistant district attorney. Helped by Henry Dane and Jill Carey, two junior members of the English literature faculty, Sampson explores the late Dr. Mersey's full closet of skeletons before coming upon the identity of the murderer. Professorial readers will appreciate the setting for Sampson's denouement speech; it is delivered at yet another department meeting. The story abounds with real and false clues, and the murderer, as Sampson reveals, had a thoroughly academic motive.

Marion Mainwaring was born in Boston. She received a B.S. from Simmons College in 1943 and a Ph.D. from Radcliffe in 1949. She then taught English at Mt. Holyoke College from 1949 until 1952. Following her short academic career, Mainwaring served as an editor for Houghton Mifflin, a newspaper correspondent in Europe, as survey director for the Massachusetts Council on the Arts and Humanities, and as a translator and writer for UNESCO. *Murder at Midyears* was the first of two mystery novels that she produced during the mid-1950s. Mainwaring is best known in the world of literature as the person who completed Edith Wharton's unfinished manuscript of *The Buccaneers* (New York: Viking, 1993).

102. WAKEFIELD, R. I. [GERTRUDE MASON WHITE (B. 1915)]. *YOU WILL DIE TODAY*. NEW YORK: DODD, MEAD & CO., 1953.

This novel of academic nastiness and murder takes place at "Greene University," an expanding school in the American city of

"Lockport." Jim Hatch, an expert in Celtic literature, is found strangled in his office. The humanities department's resident busybody, Hatch gained his primary pleasure in life from spying on his fellow faculty members and then gossiping about their darkest secrets. Since Hatch did not lack for enemies, there are suspects aplenty in the case, and Lieutenant Marshall of the Lockport police has no shortage of possible professorial killers to interrogate. Lieutenant Marshall is aided in his work by Judy Meadows, the newest member of the humanities department. Meadows is of great help to Marshall, but her attentions to her unofficial duties are sometimes diverted by Bill Griffith, a male colleague with romance on his mind. Neither Meadows nor Griffith is Jim Hatch's murderer. That individual, as readers discover at the end of the book, had an unusual reason for putting an end to Hatch's vicious tattling.

Gertrude Mason White was born in Pawtucket, Rhode Island. She received an A.B. from Mt. Holyoke College in 1936, an M.A. from Columbia in 1937, and a Ph.D. from the University of Chicago in 1950. *You Will Die Today* was her only mystery novel. Prior to the book's publication, White had taught English at the University of Chicago, McGill University, and Wayne State. At the time the book appeared, she was employed by the University of Maryland's Overseas Division as an instructor of English at Ruislip Air Force Base in Middlesex, England. In later years, White became a professor of English at Oakland University in Rochester, Michigan.

103. CANDY, EDWARD [BARBARA ALISON BOODSON NEVILLE (B. 1925)]. *BONES OF CONTENTION*. LONDON: GOLLANCZ, 1954; GARDEN CITY, N.Y.: DOUBLEDAY, 1983.

"The London Museum of Pathological Conditions in Childhood" is a part of the "Royal College of Paediatricians," which, in turn, is one of the less-distinguished units of the University of London. The skeleton of a young girl, packed in a cabin trunk, arrives unsolicited at the museum. Old Mr. Murivance, the museum's director, finds the incident unsettling, and a few days later he dies suddenly after receiving a series of injections to ease the pain in a sore shoulder. Murivance leaves a sizable bequest to impoverished Miles Latimer, the editor of the college's professional journal, but Latimer is soon grievously injured and removed to a nursing home after he mysteriously falls down a college staircase while admiring a William Kent balustrade. Professor Fabian Honeychurch, the college's founder and president, wants to get to the bottom of these troubling matters and, along with several of his faculty and staff, he turns amateur detective. The several college sleuths, who sometimes find themselves competing with a police inspector named Burnivel, eventually learn that their school has been sullied by blackmail and murder, and at the end of the story the nastiness is brought to an end during an unlikely shootout. Written with considerable humor, *Bones of Contention* offers a series of amusing situations and a collection of eccentric characters who are portrayed with proper British wit. Miles Latimer, for example, is "a man who passed unnoticed in large gatherings and hardly made his mark in small ones." As for the Royal College of Paediatricians, it is "a professional backwater, a concession to academic indolence skillfully disguised as academic necessity."

Barbara Alison Boodson Neville was born in London. She received M.B., B.S., and D.C.H. degrees from University College, London, and University College Hospital Medical School. A mainstream novelist as well as a mystery writer, she employs the pseudonym Edward Candy on many of her publications. Another Edward Candy mystery, *Words for Murder, Perhaps* (161), appears in this bibliography.

104. CASSILL, R(ONALD) V(ERLIN) (B. 1919). *DORMITORY WOMEN*. NEW YORK: LION BOOKS, 1954.

Millie Doran, an undergraduate at "Blackhawk University," encounters misfortune wherever she turns. Dolphin Myers, her big-man-on-campus boyfriend, is killed in an automobile accident after making an unsuccessful attempt on her virtue. Professor Penard of the English department begins to receive threatening telephone calls after appointing Miss Doran his research assistant, and her roommate mourns the mysterious disappearance of her pet baby chicken during a panty raid on the women's residence hall. Beset by all of these depressing events, poor Miss Doran is suffering a breakdown. *Dormitory Women* is not a conventional mystery. Nor, despite its suggestive title, is it an exposé of the sexual habits of female undergraduates. Rather, it is a skillfully written psychological suspense story detailing one young woman's mental dissolution on a Midwestern American campus.

Ronald Verlin Cassill was born in Cedar Falls, Iowa. He received a B.A. from the State University of Iowa and an M.A. from the same institution in 1947. Cassill taught at the Iowa Writers' Workshop from 1948 until 1952 and from 1960 until 1966. At the time *Dormitory Women* was published he was an editor with *Colliers Encyclopedia* in

New York City. In 1966 Cassill joined the faculty of Brown University, and he retired from Brown as a professor of English in 1983. *Dormitory Women* was Cassill's second novel. Perhaps because it was published in paperback, or because of its unfortunate title, the book received only a few, brief reviews. Many of Cassill's later works, however, have met with extensive critical acclaim. Known primarily as the author of mainstream fiction, Cassill's long list of publications includes two mainstream novels set in the world of higher education. Those books are *Night School* (New York: New American Library, 1961) and *The President* (New York: Simon & Schuster, 1965).

105. DILLON, EILIS (1920–1994). *DEATH IN THE QUADRANGLE.* LONDON: FABER & FABER, 1956; NEW YORK: WALKER, 1968.

President Bradley of "King's University" in Dublin receives threats on his life. Then someone slips nitrobenzene, a slow-acting poison, into his food, and he dies late one night in the president's lodging. A former professor of mineralogy, Bradley was unpopular at King's, and a large number of people had motive to kill him. The detectives in the story are Professor Daly and Mike Kenney. Daly is a retired King's University professor of English who has returned to the campus to deliver a series of guest lectures. Kenney is an inspector with the local police. Written in stylish prose and with considerable satirical humor, *Death in the Quadrangle* follows the two sleuths as they interrogate the eccentrics who form King's faculty and staff. The faculty members include an aged professor who is obsessed with the rats (four-legged) that he perceives everywhere in the university and a physically fit zoologist who snipes at his colleagues for doing nothing about their bulging waistlines. The book offers an interesting denouement in which Helen Bradley, the late president's widow, graciously serves tea and cakes to the detectives as she listens to their verdict on who murdered her husband and why. And, concerning the "why" of the matter, readers who monitor the misdeeds of presidents in college fiction will want to take note of the way in which the late President Bradley supplemented his academic income.

Eilis Dillon was born in Galway, Ireland. Married to Cormac O'Cuilleanian, a professor of Irish literature at University College, Cork, Dillon wrote children's books, mainstream novels, and mysteries. She taught creative writing at Trinity College, Dublin, and made several lecture tours of the United States speaking on Anglo-Irish literature. *Death in the Quadrangle* was the second (and final) Dillon mystery to feature Professor Daly and Inspector Kenney. The first was *Death at Crane's Court* (London: Faber & Faber, 1953; New York: Walker, 1963). A nonacademic tale, *Death at Crane's Court* chronicles the sleuthing of Daly and Kenney as they deal with a murder near the professor's retirement home in Galway.

106. INNES, MICHAEL [JOHN INNES MACKINTOSH STEWART (1906–1994)]. *OLD HALL, NEW HALL*. LONDON: GOLLANCZ, 1956. PUBLISHED IN THE UNITED STATES AS *A QUESTION OF QUEENS*. NEW YORK: DODD, MEAD & CO., 1956.

More a satirical exploration into academic non-manners than a conventional whodunit, *Old Hall, New Hall*, is set at a provincial university somewhere in England. The central character is Colin Clout, a young graduate of the university, who has just returned with a B.Litt. from Oxford to join the English faculty as an "Alderman Shufflеman Fellow." Clout has two lady friends. One is Sadie Sackett, a university librarian. The other is Olivia Jory, a ravishingly beautiful and wealthy woman-about-town. All three of the participants in this romantic triangle, in addition to many other members of the local community, search for a mysterious treasure trove supposedly hidden somewhere on or near the university campus. There are no murders in the story, although there is an abundance of verbal assassination. Since all of the major characters are either addled or at least mildly larcenous, there are no easily identifiable heroes in the plot. Colin Clout, whose constant bumbling cannot help but remind readers of James Dixon in Kingsley Amis's *Lucky Jim* (Garden City, N.Y.: Doubleday, 1953), is best characterized as ingenuous. Professor Gingrast, Clout's immediate supervisor in the English department, develops a sudden interest in archaeology halfway through the novel and begins to dig up large sections of the university's lawn. Milton Milder, a Yankee professor "from either Yale or Princeton," offers research appointments in America in exchange for information about the treasure. And George Lamb, another junior member of the faculty (who jousts with Colin Clout for the affections of both Sadie and Olivia), stutters so badly that his listeners often lack the patience to allow him to finish his sentences.

Old Hall, New Hall, is an atypical Michael Innes college mystery, not only in the sense that it lacks a murder, but also because John Appleby, Innes's learned, Scotland Yard series-character detective, does not put in an appearance. Three earlier Innes college mysteries, all of which include sleuthing by Inspector Appleby, appear in this bibliography. Those books are *Death at the President's Lodging* (34), *The Weight of the Evidence* (57), and *Operation Pax* (91).

107. ROBINSON, ROBERT (HENRY) (B. 1927). *LANDSCAPE WITH DEAD DONS.* NEW YORK: RINEHART, 1956.

The theft of pages from the Bodleian Library's rarest edition of *Paradise Lost* brings Inspector Autumn of Scotland Yard to Oxford. Autumn, a man of solid working-class background, initially finds the elite Oxford scene both distasteful and frustrating. However, when old Professor Manchip (the cantankerous master of "Warlock College") is murdered, Autumn begins to warm to his sleuthing tasks. Then, when the Reverend Bow-Parley (the chaplain of Warlock College) is killed shortly thereafter, Inspector Autumn finds that the mysteries of Oxford are not quite so impenetrable as he had supposed. More than vaguely Innes-esque, with its emphasis on droll professorial dialogue, and with many sketches of eccentric Oxford dons, this novel represents witty college-mystery fiction in its most pronounced state. Though the book includes some set pieces, as well as some semistock characterizations, it also incorporates considerable inventiveness. For example, when Professor Manchip is killed, the culprit drags the master's body onto the college roof for public display. Toward the end of the story, a horde of naked male Oxonians, interrupted while swimming au naturel in a secluded bywater of the River Cherwell, chases a possible suspect through the Oxford streets past all of the city's major landmarks.

Robert Robinson was born in Liverpool and received an M.A. from Exeter College, Oxford. His career included stints as a newspaper columnist, a film critic, and a BBC television personality. *Landscape with Dead Dons* was the first of three mystery novels by Robinson.

108. FARRER, KATHERINE (B. 1911). *GOWNSMAN'S GALLOWS.* LONDON: HODDER & STOUGHTON, 1957.

The charred body of a graduate student is found in a burnt haystack outside of Oxford, and Scotland Yard Inspector Richard Ringwood is assigned to the case. An Oxford graduate, and a man of independent financial means, Ringwood is the Yard's expert in murders at institutions of higher learning. He also is the master of a trusty bloodhound named Ranter, who collaborates with him in this investigation. The corpse is that of Jean Du Puys, a Frenchman. When Inspector

Ringwood learns that Tim Dawson-Glower, an undergraduate, has taken an unscheduled leave of his college and has repaired to a town in France to recuperate from a suddenly acquired illness, he and Ranter follow young Mr. Dawson-Glower across the Channel. Only the first third of this sly, witty novel takes place at Oxford, but that is long enough for several seemingly befogged dons to make their appearances. It is long enough, too, for Ringwood to come across the crucial clue that ultimately allows him to identify Mr. Du Puys's killer.

The Missing Link (95), an earlier Oxford mystery by Katherine Farrer, also appears in this bibliography.

109. HARDY, WILLIAM (MARION) (B. 1922). *LADY KILLER*. NEW YORK: DODD, MEAD & CO., 1957.

Earl Borstleman, a fortyish professor of mathematics at an American state university, wants to kill his dumpy wife. A methodical man, Borstleman calculates the advantages and disadvantages of various death-dealing methods before settling on strangulation. Then he decides that the probabilities of escaping suspicion will be better if he strangles two other dowdy, middle-aged women first, thereby creating the illusion that a mad killer is on the loose. The first of the professor's victims is the mathematics department's secretary. The second is a local landlady. And then wife Sarah goes to her reward. Although campus security officers, the local police, and state troopers all involve themselves in the affair, the most inspired detection in the novel comes from Bob Adams and Anne Miner, two of Professor Borstleman's students. Adams, a suspect in the case, becomes an amateur sleuth largely out of a sense of self-preservation. Anne Miner, a lovely young lady whose charms have not escaped Borstleman's methodical observations, discovers firsthand that her fears of a madman loose on the university campus are, in fact, well-founded.

William Marion Hardy was born in Norfolk, Virginia. He received a B.S. from Duke University in 1943 and an M.A. from the University of North Carolina in 1954. He was an assistant professor of communications at Purdue University when *Lady Killer*, his first novel, was published. Hardy later became a professor of radio, television, and motion pictures at the University of North Carolina at Chapel Hill. Although it does not qualify as a college mystery, another Hardy novel, *A Little Sin* (New York: Dodd, Mead & Co., 1959), might also be of interest to users of this bibliography. The protagonist is a professor of mathematics at "Dryden University" in South Carolina who is sentenced to death for allegedly killing a female undergraduate. Most of the story involves the effort of a newspaperwoman to overturn the professor's conviction. *A Little Sin* also was published as *The Case of the Missing Coed* (New York: Dell, 1960).

110. HOCKING, ANNE [MONA (NAOMI ANNE) MESSER (D. 1966)]. *THE SIMPLE WAY OF POISON*. NEW YORK: IVES WASHBURN, 1957.

Jocelyn Waring, a professor of drama at Oxford, is a philanderer, a liar and cheat, and something of a prankster. One night he invites all of his many enemies to meet and mingle at a party in his home. During the course of the bizarre evening, one of his guests slips him a lethal dose of poison and, unloved by all, Professor Waring departs this world. Scotland Yard Superintendent William Austen, a Mona Messer series-character detective, is called in by the local police. The prime candidate for the gallows is Juliet Waring, Jocelyn's happy-to-see-him-dead widow, but Superintendent Austen knows better than to center his investigations on the most likely suspect. Some of the other individuals whom Austen interrogates before identifying the actual killer are Oxford students and faculty members, and his attentions fall on a number of nonacademics as well. Members of the Oxford homosexual community occupy a prominent place in the story. By the end of the tale Juliet Waring, a writer of mystery fiction who is constantly searching for new whodunit ideas, has presumably traded an unwanted professor-husband for the plot of her next detective epic.

Mona Messer was the daughter of turn-of-the-century religious novelist Joseph Hocking. Beginning in 1933 and ending in 1960 she published forty-five mystery novels. *The Simple Way of Poison* was her thirty-eighth mystery. All but one of Messer's mysteries were issued under her maiden name. Under the name Mona Messer she published eleven mainstream novels.

111. KELLY, MARY (B. 1927). *DEAD MAN'S RIDDLE*. LONDON: SECKER & WARBURG, 1957; NEW YORK: WALKER, 1967.

A pleasant, inoffensive German philologist is beaten dead in the library of the University of Edinburgh. The victim, a man named Seifert, seems to have had no enemies, and the local police are baffled. Persuaded to enter the case is Scotland Yard Inspector Brett

Nightingale, who happens to be in Edinburgh to attend a concert by Clarissa, his mezzo-soprano wife. Nightingale has very few early clues from which to work. Seifert had propounded a controversial interpretation of the Runic inscriptions on a Celtic cross in the nearby town of Ruthwell, and he had recently written a will. Starting from this meager basis, Nightingale builds his evidence, and eventually establishes the identity of Seifert's killer. Along the way readers are exposed to the rudiments of the Runic alphabet, are treated to a vivid account of a student riot as the university's undergraduates campaign for their candidates for rector, and learn that quiet German philologists may have lurid pasts.

Mary Kelly was born in London and received an M.A. from the University of Edinburgh in 1951. *Dead Man's Riddle* was the second of three Mary Kelly mysteries to feature Inspector Nightingale in the role of sleuth. The first Nightingale mystery, *A Cold Coming* (London: Secker & Warburg, 1956; New York: Walker, 1968), also takes Inspector Nightingale briefly to the University of Edinburgh. In *A Cold Coming* the inspector investigates the kidnappings of two Edinburgh undergraduates. However, since almost all of *A Cold Coming* is set away from the university, the book does not have a separate entry in this bibliography.

112. ASIMOV, ISAAC (1920–1992). *THE DEATH DEALERS*. NEW YORK: AVON BOOKS, 1958. ALSO PUBLISHED AS *A WHIFF OF DEATH*. NEW YORK: WALKER, 1968.

Louis Brade is a member of the chemistry department of a large, North American university. A man of strong convictions, Brade refuses to publish until he has something truly significant to communicate to his professional peers. As a consequence, he has been an assistant professor, without tenure, for eleven years. When one of his graduate students dies in what appears to be a laboratory accident, Brade's department chairman, Professor Littleby, suggests that the loss of promising Ph.D. candidates through careless laboratory safety practices is not a way to speed up promotion. Adding to our troubled assistant professor's woes is Jack Doheny, a local police detective, who is not convinced that the student's death was accidental and who, moreover, harbors suspicions that Brade is a murderer. In the end it is Brade who discovers the truth of the matter. Before its conclusion the book touches upon faculty rivalries, the "fudging" of research data, and the poisonous properties of a host of chemicals.

Isaac Asimov was born in the Soviet Union and was brought to the United States at the age of three. He received B.A., M.A., and Ph.D. degrees from Columbia University. A veritable Renaissance man of letters, he wrote scientific texts, novels, science-fiction stories, mysteries, and a variety of other works. *The Death Dealers* was his first mystery. At the time the book was published Asimov was an associate professor of biochemistry at the Boston University Medical School.

113. CARR, JOHN DICKSON (1905–1977). *THE DEAD MAN'S KNOCK.* NEW YORK: HARPER & BROTHERS, 1958.

Mark Ruthven, a professor of English at "Queens College" in "Queenshaven," Virginia, has made an important literary discovery. An expert in the life and times of detective-story pioneer Wilkie Collins, Ruthven has found three letters from Collins to Charles Dickens. The letters, written in 1869, outline the plot of a sealed-room mystery that Collins planned to write but never actually set down on paper. Ruthven would like to give his new treasures painstaking scrutiny, but events intervene. First, his wife leaves him after a family tiff. Then Rose Lestrange, a beautiful bachelorette friend of many of Queens' male faculty members, is stabbed dead behind the locked doors of her bedroom. Happily for all concerned, with the exceptions of Miss Lestrange and her murderer, Dr. Gideon Fell happens to be visiting the Queens campus in order to inspect the Collins letters. A fat, wheezy British lexicographer, Fell is an internationally celebrated detective and a John Dickson Carr series-character sleuth. Perhaps because he has had some prior experience with American higher education—he once gave a series of lectures at Haverford—Dr. Fell is able to cut through the intricate romantic and political entanglements within the Queens College community and to bring forth a solution to the college's own sealed-room killing.

One of the giants of the "Golden Age" of mystery fiction, John Dickson Carr was born in Uniontown, Pennsylvania, and attended Haverford College. He lived much of his adult life in England where, in addition to producing a stream of popular, puzzle-filled mystery novels, he wrote radio scripts for the BBC. Carr modeled Dr. Gideon Fell after G. K. Chesterton, one of his favorite writers. A man of immense erudition and many eccentric mannerisms, Dr. Fell specializes in locked-room murders and other crimes that defy solution. *The Dead Man's Knock* was the eighteenth of twenty-three Gideon Fell mysteries.

114. DANIELS, HAROLD R(OBERT) (B. 1919). *THE ACCUSED*. NEW YORK: DELL, 1958.

The Accused is a gnarled psychological tale about an instructor of English who is arrested and put on trial for killing his wife. The instructor is Alvin Morlock, a morose, masochistic member of the faculty at "Ludlow College" in Massachusetts. Alvin's wife, Lolly, dies after a mysterious fall from a cliff. Before her demise, Lolly had affairs with various men (including at least one of Alvin's students), greatly overspent the family budget, and generally made her husband's life miserable. Thus, Alvin certainly had enough motive to murder her. But did he actually shove Lolly to her death? And, whatever the truth of the matter, what will the jury decide? The story is told though courtroom dialogue mixed with flashback narrative, and readers must persevere to the final page in order to discover Alvin's destiny. The book contains no orthodox detection, but it does include many scenes at Ludlow College. A dingy, disagreeable institution, Ludlow caters to a surly and dull-normal student clientele. It is singularly fortunate, however, in having George Gorham as its academic dean. Although he can be properly pompous, Dean Gorham has an astonishingly deep concern for the well-being of Ludlow's teaching staff. Indeed, real-life college instructors may think they have wandered into a science-fiction novel when (on page 11) Gorham offers to dip into his savings to help Alvin Morlock pay off the huge debts that his wife has accumulated.

Harold Robert Daniels was born in Winchendon, Massachusetts. He did not attend college. He began his working career as a laborer and mechanic. After serving in the U.S. Army during World War II (and rising to the rank of major), he became a freelance writer. *The Accused* was his third full-length mystery. In addition to mystery fiction, Daniels's publishing credits include articles and books on metalworking, and from 1958 until 1972 he served as senior associate editor of *Metalworking Magazine*.

115. MITCHELL, GLADYS (MAUDE WINIFRED) (1901–1983). *SPOTTED HEMLOCK*. LONDON: MICHAEL JOSEPH, 1958. NEW YORK: ST. MARTIN'S, 1985.

"Highpepper Hall" is an agricultural training college for men in the English county of Berkshire. "Calladale College," twenty-five miles away, is an agricultural training school for women. As might be expected, the romantic traffic between the two institutions is considerable, and one evening the dead body of a female, presumably a Calladale student, is discovered in an ancient stagecoach on the Highpepper grounds. Because her nephew, Carey LeStrange, is serving as a tutor in piggery at Calladale, series-character Dame Beatrice LeStrange Bradley arrives on the scene to offer her own, uniquely energetic brand of detection. With thirty published exploits already behind her, Dame Beatrice is not fazed when the corpse turns out to have a mysterious identity. Nor is she put off by the rats and rhubarb that litter the Calladale grounds as the result of a prank perpetrated by the Highpepper farmers-in-training. By the end of this lighthearted and entertaining story, Dame Beatrice has found the killer, and readers have learned a good deal about pig farming. In fact, *Spotted Hemlock* is the only college mystery to reveal the dietary regimen for piglets with oedema—sloppy bran mash mixed with an ounce and a half of Epsom salts.

Spotted Hemlock was the thirtieth Dame Beatrice Bradley mystery by Gladys Mitchell. *Laurels Are Poison* (55), an earlier entry in the Beatrice Bradley series, appears in this bibliography.

116. PILGRIM, CHAD. *THE SILENT SLAIN*. NEW YORK: ABELARD-SCHUMAN, 1958.

"Jonas B. Steele College for Women" in New England is beset by problems. President Charles Rutledge Westbridge (whose wife is known on the campus as "The Faded Bat") is being blackmailed by Isabel Respy, the cruel and crafty head of the philosophy department. Professor Respy was once President Westbridge's secret lover. She now has a secret husband, R. Pramley Thatcher, a professor of philosophy. Professor Thatcher has his own set of worries. He is trying to live down several instances in which he was accused of plagiarizing the writings of others. Bachelor Professor Robert Glynn, whose academic field is medieval French literature, has a wandering eye for his more attractive students, and Regan Bogue, one of Professor Glynn's favorite pupils, seems about to have a nervous breakdown. The difficulties at Jonas B. Steele become especially acute when Bogue disappears and is then found dead of a fractured skull in a remote area of the school's pastoral property. Matt Ruffins, the local police chief, is called in, but just when he decides that Professor Glynn is the guilty party, the professor is shot dead in his apartment. At this point, virtually everyone in the Jonas B. Steele community becomes a suspect. Chief Ruffins continues his sleuthing, striking up a romantic relationship with President Westbridge's daughter, Louisa, in the process. He stages his denouement over sherry in the library of the president's mansion. Laden with clues, characters, and subplots, and graced by occasional flashes of sardonic humor, *The Silent Slain* is an exemplar of spiteful college-mystery fiction. Isabel Respy is described as "a cat, all but the whiskers." Professor Thatcher, who suffers from ulcers, is "a bland person on a bland diet." And President Charles Rutledge Westbridge, who raises pomposity to a high art, is "conscious of each syllable of his impressive name."

The identity of Chad Pilgrim is not revealed by any of the usual biographic reference books. *The Silent Slain* was his or her only mystery novel.

117. FENWICK, ELIZABETH [ELIZABETH FENWICK WAY (B. 1920)]. *A LONG WAY DOWN*. NEW YORK: HARPER & BROTHERS, 1959.

"Stanton College," one of the oldest and most distinguished schools for men in the United States, is rocked by two mysterious deaths. First, the fiancée of a young instructor of English dies after tumbling off the town's highest bridge. Then someone shatters the skull of old Professor Gibson, the campus eccentric, all over the floor of the professor's dining room. Ordinarily, one might assume that two such violent occurrences would overtax the resources of a campus police force, but Stanton College is fortunate to have Matthew Holley as its security chief. Though Holley is more accustomed to handing out parking tickets than investigating murders (after all, in his ten years at Stanton the most serious incident has been a student suicide), he calls upon his full reservoir of latent sleuthing talent. After a few false starts, he brings the reign of terror at Stanton to an end. As Holley conducts his inquiries, readers' attentions are focused upon a lady landlord, a properly sanctimonious college president, a loud and nasty faculty wife, and an instructor of romance languages who, during his own undergraduate days, elected such criminally easy courses as practical mechanics and coed cooking.

An accomplished and commercially successful mystery writer, Elizabeth Fenwick Way has specialized in grisly stories set in isolated or tightly bounded communities. *A Long Way Down* was her fifth mystery novel.

118. GRAAF, PETER [SAMUEL YOUD (B. 1922)]. *THE SAPPHIRE CONFERENCE.* NEW YORK: IVES WASHBURN, 1959.

Joe Dust, a Peter Graaf series-character, is a wisecracking American private eye plying his trade in London. Dust's friend, Detective-Superintendent Hebden, invites him to take a holiday at "Iron Head College," where the superintendent is to attend a gathering of noted scientists. Superintendent Hebden once had ambitions to be a physicist, and he wants to listen in at Iron Head's "Sapphire Conference" in order to keep abreast of the latest developments in nuclear technology. Dust and Hebden no sooner arrive at Iron Head—located in the town of "Minster"—than one of the biggest-name participants in the think-sessions disappears. The two sleuths immediately launch an investigation that eventually resolves matters, but not until four murders have been committed. Hardly one of the more plausible works of college-mystery fiction, *The Sapphire Conference* nonetheless provides, through Joe Dust's jaundiced commentaries, some American views of the British world of higher education.

Samuel Youd was born in Knowsley, Lancashire, England. A prolific author, he has produced mainstream novels, children's books, and works on cricket as well as mystery stories. Peter Graaf is only one of Youd's many pseudonyms. Among his other aliases are John Christopher, Hilary Ford, William Godfrey, Peter Nichols, and Anthony Rye.

119. BUTLER, GWENDOLINE (WILLIAMS) (B. 1922). *DEATH LIVES NEXT DOOR.* LONDON: BLES, 1960. PUBLISHED IN THE UNITED STATES AS *DINE AND BE DEAD.* NEW YORK: MACMILLAN, 1960.

The central figure in this bizarre psychological story is Marion Manning, a University of Oxford philologist. Grey-haired, stocky, and in her fifties, Manning shares her home with a mysterious woman named Joyo. Manning is being hounded by another mysterious person known as "The Watcher." When that individual claims to be Manning's husband and is then found stabbed dead in Manning's home, series-character Inspector John Coffin from London launches an investigation. Coffin is given some assistance in his sleuthing by Ezra Barton, a scholar who has been existing on grants and bringing forth snippets of new knowledge about *Beowulf* for the past thirteen years, and by Rachael Henson, an anthropology student who is Barton's girlfriend. Toward the end of the story Henson comes down with a near-fatal fever, and her illness provides Inspector Coffin with the clue he needs to fathom what is happening. Heavy with miasmic Oxford atmosphere and very effective in generating suspense, the book is likely to keep most readers guessing (along with Inspector Coffin) until the very end.

Gwendoline Butler was born in London. She received an M.A. from Lady Margaret Hall, Oxford, in 1948. She has published over fifty mystery novels. The wife of a professor of medieval history at the University of St. Andrews, the prolific Butler writes under her own name and under the pseudonym Jennie Melville. *Death Lives Next Door* was the fourth novel in a continuing, long-running series of more than twenty-five Inspector John Coffin mysteries. Another Inspector Coffin mystery, *Cracking Open a Coffin* (345), appears later in this bibliography. One of Butler's Jennie Melville mysteries, *A New Kind of Killer, An Old Kind of Death* (159), also has an entry in this bibliography.

120. GILLA, ESKER N. *CAP AND GOWN FOR A SHROUD.* NEW YORK: VANTAGE, 1960.

Gloria Harris, a stunningly beautiful junior at the University of Cincinnati, puts herself through school by blackmailing. She has dalliances with wealthy male students and then extorts money from them to hush up supposed pregnancies. On at least one occasion she blackmailed a professor into giving her an A in an English course after she threatened to reveal their affair to the professor's wife. Because of Miss Harris's schemes, when she is stabbed dead in her apartment there is no lack of likely suspects. The detective in the novel is Percy Danton, a young University of Cincinnati law professor and the son of a late Cincinnati policeman. He is assisted by Mike Denero, a retired Cincinnati policeman who once served with Danton's father. Denero, who tells the story in a flip manner that approximates that of many private-eye narrators, now drives a taxi. Professor Danton asks Denero for help when Paul Greer, one of his more promising law students, becomes another of Gloria Harris's blackmail victims. Because Harris was also involved with underworld mobsters, Danton and Denero spend some of their time in the bars and brothels of the Cincinnati region, but there are more than enough lingering scenes at the university to satisfy college-mystery readers. Furthermore, Percy

Danton is something more than your usual professor-detective. He possesses all of the ratiocination skills required for the role, but as a former football star and Battle of the Bulge veteran he also includes physical intimidation in his sleuthing repertoire. When suspects refuse to cooperate, Danton is not above using strong-arm tactics to elucidate the information he needs.

According to Allen J. Hubin, in *Crime Fiction II: A Comprehensive Bibliography, 1749–1990*, Esker Gilla taught school in Cincinnati when this book appeared. It was her only published work of mystery fiction.

121. HULL, HELEN (1888–1971). *A TAPPING ON THE WALL*. NEW YORK: DODD, MEAD & CO., 1960.

Richard Macameny is not the happiest of men. Though he takes satisfaction in his work as a professor of English, his domestic life is a shambles. Wife Naomi is both a self-styled invalid and a shrew. She even tries to pollute Richard's professional world by circulating vicious rumors about an attractive female graduate student who is his prize pupil. As Naomi's nastiness reaches new heights, Richard begins to wish that she were dead. Not a whodunit, this novel is instead a will-he-do-it. Following Richard as he plots to improve his domestic condition, the book takes its readers deep into a tortured professional mind. In the process, it gives vent to the malodorous internal politics of the unnamed American college at which Professor Macameny is employed.

Helen Hull was born in Albion, Michigan. She attended Michigan State and the University of Michigan before receiving a Ph.D. from the University of Chicago in 1912. After two years as an instructor of English at Wellesley, she joined the department of English at Columbia, where she remained until her death in 1971. *A Tapping on the Wall* was published after Hull won a $3,000 prize offered by Dodd, Mead & Co. for the best mystery manuscript submitted by an American or Canadian college student or faculty member. Though some reviewers found the book cheerless, most praised it for the skill of its writing, for the surprises contained in the plot, and for its depiction of the darker side of academic life. *A Tapping on the Wall* appeared toward the end of Hull's distinguished writing career. A prolific author, she wrote mainstream novels and textbooks as well as mysteries. One of her mainstream novels, *The Asking Price* (New York: Coward-McCann, 1930), tells the story of yet another henpecked academic husband. Unlike Richard Macameny, however, the protagonist of *The Asking Price* passively accepts his wife's tongue-lashings because he feels that any domestic scandal will ruin his chances to become chairperson of his department.

122. DWIGHT, OLIVIA [MARY HAZZARD (B. 1928)]. *CLOSE HIS EYES*. NEW YORK: HARPER & BROTHERS, 1961.

Andrew McNeill, a visiting poet-novelist at an unnamed university in the American Midwest, dies in a plunge from the library tower. Since McNeill had chronic drunkenness among his many faults, the police dismiss the incident as either an accident or an inebriated suicide. When John Dryden arrives on the campus to catalog McNeill's papers, he begins to suspect that McNeill's death may have been murder. Dryden is a Ph.D. candidate in English at Columbia University. Alone on his first academic job, he quickly strikes up a romantic relationship with Gwyneth Jones, a clerk in the office of the university's president. Dryden pores over McNeill's letters and manuscripts; Gwyneth Jones feeds him information about various faculty members who actively disliked McNeill for his boozing, womanizing, and all-around disagreeable behavior; and together the couple identifies the poet-novelist's killer. *Close His Eyes* is a college mystery in almost undiluted form. Long on talk, relatively short on action, and laced with satire, it is built upon a network of deceptive clues, and the motive for the crime is rooted in faculty politics. The book includes among its characters a retinue of professors, administrators, and staff members whom many professorial readers will recognize as possessing traits that belong to real-life people at their own institutions. There is, for example, Horace Wooten, the university's empire-building president, who conveniently forgets about the promises he makes to faculty members. There is Dr. Quinnell, the grand old professor of English, who remains aloof from disputes within his department. And the author renders an especially compelling portrait of Alice Crabbe, the crippled, dwarfish secretary to President Wooten. Miss Crabbe lionizes her boss and would do anything to protect his reputation.

Mary Hazzard was born in Ithaca, New York. She received a B.S. from Skidmore in 1949 and an M.F.A. from Yale in 1982. She has been a freelance editor and author since 1952, and her writings include plays and mainstream novels in addition to mysteries. *Close His Eyes,* published under the pseudonym Olivia Dwight, was her first novel.

123. GORDON, ALEX [GORDON COTLER (B. 1923)]. *THE CIPHER.* NEW YORK: SIMON & SCHUSTER, 1961.

Philip Hoag holds a temporary $2,800-per-year instructorship in the extension division of a large American university. An archaeologist, he labors by day to perfect his skills in decoding Egyptian hieroglyphics, but by night he teaches Egyptian history to disinterested students. Professor Connaway, his department chairperson, constantly bullies him, and Midge, his long-suffering wife, has had enough of poverty and has just told him of her plans to file for divorce. Suddenly Hoag receives a proposition he cannot refuse. Nahj Beshraavi, a wealthy businessman and the uncle of one of Hoag's students, offers him $3,000 to translate a message written in a strange cipher that mingles English with Beshraavi's native language. The message, so Beshraavi tells Hoag, has to do with international trade matters, and time is of the essence. Hoag immediately begins work, but as mystery readers might expect, the work does not go smoothly. Murder raises its ugly head within the Beshraavi family; a visiting prime minister is threatened with assassination; and Hoag finds himself playing dangerous games with officials of both the United Nations and the United States State Department. Since much of the action in *The Cipher* takes place off campus, it is certainly not the most academic of the college mysteries in this bibliography, but it has two virtues that argue for its inclusion. First, at several junctures in the story Hoag returns from his derring-do to teach his night classes, and readers are offered opportunities to contrast the excitement of his days with the tedium of his evenings. Second, at the end of the story Professor Connaway tries to fill a sudden department vacancy by offering Hoag a permanent teaching position with a minuscule salary increase. Knowing of Hoag's dismal financial condition, Connaway is shocked when his offer is refused. Hoag's recent exploits have brought him close to breaking the code of the hieroglyphics found in the mysterious "Khev-Az-Deni" excavation in Egypt. He needs time free from teaching to bring to completion what he hopes will be a breakthrough book on the subject. Then, so he tells himself, his reputation will gain him enough research grants for life as an independent scholar. Thanks to his experiences in the bulk of the book, Hoag is now a new, more venturesome person. "Sometimes a man has to live dangerously," he tells Connaway, as he turns down the opportunity for a lifetime of drudgery in the classroom.

Gordon Cotler was born in New York City. He received an A.B. from Columbia in 1944. After working as a newspaperman, Cotler became a full-time creative writer in the late 1950s. *The Cipher* was his second mystery novel. The book was adapted for a 1966 motion picture, titled *Arabesque*, starring Gregory Peck and Sophia Loren. In the movie version of the story the protagonist is a professor of ancient languages at the University of Oxford.

124. LOCKRIDGE, FRANCES LOUISE (1896–1963), AND RICHARD LOCKRIDGE (1898–1982). *THE DRILL IS DEATH*. PHILADELPHIA: LIPPINCOTT, 1961.

It is a foggy November evening and Reginald "Reg" Grant, a visiting British poet at "Dyckman University" in New York City, leaves his apartment to deliver a lecture. In the backseat of the waiting taxi he finds the corpse of a young woman, and he and the cab driver go by the shortest route to the nearest police station. Detective Nathan Shapiro, a Frances and Richard Lockridge series-character, commiserates with Grant on his ill luck at finding the body and apologetically sends the poet off in a squad car to his appointment. Later that evening, however, Reg is picked up by two bogus policemen and held captive in an uptown tenement. The dead woman, it turns out, was a Dyckman undergraduate, and when Shapiro cannot find the visiting Englishman for further questioning, he puts out an all-points bulletin for his capture. Meantime, Reg is suddenly released by his captors, and knowing that he is now wanted by the police, he launches his own independent investigation into the whole puzzling business. Before the story reaches its final pages, Shapiro interrogates a host of Dyckman faculty members and students, the FBI and the British Special Branch enter the case, Benjamin Carter—a long-missing Oxford don—surfaces on the Dyckman campus, and the unfortunate Reg Grant suffers a series of physical beatings administered by various of the book's villains. All in all, Grant does not enjoy his stay in the United States. But at least he finds romance with Peggy Larkin, the sister of the dead woman, and he presumably takes an American bride back with him to the relative sanctity of England.

Murder Is Served (83), an earlier novel by the Lockridges, appears in this bibliography. An entry for *Twice Retired* (157), a mystery written by Richard Lockridge after the death of his wife and longtime collaborator, can also be found in the bibliography.

125. NICHOLAS, ROBERT. *THE WHITE SHROUD*. LONDON: COLLINS, 1961.

It is a dark and stormy Sunday night (and a bitter-cold one as well) when a porter discovers the dead body of Dr. Roker in the chemistry building of "Granstone University." Granstone is a redbrick located in one of the bleaker regions of northern England. On the case within minutes of the porter's phone call for help are Inspector Stone and Sergeant Crawley of the local police. A junior lecturer, Roker is dead of a bashed skull, and Stone begins calling various university officials from their beds to meet him at the murder scene. Sir Humphrey Mimms, the school's vice chancellor cannot help but wish he had never left his secure Oxford professorship for the top job at Granstone, and Charles Quantley, the chemistry department's professor and chairman, listens "grim-faced" as he is informed of the killing. Inspector Stone and Sergeant Crawley admit they have little knowledge of academic morals and manners, but they are surprised by what their sleuthing reveals about the deceased Dr. Roker. Unpopular with his colleagues, and suspected of having cheated to get his doctorate, Roker is found to have run up large gambling debts and to have paid off those debts by blackmailing a professor of English who had an affair with the wife of a colleague. *The White Shroud* is a somber police procedural, and before finding the murderer Inspector Stone doggedly sifts through a large number of suspects drawn from Granstone's students, faculty, staff, and administrators. As Dr. Roker's blackmailing is brought to light toward the end of the book, the naive Sergeant Crawley utters one of college-mystery fiction's classic lines. "Curious lot, these academics," says Crawley, "you wouldn't have thought they'd go in for that sort of thing."

The identity of Robert Nicholas is not revealed by any of the usual biographic sources. *The White Shroud* was Nicholas's only published mystery novel.

126. ROBINSON, TIMOTHY (B. 1934). *WHEN SCHOLARS FALL*. LONDON: HUTCHINSON, 1961.

When Scholars Fall is both a quintessential Oxford mystery and a spoof of the classic Oxbridge mysteries of the 1940s and 1950s. Dr. Ronald George Herriott, a singularly unpleasant historian, is shot with an eighteenth-century dueling pistol in his rooms in "St. Savior's College," and various of the book's characters try their hands at sleuthing. Charles Blakelock, Edward Donaldson, Andrew Muir, and John Quince, a quartet of energetic undergraduates, are four of the would-be detectives. Another is Dr. Browning, a crashing bore of a visiting professor from Harvard. And then there is Inspector Mild of the Oxford police. A graduate of Balliol, Mild knows that the keys to Oxford murders are inevitably found in literary quotations. Therefore, in preparation for such cases, Mild spends much of his free time studying the works of lesser British writers. Although literary clues prove crucial in solving the mystery of Dr. Herriott's death, the motivation of the killer proves to be rooted in the history of the university. Another don meets his end before the book's conclusion, but with the arrest of the evildoer the university's survivors are free, once again, to engage in the unfettered celebration of their eccentricities. No serious student of the academic mystery can ignore this novel. All of the stock Oxbridgians found in the works of Innes, Masterman, and Morrah parade across its pages, and they interact in exaggerated set-piece situations that satirize the plots and styles of those same authors.

Timothy Robinson was born in Croydon, Surrey, and read history at Magdalen College, Oxford. *When Scholars Fall* was his first novel. At the time the book was published Robinson was employed by the Church Commissioners for England in Purley, Surrey.

127. SPENCER, PHILIP (HERBERT) (B. 1924). *FULL TERM.* LONDON: FABER & FABER, 1961.

Randall Sawyer, a fellow of "St. Old's College," Oxford, is beaten to death with a wine decanter as he sits alone, late at night, in the senior common room. The police can find no motive for the crime, and in desperation they ask Reynard Hudson to help them in their investigations. Hudson is a young St. Old's graduate, now a London journalist, who is staying at the college while recuperating from a series of mysterious attacks on his person. The police reason that Hudson, friendly with the St. Old's faculty and staff, yet not a member of the self-protecting college community, can develop important information. As the case unfolds many of St. Old's denizens become suspects, and Hudson learns that Randall Sawyer, a man whom he knew to possess a private income, actually derived his extracollege funds from secret, illegal activities. Hudson learns, as well, that the attacks on him were part of a more general scheme that encompassed Sawyer's murder. *Full Term* is a richly atmospheric Oxford mystery. As they engage in lengthy discussions about their colleague's murder, St. Old's dons display the proper mix of arrogance, eccentricity, and verbosity. However, they seem to be unaware of the sleuthing lessons one can learn from reading college-mystery novels. Until the guilty party is identified, they staunchly insist that Sawyer's killer must have come from outside St. Old's walls. As Miles Fallowfell, a senior tutor in history, naively reasons, "It seems to me well improbable that one St. Old's man would ever actually kill another."

The identity of Philip Spencer cannot be established from any of the usual biographic sources. *Full Term* was Spencer's only mystery novel.

128. NASH, SIMON [RAYMOND CHAPMAN (B. 1924)]. *DEAD OF A COUNTERPLOT.* LONDON: BLES, 1962; NEW YORK: HARPER & ROW, 1985.

The sleuths in this droll British mystery are Inspector "Montero of Scotland Yard and Adam Ludlow, a lecturer in English at North London College" and a Simon Nash series-character professor-detective. The victim is Jenny Hexham, a North London undergraduate, who is found strangled dead in the rooms of Robert Trent, another of the college's undergraduates. Both Miss Hexham and Mr. Trent were active in Communist organizations. Inspector Montero is the policeman in charge of the case. Ludlow becomes involved because Trent, who disappears after Miss Hexham's murder, is one of his most promising students. The primary suspects are several student residents of the college dormitory, known as "Mudge Hall," where Miss Hexham met her death, but because Ludlow shows such interest in the murder Inspector Montero adds him to the official list of people who might have done the gruesome deed. Much of the novel depicts Ludlow traveling to various parts of London in search of the missing Mr. Trent, but there are many scenes at Mudge Hall and several episodes at other places on the North London College campus. Many literary critics have found Adam Ludlow a noteworthy academic detective. Tall and gaunt, with a "long, anxious face," he is a pipe smoker and aggressively British. He wears tweed suits, even when he goes on holiday in the Mediterranean, and he loathes the American custom of drinking ice water at meals. The middle-aged lecturer is a competent teacher, but because he has not compiled a significant record of publication he is without prospect of academic promotion. People sometimes address Ludlow as "Professor," thereby momentarily awarding him a rank that he is never likely to attain, and those salutations sometimes send him into prolonged bouts of introspective self-criticism.

Raymond Chapman was born in Cardiff, Wales. He received a B.A. in 1945 from Jesus College, Oxford, and a Ph.D from the University of London in 1978. In 1948 Chapman became a lecturer in English at the London School of Economics, a post he held when *Dead of a Counterplot* was published. After *Dead of a Counterplot,* Chapman wrote four more mysteries featuring Adam Ludlow in the role of detective. All four of the subsequent Ludlow novels take place away from academe. In later years Chapman became a professor of English studies at the University of London, and he published widely in the professional field of English literature. He became professor emeritus at the University of London in 1989.

129. PHILLIPS, STELLA (B. 1927). *THE HIDDEN WRATH.* LONDON: HALE, 1962; NEW YORK: WALKER, 1982.

June Grant is part of a four-person team of librarians cataloging books at "Braseley Adult College," a school that has recently opened in an eighteenth-century mansion somewhere in rural England. It is August, and one warm evening the attractive Miss Grant and the rest of the team relax around the college's swimming pool. Grant runs toward the water intending to dive, but she is killed when she trips over an ankle-high chainlink fence and splits her skull on the edge of the pool. The fence, which is intended to act as a warning device when no one is swimming, should not have been up at the time of Miss Grant's attempt to dive. Although Grant's death is initially considered an unfortunate accident, Inspector Matthew Furnival of the local police suspects foul play, and his suspicions are confirmed when Hugo Browne, the warden of the mansion, almost dies during a play rehearsal when ammonia is found in a cup from which the script calls for him to drink. The four librarians in the story are county employees who usually work in the local public library system. Each for his or her personal reasons has volunteered to spend some vacation time working at the college. A few of Braseley College's administrators appear in the tale, but because of the occupations of its major characters, and because the motive for murder in the story involves antique books, *The Hidden Wrath* is less a college mystery than a "library" whodunit. The book is included in this bibliography because the action takes place entirely on academic grounds. What is an "Adult College"? As explained in the text this form of institution has no full-time students. Instead, knowledge seekers spend weekends at the mansion, where they have programs on "all sorts of subjects."

Stella Phillips was born in Plymouth, England, and trained as a librarian at the University of Birmingham. At the time this book was published she was a librarian at the Walker Technical College in England. *The Hidden Wrath* was her second novel. Sometimes using the pseudonym Stella Kent, Phillips has gone on to become a successful writer of romance novels as well as mysteries.

130. EVANS, FALLON (B. 1925). *PISTOLS AND PEDAGOGUES*. NEW YORK: SHEED & WARD, 1963.

The protagonist of this often-frenzied comic mystery is Adrian Withers. Short, red-haired, and at the age of thirty a perpetual graduate student, Adrian is hired to teach English at "Saint Felicitas College," a Catholic institution in the Midwestern American town of "Stratford." The complicated plot centers on the disappearance of Jim Downey, another member of the college's English department. Foul play is suspected, and because he quickly becomes the target of the subsequent police investigation, Withers turns sleuth in his own defense. Before the book is over readers are provided with depictions of Chicago mobsters, local drug pushers, and thoroughly confused Saint Felicitas's faculty members and administrators. However, they will look in vain for anything resembling serious detection.

Born in Denver, Colorado, Fallon Evans received a B.A. from Notre Dame, an M.A. from the University of Chicago, and a Ph.D. from Denver University. *Pistols and Pedagogues* was his first mystery novel. At the time the book was published Evans was an associate professor of English at Immaculate Heart College in Los Angeles. An earlier, nonmystery novel by Evans also deals with the world of higher education. *The Trouble with Thurlow* (Garden City, N.Y.: Doubleday, 1961) follows the comedic exploits of Henry Thurlow, an associate professor of English, as he attempts to adjust to his dead-ended professional career at a small Catholic college for women in the American west.

131. HOPKINS, (HECTOR) KENNETH (1914–1988). *CAMPUS CORPSE*. LONDON: MACDONALD, 1963.

The protagonist of *Campus Corpse* is Gerry Lee, a London newspaperman. Lee travels to the University of Texas to give a series of lectures on the differences between British and American journalism. During his stay in Austin he is the recipient of some of Texas's finest hospitality—in the bed of Miss Jose Sparrow, a dean's secretary—and he turns sleuth when an assistant professor of English dies in a suspicious automobile accident. The plot of the story is very inventive and includes a phony fall-to-the-death from the Texas Tower, the disappearance from a faculty office of a complete set of Sir Walter Scott's novels, and the only tour of the Alamo in college-mystery fiction. In a preface to the narrative, author Kenneth Hopkins notes that although he "spent some months" at the University of Texas before writing the book, none of the characters is "totally based" on anyone he met on the Texas campus.

Hector Kenneth Hopkins was born in Bournemouth, Hampshire, England. A prolific professional writer, his list of publications includes works of poetry, mainstream novels, travel books, and children's stories in addition to mysteries. Gerry Lee was a Kenneth Hopkins series-character detective, and *Campus Corpse* was the last of four Gerry Lee novels that Hopkins produced during his literary career.

132. MACDONALD, ROSS [KENNETH MILLAR (1915–1983)]. *THE CHILL*. NEW YORK: KNOPF, 1963.

Dolly Kincaid, a student and part-time librarian at "Pacific Point College" in California, disappears on the second day of her honeymoon. Her perplexed husband hires series-character private detective Lew Archer to find his missing bride. Because Archer's early sleuthing suggests that the case has its roots at Pacific Point, much of his time is spent examining Mrs. Kincaid's connections with various members of the school's academic community. Many professorial readers will take special interest in the information that Archer develops about Dean Roy Bradshaw, a man who seems to be unusually attached to his ultra-protective mother. Thanks to his dogged detection, Archer discovers what the dean actually does while on out-of-town trips. The only Harvard Ph.D. at Pacific Point, Bradshaw is anxious for a college presidency. By probing Bradshaw's difficult relationships with women, Archer also provides insight into the deep-seated psychological factors that prompt such lofty administrative aspirations.

Lew Archer, a cynical private eye with his own code of ethics, was one of the most popular series-character detectives in post–World War II mystery fiction. *The Chill* was awarded the 1964 Silver Dagger by the Crime Writers' Association of Great Britain. *The Dark Tun-*

nel (63), a non-Lew Archer mystery by Kenneth Millar, appears earlier in this bibliography.

133. LANGLEY, LEE [SARAH LANGLEY (B. 1927)]. *OSIRIS DIED IN AUTUMN.* GARDEN CITY, N.Y.: DOUBLEDAY, 1964. PUBLISHED IN ENGLAND AS *TWILIGHT OF DEATH.* LONDON: HALE, 1965.

Wilson Athestan Gregg, a professor of geology at a university somewhere in New York State, is killed by a blow to the head as he sits at home in his study. His significant other, Professor of Anthropology Natalie Keith, is devastated by the news. But, as one character in the story describes her, Professor Keith is a "tough old bird," and along with Lieutenant Chris Jensen of the local police she eventually brings Professor Gregg's murderer to justice. Suspects in the case include Peter Archer, a student with whom Professor Gregg had recently quarreled, and George Durwent, the university's officious dean of arts and sciences, who suggests to Lieutenant Jensen that Professor Keith is the most likely murderer. Many more university characters appear in the book, but the star of the story is clearly Professor Keith. A widow, and a Ferry Command pilot in World War II, Keith has a sharp tongue and can make life decidedly unpleasant for anyone who dares to disagree wth her. Nor does she shrink from physical danger. At one point in the novel she rescues herself from a kidnapper by pushing him into the path of an oncoming truck.

Sarah Langley earned a B.A. in journalism and then trained as an occupational therapist. At the time *Osiris Died in Autumn* was published she was employed at Bellevue Hospital in New York City. *Osiris Died in Autumn* was the first of two novels to feature Professor Natalie Keith as detective. The second, *Dead Center* (146), appears later in this bibliography.

134. FLEMING, JOAN MARGARET (1908–1980). *NOTHING IS THE NUMBER WHEN YOU DIE.* NEW YORK: IVES WASHBURN, 1965.

The protagonist of this very different college mystery is Nuri Iskirlak, an impoverished Turkish philosopher-scholar. Though he has never before been out of his native land, Iskirlak is asked by Torgut Yemish, a wealthy Istanbul businessman, to travel to England in search of Jason Yemish, Torgut's missing son. Jason, when last heard from, was an Oxford undergraduate. Nuri Iskirlak flies to London and then takes a train to Oxford, where he attempts to discover Jason's whereabouts. As the plot develops, he finds that Torgut Yemish is, in reality, a major figure in international drug trafficking and that Jason's disappearance is connected with his father's nefarious dealings. The book contains many views of Oxford as seen through Iskirlak's eyes, and the amateur Turkish detective even has the opportunity to stay at the Randolph Hotel and to visit Blackwell's bookshop.

Joan Margaret Fleming was born in Horwich, Lancashire, England, and attended the University of Lausanne. She was a prolific and often-honored writer of mysteries, gothic novels, and short stories. *Nothing Is the Number When You Die* was the second of two Fleming mysteries with Nuri Iskirlak in the role of sleuth.

135. HART, JANET. *FILE FOR DEATH*. LONDON: T. V. BOARDMAN, 1965.

Ellie Gerald, an undergraduate at an unnamed American university, is stabbed dead with a nail file one night as she walks across the campus. The police are inclined to assume that Miss Gerald committed an especially ghastly form of suicide, but Jinsie Cartwright, Gerald's roommate, thinks otherwise. Sleuthing alongside Richard Fletcher, her boyfriend, Cartwright proves that Miss Gerald did not take her own life, and, what's more, she unmasks her roommate's murderer. The latter task puts Cartwright in considerable personal peril, but she survives her dangerous adventure. In addition to Ellie Gerald, Jinsie Cartwright, and Richard Fletcher, two other participants in the story deserve mention. George Harrington, a professor of English, is noteworthy for his lectures on the relative merits of murder and suicide. And Big King, one of the "usual pack" of campus dogs, is the only character in the book to profit from Ellie Gerald's death. As Miss Gerald lies dying in a pool of blood, Big King leads his canine compatriots to the murder scene for a nocturnal feast.

The identity of Janet Hart cannot be established through any of the usual biographic sources. *File for Death* was the first of two mysteries she published during her brief literary career.

136. SMITHIES, RICHARD H(UGO) R(IPMAN) (B. 1936). *AN ACADEMIC QUESTION*. NEW YORK: HORIZON PRESS, 1965. ALSO PUBLISHED AS *DEATH GETS AN A*. NEW YORK: SIGNET, 1968.

An Academic Question is a semiserious takeoff on drug-related college detective stories. The protagonist of the tale is Campbell Craig, a professor of Latin literature at New York City's "Kingston University," a school that bears a very strong resemblance to Columbia. One of Campbell's graduate students, an annoyingly aggressive young woman named Iris Macready, has a $500-per-month hashish habit. In search of funds, Macready attempts to blackmail the professor. Campbell, as Macready has discovered, once published under his own name the nearly completed Ph.D. thesis of a student who died in an automobile accident. When Macready is found dead in Professor Campbell's office, her throat cut with a bronze letter opener, various amateur and professional sleuths enter the case in search of her killer. Professor Campbell is, of course, involved in the detection, as are Peter Dart (a customs agent) and Inspectors McAlpin and Golgram of the New York police. As the story unfolds the author offers his readers a wide assortment of set-piece situations, literary clues, and academic character-types, and his players sometimes regale each other with quasi-witty repartee. And, oh yes, Professor Campbell's wife is a well-known writer of mystery fiction. She plays only a minor role in *An Academic Question*, however, because she is out "in the country," trying to extricate her latest fictional heroine from the washroom on the Orient Express.

Richard H. R. Smithies was born in Canberra, Australia. He received a B.A. from Harvard in 1957 and an LL.B. from Harvard Law School in 1960. *An Academic Question* was his first novel. The book was written while Smithies was employed by a large New York City law firm.

137. BLAKE, NICHOLAS [CECIL DAY-LEWIS (1904–1972)]. *THE MORNING AFTER DEATH*. NEW YORK: HARPER & ROW, 1966.

Nigel Strangeways, Cecil Day-Lewis's erudite British series-character detective, comes to America to visit an old Oxford classmate. His friend, Zeke Edwards, is now master of Hawthorne House at "Cabot University" in New England. Strangeways' sojourn proves to be a busman's holiday when a Cabot professor of classics is found shot dead on the campus. Strangeways identifies the murderer, but not until he experiences American chocolate ice cream, a Cabot-Yale football game, and the sexual delights offered by "Sukie" Tate, a free-loving graduate student who is writing a dissertation on the works of Emily Dickinson. Despite Strangeways' obvious proficiency as a sleuth, the book contains little in the way of sophisticated ratiocination. It is better read, perhaps, as the author's attempt to thrust his literary knife deep into the corpus of American academic morals and customs.

Cecil Day-Lewis was born in Ballintubber, Ireland. The Poet Laureate of Great Britain from 1968 until his death four years later, he was at various points in his career a lecturer at Trinity College, Cambridge, and a professor of poetry at Oxford. Day-Lewis was also a prolific writer of mysteries, all of which were issued under the Nicholas Blake pseudonym. *The Morning after Death*, Day-Lewis's last detective saga, was published shortly after he returned to England from Harvard, where he spent the 1964-1965 academic year as the Charles Eliot Norton Professor of Poetry.

138. DALMAS, HERBERT. *EXIT SCREAMING.* NEW YORK: WALKER, 1966.

Exit Screaming is a cat-and-mouse will-he-do-it. The cat is Whitney Trew, a self-made, multimillionaire businessman. The mouse is Philip Radnor, the reflective, pipe-smoking president of "Burlington University," an Ivy League institution somewhere in the eastern United States. Years ago, when both men were Burlington undergraduates, Radnor blackballed the socially inferior Trew when Trew tried to join a prestigious fraternity. At the outset of this novel Trew reappears at Burlington after an absence of twenty years and requests a meeting with Radnor. Thinking that Trew may be about to give the school a large donation, Radnor welcomes him into his office. Trew then announces that he plans to kill Radnor, by a means that he refuses to specify, and he promises to do the deed sometime within the next three weeks. During the body of the novel Trew toys with Radnor by arranging situations in which he might murder the president, but he stops short of doing so each time. Increasingly frightened, Radnor confides his danger to a few intimates, but their reaction is to question his sanity. The climax of the tale comes at a Burlington football game at which both Trew and Radnor are in attendance. The book is must reading for anyone who enjoys seeing college or university presidents, even fictional ones, in extreme states of discomfort.

The identity of Herbert Dalmas is not revealed by any of the usual mystery-fiction reference books. In any event, *Exit Screaming* was his first mystery novel. Dalmas's second (and last) mystery, *The Fowler Formula* (142), also appears in this bibliography.

139. DEVINE, D(AVID) M(CDONALD) (B. 1920). *THE DEVIL AT YOUR ELBOW.* LONDON: COLLINS, 1966; NEW YORK: WALKER, 1967.

This suspenseful tale of academic intrigue is set at "Hardgate University," a British institution that is generally conceded, even by its staunchest admirers, to be much inferior to Oxford or Cambridge. Edward Haxton, a nondistinguished economist, is accused of embezzling twenty pounds from the summer school budget. He retaliates by threatening to reveal new facts about an old Hardgate sex scandal. When Haxton is soon found murdered, several of Hardgate's dons are suspected of the crime. Inspector Finney of the Hardgate CID leads the investigation, but the author provides a great many real and false clues through which readers can do their own, independent detecting. *The Devil at Your Elbow* is noteworthy for the well-realized academic characters who appear in the story. Edward Haxton, whose chief failing in the minds of some members of the Hardgate community is that he allows the garden around his home to become overrun with weeds, is suitably obnoxious. Peter Bream, a neophyte member of the economics faculty, has all of the charm and good looks that real-life economists often admire in themselves. And Graham Louden, the fortyish, widower dean of the faculty of law, is appropriately sober minded as he plays amateur sleuth, finds himself on the list of suspects, and carries on the courtship of a woman who is half his age.

Born in Greenock, Scotland, David McDonald Devine was educated at the University of Glasgow and the University of London. At the time *the Devil at Your Elbow* was published Devine was deputy secretary of the University of St. Andrews, Scotland. *The Devil at Your Elbow* was his fifth work of mystery fiction. A later David Devine mystery, *Death Is My Bridegroom* (152), also appears in this bibliography.

140. BRETT, MICHAEL (B. 1928). *WE, THE KILLERS.* NEW YORK: POCKET BOOKS, 1967.

Sabrina Fentrose, a chubby student with mediocre grades at "Macedonia State College," vanishes from the campus. The police make no progress in their attempts to find her, and eight months after her disappearance a man claiming to be Sabrina's father asks Peter

McGrath, a world-weary but energetic New York City private investigator, to locate his daughter. Down to his last $200, the man has already hired and fired another private eye who took his life savings but produced no results. Against his better judgment, McGrath takes the case because he feels sorry for his visitor. He begins by traveling to Macedonia State, located in central New York near the Pennsylvania border. At Macedonia he interviews Mrs. Gahagan, the chain-smoking dean of women, and several students, and he learns that beautiful Marie Gilmore, one of Sabrina's two roommates, has also disappeared. Curiously, in the interim between disappearances Marie had begun dating the same "dreamboat" male student who had been romancing Miss Fentrose. After his visit to Macedonia, McGrath's sleuthing takes him to various unsavory places in New York City, and in terms of the relatively small amount of the book devoted to on-campus scenes *We, the Killers,* is a marginal entry in this bibliography. The strongest argument for the book's inclusion is its ending. At the conclusion of the story Sabrina Fentrose emerges from hiding to play a crucial role, and academic readers may be fascinated to learn what an overweight, academically average college dropout can accomplish if she puts her mind to it.

Series-character Peter McGrath was featured in ten paperback mysteries by Michael Brett. All of the McGrath novels were published between 1966 and 1968. *We, the Killers,* was one of six McGrath mysteries that appeared in 1967.

141. CLINTON-BADDELEY, V(ICTOR) C(LINTON) (1900–1970). *DEATH'S BRIGHT DART.* LONDON: GOLLANCZ, 1967; NEW YORK: MORROW, 1970.

An international conference on poisons at "St. Nicholas's College," Cambridge, is interrupted when distinguished Dr. Brauer is hit and killed by a poisoned dart as he is giving a speech. Since many people could have done the deed, the first matter of detection is to uncover a motive. Although Inspector Hodges of the police is quickly on the case, the person who ultimately identifies the murderer is Dr. R. V. Davie, a retired St. Nicholas's fellow who still occupies rooms at the college. Dr. Davie's area of academic specialization is Greek, but in order to identify the evildoer in this classic British college-mystery novel he must delve into some of the more unpleasant aspects of twentieth-century history. During his investigation Dr. Davie contends with a collection of nervous Cambridge dons, a college porter named Jump, many prominent visiting scientists, and a clutch of naughty faculty children. One of the most pleasant and genteel professor-detectives in the college-mystery subgenre, Dr. Davie is able to gain information from witnesses by disarming them with his nonthreatening manner. A student of meteorology, he often opens conversations by talking in detail about the weather. Thanks to a lifetime of reading detection fiction, Dr. Dave also has a facility for turning into profit the many red herrings he comes across in this story. Bogus clues, he says, are simply "real clues pointing in an opposite direction."

Victor Clinton Clinton-Baddeley received an M.A. from Jesus College, Cambridge. During his long and varied career he was an actor, a playwright, a modern history editor for the *Encyclopaedia Britannica*, a writer of historical monographs about the English stage, and a director of Juniper Records, a firm that specialized in recording poetry. He was in his late sixties when he turned to mystery writing, and he wrote five whodunits with Dr. Davie in the role of detective. *Death's Bright Dart* was Dr. Davie's initial case and the only one of his adventures that is set in the world of higher education.

142. DALMAS, HERBERT. *THE FOWLER FORMULA*. GARDEN CITY, N.Y.: DOUBLEDAY, 1967.

"Dorset University" is a high-caliber institution in southern New England. John Fowler, a prominent member of the English department, is framed for the murder of a local businessman. Knowing his arrest is imminent, Professor Fowler leaves his home, goes into hiding, and eventually discovers the identity of the actual killer. The book is set during Christmas vacation. Since Fowler chooses to conceal himself for long periods in his campus office (where no one would think to look for him during the Christmas holidays), the book provides real-life professors with insight into what happens in faculty office buildings when they are supposed to be deserted. Professorial readers also will find instruction in the portrait of Prescott Smith, Dorset University's unctuous president. Flashing a smile that "he [does] not attempt to make merry," President Smith has as his goal the prevention of any damage to the university's good name. Although John Fowler has always been a model academic citizen, President Smith roots for his speedy capture and conviction, and he provides the police with information about the professor's personal tastes and habits.

An earlier Herbert Dalmas mystery, *Exit Screaming* (138), appears in this bibliography.

143. KENYON, MICHAEL (B. 1931). *THE TROUBLE WITH SERIES THREE.* NEW YORK: MORROW, 1967. PUBLISHED IN ENGLAND AS *THE WHOLE HOG*. LONDON: COLLINS, 1967.

The Trouble with Series Three is the second (and last) novel in this bibliography to deal extensively with academic piggery. The first, Gladys Mitchell's *Spotted Hemlock* (115), is set at "Calladale College," an agricultural training school in England. *The Trouble with Series Three* has a British protagonist, Arthur Appleyard, a twenty-nine-year-old visiting swine nutritionist from Leeds University. However, it is set at "Illinois State College," deep in the American Midwest. Appleyard is at Illinois State under grants from the United States Air Force and the National Aeronautics and Space Administration to test various pig feeds. Because pigs have digestive systems similar to those of human beings, his research has important implications for space travel. International spies, interested in Appleyard's findings, kill his laboratory assistant and kidnap Humphrey, his prize hog. Captain Petty of the local police handles some of the detection in the story, but finding purloined porkers is not really his crime-fighting speciality. In the end, it is up to Appleyard and Liz Salucka, his American coworker and girlfriend, to bring the case to a successful conclusion. Humphrey, too, has an important role in the final, climactic scene. Mixing satire with serious mystery, *The Trouble with Series Three* offers a wealth of sardonic commentary on space research, on American police methods, and on life at a large Midwestern emporium of higher education where the experimental animals seem to be at least as intelligent as the school's human element.

Michael Kenyon was born in Huddersfield, Yorkshire, England. From 1949 until 1951 he was a pilot with the Royal Air Force. He received a B.A. and an M.A. from Oxford and then did graduate work during the 1954-1955 academic year at Duke University. Before moving to the isle of Jersey in 1966 to pursue a full-time career as a creative writer, Kenyon worked as a reporter and editor for several British newspapers. He was a visiting lecturer in journalism at the University of Illinois from 1964 to 1966. *The Trouble with Series Three* was his second mystery novel.

144. DEAL, BABS H(ODGES) (B. 1929). *THE WALLS CAME TUMBLING DOWN.* GARDEN CITY, N.Y.: DOUBLEDAY, 1968.

When the old "Delta" sorority house at "Druid City University" is torn down in the mid-1960s, the skeleton of a baby is found in an airshaft. The local authorities reason that the body must have been deposited in the summer of 1944, when the house was being remodeled and the shaft was briefly opened. Nine young women occupied the house that summer, and all of them immediately come under suspicion. *The Walls Came Tumbling Down* is not a conventional mystery. Instead of employing a fictional sleuth to develop clues, the author concentrates her attentions on the life, times, and thoughts of the various Delta women, now approaching middle-age, who might have committed infanticide. Since several of the suspects still reside in Druid City, and since the author includes a series of flashbacks about events in 1944, this somber book contains many descriptions of Druid City University life and Druid City University characters in both the 1960s and in the wartime years.

Babs Hodges Deal received a B.A. from the University of Alabama in 1952. Her publications include mainstream novels as well as mysteries.

145. JAY, SIMON [COLIN JAMES ALEXANDER (B. 1920)]. *SLEEPERS CAN KILL.* GARDEN CITY, N.Y.: DOUBLEDAY, 1968.

At the end of World War II, five communist agents were planted in New Zealand. Their mission was to obtain ordinary jobs and wait until called upon. The agents' big moment comes fifteen years later, when they are ordered to steal the plans of a new laser device being perfected at "Ardmore," an engineering college of the University of Auckland. Fortunately for Western civilization, Mike Conner, a former CIA agent now employed by New Zealand Intelligence, is assigned to the case. After much derring-do on and near the Ardmore campus, Conner is able to identify the well-hidden spies and to save the Allied defense establishment from a disaster of serious proportions. Although espionage stories do not ordinarily qualify for entries in this bibliography, *Sleepers Can Kill* is included because Ardmore College and several of its faculty members are crucial to the book's plot. And so, too, as readers will discover, are the sinister activities of the college's Chess Club.

A New Zealand physician, Colin James Alexander was a radiologist at Master Miserocordiae Hospital in Auckland when *Sleepers Can Kill* was published.

146. LANGLEY, LEE [SARAH LANGLEY (B. 1927)]. *DEAD CENTER.* GARDEN CITY, N.Y.: DOUBLEDAY, 1968. PUBLISHED IN ENGLAND AS *DEAD CENTRE*. LONDON: HALE, 1969.

David Jones, the star basketball player at a university somewhere in New York State, collapses and dies during a game. Among the spectators are Professor of Anthropology Natalie Keith and Police Lieutenant Chris Jensen, the crime-fighting team that solved the mystery of a murdered professor at the same university in *Osiris Died in Autumn* (133). An autopsy shows that Jones was poisoned, and once again Professor Keith and Lieutenant Jensen join forces to cleanse the university of evildoers. The case involves gambling, drugs, cheating on examinations, and the "fixing" of basketball games. Several faculty members seem to have adequate motives for murder, and one of them, sociologist Nelson Seward, comes under special scrutiny because he once gave Jones a C+, the highest mark Jones ever received in his collegiate career. Before the novel concludes three more people die violently, the chain-smoking Lieutenant Jenson consumes several cartons of cigarettes, and Professor Keith narrowly survives a near-fatal dose of the poisoner's favorite concoction.

Dead Center was the second (and final) novel in Sarah Langley's brief Professor Natalie Keith series.

147. LATHAN, EMMA [MARY J. LATSIS AND MARTHA HENNISART]. *COME TO DUST*. NEW YORK: SIMON & SCHUSTER, 1968.

Not one but three highly publicized scandals hit "Brunswick College," a select, Ivy League school in "Coburg," New Hampshire. A professional fund-raiser disappears with a $50,000 negotiable bond intended for the institution's coffers. Someone steals the files of the applicants for next fall's freshman class. Then a high-school student visiting the Brunswick campus for an admission interview is stabbed to death in the elegant Coburg Inn. Because much of Brunswick's fund-raising is done in conjunction with the Sloan Guaranty Bank in New York, John Putnam Thayer, the bank's urbane senior vice president, becomes involved in the college's troubles. Thayer is an Emma Lathan series-character detective. He ties together and resolves all three of Brunswick's difficulties, but not before he finds that even Ivy League alumni are not always as wealthy as they claim to be. Thayer does some of his sleuthing on the Brunswick campus and some of it in New York. The New York scenes include rare fictional glimpses of an Ivy League alumni admissions committee as it screens prospective students.

Emma Lathan is a pseudonym employed by Mary Jane Latsis and Martha Hennisart. Both collaborators did graduate work at Harvard. Latis is an economist; Hennisart is an attorney. Their many John Putnam Thayer mysteries have received widespread critical acclaim and have been among the most commercially successful works in late twentieth-century detective fiction. *Come to Dust* was their eighth John Putnam Thayer novel.

148. MALLOCH, PETER [WILLIAM MURDOCK DUNCAN (1909–1976)]. *MURDER OF A STUDENT.* LONDON: LONG, 1968.

Two young women are murdered in an unidentified provincial British university town. The first to die is a librarian; the second is a student at the university. The killings are separated by a few months, but the methods are the same. Both women are bludgeoned dead by blows from a hammer as they walk alone at night. *Murder of a Student* is an inverted mystery; readers know early in the story the identity of the hammer-wielding assassin. He is a demented, third-year history student named Pilgrim, whose self-determined goal in life is to commit "perfect" crimes. Because Pilgrim had no prior contact with either of his victims and because the crimes are apparently motiveless, Inspectors Swetman and Crane of the local police are appropriately baffled. Nonetheless, after some dogged sleuthing those two upholders of the law manage to end Pilgrim's nefarious nocturnal activities. There are many university scenes in the novel, but the real emphasis is on off-campus policework.

William Murdock Duncan was born in Glasgow, Scotland, and received an M.A. in history from the University of Glasgow in 1934. A full-time and prolific writer of mysteries, Duncan published well over two hundred tales of murder and detection. In addition to the pseudonym Peter Malloch, Duncan employed John Cassells, Neill Graham, Martin Locke, and Lovat Marshall as pen names. *Murder of a Student* is starkly written. Duncan tells his story with considerable skill, but he does not embellish it with elaborate descriptions of his settings or characters. This bare-bones technique is attributable, one might suspect, to the fact that *Murder of a Student* was only one of ten mystery novels that Duncan published (under his various aliases) in 1968!

149. WOODFIN, HENRY. *VIRGINIA'S THING*. NEW YORK: HARPER & ROW, 1968.

Virginia McReedy, a twenty-year-old junior at an American state university, disappears from campus. Frank McReedy, the president of "The International Dockmen's Union," hires John Foley, an ex-cop turned private detective, to find his daughter. As Foley earns his

$200-per-day fee, his sleuthing brings him into life-threatening contact with an unfriendly black civil rights leader and into only slightly less-acrimonious relationships with several university faculty members. The book includes an especially chilling portrait of Sibyl Howard, a charmless female sociologist. An expert in the reactions of people to stressful situations, Dr. Howard verbally abuses her husband, conducts decidedly unethical research, and takes her left-wing political involvements very, very seriously.

Henry Woodfin was born in Buffalo, New York. Allen J. Hubin, in *Crime Fiction II: A Comprehensive Bibliography, 1749–1990,* identifies Woodfin as a music and jazz critic. *Virginia's Thing* was Woodfin's only mystery novel.

150. ANDERSON, REX. *COVER HER WITH ROSES*. NEW YORK: SIMON & SCHUSTER, 1969.

This novel is set in and around an unidentified university in the American Southwest. Melissa Gentry, a graduate student in studio art, is stabbed dead in her off-campus apartment. The floor around her corpse is strewn with roses, and the press dub her "the rose-covered coed." The prime suspect is Holden Jones, a senior at the university who lives in the same building. Jones narrates the story, and he tells his readers how, within the space of a few days, he avoids arrest, deals with his sorority-girl fiancée, who announces she is pregnant, identifies Miss Gentry's murderer, and just barely manages to avoid being shot as the villain tries to prevent him from revealing his findings. In addition to Miss Gentry, Holden Jones, and Jones's girlfriend, several other students appear in the story, and two of them meet their deaths before the tale concludes. One faculty member plays an important role. Marvin Witt, a determined man who somehow manages to be both a member of the university's criminology department and a captain of the local police, suspects that Holden Jones killed Gentry, and he pursues him throughout the book. A dean by the name of Crane plays a small part in the proceedings. After Captain Witt decides that Holden Jones is Miss Gentry's probable killer, he initially allows Jones to remain free while his officers try to gather more incriminating evidence. When Dean Crane learns that the police think Jones may be a murderer, he calls the already-harassed student to his office. Apparently unmoved by any innocent-until-guilty considerations, Crane immediately suspends Jones from the university.

Cover Her with Roses was Rex Anderson's first novel. According to information on the book's dust jacket, Anderson is a graduate of the "well-known Southwestern university" that is the setting for the story.

151. ANTHONY, DAVID [WILLIAM DALE SMITH (B. 1929)]. *THE MIDNIGHT LADY AND THE MOURNING MAN.* INDIANAPOLIS: BOBBS-MERRILL, 1969.

Set on and near the lovely, tree-shaded campus of "Jordan College," in Jordan, Ohio, this complex and violence-filled story is narrated by Morgan Butler, the town's lone policeman. Former-marine Butler has problems. Natalie Clayborne, a beautiful Jordan undergraduate, has been strangled in her dormitory room, and the county sheriff, a gruff bully named Jack Casey, insists on handling the investigation. Sheriff Casey succeeds only in arresting a man whom Butler knows to be innocent. Butler suspects that Waldo Mason is the guilty party. Mason, a professor of history, has a long record of extracurricular contact with his more attractive female students. Meanwhile, a gang of thuggish hillbillies tries to beat up Linda Thorpe, a tavern hostess with whom Butler has fallen in love, and Madge Bell, the seductive wife of a local underworld figure, has a habit of inviting Butler to her home, stripping off her clothes, and distracting our virile hero from his sleuthing. Before the novel comes to its surprising conclusion, Butler wrestles with literary clues—a marked copy of *The Brothers Karamazov* is found alongside Natalie Clayborne's body—and he learns that lecherous old professors may not be quite as evil as some people think them to be.

William Dale Smith was born in Holliday's Cove, West Virginia. He received a B.A. from Antioch College in 1955 and became a successful writer of both mainstream novels and mysteries. *The Midnight Lady and the Mourning Man* was his first foray into the mystery field. In 1974 the novel was adapted for a motion picture starring Burt Lancaster as Morgan Butler.

152. DEVINE, D(AVID) M(CDONALD) (B. 1920). *DEATH IS MY BRIDEGROOM*. NEW YORK: WALKER, 1969.

Who kidnapped and murdered Barbara Letchworth, a student at "Branchfield University" in England? Was it one or more of the radical students currently demonstrating on the Branchfield campus? The victim, after all, was the daughter of Lord Letchworth, a staggeringly rich capitalistic chain-store owner. Or was it Michael Denton, an assistant lecturer in Greek, with whom the deceased had been carrying on a tempestuous affair. It certainly was not Vincent Sempill, the Yale Ph.D. who is Branchfield's vice chancellor. Sempill is sincerely distraught over Barbara Letchworth's death; not only because one of his undergraduates has been killed, but also because he fears that Lord Letchworth will withdraw his generous financial contributions to the new and considerably less-than-distinguished school. A veritable army of sleuths tries to track down Miss Letchworth's murderer. Brian Armour, a young lecturer in classics, is one of the detectives. Hew Rhys-Jones, the do-gooder, ecologist head of the faculty union, is another. Sheila Rhys-Jones, Hew's wife and the secretary to Vice Chancellor Sempill, also looks into the matter. Lorna Denton, Michael's older sister, arrives from out of town to help her brother prove his innocence. And, Chief-Inspector Christie and Inspector Eggo of the local police enter the story in their official capacities. Written in the slightly sardonic, clue-dropping tradition of classic college mysteries, *Death Is My Bridegroom* suffers, perhaps, from an overabundance of characters. Nevertheless, it provides considerable detail about life and death at a recently established British university.

David McDonald Devine's *The Devil at Your Elbow* (139) also appears in this bibliography.

153. GREENBAUM, LEONARD (B. 1930). *OUT OF SHAPE*. NEW YORK: HARPER & ROW, 1969.

Rudolph Reichet, an immigrant professor of medieval literature, is found dead in his office, his face blown away by a shotgun blast. The setting is "Milton State University" in Michigan. Lieutenant Paul Gold of the local police, along with Tommy Larkin, the professor's graduate-student research assistant, investigate the killing. Larkin is especially interested in the matter since he received a telephone call, ostensibly from Reichet, an hour after the professor was murdered. The complex case prompts Gold and Larkin to focus on a growing neo-Nazi movement on the Milton campus, and it also leads them to probe Professor Reichet's youthful days in pre-World War II Germany. Written with a fine ear for the melodies and rhythms of academe, *Out of Shape* carries its readers through a highly sophisticated series of puzzles before reaching its conclusion. The many Milton faculty members who appear in the story are especially well drawn, and the plot is without most of the set pieces found in more orthodox college mysteries. Furthermore, the book is certainly one of very few detective stories, college mystery or otherwise, to include two full-page photographs of Adolph Hitler.

Leonard Greenbaum was born in Boston. He received a B.A., an M.A., and a Ph.D. from the University of Michigan. *Out of Shape* was his first novel. At the time the book was published, Greenbaum was an assistant professor of English at the University of Michigan.

154. QUEEN, ELLERY [PSEUD.]. *THE CAMPUS MURDERS.* NEW YORK: LANCER BOOKS, 1969.

"Tisquanto State College" is located in that remote area of America known as "upstate." The school was once small and idyllic, but now, at the height of the Vietnam War, it has grown into a vast, sprawling institution complete with hordes of student radicals and an incompetent administration. Tisquanto's troubles finally come to the attention of Governor Sam Holland when Laura Thornton, a sophomore and the daughter of Holland's rival for reelection, mysteriously disappears from the campus. The governor sends Mike McCall, his virile special assistant, to investigate. Mike finds Laura and helps put an end to the student uprisings, but not before he is kidnapped by a gang of mask-wearing male and female students, stripped to the buff, and has his genitals burned with the lighted end of a marijuana cigarette. Although this story will never be rated among the most cerebral of college mysteries, some readers may find that it has one redeeming quality. At the conclusion of the tale, Governor Holland makes a personal visit to Tisquanto. Appalled by the goings-on, he confronts President Wolfe Wade—a man characterized by "jellyfish dampness"—and sends him off to an early retirement.

The Campus Murders marked the debut of Mike McCall, a "two-fisted troubleshooter" who eventually became a series character. The McCall stories were not written by Frederick Dannay and Manfred Lee, the originators of the Ellery Queen pseudonym. Rather, they were composed by mercifully anonymous specialists in mass-market, paperback, action sagas.

155. BERNARD, ROBERT [ROBERT BERNARD MARTIN (B. 1918)]. *DEADLY MEETING.* NEW YORK: NORTON, 1970.

The "deadly meeting" in the title of this novel is the annual convention of the Modern Language Association. In addition to the usual paper giving, socializing, and job searching, the MLA agenda this particular year includes the death by poison of Professor Peter Jackson, head of the English department at "Wilton University." An autocratic and singularly unpopular chairman, Jackson obviously was done in by one of his faculty subordinates. The puzzle for the reader is which one of Jackson's departmental antagonists is guilty. The story is told from the perspective of Bill Stratton, who becomes acting chairman after Jackson's death. Stratton aids in solving the crime. Also in the book's multiperson cast of sleuths are a sophisticated police lieutenant named Moynahan and Dame Millicent Hetherege, an aged, visiting medievalist from "St. Agatha's College," Oxford. Since Dame Millicent writes suspense stories as an avocation, her mind is especially fine-tuned for detection. Events at the MLA convention occupy most of the first third of the intricate story and then the scene switches to the Wilton campus. The descriptions of life at Wilton ring with academic verisimilitude, and many Wilton English professors and their spouses are etched in relentless detail.

Robert Bernard Martin was born in La Harpe, Illinois, and received an A.B. from Harvard in 1947 and a B.Litt from Oxford in 1950. He was a member of the English department at Princeton University from 1951 until his retirement in 1975. *Deadly Meeting* was the second of three mysteries written by Martin, all of them under the Robert Bernard pseudonym.

156. CROSS, AMANDA [CAROLYN GOLD HEILBRUN (B. 1926)]. *POETIC JUSTICE*. NEW YORK: KNOPF, 1970.

Poetic Justice is set at a large, elite New York City university that gives every appearance of being Columbia. Against a backdrop of student demonstrations and sit-ins the university is experiencing bitter intraorganizational conflict. Some influential faculty members want to end the existence of University College, a unit of the greater university that caters to adult and other nontraditional students. The protagonist of the story is Professor Kate Fansler, a member of the graduate English faculty. Unconvinced by arguments that University College cheapens the university, Fansler sides with those who want to retain it. Fansler is engaged to Reed Amhearst, a New York assistant district attorney, and the secretaries in her department hold a party in the couple's honor. As the festivities take place, Jeremiah Cudlipp, chairperson of the English department, dies after swallowing aspirin tablets. Allergic to aspirin, Cudlipp ordinarily employed a special headache remedy sent from England, but at the Fansler-Amhearst engagement festivities someone apparently substituted real aspirin for his imported pills. Cudlipp was one of University College's most outspoken opponents. After his death, Amhearst conducts an official investigation, and Fansler, whom some members of the university suspect of Cudlipp's murder, undertakes complementary unofficial sleuthing. Almost the whole of the novel takes place on university grounds, and readers are introduced to what must be a large percentage of the university's faculty and administration. The book contains many references to W. H. Auden, one of Professor Fansler's favorite poets, and late in the book Auden makes a personal appearance at the university, reads from his work, and takes part in a question-and-answer session.

Carolyn Heilbrun was born in East Orange, New Jersey. She received a B.A. in 1947 from Wellesley, an M.A. in 1951 from Columbia, and a Ph.D. in 1953 from Columbia. She joined the Columbia faculty in 1960, was the first woman to receive tenure in Columbia's English department, and retired in 1992 as Avalon Foundation Professor in the Humanities Emeritus. The author of many professional articles and monographs, Heilbrun has been the recipient of many honors and fellowships and has served as president of the Modern Language Association. Writing as Amanda Cross, she has produced a continuing series of twelve Professor Kate Fansler mysteries, and Professor Fansler has become one of the best-known series-character professor-detectives in mystery fiction. Seven of the twelve highly literate Professor Fansler mysteries are set at institutions of higher education and, consequently, qualify for inclusion in this bibliography. *Poetic Justice* was the third mystery in the Kate Fansler series. Other Kate Fansler novels with entries in this bibliography are *Death in a Tenured Position* (211), *Sweet Death, Kind Death* (238), *No Word from Winifred* (264), *A Trap for Fools* (308), *An Imperfect Spy* (402), and *The Puzzled Heart* (457).

157. LOCKRIDGE, RICHARD (1898–1982). *TWICE RETIRED.* PHILADELPHIA: LIPPINCOTT, 1970.

Twice Retired opens with Walter Brinkley, a retired professor of English at "Dyckman University" in New York City, driving from his suburban home to the Dyckman Faculty Club in order to attend a publisher's reception for his newest book. The Vietnam War is at its height, and pickets and demonstrators roam the campus. When the reception ends Brinkley prepares to drive home, only to find the dead body of General Philip Armstrong, U.S. Army (retired), in the backseat of the car. Armstrong, the right-wing chairman of Dyckman's board of trustees, has had the back of his skull bashed in and, for good measure, has had a pig mask placed over what remains of his head. Series-character sleuth Assistant District Attorney Bernie Simmons, who happens to be one of Professor Brinkley's former students, handles the investigation, while the unnerved professor, who appears in several other Lockridge novels, contents himself with offering occasional tidbits of sage advice. Among Simmons's suspects is Carl Benson, a leftish-liberal assistant professor of English whose employment at Dyckman is ending thanks to General Armstrong's orders. Another person on Simmons's list of likely killers is Lester Brownlee, a consultant on book design to the Dyckman University Press. And still another suspect is Robert Armstrong, the general's nephew. Robert is an undergraduate at Dyckman, an R.O.T.C. cadet, and a dedicated American patriot who despises those of his fellow students who find fault with America's foreign policy.

Twice Retired was written by Richard Lockridge after the death of Frances, his wife and collaborator, in 1963. Two mysteries written by Frances and Richard Lockridges appear in this bibliography. Those novels are *Murder is Served* (83) and *The Drill Is Death* (124).

158. MANER, WILLIAM. *DIE OF A ROSE*. GARDEN CITY, N.Y.: DOUBLEDAY, 1970.

Wilson Hartley, a young member of the English department at "Spotswood University," has an unpromising pupil named Steve Zlados. Mr. Zlados is a football star but a dunce in the classroom. Moreover, Zlados is something of a bully, and at one point early in the story, he threatens to reshape Professor Hartley's face with a punch to his nose. One fine morning, Zlados is found dead with Hartley's scissors in his back. A leading suspect, Hartley must now find Steve's killer or face the prospect of arrest for a crime he only wishes he had committed. Before the end of the novel, Hartley becomes involved with rustic policemen, big-time gamblers from Baltimore, local bookies, and many Spotswood faculty members and athletic department personnel. Jacques Barzun and Wendell H. Tayor, in *A Catalogue of Crime*, call *Die of a Rose* "a deplorable book." Certainly, the story is exceedingly complex and the detection implausible. However, the notion that Professor Hartley could have stabbed the obnoxious Mr. Zlados might constitute a redeeming feature for professorial readers who have had their own difficulties with Neanderthal-like football players.

Die of a Rose was the second of three mystery novels published by William Maner. None of the usual biographic resources reveal his identity. On the dust jacket of *Die of a Rose* he is identified only as a frequent contributor to popular magazines such as *Cosmopolitan* and *Redbook.*

159. MELVILLE, JENNIE [GWENDOLINE (WILLIAMS) BUTLER (B. 1922)]. *A NEW KIND OF KILLER, AN OLD KIND OF DEATH.* LONDON: HODDER & STOUGHTON, 1970. PUBLISHED IN THE UNITED STATES AS *A NEW KIND OF KILLER*. NEW YORK: MCKAY, 1971.

The "University of Midport" is a new British university. It is so new, in fact, that it is about to install its very first vice chancellor, and when radical students stage a series of campus outrages there are grave doubts that the young school can survive the upheavals. Then, when several murders occur within the Midport community, things look very black indeed. It is fortunate, therefore, that Charmian Daniels, a Jennie Melville/Gwendoline Butler series-character sleuth, is at Midport taking courses in criminology. On leave from her job as a detective with the "Deerham Hills" police force, Daniels drops her studies to investigate the killings, and, by the end of the story, Midport can look forward to a bright future. The book offers many descriptions of Midport under siege. As an added bonus for college-mystery fans, at one point in the story Daniels flies to Holland and does some field investigations among the radical students at the University of Amsterdam. During the course of her buswoman's holiday, the married Daniels begins to develop a romantic relationship with Don Goldsworthy, an American graduate student from Berkeley. As the story ends, however, Daniels's husband returns unexpectedly from a business trip to Hong Kong and reclaims his wife.

Charmian Daniels is one of several series-character detectives created by Gwendoline Butler. *A New Kind of Killer, An Old Kind of Death,* was Daniels's seventh published exploit. Two other Butler mysteries, both of them published under her real name, appear in this bibliography. Those mysteries are *Death Lives Next Door* (119) and *Cracking Open a Coffin* (395). Both novels feature another of Butler's series-character detectives, Inspector John Coffin.

160. ASHE, GORDON [JOHN CREASEY (1908–1973)]. *A RABBLE OF REBELS*. LONDON: LONG, 1971; NEW YORK: HOLT, RINEHART & WINSTON, 1972.

Radical students take over the campus of "Mid-Cal University" near San Francisco. "Gentle-faced" Dean Connell is imprisoned in his office, and two student bystanders are killed when they attempt to make an early exit from one of the radicals' more heated protest rallies. Meanwhile, in London, Deputy Assistant Police Commissioner Patrick Dawlish sees the Mid-Cal affair as the thin edge of a revolutionary wedge designed, ultimately, to destroy all the universities in the western world. A Gordon Ashe/John Creasey series-character detective, Dawlish hops the next jet to California in order to investigate matters. His findings at Mid-Cal only confirm his suspicions that all student uprisings are the product of an international conspiracy. *Rabble of Rebels* was first published in 1971. Perhaps the best testimony to Dawlish's proficient rebel quashing in this story is the fact that shortly after the book's appearance calm was restored, not only at Mid-Cal, but at most nonfictional colleges and universities throughout the world as well.

John Creasey was born in Southfields, Surrey, England. He did not attend college and, hence, never had any academic training in creative writing. Despite his lack of formal instruction, Creasey published well over five hundred mystery and adventure novels, along with assorted works of mainstream and historical fiction. Some of his books appeared under his own name, but he also used the pseudonyms Gordon Ashe, Norman Deane, Michael Halliday, Kyle Hunt, Peter Manton, J. J. Marrie, Richard Martin, Anthony Morton, Ken Ranger, William K. Reilly, Tex Riley, and Jeremy York.

161. CANDY, EDWARD [BARBARA ALISON BOODSON NEVILLE (B. 1925)]. *WORDS FOR MURDER, PERHAPS.* LONDON: GOLLANCZ, 1971; GARDEN CITY, N.Y.: DOUBLEDAY, 1984.

Words for Murder, Perhaps, is set at the extramural (evening adult extension) facility of the "University of Bantwich." Located in downtown Bantwich, a depressingly grim city in the British Midlands, the extramural division has a small permanent staff but draws most of its faculty on a part-time (and extra pay) basis from the nearby university itself. The story centers on the murder of elderly Professor Arthur Hallam, an Egyptologist, who dies after offering a guest lecture. Seeking postpresentation refreshment, Hallam sips a glass of water into which someone has dropped cyanide. The leading suspect in the case is Mr. Roberts, a Bantwich lecturer in English who is teaching an extramural course on the history of the detective novel. Roberts is divorced and once tried to commit suicide. Furthermore, after finding Hallam's body, he makes the mistake of picking up (and leaving his fingerprints on) the professor's glass of poison. Roberts is pinpointed by Inspector Hunt of the local police as a possible "nut case," but there are many, many other suspects as well, most of them extramural administrators, teachers, and students. Several of the important clues in the plot are literary in nature. Although devotees of "serious" mystery fiction will find that *Words for Murder, Perhaps,* presents a significant whodunit challenge, the book can also be read simply for its sly, witty commentaries on academic life. For example, class attendance in Bantwich's extramural division (like class attendance in almost every academic institution) declines precipitously as each term progresses. On the evening after Professor Hallam's murder, however, the classes at the facility are as full as they were on the term's first night.

Bones of Contention (103), another mystery written by Barbara Neville under her Edward Candy pseudonym, appears earlier in this bibliography.

162. GRAHAM, JOHN ALEXANDER (B. 1941). *THE INVOLVEMENT OF ARNOLD WECHSLER*. BOSTON: LITTLE, BROWN & CO., 1971.

Arnold Wechsler is a wisecracking junior member of the classics department at "Hewes University." His "involvement" begins when he is asked by Winthrop Dohrn, the harassed president of Hewes, to investigate the kidnapping of Dohrn's young granddaughter. Dohrn suspects that David Wechsler, Arnold's younger, student-radical brother, is responsible, and he wants Arnold to look into the matter. Arnold Wechsler's sleuthing brings him into closer-than-comfortable contact with Hewes's retinue of antiestablishment undergraduates, and it also leads him to a few skeletons in the Dohrn family closet. The book is written in the first person, with the cynical Arnold as narrator. This technique allows Arnold to offer a great many jaundiced opinions of the Hewes scene. A middling-status institution in eastern Massachusetts, Hewes denies that its faculty must publish or perish. However, as Arnold observes, all of the school's faculty members seem to do one or the other. President Dohrn is not long in a position to rectify this inconsistency in his administration's policy. During the first chapter of this partially inverted mystery, Dohrn is sundered into bloody bits and pieces when a bomb, planted by parties unknown, blows up his presidential mansion.

Born in New York City, John Alexander Graham received a B.A. from Columbia n 1962 and an M.A. from Brandeis in 1964. He was an instructor of mathematics at Wellesley College when *The Involvement of Arnold Wechsler*, his second mystery novel, was published.

163. HILL, REGINALD (B. 1936). *AN ADVANCEMENT OF LEARNING*. LONDON: COLLINS, 1971; WOODSTOCK, VT.: COUNTRYMAN PRESS, 1971.

Set at the "Holm Coultram College of Liberal Arts and Education" in the Yorkshire region of England, this wry, intricate mystery stars Reginald Hill's popular series-character detectives Superintendent Andrew Dalziel and Sergeant Peter Pascoe. The two policemen come onto the Holm Coultram campus when human bones are unearthed in the staff garden. The bones, it turns out, belong to Alison Girling, a former principal of the school who was thought to have died in an automobile accident (and to have been buried) in Austria. While investigating the circumstances surrounding the uncovered remains, Dalziel and Pascoe bring to light a whole series of potentially lethal romantic entanglements in the Holm Coultram community. Spiteful Professor Sam Fallowfield, for example, has apparently been falsifying grades in order to fail his former student-mistress, Anita Sewell. Franny Roote, a brilliant male student, has been carrying on with Marion Cargo, an art instructor. Marion Cargo, whose sexual tastes include women as well as men, once had an affair with Alison Girling. Before the novel concludes, two of the major participants in the story are dead and Superintendent Dalziel is thoroughly disgusted with academe. "So that's what I missed when I didn't get a college education," Dalziel muses as he and Pascoe drive away from Holm Coultram after concluding their inquiries.

Reginald Hill was born in Hartlepool, England. He received a B.A. (honours) in English from St. Catherine's College, Oxford, in 1960. *An Advancement of Learning* was Hill's second Dalziel-Pascoe mystery. At the time the book was published, Hill was a lecturer in English literature at the Doncaster College of Education in Yorkshire. Since 1982 Hill has been a full-time writer, and his mysteries, the Dalziel and Pascoe novels in particular, have achieved both critical and commercial success. Many of his Dalziel and Pascoe stories, including *An Advancement of Learning,* have been adapted for television.

164. LEWIS, (JOHN) ROY(STON) (B. 1933). *ERROR OF JUDGEMENT*. LONDON: COLLINS, 1971.

It's a bad day at "Burton Polytechnic" somewhere in England. Students are demonstrating for more representation in the conduct of the school's affairs. Her Majesty's Inspector Robert Fanshaw has arrived on campus to tell the administration that the British government, which oversees the operation of polytechnics, does not approve of some recent curriculum changes. The well-respected head of the large and growing social administration department, Vernon West, is in the hospital after suffering a severe heart attack the previous evening. To top matters off, Rosemary Harland, the pretty, nineteen-year-old secretary to Dr. Anthony Peters, Burton Polytechnic's harassed rector, disappears in mid-morning and is shortly thereafter found dead of a broken neck in an administration building elevator. In charge of investigating Miss Harland's murder is Chief Inspector John Crow of the police Murder Squad. Inspector Crow is a Roy Lewis series-character detective. Unhappily, when Crow and his men arrive at Burton the students think that the police have come to quell their demonstration, and they elevate the shrillness of their protests. With Robert Fanshaw's help, Inspector Crow identifies several suspects, including Bill Lambert, a lecturer in economics who was having an affair with Miss Harland, and Sadruddin Khan, the Marxist leader of the disaffected students, who has repeatedly threatened to employ violence to achieve his ends. Also making it to the suspect list is Rector Peters, who, as Crow discovers, recently hired the attractive Miss Harland over a long list of older women with much more secretarial experience. A grim police procedural, *Error of Judgement* takes its readers deep into the nonelite sector of British higher education. As an added attraction for those who like to match wits with the sleuths in whodunits, Miss Harland's murderer turns out to be one of the more difficult-to-guess villains in the college-mystery subgenre.

John Royston Lewis was born in Rhondda, Wales. He attended the University of Bristol and received an LL.B. in 1954. In 1957 he received a diploma in education from the University of Exeter, and in 1978 he was awarded an M.A. by the University of Durham. At the time this book was published Lewis was an inspector of schools. He later became principal of Wigan College of Technology in Wigan,

England. Lewis has written books on law and legal history as well as mystery novels. *Error of Judgement* was his third mystery and his second John Crow novel. Since writing *Error of Judgement* Lewis has produced more than thirty more mysteries employing several series-character sleuths.

165. MARIN, A. C. [ALFRED COPPEL (B. 1921)]. *A STORM OF SPEARS*. NEW YORK: HARCOURT BRACE JOVANOVICH, 1971.

A veteran of the Vietnam War, Frank Charles hopes to leave violence behind him by enrolling as a graduate student at a university in California. But, alas, during this action-packed suspense saga, he is beaten senseless on several occasions, witnesses three separate kidnappings, is forced to burglarize a top-secret campus research institute, participates in a bloody confrontation between radical students and the police, and is a party to an especially gory shooting. Why does a nice boy like Frank Charles find himself in so many nasty situations? One reason is that he is being blackmailed into acting as a campus spy by agents from Red China. Mr. Charles has had the misfortune of being photographed during a torrid sex act with an undergraduate named Antonia. Since his warmhearted wife, Joanna, is crippled and permanently confined to a wheelchair, hubby Frank cannot risk damage to her psyche by having his affair with Antonia revealed. *A Storm of Spears* contains many university scenes and offers an interesting portrait of Brock Fletcher, the university's dean of minority affairs. A sociologist by training, Fletcher is one of few African American administrators to appear in college-mystery fiction.

Alfred Coppel was born in Oakland, California, and attended Stanford University. A one-time reporter, a mainstream novelist, and critic for the *San Francisco Chronicle*, Coppel had published two mystery novels before writing *A Storm of Spears*. In addition to A. C. Marin, Coppel has employed the pseudonym Robert Cham Gilman on some of his works.

166. DAVIS, DOROTHY SALISBURY (B. 1916). *SHOCK WAVE*. NEW YORK: SCRIBNER'S, 1972.

The protagonist of this story is Kate Osborn, a well-known writer for "*Saturday Magazine*." Osborn travels to Venice, Illinois, to research a feature story on a local political kingpin. On the train to Venice she meets Professor Randall Forbes, a member of the physics department at the "State University of Venice." Shortly after her arrival in the southern Illinois town, Osborn learns of the mysterious death of Professor Daniel Lowenthal, one of Professor Forbes's colleagues, and she uses her prior contact with Forbes to conduct some ad hoc investigative reporting about Lowenthal's demise. A large number of Venice faculty members and administrators figure prominently in the plot of the novel. So, too, do assorted students, townspeople, and local policemen. By the end of the book Kate Osborn has gotten two stories, and a murderer has provided his own form of self-justice.

Dorothy Salisbury Davis was born in Chicago, Illinois, and received an A.B from Barat College in 1938. One of America's premier mystery writers, Davis served in 1955-1956 as president of the Mystery Writers of America. *Shock Wave* was her thirteeth mystery novel.

167. HOLTON, LEONARD [LEONARD WIBBERLEY (1915–1983)]. *THE MIRROR OF HELL*. NEW YORK: DODD, MEAD & CO., 1972.

Barbara Minardi, the sixteen-year-old daughter of a detective-lieutenant in the Los Angeles police force, attends summer classes at "Greenfield College." Greenfield is a Baptist institution deep in the Mohave Desert. Barbara's roommate, Susan, is found dead one morning, her head bashed in by a baseball bat. Then the school's iconoclastic poet-in-residence drowns off Catalina Island after what appears to be a violent reaction to a drug overdose. When Lieutenant Minardi and his priest-detective sidekick, Father Breeder, look into the deaths, much of their sleuthing takes place on the stark, sun-drenched Greenfield campus. Before the two Leonard Holton series-characters break the case, they must deal with a drug ring, with a crooked cop, and with more than a few suspicious Greenfield students and faculty members.

Leonard Wibberley was born in Dublin, Ireland. During his early working life he served as an overseas reporter for the *Daily Mirror* (London) and as an editor for newspapers in Singapore and Trinidad. Wibberley came to the United States in 1943. Alhough he published many mystery novels (all of them under the pseudonym Leonard Holton), Wibberley is perhaps best known for his books for juveniles and for his whimsical nonmystery adult fiction. One of Wibberley's nonmystery adult novels was *The Mouse That Roared* (Boston: Little, Brown & Co, 1955). Published in England as *Wrath of Grapes* (London: Hale, 1955), the book was adapted for a 1958 motion picture starring Peter Sellers.

168. JAMES, P(HYLLIS) D(OROTHY) (B. 1920). *AN UNSUITABLE JOB FOR A WOMAN*. LONDON: FABER & FABER, 1972; NEW YORK: SCRIBNER'S, 1973.

Set in and around the University of Cambridge, *An Unsuitable Job for a Woman* displays the sleuthing talents of Cordelia Gray, a novice private detective from London. On her first major case, Gray investigates the apparent suicide-by-hanging of Mark Callender, a recent Cambridge dropout. Although there are several on-campus scenes in this exceedingly well-written book, and even though assorted Cambridge students play major parts in the story, the book is only a marginal entry in this bibliography. The story is primarily concerned with nonacademic matters. Mark Callender, it seems, had enemies within his own family, and the explanation for his death hinges upon secret skeletons in the Callender family closet.

Phyllis Dorothy James was born in Oxford, England. Before launching her highly successful career as a mystery writer, she served as a hospital administrator and as a civil servant in the Home Office, where she worked in the criminal department. *An Unsuitable Job for a Woman* was James's fifth mystery novel and the first of a series of Cordelia Gray adventures. The book was adapted for film. The British-made motion picture, starring Pippa Guard as Cordelia Gray, was released in 1982.

169. KEMELMAN, HARRY (1908–1996). *TUESDAY THE RABBI SAW RED*. NEW YORK: FIELDS, 1973.

Rabbi David Small, whose natural habitat is the New England community of "Barnard's Crossing," is invited to offer a one-semester course in Jewish thought and philosophy at "Windemere Christian College" in Boston. Windemere Christian, charitably characterized by its regular faculty members as a "fallback school," is a classic example of an intellectually deprived institution. Most of its students are featherbrains, and its instructors are tired and cynical after years of pedagogic frustrations. The mystery in the story centers on the murder of John Hendryx, an unpleasant, bachelor professor of English. Rabbi Small, Detective Sergeant Schroeder of the Boston police, Suffolk County District Attorney Matthew Rogers, and Barnards Crossing's Irish Catholic police chief, Hugh Lanigan, all share in the detection. It is Rabbi Small's perceptive Talmudic logic, however, that finally puts Professor Hendryx's killer behind bars. The suspects include Roger Fine (an assistant professor of English whose contract has not been renewed),

Millicent Hanbury (Windemere Christian's young and attractive dean of the faculty), and Betty Macomber (the twenty-five-year-old, unmarried daughter of Windemere Christian's president). While the mystery in the novel will satisfy even the most demanding readers of detective fiction, the book also can be read exclusively for its commentaries on academe. Real-life American faculty members and administrators, especially those at nonelite institutions, will recognize themselves and many of their colleagues among the book's characters.

Harry Kemelman was born in Boston. He received an A.B. from Boston University in 1930 and an M.A. from Harvard in 1931. After teaching English at various Boston-area secondary schools and at Northeastern University, Kemelman joined the English department at Boston State College in 1964. *Tuesday the Rabbi Saw Red* was the fifth novel in Kemelman's extremely popular Rabbi Small series. Two other Rabbi Small novels, *The Day the Rabbi Resigned* (355) and *That Day the Rabbi Left Town* (429), appear in this bibliography. Users of the bibliography might also be interested in a collection of Kemelman stories that features the sleuthing of Professor Nicholas Welt. The anthology is titled *The Nine Mile Walk* (New York: Putnam's, 1967). Welt is Snowden Professor of English Language and Literature at a university in the New England community of "Fairfield." He is a master of inferential reasoning, and in *The Nine Mile Walk* he solves eight mysteries, doing so most often from a comfortable seat in the University Faculty Club.

170. LUDLUM, ROBERT (B. 1927). *THE MATLOCK PAPER*. NEW YORK: DIAL, 1973.

Who would ever think that "Carlyle University," an elite institution in Connecticut, could be the secret headquarters of an international crime ring? The FBI thinks so, and it recruits James B. Matlock II, a virile associate professor of English at Carlyle, to work as an undercover agent. Matlock finds that Carlyle is, indeed, a hub of drug dealing, gambling, and prostitution. Moreover, he learns that some of Carlyle's more distinguished faculty members and administrators are leading figures in the criminal activities. *The Matlock Paper* is a fast-paced thriller with an abundance of gore and a dearth of polysyllabic prose. A best-seller, it will never rate as one of the more intellectual works of college-mystery fiction. However, fiscal officers of real-life institutions of higher education may find that the book suggests some remedies for their schools' chronic budgetary ills.

Robert Ludlum was born in New York City. He received a B.A. from Wesleyan University in Connecticut in 1951. Before becoming one of America's most successful writers of commercial espionage and crime novels, he was an actor and New York City theatrical producer.

171. MANN, JESSICA. *THE ONLY SECURITY.* LONDON: MACMILLAN, 1973. PUBLISHED IN THE UNITED STATES AS *TROUBLECROSS.* NEW YORK: MCKAY, 1973.

Theodora ("Thea") Crawford arrives from London to take up a newly established professorship of archaeology at the "University of Buriton" in Cornwall. Separated from her husband, Crawford quickly finds that some of her new male colleagues offer the possibility of appealing bedtime adventure. Somewhat more slowly she also learns that someone at the university has the disconcerting habit of burying contemporary corpses instead of digging up ancient ones. Very much a modern-day liberated woman, Professor Crawford juggles detection, scholarship, and romance as the story unfolds. The book includes many on-campus scenes and many University of Buriton characters make appearances. Some readers may marvel at Crawford's academic professionalism. At the very end of the story, even as the police are leading the book's still-protesting villain off to prison, she constructs in her mind the opening sentences of a prospective journal article about an ancient ivory cross that has figured prominently in the case.

Jessica Mann was born in London. She holds B.A. and M.A. degrees from Newnham College, Cambridge, and an LL.B. from the University of Leicester. At the time *Troublecross* was published Mann was married to a professor of archaeology and lived in Truro, Cornwall. Another Jessica Mann novel, *Captive Audience* (182), appears in this bibliography. *Captive Audience* also features Professor Theodora Crawford as detective. In addition to writing mysteries, Mann has been a critic for the BBC and is the author of *Deadlier Than the Male* (New York: Macmillan, 1981), a study of English women mystery writers.

172. PEDEN, WILLIAM HARWOOD (B. 1913). *TWILIGHT AT MONTICELLO*. BOSTON: HOUGHTON MIFFLIN, 1973.

The "Jefferson Mafia," a group of academic scholars passionately interested in the study of the United States' third president, is holding a three-day meeting in Charlottesville, Virginia. Various mysteries are in the air. The University of Virginia is about to announce a new appointment to the Jefferson Chair of History, and several of the meeting's participants aspire to the post. Armistead Davis, the grand old man of Jeffersonian biography, is rumored to be about to announce a new discovery about the relationship between Jefferson and his slave, Sally Hemmings. And everyone wonders with whom Dorsey Jack Morgan, the beautiful and notoriously lascivious female archivist from Williamsburg, Virginia, will spend her evenings. All of these issues fade to secondary importance, however, after Armistead Davis collapses and dies of poison while he is delivering a speech at the group's final dinner. There is no classical sleuthing in the story, but all of the events are observed and analyzed by Raymond Green, a professor of history from the University of Missouri. Green's attractive wife, Margaret, a sometimes writer of mystery yarns, is along to help her husband understand what is happening. The book is must reading for those real-life historians who enjoy fictional tales of murder within their discipline. Nonhistorians who read the novel will, at the very least, come away from the experience with a greater knowledge of Thomas Jefferson's life and times.

William Harwood Peden was born in New York City. He received a B.S. in 1934, an M.A. in 1936, and a Ph.D. in 1942 from the University of Virginia. He was a professor of English at the University of Missouri when *Twilight at Monticello* was published. While his later professional publications focused upon American literature, much of Peden's early professional output dealt with Thomas Jefferson. *Twilight at Monticello* was his first novel.

173. TAYLOR, EDITH (B. 1913). *THE SERPENT UNDER IT.* NEW YORK: NORTON, 1973.

Set at "Hoyt College," in Massachusetts' Berkshire Mountains, this intricate story centers on murderous behavior in the English department. Professor Archibald and the department's secretary are the victims; numerous faculty members and graduate students are suspects; and Anne Redmond, the wife of a young instructor, is the sleuth. Some of the action takes place at the "Hoyt Memorial Gardens," a local beauty spot near the campus. Plagiarism is important to the plot, and the unique crucial clue is found deep in the English department's dusty files. For readers who have difficulty keeping up with the superenergetic Anne Redmond, she stops her investigation at many junctures to offer long, fact-filled summations of the case thus far.

Edith Taylor was born in New York City. She received a B.A. from Swarthmore in 1935 and then did graduate work at Syracuse University. After five years in the English department of the University of Buffalo, she moved, in 1951, to Buffalo Seminary, where she taught English and creative writing. In 1955 she became chairperson of the school's English department, and in 1970 she was appointed dean of studies. *The Serpent Under It* was her only mystery novel.

174. BARNARD, ROBERT (B. 1936). *DEATH OF AN OLD GOAT.* LONDON: COLLINS, 1974; NEW YORK: WALKER, 1977.

The "University of Drummondville" is a small, intellectual backwater in a remote part of Australia. Elderly Professor Belleville-Smith arrives from Oxford to deliver a series of lectures on Jane Austen. Something of a sham, Belleville-Smith has been giving the same presentations—word for word—for more than forty years. His first lecture thoroughly bores his audience, and the next morning he is found dead in his room in the "Yarumba Motel," his throat cut from ear to ear. Inspector Royle of the local police heads the inquiry. Royle is one of the least-appealing sleuths in detective fiction. Slow-witted, corrupt, and sour to the point of nastiness, he displays all of those negative qualities and more while attempting to discover the professor's killer. Many members of the Drummondville faculty enter the proceedings, as do representatives of the town's sheep-growing squirearchy. Written with considerable caustic humor, *Death of an Old Goat* adds some inventive twists to the classic college-mystery format. It also provides a surprise ending and offers readers a lingering, richly satirical look at an undistinguished academic outpost in the Australian wilds.

Robert Barnard is one of mystery fiction's most prolific and most respected writers. He was born in Burnham, England. Educated at Balliol College, Oxford, he spent six years as a lecturer in English at the University of New England in Northern New South Wales. *Death of an Old Goat* was Barnard's first novel. At the time the book was published, he had moved from Australia to become a senior lecturer in English at the University of Bergen in Norway. *Death in a Cold Climate* (204), a mystery set in a Norwegian institution of higher education, appears later in this bibliography.

175. CONSTANTINE, K. C. [CARL KOSAK (B. 1934)]. *THE BLANK PAGE.* NEW YORK: DUTTON, 1974.

"Rocksburg Junior College" is a small emporium of educational mediocrity in western Pennsylvania. Only a few of its faculty members have doctorates; its president, J. Hale Beverley, cares far more about his personal image than about his school's intellectual standards; and plagiarism and drug taking are mainstays of undergraduate life. When Janet Pistula, a slow-witted Rocksburg student, is found strangled with her own brassiere in a shabby rooming house, the killing is investigated by Mario Balzic, the local chief of police. A K. C. Constantine series-character, Balzic is an earthy, sometimes cynical, nonintellectual type who relies on dogged detection. In the process of solving the case, Balzic probes deeply into Rocksburg's academically dismal milieu. He finds the killer, and his experiences only reinforce his already-negative views about American higher education.

Carl Kosak is a resident of Pittsburgh, Pennsylvania. Before turning to writing he was a minor league baseball player and served in the Marine Corps. *The Blank Page* was the third novel in his continuing Mario Balzic series. All of the Balzic books have been published under Kosak's K. C. Constantine pseudonym.

176. FISHER, DAVID (ELIMELECH) (B. 1932). *A FEARFUL SYMMETRY*. GARDEN CITY, N.Y.: DOUBLEDAY, 1974.

One day, toward the end of the semester, Henry Keller is visited in his office by Becky Aaronson, a pretty undergraduate who asks for an A in Geology 103. Keller is a quiet forty-seven-year-old professor at an American university. He looks up Miss Aaronson's record, finds that she is only an indifferent student, and refuses her request. With Keller's stuffy response, Miss Aaronson stands, doffs her clothes, and announces that she is prepared to do anything to get the grade she wants. Aaronson's gracious offer jolts Keller out of his usual professorial stupor and propels him into a world comprised, in equal parts, of ecstasy and danger. Aaronson, it seems, has an overprotective boyfriend, and not long after Keller begins to consort with his now-favorite student, the boyfriend concocts a series of diabolical schemes to end the affair. Although the book is not a detective novel, its plot includes a violent death and more than enough suspense to keep most academic readers engrossed until the end.

David Elimelech Fisher was born in Philadelphia. He received a B.S. from Trinity College in Hartford, Connecticut, in 1952 and a Ph.D. from the University of Florida in 1958. He was a professor of geophysics at the University of Miami when *A Fearful Symmetry* was published. Although it lacks sufficient "academic" content to be given a separate entry in this bibliography, *Crisis* (Garden City, N.Y.: Doubleday, 1971), an earlier novel by David Fisher, might also be of interest to consumers of fiction about higher education. The story concerns the mental breakdown of Barney Ferber, an unhappy professor of English at New York University. As his moments of self-control grow less frequent, Professor Ferber has a series of distressing adventures. Most of his activities take place off-campus, but on one occasion he attends a department meeting and, unfettered by inhibitions, he lets his English-department colleagues know in forceful terms what he thinks of them.

177. PARKER, ROBERT B(ROWN) (B. 1932). *THE GODWULF MANUSCRIPT.* BOSTON: HOUGHTON MIFFLIN, 1974.

This novel follows Spenser, Robert Parker's popular series-character private detective, as he investigates the theft of a rare fourteenth-century manuscript from one of Boston's less-prestigious universities. Operating in his rough, tough, and wisecracking style (following in the manner of the great private eyes of American mystery fiction), Spenser finds that the case eventually involves him with radical students, with the collegiate drug scene, and with free-loving female undergraduates. Most of the action takes place on or near the university's campus, and several faculty members and administrators play key roles in the story. Professorial readers will appreciate the depiction of Bradford W. Forbes, the school's harassed president. Dr. Forbes occupies an office that resembles "the front parlor of a Victorian whorehouse," and he is one of the few university residents in literature or in real life who has the honesty to admit that his institution is "undistinguished." The same professorial readers may not be so admiring, however, of the portrait of the principal evildoer in the book. That individual is the only faculty villain in mystery fiction who wets his pants when apprehended for his misdeeds.

Robert Brown Parker was born in Springfield, Massachusetts. He received a B.A. in 1954 from Colby College in Maine and a Ph.D. from Boston University in 1970. Parker's doctoral dissertation was a study of Dashiell Hammett and Raymond Chandler. At the time *The Godwulf Manuscript* was published, Parker was an associate professor of English at Northeastern University in Boston. Although Spenser had appeared previously as the protagonist of short stories, *The Godwulf Manuscript* marked his debut in a novel-length publication. The subsequent Spenser series, of course, has met with both critical and commercial success. *Playmates* (315) and *Hush Money* (480), two more of

Parker's Spenser novels, have later entries in this bibliography. Two other Spenser mysteries, *Thin Air* (New York: Putnam's, 1995) and *Small Vices* (New York: Putnam's, 1977), also might be of interest to readers of college mysteries. In *Thin Air* Spenser travels briefly to "Merrimack State College" in Massachusetts in search of leads in the case of the missing wife of a Boston Police detective. And in *Small Vices,* he works to exonerate a black man who has been convicted of the murder of a white woman. *Small Vices* is not "academic" in nature, but the book contains several scenes at "Pemberton College" in Massachusetts, the school that the woman was attending before her death.

178. RENNERT, MAGGIE (B. 1922). *CIRCLE OF DEATH*. ENGLEWOOD CLIFFS, N.J.: PRENTICE-HALL, 1974.

"Elm Circle" is an elite residential cul-de-sac that adjoins the campus of "Lambert University." The inhabitants of the exclusive enclave become uneasy when Lambert's Afro-American Association establishes its headquarters in one of the houses. Called in to assuage the home owners' fears is young, attractive Guy Silvestri, a detective lieutenant and a human relations specialist with the local police force. Silvestri, as it happens, is also a part-time student at the university. The lieutenant's efforts are not made easier when Hilary Bridge, an associate professor of English and an Elm Circle resident, is murdered in his garage. As the story develops, Silvestri probes faculty politics, racial animosities, the Lambert homosexual scene, and the school's drug culture before bringing the case to a surprise conclusion. Lambert University is a Harvard-like, Ivy League institution located in "Buxton," Massachusetts, "just across the river from Boston." A goodly number of Lambert faculty members and administrators, many of them unpleasant, cross Silvestri's path during his investigations.

Maggie Rennert was born in New York City. A poet, editor, and teacher, she lived for many years in Cambridge, Massachusetts. Rennert was a resident of Israel when *Circle of Death* was published. The book was her first mystery novel. Her second mystery, *Operation Alcestis* (183), which also appears in this bibliography, describes the further efforts of Lieutenant Silvestri to cope with the strange and often-nasty folk who make up the Lambert University community.

179. DAVIS, MILDRED. *TELL THEM WHAT'S-HER-NAME CALLED.* NEW YORK: RANDOM HOUSE, 1975.

Three suspicious, fatal accidents occur in the small town that houses "Whitefield College," an exclusive institution in the northeastern United States. One of the victims is Ruth Wehrmann, the wife of a mild-mannered Whitefield professor of English. Mrs. Wehrmann plunges to her death from a cliff that overlooks the town. The Wehrmanns' daughter, Finley, takes it upon herself to investigate. Finley Wehrmann is a Whitefield undergraduate. The murderer tries to discourage her from sleuthing, but Miss Wehrmann, who gets little help or encouragement from the police, is a young lady of strong stuff. In the book's last scene, as she comes very close to becoming another of the book's murder victims, Miss Wehrmann discovers the identity of the Whitefield killer. A few professors appear in the story, but the emphasis is on Whitefield's undergraduate culture. The title of the book comes from a telephone message—"Tell them what's-her-name called"—that the villain delivers in a muffled voice to the victims in the story before dispatching them.

Mildred Davis was a resident of Bedford, New York, when *Tell Them What's-Her-Name Called* was published. The book was the last of eleven mystery novels that Davis published during her writing career.

180. LANG, BRAD. *CROCKETT ON THE LOOSE*. NEW YORK: LEISURE BOOKS, 1975.

The protagonist of this paperback action saga is Fred Crockett, a twenty-eight-year-old private detective who operates in a city that very much resembles Ann Arbor, Michigan. Long-haired, cynical, and impatient with authority, Crockett is a former cop who holds an M.A. in criminal science from the local state university. The story focuses on Crockett's search for Susan Samuelson, the daughter of a wealthy Detroit businessman, who has dropped out of the university and cut off all contact with her family. There are several on-campus scenes in the book, and a university security guard named Jim Ford is murdered halfway through the story. Before he locates Miss Samuelson—who is working in a massage parlor—Crockett runs afoul of sadistic policemen, drug dealers, and representatives of organized crime. He also meets and mates with Kathy Walker, a voluptuous university student who earns her tuition by working as a topless dancer.

Crockett on the Loose was the first in what was to become a three-novel series, by Brad Lang, starring private detective Fred Crockett.

181. LAWRENCE, ALFRED. *THE DEAN'S DEATH*. NEW YORK: POPULAR LIBRARY, 1975.

This fast-moving novel is set at "Meredith College," in Los Angeles, and the detective is homicide detective Lieutenant Columbo of the Los Angeles Police. Franklin Torrance, Meredith's president, is having an affair with Linda Kittredge, a beautiful undergraduate. Kittredge is starring in a college production of *The White Devil,* a seventeenth-century revenge tragedy by John Webster. Arnold Borchardt, Meredith's dean of students and the director of the play, discovers the Torrance-Kittredge relationship and begins to blackmail the president. Torrance and Kittredge then conspire to kill Borchardt. After a rehearsal, when the theater is otherwise empty, Kittredge engages Borchardt in conversation while Torrance sneaks up behind him and smashes his skull with a lead pipe. President Torrance and Miss Kittredge then put the dean's body in a coffin that is being used as a prop, and his corpse is not discovered until late the next day. All of the above is described in the first third of the story, and readers are left with no doubts about the identity of the villains, hence the mystery in the remainder of the book is how fast, and through what masterstrokes of deduction, Columbo will bring the murderers to justice. As he goes about his sleuthing, Columbo interviews many Meredith College characters and attends a performance of *The White Devil.* At the very end of the story, after he has arrested President Torrance, Colombo laments to Dean Markham of the law school that his wife will not understand this case because she has "a deep admiration" for people in the world of higher learning. Markham advises Columbo not to talk with her about his recent experiences at Meredith College. Columbo agrees to keep silent in order to preserve his wife's "faith" in academe and academics.

Yes, the Lieutenant Columbo in this novel is the same Lieutenant Columbo who appeared in the popular *Columbo* television series that starred Peter Falk in the title role. The story was adapted from a series episode titled "By Dawn's Early Light." The book was part of a series of spin-off paperbacks, sponsored by MCA Publications, that featured popular 1970s television detectives Kojak and Cannon as well as Columbo.

182. MANN, JESSICA. *CAPTIVE AUDIENCE.* NEW YORK: MCKAY, 1975.

The registry building at the "University of Buriton" in Cornwall is set afire, and the body of Winston Simpson, a male undergraduate, is found in the ashes. The authorities want to blame radical students for the conflagration, but the identity of the perpetrator or perpetrators is far from certain. The primary sleuth in the story is Theodora ("Thea") Crawford, a Buriton professor of archaeology, but some of the heavy ratiocination is done by Theodora's husband, Sylvester. A foreign correspondent, Sylvester is separated from Theodora. He rejoins his spouse for purposes of recuperation after breaking his leg. Sylvester narrates part of the story and provides an unusual twist to the proceedings at the very end of the novel. Many Buriton students, faculty members, and administrators appear in the tale. Two deserve special mention. Professor Prothro, an argumentative sociologist, is so obnoxious that "his colleagues groan at their own folly at having appointed him." And Buriton's principal, Lewis Rochester, hopes to prove, by dealing harshly with student demonstrators, that he is ready for bigger administrative posts in academe.

The Only Security (171), another Professor Theodora Crawford novel by Jessica Mann, appears earlier in this bibliography.

183. RENNERT, MAGGIE (B. 1922). *OPERATION ALCESTIS*. ENGLEWOOD CLIFFS, N.J.: PRENTICE-HALL, 1975.

Professor Clarence Putnam, a biologist at "Lambert University," is attacked and killed by three young assailants as he works in the backyard of his home. Putnam was a staunch conservative on campus political issues, and everyone assumes that his killers came from one of Lambert's radical student groups. Those assumptions are soon given weight when Allie Tuttle, a beautiful, radical student, confesses to having been one of the professor's murderers. But old Mrs. Roscoe, Professor Putnam's housekeeper, swears that all three members of the offending trio were male, so the authorities not only doubt Allie Tuttle's story but they begin to wonder about her sanity as well. The sleuth in the saga is Detective Lieutenant Guy Silvestri, a young-but-wise officer of the law for the town of Buxton, the Boston suburb in which Ivy-League Lambert University is located. Digging into the skeletons in several academic closets, Silvestri finds that Putnam's death was, in fact, part of an international espionage conspiracy and that the lovely-but-strange Miss Tuttle is indeed innocent. The story is crowded with characters and subplots. In addition to the late but generally unlamented Clarence Putnam, several professors enter the plot, as do a number of Lambert's large collection of dissident students. The novel is narrated by a New York drama critic named Herkimer, who once taught anthropology at Lambert and who returns to the school to help defend Allie Tuttle, but the text is interrupted at many points for excerpts (up to eleven pages in length) from Lieu-

tenant Silvestri's "personal journal" of the affair. The last chapter provides readers with information about what happens to several of the story's characters after the investigation of Professor Putnam's murder is closed. Narrator Herkimer returns to New York to review Broadway shows. Lieutenant Silvestri is appointed an advisor on human relations to the governor of Massachusetts. And, in an attempt to inject more relevance into its administration, Lambert University makes confession-prone Allie Tuttle an assistant dean.

An earlier novel by Maggie Rennert, *Circle of Death* (178), also appears in the bibliography. Like *Operation Alcestis*, *Circle of Death* is set at Lambert University and the sleuth in the story is Lieutenant Guy Silvestri.

184. FOOTE-SMITH, ELIZABETH (B. 1913). *GENTLE ALBATROSS*. NEW YORK: PUTNAM, 1976.

George Duddington Oldham is the president of "Barclay University," a school in the American Midwest. President Oldham drives a red Jaguar, hides $300 in "lucky money" in his wallet, and (though his wife claims that "sex just isn't his thing") keeps a mistress. Oldham also keeps a locked file that houses incriminating evidence about members of his faculty. He uses that information to blackmail professors into giving him money from grants that they receive. One day the loathsome President Oldham disappears, and private detective Wilson Woodford is asked to investigate. Woodford joins forces with Mercy Newcastle, a nineteen-year-old graduate student whose M.A. dissertation is entitled "The Literary Evolution of the Crime Novel in France, England, and America," and the duo sets out in search of the missing prexy. When Woodford and Newcastle find the object of their hunt, strangled to death, their task is to discover which of the many likely suspects in the case can claim credit for the murder. *Gentle Albatross* is not the most puzzling of college mysteries. Nonetheless, professorial president watchers may find the book to be among the more enjoyable novels in this bibliography.

Elizabeth Foote-Smith was born in Red Wing, Minnesota. After raising a family she returned to Northwestern University for a B.A. in 1964. In 1966 she was awarded an M.A. from the University of Chicago and then taught English at the University of Wisconsin at Whitewater until 1969. She had left academe to pursue a full-time writing career when *Gentle Albatross*, her first mystery novel, was published.

185. HOLLAND, ISABELLE (B. 1920). *GRENELLE*. NEW YORK: RAWSON ASSOCIATES, 1976.

This "had-I-but-known," gothic mystery is set at "Grenelle College," an Anglican-run institution in rural Virginia. The heroine of the piece is Susan Grenelle, the granddaughter of the school's major benefactor and the daughter of its late but still-beloved president. Thirtyish and unmarried, Susan returns after eleven years in California to live alone in the large and eerie family homestead on the Grenelle campus. Shortly thereafter Samantha (the preteen daughter of Susan's recently deceased twin sister) also takes up residence in the house. One of Samantha's playmates is murdered; Samantha is kidnapped; and some dastardly person or persons steals the school's most prized possession, a splinter that at least some members of the Grenelle faculty believe came from Christ's cross. Happily for Susan Grenelle, an old boyfriend named Mark Czernick is now the local chief of police. Susan and Mark not only detect together; they rekindle their old romance as well. Unhappily for Susan, Mark cannot stay constantly by her side, and when he is away sinister forces seem to lurk behind every door of the dark and creaky Grenelle mansion. The faculty of Grenelle College is comprised largely of Anglican priests. Several of those worthies play prominent roles in the story, and some of them prove, by their actions, that priest-professors can be as nasty as secular academics.

The daughter of a United States Foreign Service officer, Isabelle Holland was born in Basel, Switzerland. She attended the University of Liverpool in England before receiving a B.A. from Tulane University in 1942. Before launching a successful career as a writer of gothic novels, mysteries, and children's books, Holland held executive positions with several American publishing firms, including Crown, Lippincott, Harper's, and Putnam's.

186. LOVESEY, PETER (B. 1936). *SWING, SWING TOGETHER*. NEW YORK: DODD, MEAD & CO.,1976.

Swing, Swing Together was the seventh novel in Peter Lovesey's often-whimsical and extremely popular series of mysteries featuring Victorian-era detectives Sergeant Cribb and Constable Thackery of Scotland Yard. *Swing, Swing Together* takes Lovesey's intrepid pair of policemen to the "Elfrida College for the Training of Female Elementary Teachers" and then to Merton College at Oxford. The book's inventive plot involves a nude, midnight swim on the part of three young ladies from Elfrida College, the murder of an Oxford don, and a long boat ride on the Thames in the manner of Jerome K. Jerome's *Three Men in a Boat.* The story also takes Sergeant Cribb to the Coldbath Fields House of Correction, one of England's most cheerless prisons, where he receives the information that allows him to resolve the mystery that surrounds the don's death. As are all of the books in the Cribb-Thackery series, *Swing, Swing Together* is thick with Victorian atmosphere, and the descriptions of Elfrida College and Oxford provide rich (if somewhat fanciful) glimpses of two very different British institutions of higher education just before the turn of the century.

One of Great Britain's most successful mystery writers, Peter Lovesey was born in Whitton, Middlesex. After receiving a B.A. (honours) from the University of Reading in 1958, he served in the Royal Air Force as a flying officer until 1961. From 1961 until 1969 he was a member of the faculty at Thurrock Technical College in Essex, and from 1969 until 1975 he was head of the general education department at the Hammersmith College for Further Education. Lovesey published his first Cribb-Thackery novel in 1970; by 1975 the success of the series allowed him to leave academe for full-time mystery writing.

187. MACKAY, AMANDA. *DEATH IS ACADEMIC.* NEW YORK: MCKAY, 1976.

Set at Duke University, *Death Is Academic* centers on the murder of Bradley Brown, a longtime member of the political science department. Poor Professor Brown ingests squirrel poison that mysteriously appears in his fruit cocktail at a departmental dinner. Although various Durham and campus police officers investigate Brown's death, it remains for Hannah Land, the political science department's newest member, to come up with the explanation. Dr. Land, a tall and "willowy" thirty-three-year-old Columbia Ph.D., is a somewhat reluctant sleuth, but because people find it comfortable to confide in her she constantly finds herself coming into the possession of crucial information. She also finds that even at high-status Duke University the faculty is not above plagiarism, interdepartmental jealousies, and extracurricular sex. The cast of characters includes nearly all of Duke's political scientists as well as Henrietta Harrison, the ever-loyal secretary to Raymond Moseley, the political science department's chairperson. The book also incorporates a budding romance between Dr. Land and Lieutenant Robert "Bobby" Jenkins of the Durham police.

Amanda MacKay did her undergraduate work at Radcliffe and received an M.A. in political science from Columbia University. A native of Virginia, she lived in Durham, North Carolina, when *Death Is Academic* was published. The book was the first of two Amanda MacKay novels to feature Hannah Land as detective. The second was *Death on the Eno* (Boston: Little, Brown & Co., 1981). *Death on the Eno* is set in the countryside around Durham, North Carolina, and though it involves Professor Land looking for the killer of the brother of Luther Turnbull, a Duke professor of political science, it is not a college mystery.

188. AIRD, CATHERINE [KINN HAMILTON MCINTOSH (B. 1930.]) *PARTING BREATH*. LONDON: COLLINS, 1977; GARDEN CITY, N.Y.: DOUBLEDAY, 1978.

One of England's older and more stately institutions of higher education, the "University of Calleshire" has stood since the early Tudor times as a bastion of calm academic conservatism. However, the dismissal of a left-wing student agitator leads to the school's first sit-in, and that event is followed quickly by two murders. The first victim is an undergraduate; the second is Peter Pringle, the university's short, fat librarian. Detective-Inspector C. D. Sloan, a Catherine Aird series-character, is the sleuth on the scene. Sloan finds a plethora of likely culprits among Calleshire's students and faculty members. Many of the faculty suspects are properly addled British academics who draw suspicion to themselves through various forms of unusual behavior. Real-life social scientists will be especially intrigued by the portrait of Roger Franklyn Hedden, a Calleshire lecturer in sociology. Hedden becomes a suspect because he stays on campus and works on a book during summer vacation. Detective-Inspector Sloan's attention to Hedden is prompted by a professor of ecology who remarks to the inspector that "Hedden stayed on through the summer vacation when I did, [and] sociologists don't usually work as hard as scientists."

The daughter of a medical doctor, Kinn Hamilton McIntosh was born in Huddersfield, England. One of Great Britain's leading mystery writers, Mcintosh lived in an East Kent village near Canterbury when *Parting Breath* was published. *Parting Breath* was her seventh Inspector Sloan mystery novel.

189. DEWEESE, (THOMAS EU)GENE (B. 1934). *WEB OF GUILT*. SOUTH YARMOUTH, MASS.: JOHN CURLEY & ASSOCIATES, 1977.

Lissa Drexel receives a late-night phone call from her cousin Maureen Olson. Drexel is a graduate student in English at the University of Wisconsin at Madison. Maureen Olson, who likes to brag about her ever-increasing number of male conquests, is visiting Madison from Pennsylvania and staying in a hotel. Olson tells Drexel that she has a serious problem and, despite the hour, begs her cousin to come to her room immediately. When Drexel arrives she finds that Olson has fallen to her death from the balcony. Sometimes helped and sometimes hindered by Anson Harris, a Madison police detective, Drexel takes time from her busy academic schedule to do the book's sleuthing. She learns that Olson was pushed and that someone, perhaps the murderer, was showering gifts on her cousin during the few days she had been in town. One suspect is Professor Arthur Melton, for whom Drexel acts as a teaching assistant. Pictured as part man and part mouse, Melton is totally controlled by Astrid, his domineering wife. He begins to play a central role in the case after he falls into a near faint when Drexel tells him of cousin Maureen's death. The text of this novel is preceded by Drexel's personal horoscope. Born November 21, 1946, at 12:01 A.M., Scorpio Drexel is described in the horoscope as, among other things, intense, gracious, promising, and creative. Professorial readers might wish to add that she is also academically wise beyond her tender years. After Professor Melton's swoon, Drexel takes over his next day's classes, and does so well that a student tells her that her style of teaching is much more stimulating than Melton's. "Thank you," replies Lissa, "but just because (the class) seemed more interesting doesn't mean that it was necessarily better."

Thomas Eugene DeWeese was born in Rochester, Indiana. He received an associate degree in electronics from Valpariso Technical Institute. He also studied at the University of Wisconsin at Milwaukee. After a brief career as a electronics technician, DeWeese became a free-lance writer and produced gothic fantasies, science-fiction novels, and mysteries.

190. DEXTER (NORMAN) COLIN (B. 1930). *THE SILENT WORLD OF NICHOLAS QUINN.* NEW YORK: ST. MARTIN'S, 1977.

Nicholas Quinn, a former teacher of English and history at a grammar school in Yorkshire, joins the staff of the Foreign Examinations Syndicate, an organization near Oxford that gives O- and A-level examinations to students from countries other than England. Quinn, who is nearly deaf, attends a party for visiting Arab oil potentates and is able to lip-read secret conversations between some of the attendees. A short time later Quinn is found dead of poison in his bachelor apartment. Detective Chief Inspector Morse and Sergeant Lewis, two Colin Dexter series-characters, are assigned to the case. A man who likes his beer, Inspector Morse spends considerable time in Oxford-area pubs during this exploit, but he eventually manages to unravel the mystery. Deadly rivalries within the examining organization, a naughty motion picture playing at an Oxford theater, and a beautiful female employee of the syndicate all prove central to his detection. Several University of Oxford dons appear in the story, both as unpaid members of the syndicate's governing board and as members of the organization's various examining committees, and the book offers rich descriptions of Oxford street scenes.

Colin Dexter was born in Lincolnshire, England. He received a B.A. from the University of Cambridge in 1953 and an M.A. from Cambridge in 1958. He served as a classic master at several British schools, teaching Latin and Greek, before joining the Oxford Local Examining Board as assistant secretary in 1966. Dexter continued to work for the examining board until 1987, when he left to pursue creative writing on a full-time basis. Dexter created Inspector Morse during a holiday in Wales in 1973, and the sometimes cantankerous inspector (along with ever-loyal Sergeant Lewis) has served as the detective in a continuing series of twelve published mysteries and in over thirty television productions. *The Silent World of Nicholas Quinn* was the third in the Morse series of novels. Three other Inspector Morse novels focus sufficiently on academic matters to appear in this bibliography. Those novels are *The Riddle of the Third Mile* (228), *The Daughters of Cain* (386), and *Death Is Now My Neighbor* (422).

191. DIPEGO, GERALD FRANCIS (B. 1941). *WITH A VENGEANCE*. NEW YORK: MCGRAW-HILL, 1977.

Twenty years after the fraternity-hazing death of Randal Nye, his father, Stephen, continues to seethe with anger. Stephen Nye is a professor of English at "Iverson Junior College," a school in the American Midwest. One day professor Nye suddenly resigns his teaching post, withdraws his life savings from the bank, and sets out to kill the college-age offspring of the five boys-now-men who robbed him of his own son. Nye's travels take him to the Universities of Wisconsin and Missouri, to New York City, and to several other locales before his vengeful mission ends. There is some sleuthing in the story—by Detective Dela of the Chicago police—but the author of this exercise in parental retribution devotes most of his attentions to Professor Nye's determined pursuit of his victims.

Gerald Francis DiPego was born in Chicago. He received a B.S. from Northern Illinois University in 1963 and then did graduate work at the University of Missouri. After a brief career as a newspaper reporter and as a high-school teacher of English, DiPego became a full-time writer specializing in television dramas. His works have been produced on major American networks. *With a Vengeance* was his first novel.

192. LITZINGER, BOYD (B. 1929). *WATCH IT, DR. ADRIAN.* NEW YORK: PUTNAM, 1977.

Matthew Adrian is a Harvard Ph.D. and an associate professor of English at "Thomas Jefferson University" in Washington, D.C. Hoping to lose himself in work after a divorce, Adrian flies off to England to spend a summer researching Victorian poets in the Bodleian Library in Oxford and in the British Museum. Unbeknownst to Adrian, American intelligence has selected him to be the courier of microfilmed secret documents. When he arrives in London, he is mugged, given a false invitation to lecture to the Greater London Society for Literary Preservation, and otherwise abused by Russian, Arab, a British secret service operatives. Although Professor Adrian is hardly the first American professor in fiction to be harassed by international spies, he does perambulate through more of the high and low spots of Oxford and London than do many of his predecessors. Furthermore, he comes into contact with some very intriguing British characters. Among those whom he meets in his travels are "Barb the Busty," a luscious young lady whose outstanding attributes are suggested by her nickname, and Mrs. Brock-Partington, an elegant, widowed author of Oxbridge mystery novels. Mrs. Brock-Partington, whose works do not appear in this bibliography, is the creator of John Douglas Bruce, an urbane, Oxbridge don who doubles as a professorial series-character sleuth.

Boyd Litzinger was born in Johnstown, Pennsylvania. He received a B.S. from the University of South Carolina in 1951, an M.A. from South Carolina in 1952, and a Ph.D. from the University of Tennessee in 1956. At the time *Watch It, Dr. Adrian,* was published, Litzinger was a professor of English at St. Bonaventure University in Olean, New York. *Watch It, Dr. Adrian*, was his first novel. Litzinger is best known in English literary circles for his many professional works about Robert Browning and other nineteenth-century British poets.

193. WILLIAMS, DAVID (B. 1926). *TREASURE BY DEGREES*. NEW YORK: ST. MARTIN'S, 1977.

The protagonist of this ultra-inventive exercise in whimsical college mystery is Mark Treasure, vice chairman of Greenwood, Phipps, and Co., a London merchant bank. Treasure, a David Williams series-character sleuth, represents the bank's interests as Mrs. Amilia Hatch, a wealthy American widow, prepares to donate her late husband's fortune to a rundown, rural British institution called "University College." But, as Treasure and Mrs. Hatch discover to their astonishment, there are individuals at the school who do not want the money. After attempting to discourage the donation by such tactics as bomb scares and the sending of a severed sheep's head to Mrs. Hatch's hotel room, one member of the anti-Hatch forces takes the ultimate step of slitting the American widow's throat. With some assistance from Inspector Treet, an often-befuddled police official, Treasure does his detection amid thoroughly zany students and even zanier University College teachers and administrators. Moreover, the case is complicated by the presence of a sinister Arab sheik who wants to provide University College with his own form of fiscal assistance.

Born in New South Wales, Australia, David Williams read history at Oxford and served in the Royal Navy before entering the advertising business. At the same time *Treasure by Degrees* was published, Williams was chairman of the British advertising firm of David Williams and Ketchum, Ltd. The book was the second in a continuing series of more than fifteen novels that employ Mark Treasure as detective. *Treasure in Oxford* (304), another of David Williams's Mark Treasure mysteries, appears later in this bibliography.

194. COLLINS, RANDALL (B. 1941). *THE CASE OF THE PHILOSOPHER'S RING*. NEW YORK: CROWN, 1978.

The Case of the Philosopher's Ring is a Sherlock Holmes pastiche. It is set in the summer of 1914. Holmes and Dr. Watson journey to Trinity College, Cambridge, at the request of none other than Bertrand Russell, to investigate the bizarre behavior of philosopher Ludwig Wittgenstein. Then an Indian mathematician is killed, and Holmes and Watson are propelled into yet another post-Arthur Conan Doyle adventure. Holmesian experts must judge for themselves whether Randall Collins's effort measures up to the standards set by

Doyle. But readers from the present-day academic world will be fascinated by the portraits of Russell, Wittgenstein, Lytton Strachey, Virginia Woolf, John Maynard Keynes, and the many other famous intellectuals of the period who appear in the story.

Randall Collins received a B.A. from Harvard in 1963, an M.A. from Stanford in 1964, and a Ph.D. from the University of California at Berkeley in 1969. A prominent American sociologist, Collins was a professor of sociology at the University of Virginia when *The Case of the Philosopher's Ring* was published. The novel was Collins's first work of fiction.

195. GIFFORD, THOMAS EUGENE (B. 1937). *THE GLENDOWER LEGACY*. NEW YORK: PUTNAM, 1978.

This inventive, if somewhat contrived, thriller centers on Colin Chandler, a forty-five-year-old professor of history at Harvard. Thought to be in possession of documents proving that George Washington delivered Continental defense secrets to the British, even as the Continental army starved at Valley Forge, Chandler is chased through Boston and its environs by agents from the Boston police, the KGB, and the CIA. The interest in Chandler and in the papers that everyone believes are in his care is prompted in part by the murder of Bill Davis, a Harvard undergraduate, and in part by the desire of Maxim Petrov, the head of the KGB, to embarrass Arden Sanger, his CIA counterpart. Professorial readers may be only modestly amused at the scene in which Petrov and Sanger share hot dogs and spy gossip at a White Sox-Red Sox baseball game in Fenway Park. But they may find escapist interest in Colin Chandler's romantic exploits with Polly Bishop, a sexually generous newswoman employed by a Boston television station. And they will be positively enthralled by Bertram Prosser, the aged chairperson of Harvard's history department. A man of great wealth, Prosser is a staunch defender of academic freedom who carries both a Dunhill pipe and a "large" pistol in his professorial pockets.

Thomas Eugene Gifford was born in Dubuque, Iowa. He received an A.B. from Harvard in 1959. Before becoming a freelance writer in 1975, he held a variety of positions with publishing houses and newspapers. From 1960 until 1968 he was a college textbook salesman for Houghton Mifflin. *The Glendower Legacy* was Gifford's fourth novel.

196. LANGTON, JANE (B. 1922). *THE MEMORIAL HALL MURDER.* NEW YORK: HARPER & ROW, 1978.

Memorial Hall, the center for performing arts at Harvard, is rocked by a bomb explosion. Missing and presumed dead after the blast is Hamilton Dow, the popular, rotund conductor of Harvard's chorus. Homer Kelly, a Jane Langton series-character sleuth, happens to be in Cambridge as a visiting professor of American literature, and by the end of this sly, witty book Kelly has learned more than he cares to know about the perfidious Harvard milieu. *The Memorial Hall Murder* is an extremely descriptive mystery. It is enlivened by maps and sketches of Harvard scenes, and readers are given a literary tour through the maze of Memorial Hall's passages and rooms. The book also contains vivid portraits of several Harvard faculty members and administrators. Real-life professors will want to pay special attention to the depiction of President James Cheever, a man whose forceful handling of campus political battles reveals true Ivy League inventiveness. Professors who are overweight may want to take comfort in the book's overriding message. Fat, so the author implies, can prove to be a significant component of one's academic survival kit.

Jane Langton was born in Boston. She attended Wellesley in the early 1940s and then received B.S. and M.A. degrees from the University of Michigan and an M.A. from Radcliffe. Langton is well-known as an author of children's books as well as the writer of the Homer Kelly series of mysteries. Kelly is a Harvard graduate, was once an assistant district attorney in East Cambridge, and is retired from a post as detective lieutenant in Concord, Massachusetts. He also is an expert on Herman Melville and on Thoreau. A visiting professor at Harvard in *The Memorial Hall Murder,* Kelly becomes a full-time Harvard professor of English as his series proceeds. *The Memorial Hall Murder* was the third entry in Langton's continuing, thirteen-novel Kelly series and the first of the series in which Kelly deals with crime in an academic setting. Three later Kelly mysteries have enough academic content to warrant appearances in this bibliography. Those mysteries are *Emily Dickinson Is Dead* (244), *The Shortest Day: Murder at the Revels* (412), and *Dead as a Dodo* (432). Another Kelly mystery, *The Dante Game* (New York: Viking, 1991), also might be of interest to readers of college mysteries. *The Dante Game* is set in Florence, Italy, where Professor Kelly has come for a term to teach Italian literature at the newly established "American School for Florentine Studies." The focus of *The Dante Game* is away from academe, but characters associated with the school play important roles in the story.

197. MACDOUGALL, JAMES K. *DEATH AND THE MAIDEN*. INDIANAPOLIS: BOBBS-MERRILL, 1978.

The protagonist of this somber novel is David Stuart, a James K. MacDougall series-character private detective. Stuart is asked to find the kidnapped, five-year-old daughter of John Stanley, a member of the English department at an American state university. A wealthy man, Stanley has acquired his bulging bank account not from academic work but by marrying a wealthy woman. Stuart's initial efforts bear only bitter fruit. Thanks to some apparent bungling on Stuart's part, John Stanley and his daughter are both killed. But Stuart perseveres, and the singularly duplicitous villain in the story is eventually identified. Several members of the state university community emerge as suspects before the book's final chapter. Not under suspicion, but certainly a nefarious character, is Vincent Lightfoot, the university's dean of undergraduate studies. A man who has made his accommodations with the dismal facts of modern academic life, Dean Lightfoot disliked John Stanley because the latter showed no sympathy for students who plagiarize term papers. Such faculty members, in Lightfoot's view, do not understand the problems faced by today's ill-prepared students. By attempting to have classroom cheaters expelled, these faculty purists only succeed in "giving the university a bad name."

Death and the Maiden was the second mystery to feature private eye David Stuart. At the time the novel was published, James K. MacDougall was an associate professor of English at Ball State in Muncie, Indiana.

198. MACLEOD, CHARLOTTE (B. 1922). *REST YOU MERRY*. GARDEN CITY, N.Y.: DOUBLEDAY, 1978.

Rest You Merry is a comic mystery set at "Balaclava Agricultural College" in the rural Massachusetts town of "Balaclava Junction." The sleuth is Peter Shandy, a zany, bachelor professor of horticulture. The story has Shandy investigating the death of a faculty wife, whose body is found in his home, and the murder by poison of the college comptroller. For good measure, he looks into an act of arson that destroys the college's heating plant. The book's mystery element is well constructed, but the emphases in the tale are on absurd incidents and characterization. The many denizens of Balaclava Agricultural College, Professor Shandy in particular, are memorable for their daffiness. Short, overweight, and bespectacled, Professor Shandy does not cut an imposing figure, but his high level of energy, his blunt manner, and his playful iconoclasm make him a man whose actions can have unanticipated consequences. In *Rest You Merry*, for instance, Shandy decides that the annual display of Christmas decorations in his neighborhood is offensive. Seeking to underline his displeasure, he covers his small brick home with plastic Santa Clauses and flashing lights, blares songs such as "All I Want for Christmas is My Two Front Teeth" from a loudspeaker, and leaves town for a cruise aboard a tramp steamer. It is during Shandy's cruise that the first victim in the novel enters his home and expires, presumably after falling off a ladder while attempting to alter his decorations and/or turn off his sound system. Faculty readers may want to note that Professor Shandy, while content to live in fairly modest circumstances, has an income over and above his professorial salary. He receives a stream of royalties from seed companies for his great scientific creation, a giant rutabaga known as the "Balaclava Buster."

Charlotte MacLeod was born in Bath, New Brunswick, Canada. Trained as an artist, she joined the Boston advertising firm of N. H. Miller and Co. in 1952. By the time *Rest You Merry* was published she was a vice president of the agency. *Rest You Merry* was the first of what proved to be a highly successful, continuing series of nine mysteries with Peter Shandy in the role of detective. Other Professor Shandy mysteries with entries in this bibliography are *The Luck Runs Out* (201) *Something the Cat Dragged In* (233), and *An Owl Too Many* (337). Two more Shandy novels, while lacking enough on-campus scenes to be considered college mysteries, might nonetheless be of interest to this bibliography's users. *The Corpse in Ozack's Pond* (New York: The Mysterious Press, 1987) involes Shandy in an examination of the family tree of Balaclava Buggins, the founder of Balaclava Agricultural College. And *Exit the Milkman* (New York: The Mysterious Press, 1996) has Shandy investigating the disappearance from the college of Jim Feldster, a professor of dairy management. In addition to her Peter Shandy series, MacLeod has published other detective fiction, several nonfiction works, and books for children. Some of her mystery fiction has been issued under the pseudonym Alicia Craig.

199. BANKS, CAROLYN (B. 1941). *MR. RIGHT*. NEW YORK: VIKING, 1979.

The protagonist of this sexually explicit, psychological mystery is Lida, a thirty-five-year-old woman who teaches English at "Brady State College" in Maryland. Although she is single, Lida is far from being a virgin. She attempts to add a novelist named Duvivier to the list of thirty men with whom she already has slept, but Duvivier's apparent deviant sexual tastes seem about to prevent her from accomplishing her mission. Moreover, the now rich-and-famous Duvivier was once a professor of theater at a small college in New Hampshire, and those who remember him there are convinced that he is a homosexual sadist who once murdered a female student. Duvivier's suspicious past is uncovered by Diane, one of Lida's associates, when she travels to the New Hampshire school to give a lecture. The climax of the story comes when Paul Riley and Allan Dilworth, two of Duvivier's former New Hampshire colleagues, arrive in Washington, D.C., to help Diane prevent Lida from becoming the novelist's next victim. At this point, among the exhibits at the Smithsonian Air and Space Museum, the real villain is revealed. The story is cleverly constructed to create suspense. It includes several episodes at Brady State, a predominantly African American institution, and it also offers a graphic, flashback description of the events leading to the murder on the New Hampshire campus.

Born in Pittsburgh, Pennsylvania, Carolyn Banks received a B.A. from the University of Maryland in 1968 and an M.A. from that institution in 1969. She was an instructor of journalism and creative writing at the University of Maryland when *Mr. Right* was published.

200. CALDERWOOD, CARMELITA (D. 1950), AND JAMES HEARST. *BONESETTER'S BRAWL*. ARDMORE, PA.: DORRANCE & CO., 1979.

Set in the 1940s, this novel deals with murder and intrigue in the orthopedics department of a university teaching hospital. Although the university's location is never mentioned, clues strongly point to the state of Iowa. A nurse falls to her death from a bridge. Department members receive threatening letters. One doctor dies after apparently using eyedrops laced with poison, and another expires when he drinks poisoned whiskey. Meantime, faculty members fight over grant monies, and the heated romantic entanglements in the department cause everyone to suspect everyone else of assorted misdeeds. All the while the book's characters train future doctors and nurses, and, when they can tear themselves away from the department's internal turmoil, they wage a valiant fight against the ravages of poliomyelitis. The "Bonesetter's Brawl" is a dance held by the orthopedics department each spring, and it is the site of some significant action in this novel. The story is narrated by Peg Hunter, who holds a teaching appointment in the university's School of Nursing. More an observer than sleuth, Hunter leaves most of the detecting to the local sheriff, who distinguishes himself at the end of the book by extracting a confession from an evildoer as that individual dies an agonizing, convulsive death. *Bonesetter's Brawl* is not the most subtle mystery in this bibliography, nor is its atmosphere the most "academic." On the other hand, it features a professor of English among its important players, and readers are reminded regularly that the hospital and its staff are components of an encompassing university.

Carmelita Calderwood was a registered nurse. At her death in 1950 she left the unfinished manuscript of this novel. Her husband, James Hearst, completed the manuscript and arranged for its publication.

201. MACLEOD, CHARLOTTE (B. 1922). *THE LUCK RUNS OUT.* GARDEN CITY, N.Y.: DOUBLEDAY, 1979.

This tongue-in-cheek mystery is set at "Balaclava Agricultural College" in rural Massachusetts, and it features the antic sleuthing of Professor of Horticulture Peter Shandy. Martha Flackley, a farrier who does work for the college, is murdered. Someone slashes her throat and dumps her body in a pig feeder in the college's animal husbandry barns. Worse yet, Belinda, Balaclava Agricultural College's prize 900-pound sow, is found to be missing. Furthermore, someone seems determined to sabotage the college's entry in the annual competition of the Balaclava County Draft Horse Association. The book is loaded with college characters, all of whom display well-advanced cases of galloping eccentricity, and it includes Thorkjeld Svenson, the college's blustering and impulsive president, in a featured role. Many college presidents in mystery fiction doggedly keep their schools operating regardless of the number or nature of the crimes that occur at their institutions. President Svenson, in a burst of administrative resourcefulness, goes counter to most of his fictional peers. He immediately cancels classes after Miss Flackley is killed and Belinda the pig disappears. President Svenson announces his decision at a college assembly, and he orders the school's students to form search parties to look for indications about the identity of the murderer and for clues to the whereabouts of the missing sow.

Three other Peter Shandy novels by Charlotte MacLeod appear in this bibliography. Those novels are *Rest You Merry* (198) *Something the Cat Dragged In* (233), and *An Owl Too Many* (337). In *Rest You Merry*, the first novel in the Shandy series, the professor is a bachelor. In *The Luck Runs Out*, the second Shandy book, he is married to the former Helen Marsh, who was once a college librarian in California. As the series continues, Mrs. Shandy finds work in the Balaclava Agricultural College library. In her appearance in *The Luck Runs Out,* and in most of the subsequent Shandy novels, Helen Shandy lends her husband important sleuthing assistance.

202. PEARSON, ANN (BOWLING) (B. 1941). *MURDER BY DEGREES.* NEW YORK: KENSINGTON PUBLISHING CORP., 1979.

This unalloyed college mystery is set at "Jernigan State College" in rural Mississippi. The sleuth is Maggie Courtney, an assistant professor of English. Coming to work one morning, Courtney discovers Dr. Ruby Murdoch, dean of humanities and head of the English department, bludgeoned dead with a paperweight in her office. Murdock was an autocrat. Almost everyone in the humanities division feared and disliked her, thus suspects are in abundant supply. Maggie Courtney is drawn into detection when the police officer assigned to the case, Lieutenant Jake Travis, turns out to have been a high-school classmate, and he asks her to help him understand the unfamiliar ways of academic folk. Before Dr. Murdoch's killer is identified, George Purvis, another assistant professor of English, disappears, and Harriet McGraw, chairperson of the art department, commits suicide by swallowing a large quantity of alcohol mixed with lithium. The many suspects in the case, almost all of them Jernigan faculty members, possess a variety of skeletons in their closets, and taken together their collective wrongdoings form a virtual catalog of the sins that lead professors in college mysteries to kill each other. *Murder by Degrees* includes six full-page illustrations, four of which contain vital clues. Published only in paperback, the book was issued with its final chapter sealed, and readers were encouraged to solve the mystery on their own before reading the denouement.

Murder by Degrees was the first of three mysteries by Ann Pearson to star Maggie Courtney as sleuth. It was the only one of the three to be set at an institution of higher education.

203. ASWAD, BETSY (B. 1939). *WINDS OF THE OLD DAYS*. NEW YORK: DIAL, 1980.

Every Superbowl Sunday a group of Rosalind Chase's friends and relatives gathers in her home to mourn the death of her husband, Ben, on Superbowl V Sunday in 1971. Ben, a radical student at "Caliban College" in Pennsylvania, was gunned down by an unknown assailant and his frozen body was found in a forest near the Caliban campus. It is now Superbowl XII Sunday, in January of 1978, and though Rosalind is happily remarried and a member of the Caliban department of English, neither she nor her houseguests can avoid rehashing the mysterious circumstances that surrounded Ben's death. As the discussion continues, even while the Dallas Cowboys are defeating the Denver Broncos by a score of 27–10, the identity of Ben's killer is revealed. The book does not contain any classical detection. However, it does feature a host of suspects, many of whom take part in the confabulation, and most of whom are faculty members and/or former students at Caliban. Told in part through flashbacks, the unusually structured story includes graphic descriptions of Rosalind's active sex life and it also offers several classroom scenes.

Betsy Aswad was born in Binghamton, New York. She attended Hood College and the State University of New York at Binghamton. *Winds of the Old Days* was her first novel. At the time the book was published, Aswad was a member of the English department at the State University of New York at Binghamton.

204. BARNARD, ROBERT (B. 1936). *DEATH IN A COLD CLIMATE.* LONDON: COLLINS, 1980; NEW YORK: SCRIBNER'S, 1981.

The naked body of a man is found frozen in the snow outside of the Norwegian university city of Trumso. The man, whose skull has been shattered by a heavy instrument, turns out to have been Martin Forsyth, a British crewman from an oil exploration ship. The detective who handles the case is Inspector Fagermo of the Trumso police. During the course of his sleuthing, Fagermo has cause to view several members of the University of Trumso community as suspects. Among them are Steve Cooling (an American graduate student in history), Dougal Mackensie (a Scottish professor of geology), Professor Halvard Nicolaisen (of the university's department of language and literature), and Lise Nicolaisen (Professor Nicolaisen's young, attractive wife). Written with Robert Barnard's customary blend of sardonic wit and clever plotting, *Death in a Cold Climate* provides an intensive if often unflattering look at the manners and morals in a provincial Norwegian academic setting. The book also offers some telling commentaries about overseas visitors to Norway's shores. American readers may be especially interested in the brief but trenchant depiction of Nan Bryson, a bilingual young lady from America who works in the Trumso office of the United States Information Agency. Miss Bryson sometimes adds to her income by translating Norwegian works into English for clients at the university. Her Norwegian patrons do not complain about her talents as a translator; however, they do find that her skills in English spelling and punctuation are abysmal.

Another Robert Barnard mystery, *Death of an Old Goat* (174), appears earlier in this bibliography. At the time *Death in a Cold Climate* was written, Barnard was a professor of English literature at the real University of Trumsoe, an institution that lies three degrees north of the Arctic Circle in Norway. In an author's note that precedes the text of the novel, Barnard claims that while the "geographical facts" in the book are accurate, the characters in the story are entirely fictitious.

205. CARKEET, DAVID (B. 1946). *DOUBLE NEGATIVE.* NEW YORK: DIAL, 1980.

At the "Wabash Institute," a grant-supported research center in southern Indiana, the professional staff consists of six linguists who study the ways through which children acquire language. One of the linguists, aged Arthur Stiph, is found dead of a blow to his head, and another, Henry Philpot, is strangled to death and his body thrown into a nearby river. Jeremy Cook, still another of the institute's linguists, becomes a suspect in both killings, and he takes up sleuthing to clear his name. Meantime, Lieutenant Leaf, a local policeman who is known for bending the rules in order to solve murder cases, follows his own, sometimes bizarre, lines of inquiry. Although the Wabash Institute is not connected with any college or university, *Double Negative* has much of the flavor of a college mystery. The book is written with the wit one expects of high-quality college-mystery fiction, and the team of six linguists functions much like an academic department. Indeed, at several junctures in the story Walter Wach, the institute's director, calls staff conferences that produce banal and self-serving discussions that greatly resemble those often heard, at least in fiction, at college or university department meetings. Furthermore, at one of those conferences Wach articulates his "Rule Eight," a bit of operational philosophy that obviously guides many academic leaders in real life. "People forget things," the rule tells us, "so people who run things can safely treat past failures as if they had been stupendous triumphs."

David Carkeet was born in Sonora, California. He holds an A.B. from the University of California at Davis, an M.A. from the University of Wisconsin, and a Ph.D. from Indiana University. He was a member of the English department at the University of Missouri at St. Louis when *Double Negative* was published. *Double Negative* was his first novel.

206. FISKE, DORSEY. *ACADEMIC MURDER.* NEW YORK: ST. MARTIN'S, 1980.

Ernest Garmoyle, the distinguished head of the "Prye Library" at the University of Cambridge's "Sheepshanks College," dies at the college's high table after drinking port dosed with arsenic. The first police official on the scene is Inspector Bunce of the local constabulary, but the prominence of the victim soon brings Inspector Pocklington of Scotland Yard onto the scene. Pocklington is a former Sheepshanks student. Also involved in the sleuthing is John Fenchurch, a sixtyish Sheepshanks lecturer in architecture who is one of Inspector Pocklington's former tutors. As the several detectives try to identify Ernest Garmoyle's killer, a handwritten copy of an early Shakespeare poem disappears from the Prye Library and a rapist dressed in academic robes terrorizes Cambridge and its environs. *Academic Murder* is a throwback to the elegant British college mysteries written just before and after World War II. The book is unhurried, filled with eccentric characters, and well supplied with witty dialogue and cleverly constructed situations. And yet, despite its somewhat dated style of prose, it manages to poke satirical jabs at many modern-day academic phenomena. Homosexual and women's organizations come in for particular attention. A group calling itself the "Cambridge Queens" plays an important, albeit unintentional, part in capturing the book's villain, and a collection of young mothers petitions the university to establish a twenty-four-hour family care center, where women can leave their husbands as well as their offspring with the option of picking them up for weekends.

Dorsey Fiske was born in Hawaii, graduated from Radcliffe College, and was a research student in bibliography at Darwin College, the University of Cambridge, during the 1971–1972 academic year. Fiske lived in Delaware when *Academic Murder* was published.

Fiske's second mystery, *Bound to Murder* (279), also appears in this bibliography. Like *Academic Murder*, *Bound to Murder* is set at the University of Cambridge's Sheepshanks College.

207. GLOAG, JULIAN (B. 1930). *SLEEPING DOGS LIE*. NEW YORK: ELSEVIER-DUTTON, 1980.

Dr. Hugh Welchman is a British psychiatrist. He lives and works in Cambridge and his clients include students and faculty members from the university. One day he is visited by Alex Brinton, a first-year undergraduate at "Carol College." Alex, it seems, has a strange phobia against using a certain stone staircase in one of the college buildings. As Dr. Welchman probes Alex's curious malady, he begins to understand that his patient's problem involves dark Brinton family secrets. Furthermore, as he delves even deeper into the matter, he comes to the startling realization that Alex Brinton's phobia has sinister meanings for the Welchman family as well. *Sleeping Dogs Lie* is a slick, well-written psychological mystery. It contains several scenes at the university, and many of the primary characters have university connections. Those who read the book may not learn a great deal about the normal routines at University of Cambridge colleges, but they certainly will become acquainted with some of the malefic mental disorders that can afflict people who live and work behind the serene college facades.

Julian Gloag was born in London. He received a B.A. in 1953 and an M.A. in 1958 from Magdalene College, Cambridge. Early in his career Gloag was an editor for Hawthorne Books in New York City. *Sleeping Dogs Lie* was his fifth novel. He is known in British literary circles as a master of macabre suspense tales. At the time *Sleeping Dogs Lie* was published Gloag lived in Paris, France.

208. KEECH, (JOHN) SCOTT (B. 1936). *CIPHERED*. NEW YORK: HARPER & ROW, 1980.

This elaborately plotted, on-campus mystery takes place at "Thorpe University," a state-supported institution somewhere in the eastern part of the United States. Ernest Feith and his wife are shot dead in their home. Feith, a professor of biochemistry and director of the University Research Center, had many faculty enemies. He was also a wealthy man, and his two adult children stand to gain large legacies from his death. The detective in the case is Inspector Jeff Adams, a bachelor police officer and a part-time student at the university. Adams is ably assisted by Kate Shaw, a young and beautiful member of the Thorpe history department. Complicating matters is the fact that Kate's father, Mark Shaw, is a professor of theater at Thorpe and is himself a suspect. In addition to providing Jeff Adams with emotional support, Kate Shaw is able to decipher a set of complex cryptograms found in Professor Feith's study. Those suggest that espionage may somehow figure in the affair. Kate's deciphering talents stem from her professional work; she is writing a biography of Ignatius Donnelly, the author of that "obscure master work," *The Great Cryptogram* (New York: R. S. Pearle, 1888). Meanwhile, even as Jeff Adams hunts down Ernest Feith's murderer, and even as Kate Shaw's research on Ignatius Donnelly proceeds, student demonstrators attempt to disrupt the secret work of the research center.

Scott Keech was a resident of Berkeley, California, when *Ciphered* was published. Information on the cover of the novel tells us that Keech's interests are "mysteries (and mystery writing), history, and Ignatius Donnelly." *Ciphered* was Keech's only mystery novel.

209. SLAVITT, DAVID RYTMAN (B. 1935). *COLD COMFORT*. NEW YORK: METHUEN, 1980.

A study in parental revenge, *Cold Comfort* follows the machinations of Stanley Miller as he brings his own form of justice to "Fargate College," a "less-competitive" institution in the eastern United States. Miller is the widowed owner of a dry-cleaning shop. His son, Howie, dies after guzzling an immense quantity of alcohol during a fraternity initiation. The college authorities hush the affair, and the local police limit themselves to a cursory investigation. Knowing that only he can exact proper retribution, Miller begins to kill the people who were most directly involved in his boy's death and in the subsequent cover-up. The first to die is Roger Chelmsford, the homosexual alumni president of good old Lambda Mu. Then Miller dispatches selected members of Fargate's administration. By the end of the story Miller's personal vendetta is over, but Fargate College is just beginning its search for a new dean of students and a new president. Although there is no significant detection in the book, there is tension aplenty as Miller stalks his targets. There is an abundance of academic malignity in the story as well. Not only are Dean Robinson and President Garside guilty of protecting the questionable reputation of their school; Robinson is shown to have perfected sexual harassment into a high art, and Garside's behavior provides real-life faculty readers with insight into what college presidents really do in their hotel rooms when away on out-of-town speaking trips.

David Rytman Slavitt was born in White Plains, New York. He received an A.B. from Yale in 1956 and an M.A. from Columbia University in 1957. He was an associate professor of English at Temple University when this novel was published. A poet and writer of "serious" fiction, Slavitt has also written mysteries and thrillers under the pseudonym Henry Sutton.

210. CLINE, C. TERRY, JR. (B. 1935). *MISSING PERSONS*. NEW YORK: ARBOR HOUSE, 1981.

The protagonist of this slick commercial novel is Joanne Fleming, a thirty-six-year-old professor of criminology at Florida State University. Professor Fleming moonlights as a paid consultant to local police forces, and as part of her extracurricular work she finds herself involved in the hunt for a psychopathic killer who abducts attractive young women (some of them college students) and then beats them dead with a tire iron. Professor Fleming's own teenaged daughter, Marcie, is stalked and then kidnapped by the killer. The result, as the book proceeds, is a fevered attempt by Fleming and her police cronies to come to Marcie's rescue. The story includes several important scenes on the Florida State campus, and Dr. Thaddeus Kreijewski, the head of the university's criminology department, appears in an interesting cameo role. Poor Dr. Kreijewski is worried that all of the negative publicity that Fleming is bringing to his department will make it difficult for him to build a top-flight criminology program at Florida State. As for Professor Fleming, recently divorced from an unfeeling attorney named Ralph, daughter Marcie's peril only adds to her already well-stocked bag of woes. Her self-esteem battered by Ralph, and with Dr. Kreijewski making her professional life something less than a bed of roses, Fleming is having a difficult time maintaining a satisfactory sex life with Ken Blackburn, her policeman boyfriend. Fortunately, she can find consolation in the fact that her second book, *The Modality of Sex Crime* (published by Tulane University Press), already has sold 100,000 copies.

C. Terry Cline Jr. was born in Birmingham, Alabama. He attended Florida State University. A full-time professional writer, Cline is perhaps best known for *Damon* (New York: Putnam's, 1975), a chilling epic that features a sex-crazed, four-year-old boy in its leading role.

211. CROSS, AMANDA [CAROLYN GOLD HEILBRUN (B. 1926)]. *DEATH IN A TENURED POSITION*. NEW YORK: DUTTON, 1981.

Death in a Tenured Position is set at Harvard and the sleuth is Professor Kate Fansler, Amanda Cross's popular series-character detective. Professor Fansler goes to Harvard, from her home university in New York City, to assist Janet Mandlebaum, the only woman professor in Harvard's English department. Mandlebaum, an old friend from graduate school, has been the subject of threats and violent harassment. Fansler is not long in Cambridge when Mandlebaum is found poisoned dead in a men's room in Warren House, the English department's headquarters. Fansler's suspects include several male professors of English who might have been attempting to cleanse the department of its only tenured woman, but there are suspects from the other extreme of the Harvard political spectrum as well. Since Mandlebaum was not a feminist, and steadfastly refused to cooperate with militant women's groups on the campus, one or some of the aggressive feminists she offended also might have committed the evil deed. The story, which is sprinkled with literary allusions, offers much information about the treatment of women faculty at Harvard. In a disclaimer that precedes the story the author tells her readers that her Harvard characters bear no resemblance to real people. She notes that she knows only one member of the Harvard English department and is acquainted with that person only slightly. Moreover, she claims to have visited Warren House just once, and only to "case the joint for the purpose of writing this book."

Death in a Tenured Position was the sixth novel in a continuing series of twelve Kate Fansler mysteries. Six other Professor Kate Fansler mysteries by Carolyn Heilbrun, writing under her Amanda Cross pseudonym, appear in this bibliography. Those mysteries are *Poetic Justice* (156), *Sweet Death, Kind Death* (238), *No Word from Winifred* (264), *A Trap for Fools* (308), *An Imperfect Spy* (402), and *The Puzzled Heart* (457).

212. LEWIN, MICHAEL Z(INN) (B. 1943). *MISSING WOMAN*. NEW YORK: KNOPF, 1981.

Albert Samson, a cynical, down-on-his-luck Indianapolis private detective, is hired by a lady identifying herself as Elizabeth Staedtler, a Ph.D. in sociology. Staedtler wants Samson to find Priscilla Pynne, an old friend and classmate from her undergraduate days at the University of Bridgeport. Before Samson finishes the job, he encounters a murder and learns that a bogus Ph.D. in sociology can provide a perfect cover for nefarious activities. Samson's search for Priscilla Pynne takes him to Indiana University, to the Indiana University-Purdue campus in Indianapolis, and to Ball State University in Muncie, Indiana. Except for the enigmatic Dr. Staedtler, he meets no faculty members in the course of his labors, but he does encounter a gun-toting dean at Ball State. And at Indiana-Purdue he is treated to a meeting with the dour, harassed secretary of the sociology department.

Michael Lewin was born in Springfield, Massachusetts, and received an A.B. from Harvard in 1964. He also spent a year as a graduate student in chemistry at the University of Cambridge. A one-time New York City high school teacher, Lewin moved to England in the early 1970s. He has written many radio plays for the BBC. Albert Samson is a Lewin series-character sleuth. *Missing Woman* was Lewin's seventh novel and the fifth to feature Albert Samson as detective.

213. MARON, MARGARET. *ONE COFFEE WITH*. NEW YORK: RAVEN HOUSE, 1981.

Thanks to internal rivalries, egos, and some just plain nastiness on the part of its members, the art department at City University of New York's "Vanderlyn College" exists in an almost perpetual state of upheaval. Hence, when Associate Professor Riley Quinn, the department's much-disliked deputy chairperson, dies in the department's outer office after drinking coffee spiked with poison, the entire art faculty is immediately transformed into suspects. The police official in charge of this clue-crammed case is Sigrid Harald, a young-but-determined New York City detective lieutenant, who finds it useful to orient herself by referring regularly to a roster of the art faculty and to a map of the department offices. Both the roster and the map are included in the book and give guidance to readers as well. In the end, Lieutenant Harald scores two triumphs. First, she stages a bit of inspired theatrics that leads to the identification of Professor Quinn's killer. Second, she begins an affair with Oscar Nauman, the art department's attractive chairperson who is also an internationally known painter. Professorial readers may want to take note of what occurs immediately after Professor Quinn's death. His next class is canceled, but as word of his demise spreads through the college, all of his students (not just the few who ordinarily would have come) fill the hall outside his classroom and speculate with excitement on the identity of the murderer. "I've always wondered what it would take to get full attendance," observes a faculty member.

Margaret Maron was born in Greensboro, North Carolina, and attended the University of North Carolina at Greensboro and the University of North Carolina at Chapel Hill. After making her mystery-fiction debut with *One Coffee With,* Maron has gone on to become one of America's most popular writers. Sigrid Harald, who makes her first appearance in *One Coffee With*, is the featured detective in a continuing series of Margaret Maron mysteries. At the time *One Coffee With* was published Maron lived near Raleigh, North Carolina.

214. MARTIN, JESSICA. *CAMPUS KILLINGS.* NEW YORK: TOWER, 1981.

Poor Nan Bradley! She gave up a job at pressure-cooker Cornell to become an associate professor of English at peaceful "Moore College" in Southern California. Now she finds herself embroiled in several Moore College mysteries that are raising her stress levels to heights never experienced at her previous, Ivy League address. Who was responsible for a bomb that exploded in a campus utility shed, killing Gus Steck, Moore's head gardener? Could it have been some of Bradley's students who might have been attempting to enliven an antiwar demonstration that was taking place when the bomb exploded? Where has Erica Dawson gone? The English department's brightest student, Miss Dawson has confided to Bradley that she is pregnant, but now she has disappeared. What about Charles Thurston, an English-department colleague? Found in a compromising situation in a men's room years ago, how has he coped with being the possible target of blackmail ever since? And then there is the matter of brilliant Roy Haverill, another member of the Moore College English department. Haverill has been dismissed by the college administration for lack of publishing. Will Derek Phillips, the ambitious chairperson of English and one of Haverill's closest friends, try to save Haverill's job or, in hopes of becoming dean, will he concentrate on finishing his own book about Byron? Professor Bradley becomes a sleuth in part because of her deep concern for her colleagues and students and, in part, because George Hiltz, a detective with the local police, makes it clear that he suspects her of possible involvement in the utility-shed bombing. Bradley's efforts to solve Moore College's mysteries almost result in her own death, but she narrowly escapes the villain of the tale when, in a bit of on-the-job-training in the martial arts, she breaks one of his fingers during hand-to-hand combat. The complex case ultimately involves drugs, right-wing politics, and an unusual example of academic dishonesty. Fortunately, Professor Bradley explains it all in an end-of-book denouement, but it takes her twenty pages to accomplish the task.

Campus Killings was Jessica Martin's only mystery novel.

215. MURPHY, BRIAN (B. 1939). *THE ENIGMA VARIATIONS*. NEW YORK: SCRIBNER'S, 1981.

Dora Pennington accuses Troyte Griffith of raping her. Pennington and Griffith are students at a Midwestern American university, and in the finest traditions of academe, Dean Richard Arnold creates a special committee to investigate Pennington's charges. The committee's chairperson is Eliot Upton, a fifty-year-old professor of music. Upton does not relish this time-consuming extracurricular assignment. His book on composer Sir William Elgar is far behind schedule; his marriage is breaking apart; and he has fallen in love with two women, one of them a cool, beautiful publishing executive and the other a marijuana-smoking, sexually rapacious member of the university's advisement staff. Then, just to add another complication to Professor Upton's world, Troyte Griffith is shot dead one dark night, and Captain Sinclair and Detective Sergeant Baker of the local police arrest Dora Pennington for murder. Upton believes Pennington to be innocent, and between torrid sex scenes with his pair of consorts, he tries to identify Troyte Griffith's actual killer. Laced with musical allusions and crowded with references to religious matters (Professor Upton is a convert to Roman Catholicism), *The Enigma Variations* is less an orthodox mystery than an exploration of Eliot Upton's frenzied efforts to cope with the crescendo of crises in his personal life. The book contains many scenes on the university campus, and early in the story readers are treated to a lengthy episode in which the Upton-led investigatory panel attempts to establish precisely how and why Dora Pennington lost her virginity.

Brian Murphy received a Ph.D. from the University of Detroit, an M.A. from Harvard, and a Ph.D. from the University of London. *The Enigma Variations* was his first novel. At the time the book was published, Murphy was a member of the department of English at Oakland University in Michigan.

216. SHAW, HOWARD (B. 1934). *DEATH OF A DON*. NEW YORK: SCRIBNER'S, 1981.

Death of a Don is a throwback to the droll Oxbridge mysteries of the 1930s, 1940s and 1950s. Set at Oxford's "Beaufort College," the book centers on the murders of two Beaufort fellows, David Ashe and Norman Duncan-Smith. Ashe, a young, leftist activist, had many enemies in the college. On the other hand, Duncan-Smith, a retired professor of music, was thoroughly innocuous, and no one can imagine who might possibly have wanted to kill him. The case is investigated by Chief Detective Barnaby, a tall, gaunt gentleman, who learns that the motives behind Oxford crimes need not be immediately comprehensible to the nonacademic mind. While real-life professors from all disciplines will find *Death of a Don* rewarding reading, sociologists will want to make a close examination of the text for several items of special interest. The terrible David Ashe was a mathematician, but his colleagues feel that his antiestablishment (and antisocial) behavior was more in keeping with that of sociologists. At several junctures in the narrative, sociology is held up to ridicule, and Beaufort College (which also refuses to allow women to "live in") is determined never to create a sociological fellowship. "After all," as one of the Beaufort dons puts it over coffee in the common room, "you've only got to count the sewers in Liverpool and you're on the way to a degree [in sociology], probably a doctorate."

Howard Shaw was born in Bristol, England. He received a B.A. in 1958 and an M.A. in 1963 from Queens College, Oxford. Before becoming a full-time writer Shaw worked as a schoolmaster at King's College School, Cambridge, and at Harrow. *Death of a Don* was his second mystery novel.

217. STEIN, AARON MARC (1906–1985). *A BODY FOR A BUDDY.* GARDEN CITY, N.Y.: DOUBLEDAY, 1981.

Matt Erridge, an engineer, attends the twentieth reunion of his class at an American college. One night, as he returns to the dormitory room to which he has been assigned, he finds the corpse of Amanda Graystock in his bed. Twenty years earlier, before marrying classmate George Graystock, Amanda had been the town's lady of easiest virtue. Now she is dead of an overdose of phenobarbital mixed with an excessive amount of alcohol. A few nights later another death takes place. Rick Dowling, an undergraduate and a photography enthusiast, is found hanged in his dorm room. The son of the college's most generous benefactor, Dowling swings from a camera boom clad only in a woman's girdle. Were the two deaths murders or suicides? Matt Erridge, with the help of several other reunioners, tries to solve the pair of mysteries. Almost all of the novel takes place on the college campus, and two college administrators play roles in the story. Dean Daniel Mulligan, the school official in charge of the reunion, lends his hand to the sleuthing effort, and the college's president, Abner Dale, properly laments the death of a member of the family that financed the Dowling dorm complex, the Dowling administration building, and the Dowling tower.

Three other mysteries by Aaron Marc Stein have entries in this bibliography. Those mysteries are *The Corpse with Purple Thighs* (44), *The Case of the Absent-Minded Professor* (60), and *The Cradle and the Grave* (84). Like *A Body for a Buddy, The Corpse with Purple Thighs* (written under the pseudonym George Bagby) is a reunion mystery.

218. VALIN, JONATHAN (B. 1948). *DEAD LETTER*. NEW YORK: DODD, MEAD & CO., 1981.

Daryl Lovingwell, a sour, middle-aged professor of physics at the University of Cincinnati, has a problem. A top-secret nuclear power document has been stolen from a safe in his home, and Lovingwell suspects that Sarah, his Marxist-radical daughter, is the culprit. Lovingwell hires Harry Stoner, a series-character private eye, to investigate, but shortly thereafter the professor is murdered. Not a man to walk away from a case, even when his employer is dead, Stoner continues his sleuthing. Some of his detective work takes place on the University of Cincinnati campus, and in one especially effective scene an experienced department secretary tells him at length about the frustrations of her job. The woman also utters a pithy statement that will simply be repeated in this annotation without any editorial comment. Lovingwell was once head of the Cincinnati physics department, and the secretary says: "I haven't met a department chairman yet who wasn't a secret fascist." In any event, Stoner resolves matters by the end of the book, but not before several more killings take place, and not before some long-hidden jealousies among the physicists at Cincinnati come to the surface.

Jonathan Valin was born in Cincinnati. He received an M.A. from the University of Chicago in 1974 and did further graduate work at Washington University of St. Louis. From 1974 until 1976 Valin was a lecturer in English at the University of Cincinnati, and from 1976 until 1979 he was a lecturer at Washington University of St. Louis. *Dead Letter* was his third Harry Stoner novel.

219. CLEMEAU, CAROL [CAROL CLEMEAU ESLER (B. 1935)]. *THE ARIADNE CLUE.* NEW YORK: SCRIBNER'S, 1982.

This novel is set at an urban university in the eastern United States. The university museum is about to hold an exhibition of Aegean gold, but some of the choicer pieces are found to be missing. Also absent without trace is Ariadne Pappas, a graduate student who often did after-hours research in the museum. Detective Lieutenant Steve Caracci puts two and two together and begins a hunt for Miss Pappas. Antonia Nielson, an associate professor of classics, cannot believe that one of her graduate students could be a thief, and she sets out to prove that Caracci's calculation is incorrect. Some of Nielson's sleuthing takes her into another part of the city, to the home of the dysfunctional Pappas family, but most of her detection occurs on the university campus and, in particular, within the museum. The crucial clue referred to in the book's title is misinterpreted by poor Lieutenant Caracci, a man whose knowledge of the ancient world is scant, but Nielson, drawing upon her skills as a classics scholar, is able to interpret it correctly and thereby break the case. The book's sizable roster of characters includes handsome Professor of Classics Win Randolph, known to his colleagues as the university's "Lothario-in-residence," and Barry Greenfield, an assistant professor of English whose practiced smile never fails to stir the hearts of his female students. By the end of the story two murders have taken place, a villain has experienced a self-inflicted form of justice, and the world is about to learn of the amazing discovery of a hitherto unknown Euripides papyrus. As a bonus for readers who like their mysteries erudite, the author garnishes her tale with sprinklings of references to Greek mythology.

Carol Clemeau Esler received a B.A. from Oberlin College in 1957 and a Ph.D. from Bryn Mawr in 1965. She was an assistant professor of classics at William and Mary College when *The Ariadne Clue,* her first novel, was published.

220. DAVIES, FREDERICK (B. 1916). *DEATH OF A HIT-MAN.* NEW YORK: ST. MARTIN'S, 1982.

Early one morning Professor William Denton, visiting the University of Cambridge from the University of Texas, is discovered shot dead in the senior common room of "Carrington College." The murder weapon is found nearby, and it belongs to the distinguished master of the college, Professor Sir James Millard. Not long afterward Michele Gresset, the attractive daughter of a Carrington fellow, is found shot in the college's car park, where her body has presumably laid unseen during much of the night. Miss Gresset, whose affair with Professor Denton was known to many people at Carrington, also has been killed with the master's gun. The detective on the case is David Cooper, who heads the New Scotland Yard Murder Squad. At first, *Death of a Hit-Man* promises to be an orthodox Oxbridge mystery. Professor Millard convinces Cooper that someone stole the pistol from his office, and Cooper's suspicions quickly fall on Jane Denton, the late Professor Denton's widow. But there are darker forces at work! Cooper learns that Professor Millard was a regular contributor to the Communist Party, that Professor Denton was a CIA agent, and that a mysterious Russian undercover operative named "Zio" is lurking somewhere nearby. Indeed, two years earlier Zio was responsible for the deaths of Cooper's wife and young son after his attempt to eliminate Cooper himself went awry. MI5 soon becomes involved, and *Death of a Hit-Man* is transformed into an action-packed international spy thriller. Before the story ends, British paramilitary forces literally storm Carrington College and destroy a Russian command-and-control center in the school's basement. *Death of a Hit-Man* will never be described as cerebral, but some anti-Communist academics (and, perhaps, some antiadministration ones as well) may appreciate one of the bits of book-ending mayhem. As the British commandos force their way into Carrington College's basement they discover what is left of Professor James Millard, Carrington's master. Somehow, Millard has displeased his Communist associates. He is still alive, but he is hanging from two hooks in the ceiling, is oozing blood from several locations on his body, and has had all his teeth pulled out and all his fingernails removed.

Frederick Davies was a resident of Birkenhead, England, when this book was published. It was the first of two mystery novels he published during a brief literary career.

221. DEAN, S. F. X. [FRANCIS SMITH]. *BY FREQUENT ANGUISH.* NEW YORK: WALKER, 1982.

Neil Kelly is a quiet, introspective professor of English at "Old Hampton College," a high-prestige school in "Oldhampton," Massachusetts. Widowed after twenty-five years of marriage, he is about to take a second trip to the altar, this time with Priscilla ("Pril") Lacey, one of his students. Then disaster strikes! Miss Lacey is shot dead by an unknown assassin in the college library. When the police seem to be bungling their investigation, and after Miss Lacey's parents ask him to find their daughter's killer, Professor Kelly reluctantly turns sleuth. The story is filled with Old Hampton students, faculty members, and administrators, and by the end of the tale Kelly has learned more than he cares to know about several of the Old Hampton characters. *By Frequent Anguish* contains many literary allusions, considerable wit, and a level of poignancy that is not encountered in most of the mysteries in this bibliography. It is narrated by Professor Kelly, whose words convey both the pain of his personal loss and his discomfort about prying into the lives of his colleagues. At the end of the book Kelly is desperate to escape Old Hampton, and he accepts a fellowship for an extended stay in England.

By Frequent Anguish was the first in a series of six novels featuring Professor Neil Kelly. It is the only novel in the Kelly series with sufficient "academic" content to qualify for inclusion in this bibliography. At the time the series was written, Francis Smith, Professor Kelly's creator, was a professor of humanities at Hampshire College in Amherst, Massachussetts.

222. GARNET, A. H. [GARNET R. GARRISON AND ALFRED H. SLOTE]. *MAZE.* NEW HAVEN & NEW YORK: TICKNOR & FIELDS, 1982.

Three highly placed people are murdered at "Mid-East University" in "Harbour Woods," Michigan. Trying to discover motives for the killings, even before he can look for the perpetrator or perpetrators, is Cyrus Wilson, an untenured assistant professor in the Mid-East English department who is still working on his Ph.D. dissertation. The author of four detective mysteries for children, the energetic Wilson is asked to help in the investigation by his Uncle Harold, Harbour Woods' chief of police. Before this fast-paced story concludes Wilson makes his Uncle Harold proud, but while he has learned a great deal about the flourishing prostitution business in Harbour Woods, he is no closer to finishing his doctorate. The book is noteworthy for the ways in which the three Mid-East victims expire. All three leave this earth in grand manners that, perhaps, befit upper-echelon members of the academic establishment. After drinking water poisoned with cyanide, Geoff Goldstein, the chairman of the Mid-East English department, collapses and dies before a large audience while presiding over a university awards ceremony. Wally Lassiter, Mid-East's head football coach, is shot from the stands at the halftime of a big game against Duke and is trampled by an oncoming 10,000-member massed high-school band. And the body of Arthur Browne, a law professor, is found baked in a large oven at the University's Law Club. As a Harbour Woods morgue attendant later puts it, Browne is "done to a turn."

At the time *Maze* was published Garnet R. Garrison was a professor emeritus of speech at the University of Michigan, and Alfred H. Slote was recently retired as executive producer of the university's television center. *Maze* was the second Garrison-Slote collaboration but the first to have a campus setting. The first Garrison-Slote novel, *The Santa Claus Killer* (New Haven & New York: Ticknor & Fields, 1981), also features Cyrus Wilson in the role of detective.

223. HEALD, TIM(OTHY) (VILLIERS) (B. 1944). *A SMALL MASTERPIECE.* NEW YORK: DOUBLEDAY, 1982. PUBLISHED IN ENGLAND AS *MASTERSTROKE*. LONDON: HUTCHINSON, 1982.

The sleuth in this very droll Oxford whodunit is Simon Bognor, a special investigator for the British Board of Trade in London. Bognor is a Tim Heald series-character detective. He attends a gaudy at "Apocrypha College," where he once was a student, and he is thus on the scene when Apocrypha's master, old Lord Beckenham of Penge, dies after being poisoned at dinner. Bognor stays on in Oxford to find Lord Beckenham's killer. His primary suspects are Apocrypha's fellows, all of whom are laden with eccentricities and some of whom aspire to succeed Lord Beckenham. The master's death actually sparks a small celebration in the senior common room because his poisoning is the first murder to occur at Apocrypha in 450 years. *A Small Masterpiece* includes an ineffectual police inspector, whose name none of the other characters in the tale can ever remember, as well as Simon Vole, a visiting professor from Vermont. Vole is in Oxford researching a book on criminals who have attended Oxford University and/or have taught there. His thesis is that Cambridge will forever be tarnished by its four masterspies—Burgess, Maclean, Philby, and Blunt—but Oxford's reputation, by comparison, is unreasonably "pure." Vole's mission, as he sees it, is to "humanize" Oxford's image by giving publicity to the university's many miscreants. In the course of his work the visitor from America has uncovered some interesting information about several of Apocrypha's current dons. Unhappily, his encyclopedia of Oxford University crime will never be completed because the villain in this novel eradicates him before the end of the story.

Tim Heald was born in Dorset, England, and earned a B.A. in modern history from Balliol College, Oxford, in 1965. Before becoming a professional mystery writer, Heald was a reporter, feature writer, and editor for several British and Canadian newspapers and magazines. *A Small Masterpiece* was Heald's seventh Simon Bognor mystery.

224. MCCORMICK, CLAIRE [MARTA HAAKE LABUS (B. 1943)]. *RESUME FOR MURDER*. NEW YORK: WALKER, 1982.

Peter Simon is the director of placement at "Witherspoon College," a small Protestant fundamentalist school in "New Arcady," Pennsylvania. Simon is also a serial philanderer, and one day someone kills him in his office. The villain crushes Simon's skull and then pulls down his pants and castrates him. The finder of the bloody body is John Waltz, a Pittsburgh businessman who is at the college to recruit Witherspoon graduates for his company. The local police order Waltz to stay in town so they can continue to question him, and he uses his time in New Arcady to identify Simon's killer. He is assisted in his amateur detection by Anne Christenson, an attractive member of Witherspoon's English department. Written with considerable verve and wit, *Resume for Murder* offers some stinging satire of Witherspoon, a rural institution at which many of the students and faculty are religious fanatics. Waltz, a Jew from the big city, solves the murder mystery in the story, but he can never fully comprehend organizations such as the "Coventers." Dedicated to cleaning the body as well as the mind, the Coventers push themselves to their physical limits by engaging in long-distance "jogs for Jesus." Nonetheless, even though they profess deep Christian commitment, some of the characters at Witherspoon are capable of adultery, bigotry, and even murder.

Marta Haake Labus was born in Huntington, West Virginia. She received a B.A from Ohio University in 1965 and a Ph.D. from the University of Illinois in 1971. She was an assistant professor of English at Westminster College in New Wilmington, Pennsylvania, from 1971 until 1978. *Resume for Murder* was her first novel.

225. MINER, VALERIE (B. 1947). *MURDER IN THE ENGLISH DEPARTMENT.* NEW YORK: ST. MARTIN'S, 1982.

Most of this book is set at the University of California at Berkeley. The protagonist is Nan Weaver, an outspoken assistant professor of English who champions women's causes on the campus. Working late in her office on New Year's eve, Weaver hears a man and woman shouting. The disturbance seems to come from the office of Professor Angus Murchie, a generally unpleasant individual who is noted for his sexist attitudes and behavior. The woman's voice sounds like that of Marjorie Adams, an attractive but naive graduate student. Weaver runs down the hall and finds Professor Murchie dying of stab wounds. His pants are down and his penis is exposed. Murchie's office window is open and Weaver sees a woman who resembles Adams running away. Weaver supposes that Adams killed Murchie while trying to fend off a sexual assault, and in a spur-of-the-moment decision to protect her, she tries to cleanse the office of fingerprints, removes a scarf that Adams apparently left behind, and leaves the building without calling the police. Weaver is eventually arrested for Murchie's murder. At this point the book becomes less a whodunit and more a will-she-be-convicted, and the story moves away from the Berkeley campus into several courtroom and prison scenes. Some literary critics now consider *Murder in the English Department* an archetypical example of feminist mystery fiction. With the exception of Matt Weitz, a gay member of the English department with whom Weaver has a mutually supportive relationship, all of the sympathetic characters in the story are female. Moreover, as a divorced, middle-aged academic struggling to achieve tenure, Weaver constantly does battle with people, including her own sister, who have difficulty coping with her aggressive feminism.

Valerie Miner was born in New York City. She received a B.A from the University of California at Berkeley in 1969 and an M.J. from that institution in 1970. A prominent feminist lecturer and writer, Miner was a lecturer in the field studies program at the University of California at Berkeley when *Murder in the English Department* was published. The book was her first mystery novel.

226. MURPHY, WARREN B. (B. 1933). *DEAD LETTER.* NEW YORK: POCKET BOOKS, 1982.

Frank Stevens, the multimillionaire president of an insurance company, believes that his daughter, Allison, is an innocent young lady of unblemished virtue. Allison is an undergraduate at "Waldo College" in Boston, and when she displays some apparent unhappiness while home on vacation, father Frank asks Julian ("Digger") Burroughs, a Las Vegas-based investigator with his firm, to look into the matter. It does not take Burroughs long after arriving in Boston to discover that Allison's father knows little about his daughter's life. Allison has just ended a torrid affair with Henry Hatcher, Waldo's married dean of students, and she now shares her bed with an unpleasant young man named Danny Gilligan, a fellow Waldo student whom she considers to be a genius. Meanwhile, someone is circulating letters on the Waldo campus containing the names of people who will be killed. Wally Strickland, the owner of a local saloon, already has died in a mysterious fall after his name appeared in a letter. Shortly after Burroughs's arrival Otis Redwing, a Native American professor of history who was identified for death, is killed in a hit-and-run incident. Then a new letter appears that identifies Allison Stevens as a near-future victim. A fast-moving private-eye novel, *Dead Letter* contains more action than most college mysteries, and most of its characters speak in brief sentences with words that convey high levels of cynicism. Philosophers may take particular interest in the scene, early in the story, in which the dissolute Burroughs, whose main motives for existing seem to be cigarettes and alcohol, engages two loutish male undergraduates in a bizarre conversation about the meaning of life.

Warren B. Murphy was born in Jersey City, New Jersey, and attended St. Peter's College. After an early career as a newspaperman, Murphy has written well over one hundred novels and screenplays. His screenplays include *The Eiger Sanction*, a 1975 motion picture starring Clint Eastwood. As a mystery writer Murphy is best known for his series of seventy-three novels featuring Remo Williams, also known as "The Destroyer." *Dead Letter* was the third in a four-novel "Digger" series written by Murphy in the 1980s.

227. TAYLOR, ANDREW (B. 1951). *CAROLINE MINISCULE.* LONDON: GOLLANCZ, 1982; NEW YORK: DODD, MEAD & CO., 1983.

The protagonist of this unconventional mystery is William Dougal, a graduate student in history at a university in London. The university is located near Russell Square. As the story begins Dougal enters the office of Dr. Gumper, his tutor, only to find him garrotted dead. Rather than ruin his evening by having to answer questions, Dougal leaves the scene without notifying the police, and outside the building he is approached by a stranger who identifies himself as James Hanbury. Dr. Gumper, so Hanbury tells Dougal, was being paid by Hanbury's unnamed employer to translate a passage of medieval script known as "Caroline Miniscule," and now that Gumper is unable to continue his assignment Hanbury inquires whether Dougal would be interested in taking up the task. The script, as Dougal quickly learns, may reveal the location of a cache of diamonds. From that point in the story Dougal, along with his girlfriend, Amanda, sets out to find the jewels, and he must outsmart, and sometimes eliminate, several nasty parties as he proceeds on his quest. The book sometimes wanders away from academic turf, but the first third of the story is set in and around the London university where Dougal is a student, and midway through the tale Dougal and Amanda journey to Cambridge. The plot of this detectionless tale offers many unusual twists and some derring-do, and Dougal emerges as both charming and thoroughly amoral.

Andrew Taylor was born in Hertfordshire, England, and educated at Emmanuel College, Cambridge. After an early career as a librarian, he became a full-time writer and has written more than twenty mystery novels. *Caroline Miniscule* was his first mystery. The book received the John Creasey Award and was shortlisted for an Edgar for best first mystery novel of 1982. William Dougal, the central character in *Caroline Miniscule*, has appeared in many subsequent Taylor novels. One of the more unusual and complex series-characters in mystery fiction, Dougal is one of very few fictional sleuths who is prone to commit murder while resolving mysteries. *Caroline Miniscule* was serialized for radio by the BBC.

228. DEXTER, (NORMAN) COLIN (B. 1930). *THE RIDDLE OF THE THIRD MILE.* NEW YORK: ST. MARTIN'S, 1983.

Oliver Maximilian Alexander Browne-Smith disappears. A widely disliked fellow of "Lonsdale College" at Oxford, Browne-Smith is known to be suffering from cancer. Concerned about Browne-Smith's welfare, the master of Lonsdale alerts Chief Inspector Morse of the Thames Valley Police. Morse is Colin Dexter's immensely popular series-character detective. Shortly after Morse learns that Browne-Smith is missing, a headless, handless, and legless corpse is found in an Oxford canal. Though absolute identification of the torso is impossible, from clothing on the body Morse believes that the mutilated corpse is that of the missing don, and his task, as he sees it, is to find Browne-Smith's killer. The plot of this mystery is both clever and intricate, and to reveal more would diminish the enjoyment of the book for prospective readers. It can be noted, however, that the story involves very serious faculty politics at Lonsdale College, and it relates to events that occurred during the North African campaign in World War II. Although some of the novel takes place in the Soho district of London, Morse and his faithful assistant, Sergeant Lewis, spend considerable time sleuthing at Lonsdale. As further food for the plates of college-mystery gourmands, at the beginning of the story there is a scene in which Browne-Smith and a panel of other Oxford dons decide upon the class of degrees to be awarded the next crop of university graduates.

The Riddle of the Third Mile was the sixth book in Colin Dexter's continuing Inspector Morse series. Three other Inspector Morse mysteries by Colin Dexter have entries in this bibliography. Those mysteries are *The Silent World of Nicholas Quinn* (190), *The Daughters of Cain* (386), and *Death Is Now My Neighbor* (422).

229. FOX, PETER (B. 1946). *THE TRAIL OF THE REAPER*. NEW YORK: ST. MARTIN'S, 1983. PUBLISHED IN ENGLAND AS *KENSINGTON GORE*. LONDON: MACMILLAN, 1983.

A killer, known to the police as "The Reaper," is stalking and murdering celebrities in London. Clearly a person of superior intelligence, The Reaper never uses the same method of murder twice, and he or she taunts the police by sending them obscure, crossword puzzle clues. Detective Inspector Jack Lamarre of New Scotland Yard is in charge of the case, and he is assisted by attractive Detective Sergeant Allison Prendergast. *The Trail of the Reaper* is structured so that two stories run simultaneously. Some of the book follows Lamarre and Prendergast as they detect, and some of it describes the mundane academic activities of a set of physicists, mathematicians, and computer scientists at London University's Imperial College. Of course, by the end of the tale the two stories come together and the identity of The Reaper is revealed. The police eventually trace the killer to the Imperial College mathematics building, but as they try to make an arrest the villain kills again. The many university scenes offer fascinating detail about the ways in which academic scientists comport themselves. For example, Professor Koenig encourages the students in his "Galois theory" course to interrupt his lectures with questions. He claims that if they do not understand what he is saying they will be wasting his time, which, as he informs his pupils, "is infinitely more valuable than yours." However, when a brave student asks for the clarification of a formula the professor insults her by responding that even his pet parakeet knows the answer to her inquiry.

A resident of England, Peter Fox holds a Ph.D. in mathematical physics. *The Trail of the Reaper* was his third mystery novel.

230. HARRIS, WILL. *THE BAY PSALM BOOK MURDER.* NEW YORK: WALKER, 1983.

Link Schofield, curator of special collections at the library of "Los Angeles University," is stabbed dead in his garage. A few dollars have been removed from his wallet, but a copy of *The Bay Psalm Book*, the first book printed in the American colonies, is still clutched in his hand. The police believe that Schofield was the victim of a common mugging, but Pearl Humphrey, Schofield's daughter, asks Clifford Dunbar to investigate. A professor of English at Los Angeles University, Dunbar is a recent widower. He also is a wealthy man from textbook writing. In preparation for starting a new life Dunbar has just resigned his post at the university, though he still has a few weeks left on the school's payroll as he detects in this novel. The focus of his sleuthing quickly becomes the authenticity of *The Bay Psalm Book* found at the scene of Schofield's death, and he spends considerable time at the university library and at the offices of the university's press. He is assisted by Mona Moore, a pretty proofreader for the press, and by the end of the story the two sleuths have become such close associates that Miss Moore has moved into Dunbar's home. Real-life professors of English may find two brief sections of the book insensitive. A decorated Vietnam combat veteran, Dunbar twice fights off professional assassins who are bent on ending his life. After both events neither the police nor his assailants can believe that he really teaches English.

When *The Bay Psalm Book Murder* was published Will Harris was a senior researcher at the Rand Corporation in California. The book won Harris an Edgar Award for the best first mystery novel published in 1983. Harris's detective, Professor Clifford Dunbar, served as sleuth one more time, in a nonacademic mystery titled *Timor Mortis* (New York: Walker, 1986).

231. HUTTON, JOHN (HARWOOD) (B. 1928). *ACCIDENTAL CRIMES.* LONDON: BODLEY HEAD, 1983; NEW YORK: NEW AMERICAN LIBRARY, 1985.

More a character study than a detective mystery, *Accidental Crimes* chronicles the misfortunes of Conrad Nield, a sour, burnt-out tutor at the "Alderman Robertson College of Education" in the north of England. One of Nield's academic duties is to conduct field supervisions of student-teachers, and in that capacity he routinely journeys to towns at some distance from the college. When two young women are murdered, and their bodies left along a road that Nield often travels, the police begin to suspect him of the killings. During one of his more recent trips Nield attended a pornographic movie and gave a ride to a female hitchhiker, and when he unsuccessfully tries to deny engaging in those (and other) embarrassing activities, the police respond by searching his home and by asking his wife and faculty colleagues questions about his tastes and movements. The book offers several scenes at Alderman Robertson, a dreary institution that is housed in an eighteenth-century mansion, and on several other occasions it depicts Nield, who is something of a bully in his capacity as tutor, evaluating fledgling teachers in primary and secondary schools. The book also contains a noteworthy episode in which Nield, during one of his supervision trips, tries to pick up a woman for purposes of sex. Although Nield hopes to keep his identity a secret, the woman turns out to be a former student who instantly recognizes him.

John Harwood Hutton was born in Manchester, England. He received B.A. and M.A. degrees from the University of North Wales. After a decade of teaching English at a girls' grammar school in Ruabon, Wales, Hutton became a teacher of English at Cartrefle College in Wrexham, Wales. He was a senior lecturer at Cartrefle College when *Accidental Crimes,* his second mystery novel, was published.

232. LARSEN, GAYLORD (B. 1932). *TROUBLE CROSSING THE PYRENEES.* VENTURA, CALIF.: REGAL PRESS, 1983. ALSO PUBLISHED AS *AN EDUCATED DEATH.* NEW YORK: BALLANTINE, 1986.

The victim in this curious mystery is Ralph Pangbourne, an internationally known geologist at "El Rio University" near San Diego. Professor Pangbourne's death occurs during a medieval fair that is being held as a fund-raising exercise on the El Rio campus. At dawn one morning the professor is found dead in a set of stocks that are being used as props for the fair. His head is covered with a plastic bag and his death apparently was the result of suffocation. Scattered around the stocks are placards, printed in old English script, that proclaim Pangbourne, among other things, a "Boring Lecturer" and a "Giver of Unfair Tests." Professor Pangbourne was not a nice man and had many enemies, hence the story offers a plethora of suspects. Sylvia, the professor's estranged wife, might have been the murderer. Or perhaps it was Jeremy Bruce, a graduate student whom the professor continually harassed with cruel practical jokes. Or maybe it was John Mumford or Wendel Hazard, two El Rio deans with whom Pangbourne had bitter battles over curriculum matters. Although the police are involved in the case, the real detection is accomplished by Henry Garrett, a CIA agent. Garrett has come to El Rio to try to reclaim a listening device that the CIA lent to Professor Pangbourne for underwater mapping of the ocean floor, but which Pangbourne refused to return. Publication of *Trouble Crossing the Pyrenees* was underwritten by Gospel Literature International (GLINT), and at several points in the text the main characters discuss weighty matters having to do with the power of spiritual renewal and with the nature of good and evil. With regard to the latter, Professor Pangbourne competes well with any professorial reprobate in college-mystery fiction. As one example of his nastiness, Pangbourne once became aware that a rival was about to publish a book that would contest some of his theories. He then had a friend at the rival's publishing firm cause the book to be issued with a Library of Congress designation of PZ 24, the call number for children's fairy tales. Pangbourne's action not only caused the book to be shelved in the juvenile sections of libraries, it also made the book a joke among geologists and ensured that its arguments would never be taken seriously.

Gaylord Larsen is a resident of California who has written many television and film screenplays. He also has done extensive film editing. *Trouble Crossing the Pyrenees* was his second mystery novel.

233. MACLEOD, CHARLOTTE (B. 1922). *SOMETHING THE CAT DRAGGED IN.* GARDEN CITY, N.Y.: DOUBLE-DAY, 1983.

The cat in the title of this merry mystery is Edmund, who lives in the "Balaclava," Massachusetts, home of Mrs. Betsy Lomax. The "something" is the toupee of Professor Herbert Ungley, a lodger in Mrs. Lomax's home. Ungley, who is retired after a long career teaching history at "Balaclava Agricultural College," is not dragged into Mrs. Lomax's kitchen along with his hairpiece, and his corpse is soon found, bloody and beaten, behind the clubhouse of a fraternal organization known as the Balaclavian Society. The sleuth in this story is Balaclava Agricultural College Professor of Horticulture Peter Shandy, a popular Charlotte Macleod series-character detective. Before Shandy can identify the book's villain, another murder occurs. Ruth Smutz, the campaign manager for a local congressional candidate, is found strangled dead on the college campus. The motives for the killings in the story are not academic, but there are many scenes on the college grounds and many college characters, all of them offbeat and addled, play important parts in the story. Readers who follow the exploits of fictional college presidents will want to pay special attention to gruff, impetuous President Thorkjeld Svenson of Balaclava. A huge man, who might be "mistaken for a rampaging *Tyrannosaurus Rex*" when angry, President Svenson at one point in the novel rips in two a copy of the Boston telephone directory, and after the unsettling death of Ruth Smutz, he personally leads a group of students, whom he has transformed into security guards mounted atop college horses, on patrols of the campus.

Three other Peter Shandy mysteries, *Rest You Merry* (198), *The Luck Runs Out* (201), and *An Owl Too Many* (337) also appear in this bibliography.

234. SINGER, SHELLY [ROCHELLE SINGER (B. 1939)]. *SAMSON'S DEAL*. NEW YORK: ST. MARTIN'S, 1983.

Margaret Harley dies of a broken neck when she falls, apparently by accident, from a deck at the rear of her home. Her husband, John Harley, is a professor of political science at the University of California at Berkeley. Professor Harley thinks that foul play may be involved, and he pays Jake Samson, a private detective, $10,000 to investigate his wife's death. Samson has several promising lines of inquiry to follow. A radical group calling itself the Campus Organization for the Return of Political Sanity has targeted Harley for his insufficiently leftist political beliefs, and it has taken to picketing his office and otherwise harassing him. Margaret Harley was known to have made enemies when, before her marriage, she was a well-known artist in Berkeley. And what about Rebecca Lilly, the professor's mistress? Could she have killed Margaret? As Samson begins to earn his fee, an arsonist sets fire to Professor Harley's office. Harley is almost killed in the blaze, but he is able to save the manuscript for his new book about the absurdity of political systems. Thanks to its several extended scenes on the Berkeley campus, *Samson's Deal* qualifies for inclusion in this bibliography, but it is not the most academic of college mysteries. A good deal of the fast-moving private-eye tale takes place in the city of Berkeley and elsewhere in the San Francisco area, and while some Berkeley students play significant roles in the story, John Harley is the only Berkeley faculty member with a significant part.

A resident of Oakland, California, when *Samson's Deal* was published, Rochelle Singer was born in Minneapolis and earned a B.A. from the University of Minnesota in 1961. She has worked as a journalist, editor, antiques restorer, welfare worker, and advertising copywriter. She also has been the owner of a Chicago boutique. *Samson's Deal* marked the debut of private investigator Jake Samson. He has gone on to detect in several subsequent Rochelle Singer novels.

235. THOMAS, DONALD (B. 1935). *MAD HATTER SUMMER.* NEW YORK: VIKING, 1983. PUBLISHED IN ENGLAND AS *BELLADONNA.* LONDON: MACMILLAN, 1984.

This skillfully written novel is set in Oxford in 1879, and its central character is the Reverend Charles Lutwidge Dodgson, a senior member of Christ Church College. Now better known as Lewis Carroll, the author of *Alice's Adventures in Wonderland,* Dodgson in 1879 was the subject of considerable rumor in Oxford because of his fondness for sketching and taking photographs of nude young girls. In *Mad Hatter Summer*, Dodgson becomes a suspect in a murder case. The badly beaten corpse of Major Dicky Tiptoe, a former military officer turned professional extortionist, is found in the River Isis. Letters and photographs in Tiptoe's possession suggest that he may have been blackmailing Dodgson, and it is possible that Dodgson killed Tiptoe to bring the blackmail to an end. The police investigator is Inspector Alfred Swain from Scotland Yard in London. As he detects, Swain develops a respect for Dodgson's gentleness and intelligence. In addition to the Reverend Dodgson, the story includes several highly placed real-life British characters of the period, and thanks to Major Tiptoe's dastardly efforts readers can learn about some of those characters' guilty secrets. There are many scenes at the university. Students of absurd faculty behavior will appreciate chapter 6.

The fellows of Christ Church, some of the most accomplished men of their time, stage an extended and sometimes-bitter debate over the management of the college's wine supply.

Donald Thomas was born in Cornwall, England. He holds a B.A. and an M.A. from Oxford. Thomas taught English literature at the University of Wales before becoming a full-time writer. As a visiting lecturer he also taught in the United States at Hamline and American Universities. Sometimes employing the pseudonym Francis Selwyn, Thomas has written poetry and mainstream novels as well as mysteries. His best-known work is the mainstream novel *White Hotel* (New York: Viking, 1981). *Mad Hatter Summer* was the first of three Donald Thomas mysteries in which Inspector Swain serves as sleuth.

236. WARD, ELIZABETH C(AMPBELL) (B. 1936). *COAST HIGHWAY 1.* NEW YORK: WALKER, 1983.

This unusual mystery is narrated by Jake Martin, an associate professor of English at the University of California at Irvine. Disheartened over his failure to win promotion, Martin has taken to brooding and boozing. When a student named Jennifer approaches him for help, instead of finding out the nature of her problem Martin tells her of his own troubles instead. Then Jennifer's body turns up, shot by an apparent sniper, on the patio outside his home. A few days later, a young man named Petersen is also shot dead. Petersen had been Martin's graduate assistant and had known something about the nature of Jennifer's difficulties. Professor Martin sets out to retrace Jennifer's recent footsteps, in part to identify her killer, in part because he fears that the murderer may target him next, and in part because his failure to come to Jennifer's assistance has left him guilt-ridden. The first third of the book is set on and near the Irvine campus. The remainder takes Martin from Tijuana to San Francisco and to many places in between. At one juncture he meets a man named Hosford on the campus of Stanford. One of Martin's former college classmates, Hosford is now campaigning for the presidency of the United States. Since Hosford was expelled from Stanford for cheating on an examination, while Martin was a brilliant scholar, the professor wonders about the perverse fates that have brought the two men to such different points in life.

Elizabeth C. Ward was born in Los Angeles and received a B.A. from Stanford in 1958. At the time *Coast Highway 1* was published she lived in Newport Beach, California. *Coast Highway 1* was her second mystery novel.

237. WRIGHT, ERIC (B. 1929). *THE NIGHT THE GODS SMILED.* NEW YORK: SCRIBNER'S, 1983.

Accompanied by four of his colleagues from the English department, Professor David Summers, of "Douglas College" in Toronto, attends an academic conference in Montreal. He does not spend all of his time listening to scholarly papers. One night he attends a strip show and consumes a large quantity of alcohol. The next morning he is discovered dead in his hotel room, his skull fractured by a whiskey bottle, and a glass with lipstick on its rim is found sitting on a table. The detective in this story is Inspector Charlie Salter of the Toronto police, an Eric Wright series-character. At first, Salter suspects that a prostitute may have dispatched the professor, but when he begins interrogating Summers's four fellow conference goers, he learns that all of them had ample motive for the crime. One of those individuals, Professor Dunkley, had been carrying on a bitter feud with Summers for so many years that no one at the college, including Dunkley, can remember what originally prompted it. To complicate matters, Jane Homer, Douglas's dean of women, suddenly tells Salter that she, too, was in Montreal at the time of Summers's death. Miss Homer, who once taught in the English department, admits to an annual ritual of going each year to the conference, wherever it might be held, to engage in a once-a-year sexual tryst with the professor. The portraits of the academics in this novel are especially well drawn, and because the author offers considerable detail about Douglas College, a new university in Toronto's downtown, the book also contains interesting background material about Canadian higher education.

Eric Wright was born in England and migrated to Canada at the age of twenty-two. He received a B.A. from the University of Toronto in 1957 and an M.A. from Toronto in 1960. *The Night the Gods Smiled* was his first mystery novel and the first in a continuing series of very successful Charlie Salter novels. *The Night the Gods Smiled* won both the Ellis and Creasey first-novel awards. Another of Wright's Charlie Salter mysteries, *Death by Degrees* (376), appears later in this bibliography. During most of his writing career Wright has taught English at Ryerson Polytechnic in Toronto. In an interview, Wright once responded to a question about whether his often-negative portraits of professors alienate his departmental colleagues at Ryerson (*Contemporary Authors*, vol. 132. Detroit: Gale, 1991, p. 479). Wright told the interviewer that he has managed to convince his Ryerson colleagues that he models his professorial characters not after his present-day peers but after professors who taught him during his days as a student at Toronto.

238. CROSS, AMANDA [CAROLYN GOLD HEILBRUN (B. 1926)]. *SWEET DEATH, KIND DEATH*. NEW YORK: DUTTON, 1984.

This novel takes Professor Kate Fansler, Amanda Cross's celebrated series-character detective, from her home university in New York City to "Clare College," a school for women outside Boston. After several previous adventures Fansler has a reputation in academic circles for her mystery solving, and in this story she is asked by Clare College's president, a young woman named Norton, to investigate a death that has occurred recently on the Clare campus. The deceased was Patrice Umphelby, a world-famous novelist and historian, who was found drowned in a campus lake. The local police are content to believe that Umphelby committed suicide, but she was an outspoken woman, with a pronounced capacity to irritate, and she had many enemies. President Norton wants Fansler to discover whether Umphelby really killed herself and, if so, why she did it. Alternatively, the president would like Fansler to identify the killer if she finds that Umphelby was murdered. Under the cover of serving as an outside member on a Clare committee investigating the feasibility of a gender studies program, Fansler commutes between New York and Clare College, where she interacts with and assesses many members of the school's faculty and, in some cases, meets their spouses as well. The book offers insights into the difficult status of American women's colleges after the coeducationing, in the 1960s and 1970s, of traditionally all-male bastions of higher learning. For her part, Professor Fansler displays her usual penchant for quotation dropping, her fondness for liquor (but not sherry) and cigarettes, and her enduring reluctance to suffer fools gladly.

Sweet Death, Kind Death, was the seventh novel in Carolyn Heilbrun's Professor Kate Fansler continuing, twelve-novel series. Entries for two earlier Kate Fansler mysteries, *Poetic Justice* (156) and *Death in a Tenured Position* (211), can be found in this bibliography. Four later Kate Fansler novels also appear in the bibliography. Those novels are *No Word from Winifred* (264), *A Trap for Fools* (308), *An Imperfect Spy* (402), and *The Puzzled Heart* (456).

239. EULO, ELENA YATES. *ICE ORCHIDS.* NEW YORK: BERKLEY PRESS, 1984.

Ice Orchids is part mystery and part science-fiction thriller. It is set at "Triesius College" in the coldest, most remote part of upstate New York. Unique among the institutions represented in this bibliography, Triesius admits only young women with IQs above 170. The school's admission process includes an intense three-day physical exam, during part of which the young female geniuses are rendered unconscious and awake feeling "sore on the inside." The prologue of the book graphically describes the rape/murder of a Triesius student, hence the initial mystery interest in the story has to do with the identity of the perpetrator. However, as the novel continues readers are quickly drawn into a more complex puzzle concerning the nature of the college itself. What are the goals of the faculty? What sort of experiments are they conducting? What is happening to the Triesius students? And who is providing the financial support for this very strange outpost of higher education? Although the novel is not a conventional detective story, the answers to the above questions are ultimately revealed by the information-gathering labors of Beth Allen, an inquisitive Triesius student (with an IQ of 180) whose efforts are prompted by a need for self-preservation. Some readers may appreciate the portrait of Dr. Frederick Alan Randelar, a world-famous geneticist who directs a top-secret research project at Triesius. Dr. Randelar was only an average student in high school, but his brain suddenly "woke up" one day while he was attending a theoretical physics class at a middling state university. He immediately transferred to Cornell and stopped using his first name ("if I were to call myself Frederick the electric current would shut off."). Reinvented as Alan Randelar, he eventually acquired a medical degree as well as a Ph.D., and he now considers himself so mentally superior that he need not follow the conventional social and legal codes that constrain lesser mortals.

Ice Orchids was Elena Yates Eulo's first book-length work of fiction.

240. HARRIS, CHARLAINE (B. 1951). *A SECRET RAGE.* BOSTON: HOUGHTON MIFFLIN, 1984.

The narrator of this grim novel about campus rape is Nickie Callaghan, a twenty-seven-year-old woman who gives up a modeling career in New York to finish her undergraduate education at "Houghton College" in "Knolls," Tennessee. Shortly after she arrives at Houghton, Callaghan becomes the third victim of a knife-wielding rapist who is terrorizing women at the college. The man's identity is unknown because he never lets his victims see his face. Soon another woman is stabbed dead, presumably by the same person. In concert with Barbara Tucker, a Houghton admissions counselor who was the rapist's second victim, Callaghan draws up a list of nine campus men who might be the perpetrator, and she begins to gather information about each of her suspects. The list includes several professors and administrators, among them Jeffrey Simmons, Houghton's youngish president. *A Secret Rage* has little of the humor often associated with college mysteries, but it is unequaled in the subgenre for reflecting the anguish and anger felt by women who have been subjected to sexual assault. Indeed, at the end of the story Callaghan, Tucker, and a female companion capture the guilty party after a vicious fight. Only the intervention of a male, who comes upon the struggle after the rapist has been subdued, prevents Callaghan and Tucker from killing the man who attacked them.

Charlaine Harris was born in Tunica, Mississippi, and received a B.A. from Southwestern at Memphis. *A Secret Rage* was her second mystery novel.

241. HORNIG, DOUG (B. 1943). *FOUL SHOT.* NEW YORK: SCRIBNER'S, 1984.

Leigh Majors, an undergraduate at the University of Virginia, disappears. Fearing that various extended family scandals will come to light if they notify the police, Miss Majors's parents ask Loren Swift, a private detective, to find her. The wisecracking Swift, who narrates the story, does find Leigh, but not before he becomes a suspect in the murder of an insurance investigator from California who was trying to pry open some of the Majors family's secrets. Before her disappearance, Leigh Majors had a relationship with Delmos Venable, the black star of the Virginia basketball team, and as Swift, by his sleuthing, stirs the passions of those who oppose interracial couples, Venable comes close to death when someone tries unsuccessfully to shoot him. Meantime, Ward Williams, a black civil rights activist, is stabbed dead in prison after being falsely charged with raping a white woman, and Charlottesville erupts in racial disturbances. Although *Foul Shot* is, in essence, the story of a wealthy family in the process of dissolution, the book contains many scenes on and near the University of Virginia campus, and it offers a speaking part to Virginia basketball coach Storm Taylor. Moreover, the last two pages of the book are given over to a running account of a University of Virginia versus North Carolina basketball game, and

Foul Shot is the only college mystery in which North Carolina's legendary Dean Smith can be observed coaching his way toward the Basketball Hall of Fame.

Doug Hornig was born in New York City and received a B.A. from George Washington University in 1965. *Foul Shot* was the first of what has become a series of mysteries featuring private-eye Loren Swift.

242. JORDAN, CATHLEEN. *A CAROL IN THE DARK*. NEW YORK: WALKER, 1984.

This several-stranded mystery is set during the Christmas season at "Crosscreek University" in "Crosscreek," South Dakota. The frozen corpse of Tom Donahue, a junior member of the English department, is found late one night in a field outside town. His car, with an empty gas tank, is discovered three miles away. The police assume that Donohue ran out of fuel and then foolishly tried to walk to safety in a windchill of seventy-five degrees below zero. Donohue's friend Will Gray, a member of the history department, suspects foul play, and he takes on the role of sleuth in the story. A few nights later, at a Christmas party held in the home of a retired professor of Greek named Will Mellon, a killing occurs that is manifestly murder. Lucy Mellon, the professor's undergraduate niece, is beaten dead in a deserted area of the house. Her uncle, presumably attacked by the same person, is badly injured. As matters develop, Will Gray finds himself following multiple leads, some of them having to do with the popular Tom Donohue's love life, and some of them having to do with the lost fortune of elderly Maisie Moffat, a Crosscreek resident and a major university benefactor. Once a wealthy heiress, Mrs. Moffat recently squandered much of her money by backing a play that failed on Broadway. Now, in order to retain her lifestyle and to continue her donations, she has asked several university people to help her locate additional financial assets that her late father is thought to have hid decades ago somewhere in Crosscreek. Many members of the Crosscreek faculty, as well as many Crosscreek students, make appearances in the book. The crimes in the novel are, in part, the product of an understandable motivation; the villain's misdeeds are designed to raise the money needed to pay the expenses of a daughter who attends an Ivy League college.

Cathleen Jordan was an editor of *Alfred Hitchcock's Mystery Magazine* when *A Carol in the Dark*, her first novel, was published.

243. KELLY, NORA [NORA HICKSON (B. 1945)]. *IN THE SHADOW OF KING'S.* NEW YORK: ST. MARTIN'S, 1984.

Gillian Adams returns to the University of Cambridge to give a guest lecture. Adams, who earned a doctorate in history at Cambridge, is now a professor at the "University of the Pacific Northwest" in Vancouver. Her talk is held in the Chetwynd Room at King's College. She is introduced by Professor Alistair Greenwood, Cambridge's most celebrated historian, who then takes a seat on the platform. Adams's lecture is well received, but her triumph quickly turns to tragedy. As the audience applauds at the end of her presentation, someone shoots Professor Greenwood. He topples out of his chair, bleeds profusely from a chest wound, and dies as Adams desperately tries to keep him alive with artificial respiration. Unfortunately for Greenwood's killer, Chief Inspector Edward Gisborne of Scotland Yard has come from London to attend the lecture. Inspector Gisborne is Professor Adams's significant other. As the story unwinds, Gisborne conducts an official inquiry and Adams assists in unofficial ways until the murderer is brought to justice. The book is rich with Cambridge atmosphere and it takes its two detectives to many Cambridge locales. For his part, Professor Greenwood emerges as one of college-mystery fiction's more maliciously offensive academics. Early in the story he holds a luncheon in his home. The gathering, held in honor of Professor Adams, is described at length. Greenwood, the master of the venomous comment, insults and angers all his guests, thereby giving many of them motive for his murder.

Nora Hickson was born in New Jersey and grew up in New York City. She has a B.A. from the University of British Columbia and a Ph.D. from Simon Fraser University. She also studied at Cambridge. At the time *In the Shadow of King's* was published Hickson lived in Vancouver, British Columbia, where she was a professor of history. *In the Shadow of King's* was Hickson's first Professor Gillian Adams mystery. *My Sister's Keeper* (354), *Bad Chemistry* (367), and *Old Wounds* (463), three later Professor Gillian Adams mysteries, also appear in this bibliography.

244. LANGTON, JANE (B. 1922). *EMILY DICKINSON IS DEAD.* NEW YORK: ST. MARTIN'S, 1984.

The University of Massachusetts and Amherst College jointly sponsor a symposium on Emily Dickinson. The conference is to mark the one-hundredth anniversary of the poet's death in 1886. The meeting does not go smoothly. Groups of women noisily protest the exclusion of women from the list of speakers. A mysterious fire occurs in a University of Massachusetts dormitory and two male students die in the conflagration. Winifred Gaw, a grossly obese graduate student at Massachusetts, is found dead in Emily Dickinson's bedroom at the Dickinson Homestead. Alison Grove, a sophomore English major at Massachusetts, disappears. A young woman of rare beauty, Miss Grove is the favorite student of several of her professors. Furthermore, Professor Peter Wiggins, who has come to the symposium from the "University of Central Arizona" in the remote town of "Pancake Flats," is attempting to convince the conference attendees that he is in possession of a rare photograph of Dickinson, and, at the same time, he is trying to use the conference to obtain a new academic job. The sleuth in the story is Jane Langton's series-character detective Homer Kelly. A former police detective who is now a distinguished Thoreau scholar, Kelly is spending a semester as a visiting professor at nearby Mt. Holyoke College, and he attends the symposium to lend support to his old friend Professor Owen Kraznick, the world's leading Dickinson authority and one of the conference organizers. Although *Emily Dickinson Is Dead* contains several mysteries for Kelly to solve, it is less a conventional detective tale and more a highly satirical novel of incident and imagery. The author offers scene after scene in which her characters, almost all of them academics obsessed with Emily Dickinson, with Dickinson scholarship, and/or with personal advancement, behave in ways that are absurd and sometimes life-threatening. She also illustrates the book with exterior and interior sketches of many of the Amherst, Massachusetts, places—including the Dickinson Homestead—that figure in her story.

Three other Homer Kelly mysteries by Jane Langton appear in this bibliography. Those mysteries are *The Memorial Hall Murder* (196), *The Shortest Day: Murder at the Revels* (412), and *Dead as a Dodo* (431).

245. LEMARCHAND, ELIZABETH (WHARTON) (B. 1906). *LIGHT THROUGH GLASS.* LONDON: PIATKUS, 1984; NEW YORK: WALKER, 1986.

When John Paterson announces plans to take early retirement at age fifty-five, there is rejoicing at the "Minstow College of Education" somewhere in the northern parts of England. The head of the school's geology/geography department, Paterson is an acid-tongued, self-centered individual who is thoroughly disliked by everyone on the campus. One person who eagerly awaits Paterson's exit is Ronald Grimshaw, the deputy department head. Not only will Grimshaw be free from Paterson's constant browbeating, he also has a good chance to succeed Paterson as head of the department. One day, just as the school's week-long October vacation is about to begin, Paterson tells Grimshaw that he has reconsidered; he will stay on as department head until mandatory retirement at age sixty. The next day Dr. Paterson's van is spotted at the bottom of a thousand-foot rock face, and his corpse is discovered on a ledge halfway down the cliff. The first detective on the case is Charles Nevinson of the local police, but just as Nevinson concludes that he has a murder, not an accidental death, on his hands, he is badly burned when he opens a letter bomb. The detection in the novel is then taken up by Superintendent Tom Pollard and Inspector Gregory Toye of Scotland Yard. In the course of their inquiries Pollard and Toye make many trips to the Minstow campus, and in addition to Ronald Grimshaw they identify several other college suspects. They also spend time with the members of Dr. Paterson's extended family, and *Light through Glass* is the only college mystery that includes the complete family tree of a faculty victim. The book also contains a map of Minstow College and a roster of the main characters in the story.

Elizabeth Lemarchand was born in Devonshire, England. She received an M.A. from the University of Exeter in 1929. Lemarchand spent thirty-two years as a teacher and headmistress before retiring in her early sixties to a very successful second career as a mystery writer. Lemarchand is best known for her genteel, classic British whodunits, many of which feature the detection of Superintendent Pollard and Inspector Toye. *Light through Glass* was Lemarchand's fifteenth Pollard-Toye novel.

246. O'MARIE, SISTER CAROL ANNE. *A NOVENA FOR MURDER*. NEW YORK: SCRIBNER'S, 1984.

The sleuth in this story is Sister Mary Helen, a septuagenarian nun. After fifty years in the classrooms of parish schools, Sister Mary Helen has been forcibly retired to "Mount St. Francis College for Women" in San Francisco. There she is assigned to do research for Professor Phillip Villanueva, an immigrant from Portugal who heads the school's history department. Sister Mary Helen is not long at Mount St. Francis before Villanueva is murdered, and it is she who finds him, dead of a crushed skull, in his office. A few days later Sister Mary Helen comes upon another body, this one in the college chapel. The second corpse belongs to Joanna Alves, the sister of Professor Villanueva's secretary. Readers might assume that the discovery of two corpses would be enough excitement for an elderly nun, but they would be underestimating Sister Mary Helen. Invigorated by the murders, and informed by a lifetime of reading detective whodunits, she sets out to help the police find the villain or villains. She conducts library research, collects physical evidence from crime scenes, interviews suspects, and survives a dangerous face-to-face encounter with a drunken college groundskeeper whom she thinks may want to murder her. *A Novena for Murder* is set almost entirely at Mount St. Francis, and it includes many of the school's faculty and staff among its characters. The evildoers in the case are employed by the college, but fortunately for Mount St. Francis's academic reputation, the motive for the killings proves to be unrelated to the school's educational function.

Sister Carol Anne O'Marie was born in San Francisco. She entered the Order of Sisters of St. Joseph of Carondelet in 1951. She received a B.A. from Mount St. Mary's College in 1960 and an M.A.T. from that institution in 1973. She has worked as an elementary school teacher and principal, as the director of a homeless shelter for women, and at the time *A Novena for Murder* was published she was director of development at Carondelet High School in California. *A Novena for Murder* was the first in what was to become a successful series of mysteries starring Sister Mary Helen.

247. SILVER, VICTORIA. *DEATH OF A HARVARD FRESHMAN.* NEW YORK: BANTAM, 1984.

The sleuth in this mystery is Lauren Adler, a first-year student at Harvard. A young Jewish woman from New Jersey, Adler finds herself romantically attracted to Russell Bernard, one of eleven students in a freshman seminar she is taking on the Russian Revolution. Bernard is an African American from Atlanta who, in keeping with the overachieving nature of Harvard students, plays soccer and the violin and already has published fiction in *The New Yorker*. Bernard's corpse is soon found floating in the Charles River, and the person who killed him apparently wanted to make certain he was dead. The villain crushed Bernard's skull with a heavy object, stabbed him three times, and shot him through the heart. Because her seminar group has just finished discussing the multiple methods used to kill Rasputin, Adler deduces that a student copycat killer from the class dispatched Bernard, and she sets out to identify which of the nine possible killers in the seminar is the actual murderer. She is assisted in her detection by Michael Hunt, a "delicate" young man who is her best friend at Harvard. Hunt, who despises the student engineers and football players who populate the dormitory in which he lives, brews tea in a British china teapot decorated with roses and covers his bed with a baby blue silk comforter. Adler and Hunt successfully identify Bernard's killer, but before they do so another member of the seminar, Tracy Nicholson, is shot dead on the Cambridge Common. A young woman from Chicago who had "enough sexual energy to sink a ship," Miss Nicholson carried a pistol for self-protection while pursuing her Harvard education, and the police discover that the gun used to murder her was her own weapon. Professor Tatiana Baranova, the director of the Russian Revolution seminar and the only tenured woman in the Harvard history department, plays a role in the story. The other major characters are all Harvard undergraduates.

Victoria Silver graduated from Radcliffe and was a resident of San Francisco when *Death of a Harvard Freshman* was published. Another Silver mystery with Lauren Adler in the role of sleuth, *Death of a Radcliffe Roommate* (272), appears in this bibliography.

248. CARLSON, P(ATRICIA) M(CELROY) (B. 1940). *AUDITION FOR MURDER*. NEW YORK: AVON, 1985.

Professional actors Nick and Lisette O'Connor are hired to spend a semester at "Hargate College" as artists in residence. Hargate College is in upstate New York near Binghamton. The O'Connors are to teach acting classes and star in a production of *Hamlet*. Lisette O'Connor has a history of drug use and mental instability, and when someone at Hargate drops her picture in a urinal and starts leaving other threatening signs and symbols, she becomes increasingly anxious. More a suspense novel than a conventional detective story, *Audition for Murder* teases its readers by keeping them guessing about Lisette O'Connor's ultimate fate. Several Hargate faculty members figure prominently in the plot, as do many of the college's students. The person who finally resolves matters is Maggie Ryan, a vibrant and independent-minded English major, and it is she, along with Nick O'Connor, who apprehends the villain of the piece in a late-in-the-story bit of derring-do. The book, which is set in the mid-1960s, offers a wealth of detail about the staging of a college play, and readers can learn how Hargate College employs theatrical productions as part of its fund-raising.

Patricia McElroy Carlson was born of American parents in Guatemala City, Guatemala. Her father was an engineer and her mother a teacher. She received B.A., M.A., and Ph.D. degrees from Cornell. From 1973 to 1978 she was an instructor and lecturer in psychology and human development at Cornell. *Audition for Murder* was her first mystery novel. Maggie Ryan, the sleuth in *Audition for Murder*, became a series-character detective. Three later Maggie Ryan novels have entries in this bibliography. Those novels are *Murder Is Academic* (249), *Murder Is Pathological* (262), and *Murder Misread* (330). At the time her Maggie Ryan mysteries were being written, Patricia McElroy Carlson lived in Bloomington, Indiana, where she was the wife of a professor.

249. CARLSON, P(ATRICIA) M(CELROY) (B. 1940). *MURDER IS ACADEMIC*. NEW YORK: AVON, 1985.

The protagonist of this adroitly crafted mystery is Maggie Ryan, a graduate student in statistics at a large university in "Laconia," New York. A young woman of many talents, Ryan is an accomplished flutist and gymnast as well as an ace at number crunching. A serial rapist-murderer is killing women near the campus, and Ryan, as well as everyone else at the university, is increasingly concerned. Ryan joins a group known as WAR (Women against Rape) sponsored by psychology professor Jane Freeman, and she and the other members of the organization hear presentations on rape and learn to protect themselves from potential rapists. Nevertheless, Jackie Edwards, a member of WAR and one of Professor Freeman's graduate students, is killed in what seems to be one more in the series of sexual attacks, and then Maggie Ryan herself barely escapes becoming an additional victim. The rapist-killer is arrested after his attempt on Ryan, and the story would seem to be over. However, Ryan learns that another villain lurks on the campus, and in the last few chapters of the book she brings this loathsome person to an unusual, but fully academic, form of justice. The story is set in 1968, and real events of the year, including the assassinations of Martin Luther King Jr. and Robert Kennedy, are used as a backdrop.

Three other Maggie Ryan mysteries by P. M. Carlson appear in this bibliography. Those mysteries are *Audition for Murder* (248), *Murder Is Pathological* (262), and *Murder Misread* (330).

250. FRASER, ANTONIA (PAKENHAM) (B. 1932). *OXFORD BLOOD.* NEW YORK: NORTON, 1985.

Megalith Television in London plans a documentary on Britain's "Golden Lads and Girls"—Oxford undergraduates who are the sons and daughters of the ultrawealthy. Jemima Shore, Megalith's ace reporter, is assigned to the project, but because she has little sympathy for the overprivileged she is initially unenthusiastic about her assignment. Shore's interest grows, however, when she learns that the lineage of one superrich Oxford student, the loutish Viscount Ivo Charles Iverstone Saffron, may not be what he thinks it is, and when Ian Marcus, another Oxford undergraduate, dies after mysteriously falling down a steep staircase in "Rochester College." Then, when someone makes an attempt on Viscount Saffron's life, Shore becomes convinced that some good journalistic sleuthing may yield her a television program capable of getting very high ratings. Although part of this tale takes place away from the university, while Shore is following the wealthy to their homes and haunts, the book has more than enough university scenes to qualify as a college mystery. The focus is on the undergraduate milieu, and most of the affluent students whom Shore meets and interviews have nicknames such as "Bim," "Tiggie," and "Muffet." The story also includes a professor, named Claud Mossbanker, who was once a British intelligence agent. Mossbanker, who is known as "Proffy" to his students, has a wife and eight children in North Oxford. To escape the chaos in his home the professor spends as much time as he can at raucous undergraduate parties where he can relax in the relative quiet.

Antonia Fraser was born in London. She holds B.A. and M.A. degrees in history from Oxford. Among her many activities, she has been the wife of a member of the British Parliament, a television broadcaster, a biographer of British royalty, and the writer of the popular Jemima Shore series of mysteries. *Oxford Blood* was her fifth Jemima Shore novel.

251. GILLESPIE, ROBERT B(RYNE) (B. 1917). *HEADS YOU LOSE.* NEW YORK: DODD, MEAD & CO, 1985.

David Black is a divorced professor of law at "Stuyvesant University," an Ivy League institution in New York City. Professor Black's private practice has made him a millionaire, and he owns a large house on Long Island to which he often invites some of his favorite students for weekends of sun, booze, drugs, and sex. One particular

Sunday morning, after a Saturday night party that was highlighted by cottage cheese mixed with hallucinogens, Dave is found in two pieces. His body is located behind the house of his next-door neighbor, retired advertising executive Ralph Simmons. His head is discovered protruding from an ice bucket in the nearby home of Dick O'Kane, a former right fielder for the New York Mets. The colorful story contains detection by the local police, but the attention of the book's readers is focused on the amateur sleuthing of Ralph Simmons. Simmons is prompted to do his own investigation because he knows the police consider him a suspect. As it happens, five law students (three of them female) were staying over at the Black residence, as were Susan Bollinger, a beautiful former student, and Black's nineteen-year-old son, Oliver Hugo Black, an undergraduate at the University of Southern California. As Ralph Simmons detects, Miss Bollinger, Oliver Hugo, and all of the law students make Ralph's own list of suspects. At one point in the book Simmons searches for clues on the Stuyvesant campus, but most of the story is set on Long Island. *Heads You Lose* is included in this bibliography because of its large concentration of characters from the world of higher education, and because much of what Ralph learns about the decapitated David Black relates to the friends and enemies Black acquired in his role as a professor.

Robert Byrne Gillespie was born in Brooklyn, New York. He received an LL.B. in 1940 from St. Johns University. In addition to writing mystery novels, his long and varied career has included work as an attorney, as an editor of comic strips, and as a constructor of crossword puzzles.

252. GOSLING, PAULA (B. 1939). *MONKEY PUZZLE.* GARDEN CITY, N.Y.: DOUBLEDAY, 1985.

This story is set in motion when, early one Saturday morning, a security guard finds Professor Aiken Adamson brutally murdered in his English department office. Adamson has been stabbed dead with his own paper knife and, to add zest to the proceedings, the killer has cut out the professor's tongue. The setting for this thoroughly academic mystery is "Grantham University," somewhere in the northern United States, and the police detective is Lieutenant Jack Stryker. The unofficial detective is Kate Trevorne, a young instructor of English, who enters into sleuthing after she takes offense at Stryker's heavy-handed tactics and, not incidentally, after she becomes one of Stryker's suspects. Grantham is a large institution, and the English department has sixty faculty members, but fortunately for the readers of this book Detective Stryker is able to narrow the number of possible villains to eleven—those members of the English faculty, including Kate Trevorne, who stayed late on Friday evening to discuss departmental problems. As Stryker pursues his inquiries, he finds that almost all of his suspects have guilty secrets, and that the late Professor Adamson was hiding some sins of his own. The book contains several interesting scenes in the Grantham University library where, late in the tale, Kate Trevorne finds herself in a life-and-death wrestling match with the guilty party. That individual turns out to have had a perfectly academic motive for murder.

Paula Gosling was born in Detroit and received a B.A. from Wayne State University in 1962. After a career as an advertising copywriter she began writing mysteries. Her novels have won many awards and several have been adapted for film. *Monkey Puzzle* won a Gold Dagger Award in 1986, and it became the first in a three-novel series of mysteries to feature Lieutenant Jack Stryker and Professor Kate Trevorne. At the time *Monkey Puzzle* was published Paula Gosling lived in England.

253. HINKEMEYER, MICHAEL (THOMAS) (B. 1940). *FOURTH DOWN DEATH.* NEW YORK: ST. MARTIN'S, 1985.

An undergraduate named Alicia Stanhope is found raped and murdered on the campus of "North Star University" near St. Cloud, Minnesota. A miniature toy football is stuffed in her mouth. Emil Whippletree, the shrewd, tobacco-chewing local sheriff, is in charge of the case, and his investigation leads him straight to the university's nationally prominent football team. Whippletree's detection does not go smoothly. Butch Lodge, the director of North Star's campus security, provides the sheriff with only minimal cooperation because he would like to run for Whippletree's office at the next election. Nor does "Snopes" Avano, the veteran coach of the team, go out of his way to facilitate Whippletree's sleuthing. Nonetheless, the persistent sheriff winnows his list of suspects until he knows that the guilty party is one of three star players. Several high-level North Star administrators appear in the story, most notably President Rexford ("Rector Rex") Anderson, a man who understands how dependent his institution is on football and who prefers to believe that no North Star player could ever commit rape or murder. A secondary plot has Bunny Hollman, the wife of history department chairperson Charlie Hollman, seeing visions of the Blessed Virgin. Whippletree fears that once the word of Mrs. Hollman's apparent miracle has been publicized the area will be overwhelmed by religious pilgrims and his inquiry into Miss Stanhope's death will be impeded. The book's climax comes on a Saturday afternoon, at the end of a football game between North Star and the University of Illinois. Miss Stanhope's assailant receives an unusual form of justice, and canny Sheriff Whippletree profits from a once-in-a-lifetime investment opportunity.

Michael Thomas Hinkemeyer was born in St. Cloud, Minnesota. He received an A.B. from St. John's University in Collegeville, Minnesota, and a Ph.D. from Northwestern. Before becoming a full-time writer in the late 1970s, Hinkemeyer held several academic postions, the last being associate professor of education at Queens College of the City University of New York. *Fourth Down Death* was the third Hinkemeyer mystery to feature Sherifff Whippletree as detective.

254. JANESHUTZ, TRISH [PATRICIA MAINE JANESHUTZ (B. 1947)]. *IN SHADOW.* NEW YORK: BALLANTINE, 1985.

Denise Markham, a beautiful, young research chemist, is stabbed dead late one night on the campus of an unidentified university in Miami, Florida. Heading the police investigation is Detective John Conway. The married Dr. Markham, as Detective Conway soon discovers, was a swinger, and any one of several extramarital sexual partners might have been her killer. Or perhaps it was Dan Markham, her golf-professional husband, who tells Conway that he had reluctantly adjusted to his wife's wandering ways. In addition to her research, Dr. Markham also taught classes, and one of her faculty colleagues tells Conway, only half facetiously, that the murderer might have been one of Markham's students since she seldom gave grades above the mark of C. There is also the matter of the new, illegal designer drug that Markham had secretly created and that Conway finds in her office. And what about the obviously deranged man who makes threatening phone calls to Laura Perkins, a teacher of languages at the university, who was one of Dr. Markham's few female acquaintances? To his credit, the intrepid Detective Conway is able to digest his banquet of leads, and he finds Markham's murderer by the end of the story. While doing so he copes with a corrupt clergyman, with an adjunct professor of law whose tax returns grossly understate his actual income, with a female professor of law who would like to trade in her husband and replace him with Conway, and with an aspiring magician who finds hand puppets more desirable companions than human beings.

Patricia Maine Janeshutz was born to American parents in Caracus, Venezuela. She received a B.A. from Utica College in 1970 and an M.A.L.S. from Florida State University in 1973. Janeshutz has worked as a prison librarian in Florida, as a teacher of Spanish, as a social worker, and as a teacher of English to Cuban refugees. She has published mainstream fiction and mysteries, and she has employed T. J. McGregor as well as Trish Janeshutz as pen names. *In Shadow* was her first mystery by Trish Janeshutz. At the time the book was published Janeshutz lived in South Florida.

255. JEVONS, MARSHALL [WILLIAM BRIET (B. 1933) AND KENNETH G. ELZINGA (B. 1941)]. *THE FATAL EQUILIBRIUM*. CAMBRIDGE, MASS.: THE M.I.T. PRESS, 1985.

It is time once again for the dreaded eight-person Promotions and Tenure Committee at Harvard to decide which junior faculty members get tenure and which do not. This year Dennis Gossen, an assistant professor of economics, is turned down. Shortly after receiving that dismal news Gossen apparently commits suicide. He is found dead of carbon monoxide poisoning in his closed automobile. Over the next few days, mathematician Morrison Bell and classicist Foster Barrett, two members of the committee, are brutally murdered in their homes. Melissa Shannon, a Boston University graduate student and Gossen's fiancée, is arrested for the pair of murders, tried, and sentenced to life in prison. Case closed? Not as far as Harvard economist Henry Spearman is concerned. A brilliant man, known among his colleagues for "logic-chopping," he considers all of the evidence. Then, during an end-of-the-story "Harvard at Sea" cruise on the *Queen Elizabeth II,* a voyage on which most of the surviving characters in the tale are present, he identifies the real villain. A man who applies economic principles to "every nook and cranny of life," Professor Spearman is depicted throughout the book analyzing various mundane activities, including shopping in a Boston department store, through the piercing light of economic theory. Spearman is also a member of the Promotions and Tenure Committee, and the book includes many, many scenes in which the committee members discuss the pros and cons of the various candidates who are being considered for lifetime employment at Harvard.

Marshall Jevons is the joint pseudonym of William Briet and Kenneth G. Elzinga. At the time this book was published William Briet was a professor of economics at Trinity University in San Antonio, Texas, and Kenneth G. Elzinga was a professor of economics at the University of Virginia. Their pseudonym pays tribute to the real Marshall Jevons, an economist who, as the authors point out in the book's text, is widely considered to have been the founding father of modern utility theory. Henry Spearman made his first appearance as a detective in *Murder at the Margin* (Glen Ridge, N.J.: Thomas Horton and Daughters, 1978), a mystery that takes the sleuthing Harvard professor on vacation to the Virgin Islands. Another Spearman mystery, *A Deadly Indifference* (408), is set at the University of Cambridge and appears later in this bibliography. Because he often stops and delivers minilectures on assorted subjects, Henry Spearman is one of the more boorish sleuths in mystery fiction, but there is method behind what might seem to be the authors' literary madness. Many of Spearman's seemingly gratuitous explanations of economic phenomena are, in reality, relatively painless lessons in "the dismal science" for undergraduates, and all of the Spearman mysteries have been used as classroom reading in economics courses.

256. KENNEY, SUSAN (B. 1941). *GRAVES IN ACADEME.* NEW YORK: VIKING, 1985.

The protagonist of this literate college mystery is Roz Howard, a woman in her early thirties who comes to "Canterbury College" in Maine to take up a one-year temporary appointment as an assistant professor of English. Howard is to replace a veteran professor who has recently died in an apparent accident while chopping wood. Shortly after she arrives, Howard learns that another unusual death—that of a female undergraduate who expired from hypothermia—has also occurred recently at Canterbury. Then more bizarre incidents take place, some of them with fatal consequences, and Howard begins to fear that the college has fallen victim to a serial killer. Furthermore, Howard suspects that the clues to that person's identity may lie in the syllabus, which she inherited from her predecessor, that she is employing in her survey course in medieval English literature. A large array of Canterbury characters takes part in the story, including Dean Luke Runyon, a man who dresses in a fringed leather jacket and a cowboy hat and looks "like a cross between General Custer and the Marlboro Man." Runyon is something of a sexist and often patronizes women, but he is also very macho, and despite strong feminist leanings Roz Howard is attracted to him. The book keeps its readers guessing by offering several red herrings, but it also provides many valuable clues in the form of literary allusions. Indeed, medieval English literature buffs will immediately realize that the surnames of the two faculty victims in the story—Parsons and Manciple—are very likely to hold significance for sleuthing.

Susan Kenney was born in Summit, New Jersey. She received a B.A. from Northwestern in 1963 and a Ph.D. from Cornell in 1968. At the time *Graves in Academe* was published Kenney was an associate professor of English at Colby College in Waterville, Maine. Roz Howard is a Susan Kenney series-character professor-detective. *Graves in Academe* was Professor Howard's second published adventure.

257. NOWAK, JACQUELYN. *DEATH AT THE CROSSINGS.* NEW YORK: DODD, MEAD & CO., 1985.

When the smell of decomposing flesh begins to permeate Bayard House, the home of the art history department at a large American university, the rotting body of graduate student Colleen Blakeley is found in the little-used basement. Sergeant Mike Minor, a homicide officer, is one of the first policemen on the scene. An autopsy shows that the cause of death was a lethal amount of "henbane," a hallucinogenic drug, and the authorities are willing to assume that Miss Blakeley either committed suicide or overdosed. But with strong suspicions that the young woman was murdered, Sergeant Minor pursues the case against the wishes of his superiors, and with the help of Sue Singer, the art department's secretary, he delves not only into Colleen Blakeley's life history but into the pasts of many of the department's faculty members and students as well. *Death at the Crossings* is an almost undiluted college mystery. All of the major suspects are connected with the university, and the motive for Miss Blakeley's murder turns out to be rooted in academe as well. Indeed, as the case concludes an incredulous Sergeant Minor asks the guilty party if his lethal misdeeds could really have been prompted by a matter so esoteric as a disputed theory about medieval church transepts. In the book's final chapter the author tells her readers what the principals in the story are doing six months after the villain has been apprehended. The art history department has lost three of its nine members, two by voluntary resignation and one by arrest. Secretary Sue Singer, tired of the department's corrosive atmosphere, has left to pursue other interests. And Sergeant Minor, badly bruised by his experiences with academe and academics, has resigned from the police force.

Jacquelyn Nowak has been an art history instructor. *Death at the Crossings* was her first novel. At the time the book was published Nowak lived in southeastern Arizona.

258. RESNICOW, HERBERT (1922–1997). *THE SEVENTH CROSSWORD*. NEW YORK: BALLANTINE, 1985.

Fabian Humboldt is "University Professor" at "Windham College" in Vermont. He is not assigned to any academic department, nor is he expected to teach. Instead, he heads an interdisciplinary team of six assistant professors that is developing a technique for increasing the reasoning skills of high-school students by having them solve crossword puzzles. None of Professor Humboldt's six research associates has tenure, and he works all of them so hard they do not have time to turn out independent publications. Thus, all six team members will have to depend on Humboldt to testify that the quality of their research on the crossword project deserves continuing appointment. A man who certainly knows how to make enemies, the nasty Professor Humboldt sometimes implies that several or more of his reports to the tenure committees will be disparaging, and one night he is stabbed dead in his home with a sword from his collection of antique weapons. Although the local police and the Windham College security force conduct investigations, the principal detective in the story is Isabel ("Sourpuss") Macintosh, Windham's nature-loving dean of the faculty. Although she can certainly afford better, Dean Macintosh prefers to live in a simple cabin in a forest near the Windham campus. Dean Macintosh is assisted in sleuthing by Giles Sullivan, a retired criminal lawyer with whom she is experiencing a late-in-life romance. Professor Humboldt's six research-team members, all of whom have incriminating skeletons in their closets, are the major suspects in the case, along with Virginia Wagner, Humboldt's Reubenesque secretary. Miss Wagner was having an affair with the unmarried Humboldt, and she enjoyed stimulating his ardor by arriving at his home clad in erotic attire. Academic readers may appreciate the scene in which the hysterical Miss Wagner, clad in a scanty French maid's costume, bursts into a party at the nearby home of Morehead ("Fathead") Jordan, Windham's president, after she discovers Professor Humboldt's bloody corpse. The text of this full-blown college mystery is interrupted at five junctures with crossword puzzles that contain clues to the identity of Professor Humboldt's killer.

Herbert Resnicow was born in New York City and graduated from the Polytechnic Institute of Brooklyn. After a long career as a civil engineer he began writing mysteries at age sixty. His mysteries emphasized puzzle solving and the application of logic. *The Seventh Crossword* was the second of five mysteries in which Dean Isabel Macintosh plays the role of detective. Another of Resnicow's Isabel Macintosh novels, *The Crossword Hunt* (287), appears later in this bibliography.

259. TOWNSEND, GUY. *TO PROVE A VILLAIN.* MENLO PARK, CALIF.: PERSEVERANCE PRESS, 1985.

This novel is narrated by John M. Forest, a young professor of history at "Brookleigh College." Brookleigh is an American institution of higher education that, according to Forest, tries to make up in pleasantness for what it lacks in academic distinction. During the course of the book Professor Forest achieves two objectives. First, in conjunction with the local police he discovers who killed Marian James-Tyrell, the widely disliked chairperson of the Brookleigh English department. James-Tyrell is smothered dead in the bedroom of her home at the beginning of the story. Second, in his evening class in British history Forest brings to bear a mountain of historical evidence to prove (at least to his own satisfaction) that King Richard III of England was, indeed, responsible in 1483 for the killing of his two young nephews in the Tower of London. Forest's thesis, as he takes great pains to tell his students, runs counter to the more favorable, revisionist view of Richard III that Jacqueline Tey presented in her well-known novel *Daughters of Time* (London: Davies, 1951; New York: Macmillan, 1952). Although Forest's classroom discussions of Richard III generally stand apart from the contemporary murder mystery, the two texts are brought together late in the proceedings when the person who killed James-Tyrell deliberately drops clues that only a person familiar with Richard III's history would find meaningful. *To Prove a Villain* is well stocked with Brookleigh College characters, many of whom become suspects in the James-Tyrell murder, and at those points in the story at which Professor Forest makes his protracted case against Richard III, the book offers its readers more exposure to classroom discourse than does any other mystery in this bibliography.

The holder of a Ph.D. from Tulane, Robert Townsend was for many years a college professor specializing in nineteenth-century British history. He eventually left academe to become an attorney in Madison, Indiana. At the time *To Prove a Villain* was published Townsend was editor of *The Mystery Fancier*, a mystery fanzine. *To Prove a Villain* was Townsend's only mystery novel.

260. WENDER, THEODORA. *KNIGHT MUST FALL.* NEW YORK: AVON, 1985.

The victim in this light college mystery is Henderson N. Knight, the autocratic president of "Turnbull College," a school for wealthy young ladies in "Wading River," Massachusetts. Knight is found dead in the college's swimming pool, his skull demolished by a baseball bat that is found lying at the pool's edge. About to take a post with a foundation after nine years at Turnbull, Knight was in his last weeks at the college and, surrounding the time of his murder, six candidates for his job are being interviewed on the campus. The detectives in the story are Alden Chase, the handsome, divorced chief of the Wading River Police, and Gladiola ("Glad") Gold, a single, thirtyish professor of English. A member of the committee to select the new president, the chain-smoking Professor Gold initially serves as a police informant about the six candidates for Turnbull's presidency, but as the novel proceeds she finds other ways to help the attractive Chief Chase. The novel is stuffed with Turnbull College characters, most of whom actively disliked Knight, and several of the presidential candidates prove to have interesting skeletons in their closets. Professorial readers will appreciate the many scenes in *Knight Must Fall* in which the minutiae and frustrations of academic life are described. Members of academic search committees, in particular, will recognize the problems faced by Professor Gold as she telephones the presidential candidates' references and receives banal responses and misinformation.

The identity of Theodora Wender has eluded those who compile biographic compendia. However, in Willetta L. Heisling's *Detecting Women 2*, Theodora Wender identifies herself briefly as "a Latin professor who wrote 'punny' stories while relearning to speak after a stroke." *Murder Gets a Degree* (274), the second and final Professor Glad Gold mystery by Theodora Wender, appears later in this bibliography.

261. BORTHWICK, J. S. [JOAN SCOTT CREIGHTON (B. 1923)]. *THE STUDENT BODY.* NEW YORK: ST. MARTIN'S, 1986.

The strangled corpse of Alice Marmott is found frozen in an ice sculpture during a winter carnival at "Bowmouth College" in Maine. Miss Marmott was a brilliant English major who sometimes angered her professors by challenging their ideas. A few nights later the dead body of Rosalind Parker is discovered in the English department's office building while a snowstorm rages outside. The victim of poisoned cocoa, Mrs. Parker was the department's powerful secretary. Trying to tie the two killings together, and identify the villain or villains, is Sarah Deane, a Boston University graduate student and the Bowmouth English department's newest faculty recruit. Miss Deane is assisted by her boyfriend, Dr. Alex MacKenzie, who teaches at Bowmouth Medical School. Since almost all of the principal characters in this story are connected with the Bowmouth English department, and since the murders were prompted by a thoroughly academic motive, *The Student Body* is college mystery in almost undiluted form. The book even includes a map of the Bowmouth campus. The late Mrs. Parker kept secret files on the members of the English faculty. As Miss Deane and Dr. MacKenzie search for clues, they examine those caches of disagreeable information, and readers are treated to a veritable catalog of the past and present misbehaviors that faculty in college mysteries try desperately to keep secret.

The Student Body was the third in a continuing series of Sarah Deane mysteries. Joan Scott Creighton was born in Buffalo, New York, and attended the University of Buffalo. She was a resident of Thomaston, Maine, when the *The Student Body* was published.

262. CARLSON P(ATRICIA) M(CELROY) (B. 1940). *MURDER IS PATHOLOGICAL.* NEW YORK: AVON, 1986.

This novel is set at a university in the small American town of "Laconia." Someone is apparently trying to sabotage the groundbreaking tumor-reversal research of Dr. Weisen, a jolly, bearded professor of chemistry who resembles Santa Claus. Many of Dr. Weisen's most crucial experimental rats are mysteriously slaughtered, and then Norman, the night custodian of Dr. Weisen's laboratory, dies in an unexplained fall off a bicycle. Maggie Ryan suspects that Norman's death was murder and she launches an investigation. Ryan is a graduate student in statistics who has been hired to analyze

Dr. Weisen's data. She is joined in her sleuthing by Nick O'Connor, a stage and television actor who comes from New York City to be of assistance. A widower, O'Connor would like to marry the younger Ryan, but as a thoroughly modern woman, Ryan prefers to treat him as an uncle. Eventually, the energetic Miss Ryan and her lovelorn suitor discover what really is happening in Dr. Weisen's lab, but before they successfully complete their detection they are almost killed in a homemade gas chamber that the villain has constructed in a room of the chemistry building. The story provides considerable detail about small-animal laboratory research, and several graduate-student research assistants play important roles.

Three other Maggie Ryan mysteries by P. M. Carlson have entries in this bibliography. The other Ryan mysteries are *Audition for Murder* (248), *Murder Is Academic* (249), and *Murder Misread* (330).

263. CARRIER, WARREN (B. 1918). *DEATH OF A CHANCELLOR.* NEW YORK: DODD, MEAD & CO., 1986.

Bill Train, the chancellor of the "University of Wisconsin at Silvertown," is murdered in his office one Saturday morning. Chancellor Train's wife, Hannah, asks Sean Fogerty, a local attorney, to investigate. Because Fogerty and Hannah distrust the Silvertown police, Fogerty works outside the law to develop a long list of suspects—people with whom Train had quarreled during his tenure as the university's top executive officer. Among the possible murderers are a truculent sociologist who was denied tenure, a mathematician dismissed for sexually harassing female students, a black former student who is connected with campus drug trafficking, and a female English professor whose loud left-wing politics seem inconsistent with the syrupy romantic poetry she publishes. There is some derring-do in the novel, when Sean Fogerty's life is imperiled by some of those whom he is investigating, but for the most part Fogerty (who narrates the tale) is pictured as a dogged collector of information. As for the University of Wisconsin at Silvertown, it emerges from the pages of this novel as a thoroughly provincial institution, and its denizens come forth as people who have overcome unfortunate pasts to achieve mediocre presents.

Warren Carrier was chancellor of the University of Wisconsin at Platteville from 1975 until 1982, when he became chancellor emeritus. Before becoming chancellor at Wisconsin-Platteville, Carrier held positions in the English departments of Bard College, Sweet

Briar College, the University of Montana, Rutgers, San Diego State College, and the University of California at San Diego. *Death of a Chancellor* was his fifth mystery novel.

264. CROSS, AMANDA [CAROLYN GOLD HEILBRUN (B. 1926)]. *NO WORD FROM WINIFRED.* NEW YORK: DUTTON, 1986.

The Winifred in the title of this novel is Winifred Ashby, referred to in the text as the "honorary niece" of the late Charlotte Stanton, a popular British novelist and principal of an Oxford college. Miss Ashby disappears just after promising to cooperate with Charlotte Lucas, a young woman who wants to write the eminent Ms. Stanton's biography. Lucas asks Professor Kate Fansler, Amanda Cross's eminent series-character detective, to find Ashby, and after some initial reluctance Fansler accepts the challenge. Unlike many novels in the Fansler series, *No Word from Winifred* does not center on academic infighting. Nonetheless, it contains enough characters from academe and more than enough scenes at academic locales to qualify for this bibliography. During the course of her missing-person labors Professor Fansler is seen at her home institution (a large, high-status university in New York City) and at the University of California at Santa Cruz. She also looks for clues at a meeting of the Modern Language Association, and at an early point in the story she makes a foray to the association's offices in New York City. At yet another point in the proceedings Fansler has dinner at the Harvard Club of New York, where, in characteristic fashion, she has some bitter-but-witty thoughts about the club's former all-male admissions policy. Readers from the world of higher education will applaud a scene, at the Modern Language Association meeting, in which Stan Wyman, an academically ambitious professor from Hofstra, demands a reward from Fansler in exchange for vital information about the whereabouts of Winifred Ashby. Rather than asking for money, Professor Wyman guarantees himself a place in the college-mystery hall of fame by requesting faculty-access privileges at the resource-rich library at Fansler's university.

Six other Professor Kate Fansler mysteries have entries in this bibliography. Those mysteries are *Poetic Justice* (156), *Death in a Tenured Position* (211), *Sweet Death, Kind Death* (238), *A Trap for Fools* (308), *An Imperfect Spy* (402), and *The Puzzled Heart* (457).

265. EPSTEIN, CHARLOTTE. *MURDER IN CHINA*. LONDON: COLLINS, 1986; NEW YORK: DOUBLEDAY, 1989.

Janet Eldine takes a year's leave of absence from a college of education in Philadelphia to teach English at an engineering college in the suburbs of Beijing. In her fifties, and a professor of social psychology at her home institution, Eldine soon becomes a suspect when Li Mei Ling, the domineering woman who is the engineering college's chief political officer, is killed by simultaneous strangulation and stabbing. Fearful of arrest by the People's Liberation Army, which is ineptly handling the murder investigation, Eldine turns to sleuthing in order to clear her name. Since almost everyone at the college hated "Comrade" Li, there is an abundant supply of people who could have done the deadly deed. Mystery fans will appreciate the book's complex whodunit component. However, many academic readers will take even more interest in the detail that the novel offers about life in a Chinese institution of higher education shortly after the Cultural Revolution. For example, they can learn that the college's staff and faculty take student complaints very, very seriously because during the Cultural Revolution many of the school's teachers were denounced by their students and sent into the countryside to perform forced manual labor.

Charlotte Epstein is a former professor of human relations. At the time *Murder in China* was published she lived in Philadelphia. Like Janet Eldine, her protagonist, Charlotte Epstein spent a year teaching English in the People's Republic of China. *Murder in China* was her first mystery novel.

266. FINE, ANNE (B. 1947). *THE KILLJOY*. LONDON: BANTAM, 1986; NEW YORK: THE MYSTERIOUS PRESS, 1987.

When Ian James Laidlaw was five years old he was attacked by a dog and the left side of his face was horribly scarred. Now Ian is forty-nine, a political scientist, and the head of his department at a Scottish university. Sensitive about his disfigurement, he tries to keep the left side of his face in shadow or turned to a wall while he conducts classes. Ian was once married but is now divorced. Suddenly he begins an affair with Alicia Davis, a student in one of his seminars. As Ian narrates this tale, it becomes evident that his mind has become profoundly disturbed by his physical affliction. *The*

Killjoy is not a conventional detective mystery. It is a study in abnormal psychology that prompts its readers to ask whether Ian will be able to deal successfully with his new romance. At the end of the book the answer becomes apparent. Because one of Ian's difficulties is obsessiveness, during his narrative he provides some minute details about the ways in which he executes his teaching and administrative duties at the university.

Anne Fine was born in Leicester, England, and received a B.A. from the University of Warwick in 1968. Married to a university professor, she lives in Edinburgh and has written several books for children. *The Killjoy* was her first novel for adults.

267. GALBRAITH, RUTH. *A CONVENIENT DEATH.* NEW YORK: PAPERJACKS, 1986.

The speaker at this year's graduation at "Lockland University" in Canada is J. Richardson Dewar, once a Lockland undergraduate but now a famous inventor and a wealthy drug-company executive. As the crowd files slowly out of the ceremony, Audrey Benedict stays slumped in her seat. Mrs. Benedict is the wife of Lockland's dean of graduate studies. A security guard finds that she is unconscious. He attempts to rouse her, but without success. Mrs. Benedict is rushed to a hospital and pronounced dead. She is later found to have died from a rare poison. Mrs. Benedict was not universally popular in the Lockland community, in part because of her strong stance in favor of women's rights to abortions. Nonetheless, the local police lack a motive for murder, and the task of identifying the killer falls to Grace Forrester, Lockland's septuagenarian retired dean of women. The former chemistry professor is in frail health, but she knows her poisons. She also can remember decades-old events on the Lockland campus, including incidents that occurred when J. Richardson Dewer was a student in her classes, and her memory proves important in finding the person who ended Mrs. Benedict's life. *A Convenient Death* is a quieter, more somber mystery than many entries in this bibliography. The principal characters, most of whom are connected with the university, are allowed to be unusually introspective, and the novel is noteworthy for its character development. Retired readers may appreciate a scene in which Grace Forrester ponders a request from an aged colleague to chair a plenary session at the annual conference of the Federation of Women Scientists. She decides to refuse and agonizes over her written response. She gropes for the words to tell her friend that it is "time for them both to step aside."

A Convenient Death was Ruth Galbraith's first mystery novel.

268. HESS, JOAN (B. 1949). *STRANGLED PROSE.* NEW YORK: ST. MARTIN'S, 1986.

The narrator of this light mystery is Claire Malloy, the widowed owner of a bookshop in the American town of "Farberville." Carlton Malloy, Claire's deceased husband, was a professor of English at "Farber College." Mildred Twiller, the wife of another Farber College professor of English, publishes a steamy novel titled *Professor of Passion*. With only modest attempts to alter the identities of the participants, the novel features real incidents, most of a sexual nature and all of them embarrassing, that involved actual members of the Farber English department. In fact, one of the characters in the book is a thinly veiled version of Claire Malloy's late spouse. To the surprise of few, the suddenly unpopular Mrs. Twiller is soon strangled dead in her home, and several days later her husband Douglas meets the same fate. Malloy takes up detection when Lieutenant Peter Rosen of the Farberville police puts her high on his list of suspects. There is only one on-campus scene in the book—when Malloy breaks into the English department late one night and searches for clues—but there are many episodes, some of them at Malloy's bookshop, in which Farber faculty members have the opportunity to display acute levels of fear and loathing. The book is noteworthy for the cynicism in its dialogue and interior monologues, and Mrs. Malloy, with years of experience as a faculty wife, proves more than able to compete with anyone in the English department when it comes to hurling flip, irreverent wisecracks.

Joan Hess was born in Fayetteville, Arkansas. She holds a B.A. from the University of Arkansas and an M.A. from Long Island University. After brief careers as a real estate agent and as an art teacher Hess became a full-time writer in 1984. *Strangled Prose* was her first novel. Since *Strangled Prose,* Hess has gone on to become one of America's most successful mystery writers, and Claire Malloy has become a frequently employed series-character detective. Another Claire Malloy novel by Joan Hess, *Poisoned Pins* (365), appears later in this bibliography.

269. HULLAND J(ENNIFER) R(OSEMARY) (B. 1936). *STUDENT BODY.* LONDON: HODDER & STOUGHTON, 1986. PUBLISHED IN THE UNITED STATES AS *AN EDUCATED MURDER.* NEW YORK: ST. MARTIN'S, 1987.

Kate Henderson is a fortyish graduate student in the teacher-training program at a British university. Although she befriends and mothers many of her younger fellow students, she is never entirely forthcoming about herself because she has several disturbing personal secrets she would not like revealed. Readers learn about these secrets because the text of the novel includes flashbacks about them. When the naked and headless body of a male acquaintance is found frozen in a campus goldfish pond, Henderson's reticence about her past makes her a murder suspect. The official sleuthing in this intricate story is handled by Detective Chief Inspector McPherson of the local police, but Henderson also becomes involved in the detection and almost loses her life in the process. *Student Body* has a large cast of student and faculty characters, several surprising twists of plot, many scenes on the university campus, and is a solid college mystery. With its continuous focus on Kate Henderson's past and present problems it is also a compelling story of a woman's persistence throughout a lifetime of travails.

The daughter of a British civil servant, Jennifer Rosemary Hulland was born in India. She received a B.A. from the University of London in 1957 and a diploma in education from the University of Bristol in 1958. She has taught in British schools and in the extension division of the University of Liverpool. *Student Body* was her first novel.

270. KNIGHT, KATHRYN LASKY (B. 1944). *TRACE ELEMENTS.* NEW YORK: NORTON, 1986.

Tom Jacobs, a Harvard physicist, develops a device ("The Time Slicer") for obtaining geological dating information extrapolated from magnetic variations in rocks. To perfect the instrument he travels to a Harvard archaeological dig being conducted in the Nevada desert. There he meets his death when bitten by a rattlesnake. A snakebite kit, which might have saved his life, had been rendered inoperative. Jacobs leaves a widow, Calista, and a ten-year-old son, Charley. Calista Jacobs is a feisty illustrator of children's books, and Charley is a budding genius. When Peter Gardiner, a Harvard archaeologist, dies of yet another rattlesnake bite at the same Nevada site,

Calista and Charley suspect that a murderer is on the loose, and they become a mother-son detection team. During the course of the story they spend much of their time in Harvard's Peabody Museum, where Calista has taken on a new role as catalog illustrator and where Charley, who simply cannot throttle his hyperactive mind, unintentionally commits to memory the catalog numbers of the artifacts on display. They also travel to the Smithsonian in Washington, where they consult Archibald W. Baldwin, the interim chairman of the institution's Department of Archaeology and Anthropology. Baldwin is America's leading expert in archaeological matters pertaining to Western deserts. By the end of the story Calista and Charley learn that Tom Jacobs's death was the violent consequence of an archaeological scam run from Harvard, and Calista has succumbed to the erotic charms of the pipe-smoking, Dartmouth-educated Baldwin. In addition to Tom Jacobs and Peter Gardiner, several other Harvard professors (as well as several members of the Peabody Museum staff) play parts in the story, and Harvard's president, Derek Bok, can be observed personally offering Calista his condolences after her husband's unfortunate death.

Kathryn Lasky Knight was born in Indianapolis, Indiana. She received a B.A. from the University of Michigan in 1966. She has written many books for children. *Trace Elements* was her first mystery novel. At the time *Trace Elements* was published Knight lived in Cambridge, Massachusetts. *Mortal Words* (335), another Calista and Charley Jacobs mystery, appears later in this bibliography.

271. RISENHOOVER, C. C. *WINE, MURDER & BLUEBERRY SUNDAES.* WAXAHACHIE, TEX.: MCLENNON HOUSE, 1986.

When unpopular Dean Reginald Masters is found hanged in his office at Southern Methodist University, the police are willing to write off the incident as a suicide. Then, when Franklin Becker, the chairman of the journalism department, drowns after his car suddenly veers off the road into a lake, the authorities consider that event an unfortunate accident. Some of the Southern Methodist faculty have doubts about the deaths of these two important campus figures, and they ask Brian Stratford to investigate. A young, handsome professor in Franklin Becker's journalism department, Stratford was once a CIA agent, and his colleagues feel that his experiences as a spy will provide him the background he needs to detect. With the help of Deseret Anares, a strikingly beautiful undergraduate, Stratford does, indeed, discover the real circumstances behind the deaths of Masters and Becker, but not before he is kidnapped and almost killed by the book's villain. The kidnapping occurs in Oklahoma, after the light plane in which Stratford is flying is forced down by hostile helicopters, but most of this fast-paced novel takes place on or near the Southern Methodist campus. Deseret Anares, whose unexpected talent for firing an Uzi helps endear her to Stratford, also tries to win her professor's heart by plying him with the blueberry sundaes referred to in the book's title. Many college-mystery readers will appreciate the scene late in the novel in which Stratford finds a unique way to deal with Dean Masters's murderer. They may also agree with Stratford that hanging was not necessarily an improper fate for Dean Masters, a man who had millions of dollars in a secret Swiss bank account.

A native of Broken Bow, Oklahoma, C. C. Risenhoover holds B.A. and M.A. degrees from Baylor University. Risenhoover has been a journalism professor at Southern Methodist University, Sam Houston State University, and Eastfield College, and he has been director of public relations at Baylor. He also has been a reporter for the *Fort Worth Star-Telegram.*

272. SILVER, VICTORIA. *DEATH OF A RADCLIFFE ROOMMATE.* NEW YORK: BANTAM, 1986.

Debbie Doyle, an undergraduate at Harvard, is beaten unconscious in her dormitory room and then strangled with a string from a harp on which she was an aspiring virtuoso. Although the Cambridge police try diligently to find Miss Doyle's killer, the person who does the most effective sleuthing in the story is Lauren Adler, another Harvard undergraduate. Miss Adler suspects that one of Miss Doyle's four suitemates is the murderer, and as she pushes forward in her search for the killer she is helped by Michael Hunt, a gay Harvard student who is her closest friend on the campus. The story involves Adler and Hunt in the examination of letters sent between Helena Dichter, one of the suitemates, and Augustine Wedgwood, a celebrated British poet. It also takes them into a matter involving two royal families. Why did no less a personage than Queen Elizabeth personally bar another of the suitemates, Princess Yazmin from one of the oil emirates on the Persian Gulf, from attending Oxford or Cambridge? While the murder mystery in this book is entertaining, some readers may find themselves equally interested in the close relationship between the heterosexual Lauren Adler, who admits to sexual stirrings when she sees fire engines, and the homosexual Michael Hunt. Portrayed as "pretty" and decidedly effeminate, Hunt not only helps Adler with detection, he also allows her to draw freely from his private stock of exotic moisturizing lotion. At the end of the tale Adler and Hunt walk arm in arm across Harvard Yard, friends forever. In the words of the author they are linked by their "common interest in Henry James, chocolate marzipan, and boys."

Death of a Radcliffe Roommate is the second mystery by Victoria Silver in this bibliography. The first, *Death of a Harvard Freshman* (247), also features Lauren Adler and Michael Hunt as undergraduate sleuths.

273. STEPHENS, JUDITH. *BORROWED RITES.* BERKELEY, CALIF.: CAYUSE PRESS, 1986.

A broken water pipe forces workers to remove the seldom-disturbed remains stored in the basement of an anthropology laboratory at the University of California at Berkeley. Among the grisly specimens is the mummy of a young woman. Upon examination, the mummy proves to be of very recent vintage, perhaps no more than ten or twenty years old. The detective in this story is Sergeant Harry Evans of the Berkeley police. Even in Berkeley a mummified murder victim is rare, but with the help of Lily West, an attractive graduate student recently returned from fieldwork in Afghanistan, Sergeant Evans cracks the case. Many Berkeley anthropologists appear in the story. One is the department chairman, Professor Albert B. Lee, who is described by the book's author as "a great bureaucrat in a great university." Another is the elderly Samuel "Cannibal" Cane, a professor emeritus, whose nickname stems from his partaking of cannibal feasts while studying native customs in New Guinea. Something of a lecher, despite his advanced years, Professor Cane is killed during the story, and his body is found naked except for his socks and garters. Then there is Tony Clarke, whose arrogance and good looks draw Harry Evans's quick dislike. Always on the prowl for good-looking female students, Professor Clarke's idea of a romantic activity is to take a girl target shooting. Spiced with many references to the more shocking cultural practices of primitive peoples, *Borrowed Rites* is one of the spookier mysteries in this bibliography. Chapter 1, a flashback that details how the story's first victim was prepared for eternal preservation, would be good hand-out material for a course titled Mummification 101.

Borrowed Rites was Judith Stephens's first novel.

274. WENDER, THEODORA. *MURDER GETS A DEGREE.* NEW YORK: AVON, 1986.

On Halloween night the historic home of octogenarian Adah Storm burns to the ground, and Mrs. Storm and her twelve cats burn along with it. The Storm abode stood near the campus of "Turnbull College," an institution for women in "Wading River," Massachusetts. Local police chief Alden Chase suspects arson, and he is assisted in his investigations by his chain-smoking girlfriend, Turnbull College Professor of English Gladiola ("Glad") Gold. As the novel proceeds Chief Chase and Professor Gold learn more than they want to know about genealogy, witchcraft, and black magic. Although some of this quick-reading story focuses on the officials of the Wading River local government, several Turnbull College students and faculty members are given important parts. One of the students, Mary Anne Wormerey, is murdered and her body dropped down a well, and one of the teachers, overweight archaeologist Zoe Doulodike, develops evidence through digs, even while subsisting on a diet consisting largely of beer and Oreo cookies. The book also features an unusual faculty party. Held on Halloween night, shortly before the fire in Adah Storm's home, the affair is attended by costumed faculty and administrators. Professor-readers may or may not be surprised to learn that two of Turnbull College's more distinguished political scientists choose to come dressed as gorillas.

Knight Must Fall (260), another Professor Glad Gold mystery by Theodora Wender, appears earlier in this bibliography. The two-novel Glad Gold series ended with *Murder Gets a Degree.*

275. ADAMSON, M(ARY) J(O) (B. 1935). *NOT TILL A HOT JANUARY.* NEW YORK: BANTAM, 1987.

Three young women, two of them undergraduates at the University of Puerto Rico, die at the hands of someone the press begins to call "The San Juan Strangler." Fortunately for the cause of justice, Lieutenant Balthazar Marten, a homicide detective with the New York City Police, happens to be on temporary duty in San Juan. Although he is supposed to be investigating crime in Puerto Rican casinos, Marten leaps into action in the Strangler case. Along with Sixto Cardenas, his contact with the San Juan Police, Marten makes several trips to the university in search of clues, and on one campus visit he is almost assassinated by a bomb concealed within a notebook. Maira Knight, an attractive professor of English, figures prominently in the story, and *Not Till a Hot January* is the only novel in this bibliography that accords a speaking part to the janitor at a university baseball stadium. By the end of the tale the guilty party has been apprehended. The month is January and New York is in the cold, cruel grip of winter. As his reward for finding the villain, Lieutenant Marten is informed that his temporary assignment in San Juan has been extended until June.

Mary Jo Adamson was born in Moline, Illinois. She received a B.A. from Marycrest College in 1956 and a Ph.D. in English from the University of Denver in 1979. She has held academic posts at Humboldt State College and the University of Denver. Adamson began writing fiction in 1984. She has published many historical romances, and *Not Till a Hot January* was her first mystery novel. The book became the initial entry in a continuing series of mysteries featuring detectives Balthazar Marten and Sixto Cardenas.

276. BECK, K. K. [KATHRINE MARRIS]. *THE BODY IN THE VOLVO.* NEW YORK: WALKER, 1987.

Charles Carstairs, a junior faculty member at the University of Washington, is told by Professor Roland Bateman, his department chairperson, that he will not be given tenure. As Carstairs is digesting this unpleasant information, good fortune seems to strike. His uncle, Cosmo Sweeney, wins the lottery, gives Carstairs his automobile repair shop, and immediately leaves for an extended period of debauchery in Las Vegas. Carstairs prepares to give up academe and begin a new career in the auto-repair game when disaster hits again. A Volvo with a broken windshield is brought into his just-acquired business, and when the trunk is opened the battered corpse of Professor Bateman is found inside. The official detection in the story is handled by Detectives McNab and Lukowski of the Seattle police, but Charles Carstairs, the detectives' prime suspect, engages in sleuthing of his own in order to avoid being charged with Bateman's murder. Since the unctuous Bateman was widely disliked by most members of his department, Carstairs has the idea that one of his faculty colleagues may have killed him. Much of this novel takes place away from the University of Washington campus, and in that regard the book is only a marginal entry in this bibliography. However, many of the primary players in the often-funny tale are from the university, and several of the scenes in which those academic characters appear rank with the most sardonic in college-mystery fiction. Many academic readers will savor the episode in which Bateman invites Carstairs to an elegant Seattle restaurant to inform him of his tenure denial. Carstairs is a popular teacher and has published widely, but Bateman finds a variety of insulting and irrelevant reasons to justify the no-tenure decision. At the end of the lunch Bateman reaches for the check, and Carstairs assumes that his chairperson, having just delivered the ultimate in academic bad news, is paying for the meal. Instead, Bateman mentally divides the bill in two and tells Carstairs the amount of his share. Carstairs's academic discipline is never identified in the story, but perceptive readers might be able to deduce it from the title of one of his article-length publications. That title is: "Establishing Primary Performance Matrices in Analysis of Social Organization of Hitherto Unclassified Primates of Large Dimensions."

Kathrine Marris attended San Francisco State University. At the time *The Body in the Volvo* was published she was a resident of Seattle, Washington. Before becoming a mystery writer she worked in the advertising business and edited a trade magazine. Although *The Body in the Volvo* takes place in the 1980s, Kathrine Marris (writing as K. K. Beck) is probably best known to mystery-fiction readers for her several mysteries, featuring Iris Cooper as detective, that are set in the 1920s.

277. BIGGLE, LLOYD, JR. (B. 1923). *INTERFACE FOR MURDER.* NEW YORK: DOUBLEDAY, 1987.

A young man wielding a knife is attacking women students at "Sparta College" in Ohio as they walk on the campus at night. Happily for the students, his interests seem to be limited to slashing their clothing, and no one has been badly injured. Arthur Keeton, a Sparta High School student, invents a computer program that he claims will identify the slasher, but Arthur is murdered and his computer program disappears. Enter Januarius "Jay" Pelcher, an energetic Los Angeles private detective! Pelcher is asked to investigate matters at Sparta by Carlton Channer, a local industrialist and the father of one of the slasher's victims. Operating on unfamiliar turf, Pelcher meets and suspects a great many college and high-school students. He also interacts with a large number of adults from both the town and the college. Interspersed between his extensive personal contacts he gets several lessons in the niceties of computers and almost loses his life when he is the target of a drive-by shooting. Eventually, Pelcher finds that the slashing incidents are only part of a much deeper Sparta problem, and by book's end Sparta and its college are rid of the slasher and of several other undesirables as well. Not gone, however, is the inferior cuisine in the Sparta College dining hall. Fond of eating meals in Los Angeles's better restaurants, Pelcher laments throughout the novel that the food at Sparta College alternates between being undercooked and overdone, and on several occasions, as he narrates the tale, he offers his negative appraisals of specific dining hall dishes.

Lloyd Biggle Jr. received a Ph.D. in musicology from the University of Michigan. He has written science-fiction novels as well as detective fiction. *Interface for Murder* was his second mystery novel and the first in a continuing series of books with Januarius Pelcher as detective.

278. CURRAN, TERRIE (B. 1942). *ALL BOOKED UP.* NEW YORK: DODD, MEAD & CO., 1987.

The sleuths in this droll novel are Basil Killingsley, an eccentric professor of medieval English history, and his waspish wife, Hortense. The setting is the "Smedley," a vast, privately funded library located in a large city somewhere in the United States. While conducting research, Basil finds a very rare book in the Smedley, but when he goes back five weeks later the book is gone and so is the book's entry in the noncomputerized library's card catalog. Not a couple to leave a mystery uninvestigated, Basil and Hortense begin interviewing the library staff to try to learn what has happened, but as they begin to close in on an answer two murders occur. Leon Boehm, the Smedley's internal auditor, is found strangled with, ironically, a computer cord. And then Giles Moraise, the library's director, is killed by a blow to the back of his head. Meantime, other rare books vanish and still others mysteriously appear. Since the Smedley has its own board of directors and does not appear to have direct university connections, *All Booked Up* is not set on higher-education turf. However, Basil Killingsley lends both academic status and professorial brainpower to the proceedings, and the text contains much about the intricacies of research libraries, the very kind of places that real-life academics often frequent. I had always believed that theology students purloined more books than any other group because, in the words of a Smedley staff member, "they can concoct the best rationalizations for stealing".

Terrie Curran was born in New York City. She received a B.A. from the City College of New York in 1964, an M.A. from Indiana

University in 1966, and a Ph.D. from the University of Wisconsin in 1973. At the time *All Booked Up* was published, Terrie Curran was a professor of medieval literature at Providence College. The novel was Curran's first work of fiction.

279. FISKE, DORSEY. *BOUND TO MURDER.* NEW YORK: ST. MARTIN'S, 1987.

The illustrations from rare books are being stolen from the library at the University of Cambridge's "Sheepshanks College." Investigating the thefts are John Fenchurch, a sprightly sixty-five-year-old Sheepshanks lecturer in architecture, and Inspector Bunce of the local police. The culprit seems to be an undergraduate named Maunders, but when Maunders is stabbed dead just outside the college gate, Fenchurch and Bunce turn their attentions from book thefts to finding a killer. *Bound to Murder* is the second of two Dorsey Fiske mysteries in this bibliography. The first, *Academic Murder* (206), also takes place at Sheepshanks College, and many of the characters in *Bound to Murder*, including Fenchurch and Inspector Bunce, made their debuts in Fiske's earlier novel. Like *Academic Murder*, *Bound to Murder* is written in the leisurely-but-barbed style of the classic, murder-is-fun British college mysteries of the 1930s, 1940s, and 1950s. At one point in the story Sheepshanks holds its annual "Pullet Feast," which, by college tradition, is an all-male affair. After the diners consume their meals they are entertained by a bevy of energetic prostitutes who arrive nude beneath academic gowns. At another juncture John Fenchurch reveals that his skills at detection are the consequence of his own writing of Cambridge whodunits. Fenchurch's pen name is Geoffrey Saltmarsh, and his best-known work is *A Killer at King's.* Because Fenchurch's Cambridge mysteries were not available for examination, none of them is included in this bibliography.

280. HAYNES, CONRAD. *BISHOP'S GAMBIT, DECLINED.* NEW YORK: BANTAM BOOKS, 1987.

This lively mystery is set at "John Jacob Astor College" in Portland, Oregon. John Jacob Astor is an "abominably expensive" private liberal arts school attended principally by the children of the wealthy. It is also the employer of political science professor Harry Bishop, a onetime Korean War army officer who is now a caustic, gone-to-seed wreck of a man who is slipping toward alcoholism. The victim in the story is David Wasserman, editor of the student newspaper and one of Professor Bishop's students. Wasserman is found on the campus early one morning dead of a bashed skull. The sometimes slothful Professor Bishop reluctantly takes on the role of amateur detective in the story after someone, presumably Wasserman's killer, tries unsuccessfully to shoot him. Eventually, after he survives another attempt on his life, this one in the college library, Professor Bishop identifies Wasserman's murderer and ties his killing to the disappearance, fifteen years earlier, of a John Jacob Astor female undergraduate. The police are represented in the tale by Detective Sergeant Clair Dupree, an assertive woman who does not always approve of Professor Bishop's meddling in official business. Also involved in the detection are Kate Fairbain, a politically conservative professor of economics who is the current love of Professor Bishop's life, and Tucker Nelligan, a reporter for a Portland newspaper. Several John Jacob Astor administrators appear in minor roles. Dean Lee Connar is known to the faculty as "The Peter Principle That Walks Like a Man," and Lyman Bledsoe Jr., chairperson of political science, worries that because the late David Wasserman was a political science major, his murder may provoke someone in authority to reduce his department's budget.

Conrad Haynes was a resident of Milwaukie, Oregon, when this book was published. Two more Professor Harry Bishop mysteries by Conrad Haynes appear in this bibliography. Those mysteries are *Perpetual Check* (295) and *Sacrifice Play* (333).

281. HEALY, JEREMIAH (F., III.) (B. 1948). *SO LIKE SLEEP.* NEW YORK: HARPER & ROW, 1987.

Jennifer Creasey, a white undergraduate at "Goreham College" in Massachusetts, is shot dead in the basement of a building in which a psychotherapist rents consulting space. Almost immediately thereafter William Daniels, a black Goreham student whom Jennifer had been dating, bursts into a group therapy session upstairs in the doctor's office and confesses to the crime. Moreover, as William admits the killing he displays what laboratory examination later shows to be the murder weapon. All of the above would seem to suggest an open-and-shut case, but Lieutenant Robert Murphy, a black Boston police officer, is not so sure, and because he lacks authority in the suburban town in which the shooting took place, he asks private investigator John Francis Cuddy to look into the matter. Eventually, Cuddy finds enough evidence to exonerate Daniels and to identify Miss Creasey's actual murderer. As he detects, Cuddy looks for clues on the Goreham" campus and at the "University of Massachusetts at Columbia Point," where Daniels began his college career before transferring. Cuddy also finds himself briefly at Boston University, where he interviews a faculty expert in hypnosis and posthypnotic suggestion. Although Cuddy makes appearances on three campuses, most of the scenes in the book are not set on academic grounds. The novel deserves inclusion in this bibliography primarily because most of Cuddy's informants, wherever he finds them, furnish information about William Daniels's distressing experiences as a poor-but-brilliant black student in the predominantly white and very high-prestige world of Goreham College.

Jeremiah F. Healy III was born in Teaneck, New Jersey. He holds an A.B. from Rutgers and a J.D. from Harvard. At the time *So Like Sleep* was published Healy was a professor of law at the New England School of Law in Boston. *So Like Sleep* was his third John Francis Cuddy mystery novel.

282. HOWARD, TOM (B. 1937). *HOWARD'S PRICE.* SYDNEY, AUSTRALIA: RASTAR PRESS, 1987.

The "University of Warrigal" in New South Wales, Australia, extends an invitation to Tom Howard to be a writer-in-residence. Howard, who not only narrates this tale but gets author credit as well, is a former Sydney policeman and a successful writer of mysteries. Once at Warrigal, Howard finds that he has been tricked; the university really wants him on campus to investigate a series of rapes that it does not want to report to the police for fear of bad publicity. Howard stays at Warrigal only after demanding, and receiving, an immediate honorary doctorate. His investigation eventually comes to encompass the murder of a senior lecturer who, before his death, was somehow both unmarried and a participant in a wife-swapping ring. Howard also deals with the mysterious fall from the campus tower of a male undergraduate. With dialogue peppered with Australian slang and its story sometimes dealing irreverently with the traditions of Australia's institutions of higher education, *Howard's Price* is as much a satirical college novel as it is a mystery, and the book offers some wildly inventive scenes that strip the pretense from Warrigal's studied public pomposity. Written in eighty-two very brief chapters, it also offers a compelling whodunit. According to information at the front of the book the city of Warrigal is modeled after Adelaide but the University of Warrigal "is wholly imaginary."

Tom Howard is an Australian who writes books about the history of motion pictures in addition to mystery novels. *Howard's Price* was his fourth mystery.

283. KELMAN, JUDITH (ANN) (B. 1945). *WHERE SHADOWS FALL.* NEW YORK: BERKLEY BOOKS, 1987.

Sarah Spooner, an assistant district attorney in New York City, receives the shocking news that her son, Nicholas, has committed suicide at "Cromwell University" by throwing himself into a gorge. A high-status, Cornell-like institution in upstate New York, Cromwell has experienced eleven student suicides in the current academic year, and seven of the victims, like Nicholas, were English majors. Unable to believe that her son would kill himself, Sarah flies to Cromwell and looks into the particulars of his death. She is assisted by Aldo Diamond, a corpulent "forensic graphologist" whom she meets on the plane. Diamond, who spends as much time eating as he does detecting, has been asked by the Cromwell police to shed light on the suicides by examining the victims' handwriting. As readers of college mysteries might suspect, Sarah and Aldo eventually discover that there was considerably more to the students' deaths than simple self-destruction, and both almost lose their own lives as their investigations bring them ever closer to the truth. Several professors of English play important roles in this "psychological thriller," including Warren Lawrence, a man whose speech consists almost entirely of quotations from Shakespeare. Representing the administration in the book's cast of characters is Warren's brother, Wallace Lawrence, Cromwell's president. The academic Lawrences are two-thirds of a set of triplets. The third triplet, Winston, operates the Cromwell hotel in which Sarah and Aldo stay while conducting their inquiries. Cold and often inaccessible, President Lawrence is, appropriately, the least likeable Lawrence brother, and some readers may applaud the scene in which he is shouted down at the annual Cromwell graduation ceremony after he publicly excoriates the suicide victims for selfishly killing themselves without considering the negative consequences their deaths would have on Cromwell's reputation.

Judith Kelman was born in New York City. She holds a B.A. from Cornell, an M.A. from New York University, and another M.A. from Southern Connecticut State University. Before becoming a full-time writer in 1981 she worked as a teacher of handicapped children on

Long Island and later as a speech pathologist in Greenwich, Connecticut. *Where Shadows Fall* was Kelman's second mystery novel, and the first in a continuing series of mysteries featuring Sarah Spooner.

284. LAPIERRE, JANET. *UNQUIET GRAVE.* NEW YORK: ST. MARTIN'S, 1987.

Unquiet Grave is set in the town of "Port Silva," California, the site of the newest and smallest campus in the University of California system. Illona Berggren, a beautiful graduate student, disappears. The book's primary detective, Chief Vince Guitierrez of the local police, suspects foul play, and when Miss Berggren's badly beaten corpse is found buried on the outskirts of town, his attentions center on Joe Mancuso, a computer science professor at the university. Mancuso, a middle-aged bachelor, was known to have shown interest in the deceased and was seen with her on the night of her death. Unaccustomed to the stress of being a murder suspect, the professor asks for leave from the university, and he then spends much of his time pacing the floor of his home hoping the real killer will be arrested. That event does, in fact, occur at the end of the story, when Cat Smith, a young, female hippie who lives in Joe Mancuso's house, is attacked by the villain and disables him by throwing a pail of carburetor-cleaning fluid in his face. The book offers many scenes on the university campus and, in addition to Illona Berggren and Joe Mancuso, it includes several university students and faculty members in prominent roles. Professorial readers may find special interest in the scene, midway through the novel, in which Joe Mancuso, who considers himself an invaluable member of the university faculty, laments the speed and enthusiasm with which the school's administration accepts his request to take a leave of absence.

At the time this book was published Janet LaPierre lived in Berkeley, California. *Unquiet Grave* was her first novel.

285. LYALL, FRANCIS. *A DEATH IN TIME.* LONDON: COLLINS, 1987.

A small conference of academic economists is held at "Ebony House," a hotel in rural Scotland. Among the attendees is a professor named Benedict, who, despite his English surname, is an emigre from Eastern Europe and a man who is under constant surveillance by British Intelligence. Another person at the conference is Jarvis, a former British security operative who is now a professor of law. Jarvis has been asked by his former employers to watch Benedict during the meeting. During the conference several attendees (including Professor Benedict) lose their lives, and Jarvis, along with Superintendent Mason of the local police, must try to decide whether the deaths were murders, accidents, or suicides. A cold-war espionage novel, with echoes from World War II as well, *A Death in Time* is deliberately opaque, and the motives and full identities of many of its characters are not revealed until the end of the story. Nonetheless, as the conference proceeds it is clear that the assembled British academics have brought to Ebony House their many personal and professional rivalries, and the book contains a great deal of biting dialogue as the conferees criticize each other's presentations. There are no campus scenes. The book is included in this bibliography because the cast of characters consists for the most part of professors behaving in thoroughly professorial ways at an academic meeting.

A Death in Time was Francis Lyall's first mystery novel.

286. MATERA, LIA. *WHERE LAWYERS FEAR TO TREAD*. NEW YORK: BANTAM, 1987.

Four people are murdered at "Malhousie Law School" in San Francisco. The first to die is Susan Green, the brilliant editor of the school's law review. The back of Ms. Green's skull is demolished as she sits in the law review office examining articles that have been submitted for publication. Then two more law review staff members are killed, as is Virginia Miles, a middle-aged, intellectually "mummified" professor of trusts and wills. Filling the book's detective role is Willa Jansson, who is elected to succeed Ms. Green as the law review's editor. A dogmatic liberal, supercynical, and an occasional smoker of pot, the prickly Ms. Jansson comes under immediate suspicion of eliminating her editor-predecessor (and perhaps the three other victims as well), and she engages in sleuthing in order to establish the identity of the real villain. As she labors to clear her name Ms. Jansson barely survives two attempts to make her the book's fifth corpse. Malhousie Law School is noteworthy for the unceasing nastiness of its students, faculty members, and wealthy alumni, and readers may have difficulty developing sympathy for any of the novel's major characters. Indeed, they are likely to agree with Dean Sorenson, the school's hapless chief administrator. After the fourth murder, Sorenson reasons that the only way to end the unpleasantness at Malhousie may be to close the place permanently, and he begins to explore the possibility of having Malhousie's surviving students transfer to other law schools.

Lia Matera graduated from the Hastings College of Law. While a student at Hastings she edited the school's law review. Matera later held a teaching fellowship at Stanford Law School. *Where Lawyers Fear to Tread* was the first in a continuing series of Willa Jansson mysteries. Lia Matera was a resident of Santa Cruz, California, when the book was published.

287. RESNICOW, HERBERT (1922–1997). *THE CROSSWORD HUNT.* NEW YORK: BALLANTINE, 1987.

Abraham Hardwick, a wealthy industrialist, wants to establish an "Institute for Generalist Studies" at "Windham College" in Vermont, and he offers the school an initial gift of fifty million dollars (with much more money to come) if it will carry out his idea. Hardwick insists upon selecting the institute's director himself, and when the six finalists for the job are invited to Windham he reveals that his decision will hinge on the candidates' skills at solving several crossword puzzles that he has composed. As the competition is beginning, Hardwick is choked dead in his home near the Windham campus, and the six candidates for the directorship—all of them prominent academicians—become instant suspects. Handling the detective chores is Isabel Macintosh, a high-level Windham administrator. She is assisted by Giles Sullivan, the retired criminal lawyer who has become the love of her life. As *The Crossword Hunt* proceeds Giles Sullivan shows an impressive facility not only for solving crossword puzzles but for composing them as well. Readers, too, can become involved with crosswords, because five puzzles are spaced within the book's text, and each contains clues to the murderer's identity. Some academic readers might feel that the generalist studies proposed by Mr. Hardwick could prove unworkable in the modern academic world. In addition to several generalist seminars, students enrolled in the institute would be expected to take two courses from each of Windham's many academic majors, and by the end of their college careers they would have taken double the number of courses required for regular degrees. Nonetheless, those same readers will probably admire Abraham Hardwick's strategies for minimizing campus opposition to his scheme. Students enrolled in generalist studies would be given all-expenses-paid scholarships, and upon graduation they would be offered high-paying positions in the Hardwick industrial empire. Moreover, upon college approval of the generalist plan Hardwick proposes to distribute twenty-five million dollars among Windham's existing academic departments so that they might raise faculty salaries.

Isabel Mcintosh and Giles Sullivan can be found detecting in *The Seventh Crossword* (258), an earlier Herbert Resnicow mystery. Successful detection can apparently facilitate administrative promotions in the world of colleges and universities. In *The Seventh Crossword* Isabel Mcintosh was the lowly dean of the college's faculty. In *The Crossword Hunt* she is Windham's president.

288. TAYLOR, ELIZABETH ATWOOD (B. 1936). *MURDER AT VASSAR.* NEW YORK: ST. MARTIN'S, 1987.

Reunion week at Vassar College is marred by two murders. First, Chloe Warren, an elderly lady of immense wealth, is shot dead as she walks across the campus. Then Deborah Marten, an undergraduate, is strangled dead in the costume room of the college theater. The police believe that the two violent deaths may be related, and they suspect Vassar graduate Pudgie Brown, Mrs. Warren's niece, who stands to inherit the bulk of her aunt's fortune. When they find incriminating evidence in Mrs. Brown's home, they arrest her, and she is incarcerated in the Dutchess County jail in Poughkeepsie. Desperate to clear Mrs. Brown of suspicion, some members of the Warren family hire Vassar alum Maggie Elliott to investigate. Eliott is a San Francisco private detective who is in town to attend her fifteenth reunion. She narrates the story. Because much of Elliott's sleuthing involves warfare between Chloe Warren's potential heirs, some of her work takes place off campus. However, there are more than enough scenes at picturesque Vassar to qualify the book for this bibliography, and though the plot does not include any Vassar faculty members, the school's president plays a vital role by saving Elliott's life when the female private eye finds herself in extreme peril. One of the stops in Elliott's travels away from Vassar is Princeton University. There she interviews Professor Paul Lombardi, the director of a genetics research institute, who hopes his facility will get a million dollars from Chloe Warren's estate. In another Princeton scene Elliot comes across the crucial clue that allows her to identify the book's villain.

Elizabeth Atwood Taylor was born in San Antonio, Texas. She received a B.A. from Vassar College in 1957 and an M.S. from Bryn Mawr in 1960. She has worked as an editor of documentary films, as a television news reporter, and as a social worker. *Murder at Vassar* was her second Maggie Elliot mystery.

289. WALTCH, LILLA M. (B. 1932). *THE THIRD VICTIM.* NEW YORK: DODD, MEAD & CO., 1987.

On the morning of April 24, 1984, Professor of English Sheldon Silverman is discovered shot dead in his office at "Addison University." Addison is located somewhere in or near Boston. Lieutenant Irving Cohen of the local police is quickly on the scene. Cohen learns that Silverman had several skeletons in his closet. More than a few female students and faculty members despised him for the unwanted sexual attentions he had paid them, and in 1968, while an undergraduate at "Page University" in upstate New York, the left-leaning Silverman had been arrested in the bombing of a campus research laboratory. Two people were killed in the explosion, but a grand jury found insufficient evidence to put Silverman on trial. Also in on the sleuthing is Lisa David, a graduate student who finds the professor's body. Miss David survives several attempts on her life before the story's conclusion. Many members of the Addison English department appear as suspects. One is Assistant Professor Louis Jason Hammer, who was an undergraduate at Page University at the same time as Silverman and whose grand jury testimony, that he was with Silverman at the time of the laboratory bombing, allowed the future professor to escape trial. Professor Hammer fails to appear for a scheduled interview with Lieutenant Cohen the day after the murder and is scrubbed from the suspect list when he dies in what appears to be the second half of a murder-suicide. Another possible murderer is Mary Reardon, a feisty visiting professor from Ireland. While rejecting one of the diminutive Silverman's advances, Professor Reardon possibly imperiled her professional career by calling him a "leprechaun-sized lecher." For devotees of college mysteries *The Third Victim* contains a bonus. In addition to the many scenes at Addison, there are flashbacks to Silverman's life as a student radical at Page University, and during the Page episodes readers get a glimpse of a harried Vietnam-era college president trying to prevent a catastrophe on his campus.

A resident of Cambridge, Massachusetts, Lilla M. Waltch received a B.A. from Radcliffe College, an M.A. from Boston College, and a Ph.D. from Brandeis University. She has written short stories and mysteries for older children. *The Third Victim* was her first mystery novel for adults and the first of two mysteries to feature the sleuthing of Lisa David.

290. CRIDER, BILL (B. 1941). *ONE DEAD DEAN.* NEW YORK: WALKER, 1988.

This clever, sardonic mystery takes place at "Hartley Gorman College," a small Baptist school in "Pecan City," Texas. The victim in the story is Hartley Gorman's autocratic dean, a man with the last name of Elmore, who dies in his office after someone delivers a fatal blow to his skull. Since Dean Elmore was widely disliked, Sheriff "Boss" Napier of the Pecan City police has a campus full of people with motives for the murder. The person who solves the mystery is Carl Burns, a sour, middle-aged Hartley Gorman professor of English. *One Dead Dean* is crammed with satirical vignettes about life on the bottom rung of the academic ladder, and Professor Burns, who is only too aware of the dismal nature of the school at which he teaches, vents some of his frustration by constantly making lists of the things he dislikes. Like Burns, many of the other Hartley Gorman faculty are victims of a nationwide glut of Ph.D.s. They are unable to escape their academic fate, and like Burns they have developed eccentricities as devices for coping with Hartley Gorman. Students of fictional academic administrators will want to pay special attention to this novel. Not only is nasty Dean Elmore murdered, but A. Clark Rogers, Hartley Gorman's long-suffering president, is pushed to the limit of his endurance by the challenge of presiding over one of America's least distinguished institutions of higher learning.

Bill Crider was born in Maxia, Texas. He was chairperson of the English department at Alvin Community College, Alvin, Texas, when this book was published. He is a prolific and frequently honored writer of mysteries, some of which feature Sheriff Dan Rhodes as sleuth. Three other Crider mysteries appear in this bibliography. Those mysteries are *Dying Voices* (307), . . . *A Dangerous Thing* (383), and *Murder Is an Art* (473). *Dying Voices* and . . . *A Dangerous Thing* are Carl Burns mysteries set at Hartley Gorman College. *Murder Is an Art* is set at "Hughes Community College" and features the detection of Sally Good, chair of Hughes Community's Division of Arts and Humanities.

291. DEIGHTON, BARBARA. *A LITTLE LEARNING.* LONDON: QUARTET CRIME, 1988.

As much a character study of its protagonist as it is a mystery, *A Little Learning* is narrated by Felicity Travers, a young lecturer in social sciences at a British polytechnic somewhere near Birmingham. Throughout the story Miss Travers blunders and bulldozes her way through a variety of personal difficulties. She also engages in a modest amount of detection. When two male students in one of her classes are thrown out of their lodgings for using drugs, Travers allows them to stay in her spare bedroom. Then, when Ken Scott, a lecturer in economics and social history, kidnaps his two small daughters in order to keep his estranged wife from taking them to her native Germany, Travers adds two more members to her household by allowing Scott to leave the girls with her. Next, Sharon Moss, another of Travers's students, is brutally murdered, and Ken Scott is arrested for the crime. Toward the end of the story several other students break into Travers's home and hold her hostage. Meantime, she has an on-again, off-again sexual relationship with a young man named Matt, another of her students, and throughout her narrative she makes it clear that her tumultuous existence is forever fragmented by the continuous need to be on campus at specified times to meet her classes. By the end of this novel Sharon Moss's killer has been apprehended, and some of Travers's immediate personal concerns have become less acute. But as Travers herself tells readers in her narrative, she has poorly developed organizational skills, many students at the polytechnic at which she teaches are little more than thugs, and when it comes to friends and sexual partners, she has a long record of making poor choices. Even though the mystery of Sharon Moss's murder has been solved, many readers will suspect that Felicity Travers's life will continue to be frantic and problem prone.

Barbara Deighton was born in the north of England. She attended a polytechnic, where she studied modern languages. She has worked as a teacher of English in Germany. *A Little Learning* was her first novel.

292. EVERSON, DAVID (B. 1941). *REBOUND.* NEW YORK: BALLANTINE, 1988.

Only a few years ago the men's basketball team at "Lincoln Heritage University" had a 1–20 season record. Now, under new coach "Showboat" Green, and with new, academically deficient players recruited from junior colleges, the team is fighting for the national championship. Lincoln Heritage University is located in Springfield, Illinois, and the Speaker of the Illinois House of Representatives is concerned that a basketball scandal might be brewing right under his nose. Hoping to head off any problems before they cause him political embarrassment, the Speaker asks private investigator Robert Miles to look into the Lincoln Heritage team's recent success. As might be expected, Miles finds arrogant athletes who drive Porsches, drug dealing, and point shaving. He also witnesses the killing of the team's best player and eventually helps bring the murderer to justice. Because Miles's sleuthing focuses on the athletic side of the university, readers learn a great deal about the lives (and sometimes the deaths) of "student-athletes," team doctors, and coaches, but they are not given any extensive looks at the academic goings-on at Lincoln Heritage. Perhaps that is just as well, since the book contains hints that such a view would not be pretty. Marvel Turner, the murdered star player, was majoring in "holistic recreation," and Kirby Cox, Lincoln Heritage's president, believes that the university's new prominence in basketball "is just one piece of the puzzle in our drive for excellence."

David Everson was born in Rochester, Minnesota. He received a B.S. from Indiana State University in 1963 and a Ph.D. from Indiana University in 1969. He was a professor of political science at Sangamon State University in Springfield, Illinois, when this book was published. Everson is the author of several political science textbooks and monographs. *Rebound* was his second mystery novel. Readers of college mysteries might be interested in a later Everson mystery, *A Capital Killing* (New York: Ballantine, 1990). *A Capital Killing* also features private investigator Robert Miles. The novel deals primarily with high-level political and business corruption in Springfield and is not sufficiently "academic" to be given a separate entry in this bibliography. Nonetheless, it contains several scenes at "Lincoln Heritage University," and it offers interesting portraits of the school's new president, Dr. Andrew Slack, and his nubile twenty-four-year-old wife.

293. FERRARS, E. X. [MORNA DORIS BROWN (1907–1995)]. *A MURDER TOO MANY.* LONDON: COLLINS, 1988; NEW YORK: DOUBLEDAY, 1989.

Professor of Botany Andrew Basnett, five years retired from London University, attends a conference at the "University of Knotlington," the school where he began his teaching career. As the conference is beginning Ken Marriott, the university registrar, is found strangled in his home. An E. X. Ferrars series-character sleuth, Basnett learns to his displeasure that his reputation for detecting has preceded him, and a former student, now on the faculty, prevails upon him to help the police in their investigations of Marriott's death. Professor Basnett soon finds that Marriott's murder is linked to another killing, that of fine arts lecturer Carl Judd, two years earlier. Then, after yet another death, this one the apparent suicide of botany professor Walter Greenslade, Basnett discovers that a blackmailer is at work on the campus. *A Murder Too Many* is a smoothly written, leisurely college mystery, and Basnett is a pleasant, low-keyed man who worries that increasing age is diminishing his mental capacities. Some academic readers may find Gwen Sharland another appealing character. She is the wife of botanist Stephen Sharland, who was found guilty of Carl Judd's killing and sentenced to life in prison. Every evening Mrs. Sharland silently asserts her husband's innocence by marching into the university's faculty club, consuming one drink, and leaving after pointedly ignoring the presence of her husband's former colleagues.

After earning a certificate in journalism from University College, London, in 1928, Morna Doris Brown became one of England's most popular and most prolific mystery writers. Over a fifty-year writing career she wrote more than sixty novels under her maiden name, Morna Doris Brown, under her married name, Morna Doris MacTaggart, and under two pseudonyms, E. X. Ferrars and Elizabeth Ferrars. Retired Professor Andrew Basnett appeared in eight mysteries by E. X. Ferrars. *A Murder Too Many* was the fifth mystery in the Professor Basnett series and the only one to have a campus setting. Another novel by E. X. Ferrars, *Thy Brother Death* (363), appears later in this bibliography. Like *A Murder Too Many, Thy Brother Death* takes place at the "University of Knotlington," but Andrew Basnett is not a character in the story.

294. GOLDSBOROUGH, ROBERT (B. 1937). *THE BLOODIED IVY.* NEW YORK: BANTAM, 1988.

The Bloodied Ivy is a Nero Wolfe pastiche. The original Nero Wolfe, now generally considered one of the outstanding detectives in the history of mystery fiction, was created by Rex Stout, and he was the featured sleuth in a popular series of novels that ended with Stout's death in 1975. *The Bloodied Ivy* is set in the 1980s, and it depicts Wolfe, along with his energetic assistant Archie Goodwin, solving the mystery of a murder at an institution of higher education. The school in question is "Prescott University," a high-prestige institution on the Hudson River seventy-five miles north of New York City. The victim is Hale Markham, a politically conservative professor of political science. Markham falls to his death in a ravine in a remote area of the Prescott campus. Wolfe is asked by Walter Cortland, one of Markham's faculty colleagues, to investigate. Though the police are ready to attribute Markham's death to an accident or to suicide, Professor Cortland believes the deceased was murdered, and he presents Wolfe with a list of Markham's campus enemies. The list contains several left-wing political science professors who opposed Markham's views. It also includes Keith Potter, Prescott's president, who feared that Markham's conservatism was preventing Prescott from receiving gifts from liberal donors. In the original Wolfe novels the corpulent detective seldom left his brownstone home on West 35th Street in New York City. In *The Bloodied Ivy* he makes a brief appearance at Prescott when he must rescue Archie Goodwin, who does most of the on-campus legwork in the story, after Goodwin is arrested for illegally entering the home of a suspect. There are many scenes at Prescott, as Goodwin trolls for clues, but the denouement is held in Wolfe's home. It is testimony to Wolfe's status as a sleuth that all of the participants in the tale, even President Potter, make the journey down to Manhattan to hear his words of wisdom. Their trips are worth the effort. Wolfe identifies Professor Markham's killer, and he further reveals that Markham's death was the result of a persistent professorial activity that, almost since the inception of college-mystery fiction, has motivated many aggrieved parties to murder many members of college and university faculties.

Robert Goldsborough was born in Chicago. He received B.A. and M.A. degrees from Northwestern University. At the time *The Bloodied Ivy* was published Goldsborough was executive editor of *Advertising Age. The Bloodied Ivy* was Goldsborough's third Nero Wolfe pastiche.

295. HAYNES, CONRAD. *PERPETUAL CHECK.* NEW YORK: BANTAM, 1988.

"John Jacob Astor College" in Portland, Oregon, assigns Professor Harry Bishop to serve for a semester as faculty liaison to the school's board of trustees. Professor Bishop, a downbeat political scientist who nips shots of whiskey before his classes and takes afternoon naps in his office, would rather avoid the duty, but Dean Lee Connar insists that he cannot shirk his college responsibilities. The professor no sooner takes up his charge when board member Richard Llewellyan, an unpleasant young financial planner, is found stabbed dead in downtown Portland. The police suspect that Geoffrey Erickson, the board's chairperson, may be the villain, and because Erickson is pushing to reduce the number of John Jacob Astor College faculty members who can be tenured, many academic readers also will mark him immediately as a suspicious character. Professor Bishop thinks that Erickson is innocent of Llewellyan's murder, and with the help of Portland newspaper reporter Tucker Nelligan, he eventually finds the real culprit. The often satirical story includes many lengthy scenes at college board-of-director meetings. It also provides several glimpses into the sumptuous homes of the board's wealthy members, some of whom are not quite the paragons of virtue they pretend to be.

Bishop's Gambit, Declined (280), and *Sacrifice Play* (333) are two other Professor Harry Bishop mysteries that appear in this bibliography.

296. KELLY, SUSAN (CROCE) (B. 1947). *TRAIL OF THE DRAGON.* NEW YORK: WALKER, 1988.

Liz Connors is a former college English teacher who now writes freelance crime articles for magazines and, when called upon, acts as a Susan Kelly series-character detective. Connors receives a strange request from Carl DiBenedetto, a professor of English at "Thatcher College" in suburban Boston, for whom she once ghostwrote an instruction manual for his textbook on Elizabethan tragedy. Knowing of Connors' expertise in matters criminal, DiBenedetto asks her to find Bonnie Nordgren, a beautiful young member of the Thatcher English department, who has recently disappeared. DiBenedetto, so he tells Connors, recently lent Nordgren $3,500 to help her obtain an experimental treatment for advanced brain cancer. He has not seen or heard from her since, and he is concerned about her welfare. With the help of her boyfriend, Detective Lieutenant John Lingemann of the Cambridge, Massachusetts, Police, Connors begins to investigate, but Nordgren quickly turns up dead in a Cambridge apartment, the victim of an apparent overdose of drugs. At this point Connors's sleuthing becomes propelled by new questions. Was Bonnie Nordgren really murdered, and if so, who was the culprit? *Trail of the Dragon* takes some sharp turns as it unfolds, and by the end of the tale Connors's detection has directed her toward several characters from the sordid world of Massachusetts politics, one of whom almost ends her life. In spite of its digressions, the book focuses sufficiently on academe to qualify for this bibliography. During the earlier parts of the story Connors spends much of her time interviewing faculty members at Thatcher College and at nearby "Currier College." She also spends time at and around Harvard, including one interlude in the Fogg Museum. Furthermore, she twice impersonates academics in order to draw information from informants. Claiming to be a member of the English department at Brown University, she telephones Bonnie Nordgren's mother, and after telling her that she is doing a follow-up study of Brown graduates, she convinces the woman to give her Nordgren's address. Then, in order to penetrate the protective layers of bureaucracy that surround a Boston businessman who once dated Nordgren, Connors makes contact by pretending to be on the faculty of the Harvard Business School.

Susan Kelly holds a Ph.D. in medieval literature from the University of Edinburgh. At the time this novel was published she was a teacher of English at an institution of higher education in the Boston area. She also taught classes in crime-report writing at the Cambridge, Massachusetts, police academy. *Trail of the Dragon* was her third Liz Connors mystery novel.

297. KELVIN, NED [NORTON D. KLINGHORN]. *PEGGED FOR MURDER.* NEW YORK: PAPERJACKS, 1988.

Richard Lawson, dean of arts and sciences at a large university in the American Midwest, is shot dead in his office. The death-dealing revolver is found near his body, and the local police quickly conclude that the dean committed suicide. Ned Kelvin, a professor of English, suspects murder because Lawson, with whom he often played cribbage, left an unusual arrangement of cards scattered across his desktop. Professor Kelvin, who not only narrates the story but receives author credit as well, takes time from his Twain seminar to serve as the book's sleuth. In something approaching private-eye fashion, Kelvin jousts verbally with most of the book's other participants and at one point he breaks into the university's administrative offices in search of clues. The suspects include Laura, Dean Lawson's estranged wife, and Colonel Chisholm, the former commander of the school's ROTC unit. Dean Lawson, a man of leftist political leanings, recently led a successful effort to eliminate ROTC from the university, and the embittered Chisholm, now retired from the military, operates a religious bookstore near the campus. Also in the book's complement of characters are Beverly Slide, the foul-mouthed, 300-pound local police chief who constantly munches balls of milk chocolate, Jason Stone, the university's politically conservative provost, and Charles Nordlich, the school's in-over-his-head president. Each for his or her own special reason, Slide, Stone, and Nordlich all try to prevent Kelvin from detecting. Professorial readers may appreciate the scene in which President Nordlich, who fears the unfavorable press reports that a murder case would generate about his institution, offers Professor Kelvin the now-vacant deanship if he will halt his investigations.

Pegged for Murder was the only mystery by Norton D. Klinghorn.

298. LUPICA, MIKE (B. 1952). *EXTRA CREDITS*. NEW YORK: VILLARD, 1988.

The protagonist of this sprightly mystery is Peter Finley, a wisecracking New York City television personality. Finley stars in a highly rated show devoted to sensationalistic investigative journalism. He decides to do a program on the bizarre public suicide of Julie Samson, an undergraduate at "Washington Square University" in Greenwich Village. Miss Samson walked into Washington Square Park, stripped to her bra and panties, and shot herself through her head. As Finley begins work on his story, Miss Samson's former roommate, Sara Hildreth, is found murdered in Queens. With Hildreth's death, Finley's focus changes from explaining a suicide to solving a murder mystery. Finley does much of his sleuthing on the Washington Square campus, and his attentions turn to several students and faculty members. One of the latter is supersuave Desmond Akeem Powell, an associate professor of African history. Another is Gus Dancy, chairperson of an academic unit known as the "Department of Contemporary Thought." A campus hippie in the 1960s, Dancy now spends much of his time at Meadowlands Racetrack in New Jersey, and his office is littered with copies of *The Daily Racing Form.* Readers of this tale receive little direct information about the classroom environment at Washington Square, but they are left with the definite impression that the school is an effective training ground for entrepreneurs. The "Extra Credits" in the book's title refers to a student-run escort service, and not to be outdone by their pupils, some of the school's faculty members augment their own incomes by selling grades.

Mike Lupica was born in Oneida, New York. He received a B.A. from Boston College in 1971. At the time *Extra Credits* was published Lupica was a broadcast sports journalist and a syndicated sports columnist for the *New York Daily News*. *Extra Credits* was Lupica's second Peter Finley mystery.

299. MINAHAN, JOHN (B. 1933). *THE GREAT HARVARD ROBBERY*. NEW YORK: NORTON, 1988.

The sleuth-narrator in this unusual mystery is "Little John" Rawlings, a robbery detective with the New York City Police. Rawlings is assigned to guard New York City Police Commissioner Bill Reilly as the latter attends the 350th anniversary of the birth of Harvard, his alma mater, on September 3, 1986. In New York, Reilly has been receiving strange threats from what seems to be a satanic cult. At Harvard, Detective Rawlings finds that he must protect the commissioner from another, presumably unrelated danger. Despite state-of-the-art, high-tech security, the Gutenberg Bible has been taken from the Widener Library, and the Bible-napper, who wants Harvard to divest itself of its holdings in firms doing business in South Africa, insists that Reilly act as the go-between in the negotiations to have the treasure returned. During the first third of the book Rawlings is busy investigating the threats made to Commissioner Reilly in New York City, before their trip to Harvard, but once the action in the novel shifts northward to Cambridge, college-mystery readers will find themselves rewarded with a deluge of Harvard characters and Harvard scenes. Derek Bok, the president of Harvard in 1986, makes an appearance, and Rawlings learns that while Harvard professors sometimes fly first-class, President Bok always insists on going coach. And, in what is his only appearance in a college mystery, Prince Charles, draped in the "dragon-emblazoned gold silk robe" that signifies that he is chancellor of the University of Wales, gives a well-received speech to the assembled Harvard birthday celebrants.

John Minahan was born in Albany, New York. He attended Cornell, Harvard, and Columbia. He is the author of more than a dozen novels. At the time *The Great Harvard Robbery* was published Minahan lived in Miami, Florida. According to information on the cover of the book, he formerly commuted to Cambridge, Massachusetts, every week to teach a course in writing novels at Harvard's Center for Lifelong Learning.

300. QUOGAN, ANTHONY. *THE FINE ART OF MURDER*. NEW YORK: ST. MARTIN'S, 1988.

Matthew Prior, a down-on-his-luck British playwright, is asked by Roger Mold, a former Cambridge classmate, to spend three months as a visiting professor of theater at "Wacousta University" in "Mapleville," Ontario. Professor Mold is head of the university's theater department. Mapleville is forty miles west of Toronto, and Wacousta is, by any standard, one of Canada's least-distinguished institutions of higher learning. Prior's assignment is to teach a playwriting class and to direct a production of his newest work, titled "Armageddon Excuse—Me Fox-Trot," which is intended to be nothing less than the full history of the world as told through the adventures of a theatrical troupe. Soon two student-members of the play's company are murdered and another survives three separate attempts on her life. Prior becomes a detective when the Ontario Provincial Police, believing that he might have insights that they do not possess into the strange world of Wacousta's theater department, ask him to help them with their investigations. Almost all of *The Fine Art of Murder* takes place on the snowy Wacousta campus, and even Matthew Prior has difficulty remembering the identities of the many, many students, faculty members, and Wacousta administrators who appear on the novel's pages. The book contains heaps of satire directed at Canada, its universities, and the theater departments within them. As a college mystery the tale has at least one distinction. It is the only on-campus whodunit in which a petrified elephant penis is employed as a murder weapon.

Born in England, Anthony Quogan received his undergraduate education at Cambridge University. He received a Ph.D. in drama from the University of Toronto. At the time *The Fine Art of Murder* was published Quogan was an associate professor of theater at York University in Ontario. *The Fine Art of Murder* was Quogan's first mystery novel.

301. ROSENTHAL, ERIK. *ADVANCED CALCULUS OF MURDER*. NEW YORK: ST. MARTIN'S, 1988.

An international conference of mathematicians is being held at St. Catherine's College, Oxford. Among the two hundred attendees are Americans Paul Hobart and Martin Kloss. Paul Hobart is a professor of mathematics at the University of California at Berkeley. Martin Kloss is a professor of mathematics at the University of Texas. Professors Hobart and Kloss are archenemies. Kloss once stole a mathematical breakthrough from Hobart and published it as his own. As the conference begins Martin Kloss is shot dead and his body dumped in a field near Oxford. Hobart, whose rented car is identified by a passerby as the vehicle from which Kloss's corpse was unloaded, is arrested. Also attending the conference is Dan Brodsky, a part-time teacher of mathematics at Berkeley who supplements his meager academic wages by working as a private detective. Brodsky and Hobart are good friends, and because he is certain that Hobart is innocent, Brodsky tells the British police about his private-detective work and prevails upon them to allow him to take part in the murder investigation. Without sufficient evidence to hold him, the police eventually release Hobart. Shortly thereafter another conference attendee, University of Texas graduate student Barry Donardy, is killed with the same weapon that extinguished Professor Kloss. Dan Brodsky, who narrates the story, uses the logical skills derived from his mathematics training to identify the guilty party, but not before the surviving conference participants complain bitterly that his inquiries are disrupting the meeting's scholarly atmosphere. Most of the book is set in and around Oxford, but there are some early scenes at Berkeley as Brodsky and Professor Hobart prepare for their trip to England.

Erik Rosenthal was a member of the mathematics department at the University of New Haven when *Advanced Calculus of Murder* was published. The book was Rosenthal's second Dan Brodsky mystery. The first, titled *The Calculus of Murder* (New York: St. Martin's, 1986), is a nonacademic tale in which Brodsky investigates the murder of a San Francisco industrialist. When *The Calculus of Murder* was published Eric Rosenthal was a member of the faculty at Wellesley.

302. SPRINKLE, PATRICIA HOUCK (B. 1943). *MURDER AT MARKHAM.* NEW YORK: ST. MARTIN'S, 1988.

"The Markham Institute" is a prestigious graduate school in Chicago that trains men (no women admitted) for careers in high-level government service. Melanie Forbes, a model, is found strangled dead and wrapped in a rug in the basement of the school's library. Forbes was dating several of Markham's students. The police detective on the case is Mike Flannigan, but the book's focus is on the unofficial sleuthing of Sheila Travis, a late-thirtyish widow who has just taken the job of administrative assistant to John Dehaviland, Markham's icily efficient president. Sheila Travis, in turn, is assisted by her aunt, Mary Beaufort, who has come to Chicago from Florida to look out for her niece's welfare. One of the early suspects in the story is Evelyn Parsons, Travis's immediate predecessor in President Dehaviland's office. Parsons was fired after being accused of stealing a valuable clock. Her strangled corpse is found in a dumpster midway through the story, and the attention of the book's detectives turns to the students with whom first-victim Melanie Forbes had consorted. *Murder at Markham* contains many academic characters and almost all of the action takes place on the Markham campus. In view of the recurring presidential scandals in the late twentieth century, some readers may find the career of the late Evelyn Parsons interesting. After being dismissed by Markham for stealing, Parsons quickly found a new position in Washington on the staff at the White House.

Patricia Houck Sprinkle was born in Bluefield, West Virginia. She received an A.B. from Vassar in 1965. Sprinkle has worked as a hospital patient relations counselor and as director of public relations for a junior college. She also has worked in several capacities in the cause of ending world hunger. *Murder at Markham* was her first novel. At the time *Murder at Markham* was published Sprinkle lived in Georgia. *Murder at Markham* proved to be the first in a continuing series of Sheila Travis mysteries.

303. SUCHER, DOROTHY (B. 1933). *DEAD MEN DON'T GIVE SEMINARS.* NEW YORK: ST. MARTIN'S, 1988.

This novel is narrated by Victor Newman, a young private investigator. Newman is employed by Sabrina Swift, the wife of Bruno Swift, a physicist. Bruno Swift is invited to attend a month-long physics conference at the "Champlain Valley Physics Institute" in Vermont, and Sabrina and Victor Newman tag along to sample the New England air. As the conference is convening, Herve Moore-Gann, a Nobel Prize winner and M.I.T professor, dies after being poisoned. Saul Sachs, a Yale professor and the holder of yet another Nobel Prize, is the chief suspect because he and Moore-Gann had been conducting a twenty-year feud. Other suspects include Theresa Moore-Gann, the professorial victim's long-suffering wife, and Magda, his beautiful and brilliant graduate assistant. The detection is shared by Victor Newman, Sabrina Swift, and Captain Wayne Eaken of the local police, and they find that so many of the conference attendees have reason to murder each other that it takes narrator Newman twenty pages at the end of the story to reveal who killed whom and why. There are no campus scenes. The book is accorded an entry in this bibliography because it offers a rare chance to observe how forty physicists, almost all of them professors, behave in a situation where, according to the conference organizers, they have the opportunity to "eat, sleep, and breathe physics twenty-four hours a day."

Dorothy Sucher was born in Brooklyn, New York. She earned a B.A. from Brooklyn College in 1954 and an M.M.H from Johns

Hopkins in 1975. She has been a psychotherapist in Maryland and the editor-in-chief of a small-town weekly newspaper. *Dead Men Don't Give Seminars* was her first novel.

304. WILLIAMS, DAVID (B. 1926). *TREASURE IN OXFORD*. NEW YORK: ST. MARTIN'S, 1988.

Ernest Cormit, an Oxford dealer in secondhand books, comes into possession of three nineteenth-century sketches of Oxford landmarks. Presumably by John Constable, the sketches seem to have great value, and Cormit hopes to locate a well-heeled customer. One prospective institutional buyer is the nearby "Theodore P. Moneybuckle Architectural Endowment." Located in Oxford just across the street from "All Saints College," the Moneybuckle houses a small museum and a collection of architectural drawings so large that it has never been completely cataloged. When the Moneybuckle's board of directors holds its annual summer meeting in Oxford, its members go as a group to Ernest Cormit's shop to inspect the endowment's prospective purchase. The board members do not know that Cormit, in addition to his interests in books and art, is also a devotee of kinky sex. Shortly after the Moneybuckle directors examine his sketches, someone comes into Cormit's home, ties a bag over his head, and asphyxiates him as he lies shackled to his bed. Although the Oxford police do their share of detecting in this story, the primary sleuth is Mark Treasure, a London merchant banker. Treasure is in Oxford to chair the Moneybuckle board meeting. Many Oxford students and professors, as well as a veteran university servant, appear in the novel, and because the board of the Moneybuckle stays and convenes in All Saints while holding its meeting, readers are taken into some areas of the college to which they would not have access on one of the institution's popular public tours.

Treasure in Oxford was the twelfth novel in David Williams's popular Mark Treasure series. An earlier Mark Treasure tale, *Treasure by Degrees* (193), appears in this bibliography.

305. YAFFE, JAMES (B. 1927). *A NICE MURDER FOR MOM*. NEW YORK: ST. MARTIN'S, 1988.

Stuart Bellamy, an unpopular member of the English faculty at "Mesa Grande College" in Colorado, should be attending a party at the home of his department chairman. Instead, he stays home with the flu. During the evening, Bellamy phones the chairman's house, asks to speak with one of his colleagues, and reads her a quotation over which they have argued. Moments later he is murdered in his living room by someone who crushes his skull with a paperweight. The most likely suspect is Mike Russo, another member of the English faculty. Russo had been competing with Bellamy for their department's one available tenure position, and he had recently lost the battle. Moreover, Russo arrived at the party late, after Bellamy was killed, and his only explanation is that he overslept. There are two detectives in the story. One is a fifty-three-year-old recent widower named Dave. A former New York City policeman, Dave has moved to Colorado to start a new life as an investigator for the Mesa Grande public defender's office. Dave takes up the case when Russo, a fellow New Yorker, is arrested. The other sleuth is Dave's spirited Jewish mother, who has come from New York for a brief visit. Dave does the legwork in the case and makes several visits to the Mesa Grande campus. His mother stays at home, prepares his meals, and provides sage analysis of the clues her son develops. Toward the end of the book Mike Russo commits suicide, and most members of the Mesa Grande community are content to believe that he was Bellamy's murderer. On the flight back to New York, Mom writes Dave a letter in which she names the actual killer and suggests how her son should deal with this revelation.

James Yaffe was born in Chicago. He received a B.A. from Yale in 1948. A writer of books and articles about the Jewish experience in America, Yaffe also has written mainstream novels, mysteries, and television plays. He was a professor of English at Colorado College when *A Nice Murder for Mom* was published. *A Nice Murder for Mom* was the first in a continuing series of "Dave and Mom" mysteries.

306. CAPE, TONY (B. 1951). *THE CAMBRIDGE THEOREM.* NEW YORK: DOUBLEDAY, 1989.

Simon Bowles, a brilliant graduate student, is found hanged in his rooms at Cambridge University's "St. Margaret's College." Since Mr. Bowles had tried unsuccessfully to kill himself two years earlier, almost everyone thinks his death a suicide. Detective Sergeant Derek Smailes of the Cambridge police is not so sure, and as he investigates he discovers that he has an espionage case on his hands as well as a murder inquiry. Then, because Smailes stumbles onto very sensitive matters having to do with the notorious, prewar Cambridge spy ring known as "The Ring of Five," he is soon pressured by British Intelligence to discontinue his sleuthing. Many St. Margaret's characters parade across the pages of this long, intricate novel, including Nigel Hawken, the college's senior tutor. Not always the most pleasant of men, Hawken at least has the kindness to allow the badly shaken Mrs. Allen, a college servant, to take the rest of the day off after she finds Simon Bowles's corpse. The book is also graced with brief appearances by Margaret Thatcher and Kim Philby. By the end of the tale several more university characters join Mr. Bowles in the ranks of the deceased, and Sergeant Smailes, who admires America and Americans to such an extent that he wears lizard-skin cowboy boots and listens regularly to Willie Nelson records, is offered a job as second in command of security at the British United Nations office in New York.

Tony Cape is a graduate of Cambridge University. At the time *The Cambridge Theorum* was published Cape was a resident of New Haven, Connecticut. *The Cambridge Theorum* was his first mystery novel.

307. CRIDER, BILL (B. 1941). *DYING VOICES.* NEW YORK: ST. MARTIN'S, 1989.

The celebrated writer Edward Street returns to undistinguished "Hartley Gorman College" in "Pecan City," Texas, for a conference on his works. Once an impoverished member of the school's English department, Street has become famous and wealthy. He is best known for a book of poems titled *Dying Voices* and for *We All Die Today!* a best-selling adventure novel. Some members of the Hartley Gorman community fear Street's visit because they suspect he is collecting information for a fictional exposé of the school. Before the conference can begin, Street is shot dead in his motel room. The person who finds his corpse, and then becomes the primary sleuth in the story, is Carl Burns, a dour Hartley Gorman professor of English. A few days later, upon entering his office in an ancient, three-story Hartley Gorman building known as "Main," Professor Burns discovers another shooting victim. The second corpse belongs to Harold Duncan, a Dallas newspaper reporter who came to Pecan City to cover the Street conference and who has stayed in town to cover the murder investigation. This novel contains heaps of corrosive irony, and in that context professorial readers who teach at less-than-elite schools (and perhaps those who teach at elite institutions as well) may understand Professor Burns's problem with pigeons. His third-floor office in Main is just beneath the building's attic. Ever since Main was constructed pigeons have been flying into the attic and defecating in its rafters. Burns can constantly hear pigeons above him, and he fears that someday the accumulated weight of their droppings will reach a critical point, collapse his office ceiling, and bury him in hundreds of pounds of bird excrement.

One Dead Dean (290) and . . . *A Dangerous Thing* (383), two other Professor Carl Burns mysteries by Bill Crider, have entries in this bibliography. Still another mystery by Bill Crider, *Murder Is an Art* (473), also appears in the bibliography. *Murder Is an Art* is set at "Hughes Community College" in Texas and the detective is Sally Good, Hughes Community's chair of the Division of Arts and Humanities.

308. CROSS, AMANDA [CAROLYN GOLD HEILBRUN (B. 1926)]. *A TRAP FOR FOOLS.* NEW YORK: DUTTON, 1989.

Canfield Adams, a universally unpopular history professor, dies after falling seven stories from his open office window. Perhaps his death was suicide, but because so many people had motives to kill him, the police suspect murder. So, too, do several members of the administration at the large, urban university in New York City where Adams was employed. The sleuth in the story is Kate Fansler, a professor of English at the university. An Amanda Cross series-character detective who is well-known on the campus for her mystery-solving skills, Professor Fansler is asked by several deans to look into Adams's death and uncover the actual circumstances behind it. Her inquiries take her into the politics of the Department of Middle East Culture and Literature, of which Adams was a member and former chairperson, into Professor Adams's domestic affairs, and into the life and times of Humphrey Edgerton, a black professor of African American literature whom the police consider their main suspect. Before she resolves the Adams matter, Fansler must deal, as well, with the mysterious death of Arabella Jordan, a black undergraduate. Seen near Professor Adams's office just before his fatal plunge, Jordan also dies in a fall, in her case a ten-story drop from the window of her family's apartment. A major theme in this novel is Fansler's distrust of administrators, and even as she detects she fears that there is more than meets the eye to the deans' request for her assistance. As are all the novels in the Kate Fansler series, *A Trap for Fools* is literate, peppered with dry wit, and written with a strong feel for the gender-related problems of women in higher education.

A Trap for Fools is one of seven Professor Kate Fansler mysteries to appear in this bibliography. The others are *Poetic Justice* (156),

Death in a Tenured Position (211), *Sweet Death, Kind Death* (238), *No Word from Winifred* (264), *An Imperfect Spy* (402), and *The Puzzled Heart* (457).

309. HART, CAROLYN G(IMPEL) (B. 1936). *A LITTLE CLASS ON MURDER.* NEW YORK: DOUBLEDAY, 1989.

A Little Class on Murder is set at "Chastain College" in the coastal town of "Chastain," Georgia. R. T. Burke, chairperson of the school's journalism department, is desperate for an adjunct professor, and he asks Annie Laurance Darling, the recently married owner of a local detective-story bookstore, to teach a twice-a-week class. Mrs. Darling is allowed to choose her own topic, and she selects the writings of mystery authors Mary Roberts Rinehart, Agatha Christie, and Dorothy L. Sayers. Mrs. Darling hardly begins the semester when the Chastain College is disrupted by a series of shocking events. Brad Kelly, the editor of the school newspaper, prints a story that reveals embezzlement on the part of Charlotte Porter, a member of the journalism faculty. Mrs. Porter is then found dead of slashed wrists in her home. Chairperson R. T. Burke is beaten to death in his office. Then a bomb explodes in the school newspaper's office. The principal sleuth in the story is Annie Darling, but she has help from a small army of assistants. Chief Wells of the local police is on the case, as is Max Darling, Annie's private-detective husband. Then there are three adult women students in Mrs. Darling's twelve-student class who, along with their teacher, seem to know all there is to know about mystery fiction. As the hunt for Chastain College's villain progresses, Mrs. Darling and her three students constantly refer to well-known mystery novels for guidance and inspiration. At the end of the tale Annie Darling is ready to leave the world of higher education for the sanctity of her bookshop. She has experienced firsthand the murder-producing environment of academe, and, as she tells herself, she now "knows why so many mysteries (have) academic settings."

Carolyn Gimpel Hart was born in Oklahoma City, Oklahoma. She earned a B.A. from the University of Oklahoma in 1958. Hart began her working life as editor of *Sooner Newsmakers*, a University of Oklahoma alumni newsletter, and for several years in the early 1980s she was an assistant professor in the University of Oklahoma's School of Journalism and Mass Communications. She became a full-time creative writer in 1986. Since then she has become one of America's more popular and prolific authors of mystery fiction. *A Little*

Class on Murder was Carolyn Hart's fifth Annie Laurance Darling mystery. A second mystery by Carolyn Hart, *Death in Lovers' Lane* (444), appears later in this bibliography. *Death in Lovers' Lane* features "Henrie O" Collins, another Carolyn Hart series-character detective.

310. HART, ELLEN [PATRICIA BOEHNHARDT (B. 1949)]. *HALLOWED MURDER.* SEATTLE, WASH.: SEAL PRESS, 1989.

While out for a walk one November morning, Jane Lawless, the owner of a Minneapolis bookstore, finds the body of a young woman in a lake. The corpse belongs to Allison Lord, a student at the University of Minnesota. Miss Lord is also a member of the "Kappa Alpha Sigma" sorority, an organization for which Lawless acts as an alumni advisor. The police conclude that the death was a suicide, but Lawless disagrees, and with the help of Cordelia Thorn, her longtime friend and housemate, she undertakes her own investigation. Lawless quickly learns that Miss Lord was sexually ambivalent and torn between two significant others—Mitch Page, a student-busboy at the sorority, and Emily Anderson, a Minnesota graduate student in English literature. Miss Anderson soon disappears, and Mr. Page is found dead of exposure on the banks of the Mississippi River. Lawless, who is openly lesbian, eventually finds the villain of the piece, but not before she almost becomes the third victim in the story when, late in the tale, she literally finds herself on thin ice. The case involves homophobia and religious extremism. The book has many scenes at the Kappa Alpha Sigma house and elsewhere on the Minnesota campus, and several sorority sisters and sorority-house staff people are the primary suspects.

Patricia Boehnhardt received a B.A. from Ambassador College in 1971. *Hallowed Murder* was the first in a continuing series of Jane Lawless mysteries. At the time *Hallowed Murder* was published Patricia Boehnhardt lived in Minneapolis.

311. HAYMON, S(YLVIA) T(HERESA) (B. CIRCA 1918). *A VERY PARTICULAR MURDER*. NEW YORK: ST. MARTIN'S, 1989.

Professor Max Flaschner drives from Cambridge to the city of "Angleby" to attend a physics conference. The winner of a Nobel Prize, Flaschner is lionized by the other delegates, but as he attends a ceremonial dinner he dies after drinking poisoned orange juice. The detective in this opaque and complex novel is Inspector Ben Jurnet of the Angleby police. Jurnet has been assigned as a security officer at the conference, and after Flaschner is murdered he takes charge of the investigation. An early suspect is physicist Tawno Smith, Flaschner's adopted son, who handed the professor the fatal potion. But why should Tawno, who is about to give a paper that may well gain him his own Nobel Prize, want to murder the man who rescued him from possible starvation in post–World War II Germany? Why did Professor Flaschner, a Jew, keep an autographed picture of Herman Goering on the mantlepiece of his study? And is Esther Ahilar, a Cambridge undergraduate from Isreal who is desperately in love with Tawno, really the virgin she claims to be? In searching for the answers to these and other questions, Jurnet does some of his work away from academe. However, the book contains several scenes at the University of Cambridge and at the "University of Angleby," and many of the central characters are professors or students. Furthermore, for those readers who like intellectual depth to their mysteries, the author incorporates references and allusions to physics theories. According to the book's dust jacket, "A theory in quantum physics holds that the mere act of observation changes and shapes events." Inspector Jurnet is portrayed, through his sleuthing, changing and shaping the actions of those he investigates.

Sylvia Theresa Haymon was born in Norwich, England. She has written children's books and nonfiction, but her greatest success has come as the author of richly textured mysteries. *A Very Particular Murder* was the fifth of her mystery novels to feature Inspector Benjamin Jurnet.

312. JAMES, SUSAN [PSEUD.] (B. 1944). *FOUL DEEDS*. NEW YORK: ST. MARTIN'S, 1989.

"Charles College" in upstate New York is staging a production of *King Lear*, but before the play can open two of its participants are murdered. Melissa Richardson, who is to play Cordelia, is strangled and then hung in the college theater's property room. Then, while everyone else is out and about on the campus investigating Melissa's death, Professor Morton Weinstein, one of the play's two faculty directors, is run through with a sword on the theater's stage. Many of the suspects in the story come from the Charles College English department, under whose auspices the show was to have been produced. Among them are Tom Hammock, a young professor whom Melissa was trying to seduce, and Richard Brook, recently rejected for tenure but likely to have his case reconsidered in light of the department's need to replace Professor Weinstein. Although the official detective in the story is Lieutenant Polly Winslade of the New York State Police, Tom Hammock renders invaluable sleuthing assistance. *Foul Deeds* includes several subplots having to do with the general absence of morals and manners at Charles. For example, as the harried Professor Hammock detects he discovers that his wife is having an affair with Peter Nicely, an unemployed man of wealth, who has twice unsuccessfully sought appointment to the English department faculty. The methods of murder in this story (as well as several methods of attempted murder) are drawn, of course, from those depicted in Shakespeare's plays, and when the villain is apprehended he claims that he took his inspiration from an old Vincent Price motion picture (*Theatre of Blood*, 1973) in which a disaffected actor uses forms of murder found in Shakespeare to take revenge on agents, critics, and fellow actors. Clearly, the villain in *Foul Deeds* did not prepare for his deadly activities by an extensive reading of college mysteries. Had he been familiar with the older works in the subgenre, he might have taken his cues from Amelia Reynolds Long's *The Shakespeare Murders* (46), in which another on-campus killer uses Shakespearean techniques to dispatch his victims.

Foul Deeds was the first mystery by "Susan James." Information on *Foul Deeds'* cover tells readers that Susan James is the pseudonym of an academic couple who teach at a college in the American southeast.

313. LAKE, M. D. [JAMES ALLEN SIMPSON]. *AMENDS FOR MURDER*. NEW YORK: AVON, 1989.

It is late on a Friday afternoon during exam week at a large Midwestern university, and poor Professor Adam Warren is in his English department office trying to grade blue books. Unfortunately, across the street rock-and-roll music is blaring from a fraternity house, and the professor calls campus security to get the noise turned down. The campus cop sent to deal with the situation is Peggy O'Neill, a former student at the university who is armed for her job with a layer of protective cynicism. When O'Neill enters Professor Warren's office, she finds him dead in a pool of blood, his skull cracked open by a hammer. Because the professor's desktop computer had been pushed from its table, and was found upside down on the floor beside his corpse, the local police assume that his killing was part of a botched attempt at computer theft. O'Neill, who once studied under Professor Warren, thinks otherwise and conducts her own, independent investigation. The book's important characters include Doris Parker (the English department's loyal secretary), Lee Pierce (a burnt-out poet whose office is next to Professor Warren's), and Arthur Fletcher (the department's harried assistant chairperson). As Officer O'Neill labors to expose the murderer, readers find that the university's English department, rife with abuse of power and sex between professors and students, can compete with any English department in college-mystery fiction in the matter of moral corruption.

Before he retired in 1992, James Allen Simpson was for twenty-eight years a professor of Scandinavian language and literature at the University of Minnesota. He has spent his retirement turning out a stream of Peggy O'Neill mysteries. Eight of his subsequent O'Neill novels are college mysteries and, like *Amends for Murder*, they appear in this bibliography. Those eight novels are *Cold Comfort* (325), *A Gift for Murder* (356), *Poisoned Ivy* (357), *Murder by Mail* (368), *Grave Choices* (410), *Once Upon a Crime* (411), *Flirting with Death* (431), and *Death Calls the Tune* (479). Another Peggy O'Neill mystery, *Midsummer Malice* (New York: Avon, 1997), is set primarily off the campus of the university that employs Officer O'Neill, and it does not have an entry in the bibliography.

314. NAHA, ED (B. 1950). *ON THE EDGE.* NEW YORK: POCKET BOOKS, 1989.

A serial villain is torturing, raping, and murdering female undergraduates on and near the campus of "Bay City College" in the Los Angeles area. Tough-but-vulnerable Lieutenant Kevin Brodsky of the local police is the chief investigating officer. During the course of his inquiries Brodsky meets many of Bay City's students, faculty members, and administrators. One of the student victims was an actress in pornographic films, and one of the professors in the story is former showgirl Cheryl Williams, who now teaches Acting 101. Williams tries to seduce Lieutenant Brodsky, but he already has found a younger sex partner in Melanie Melnick, coeditor of the Bay City student newspaper. Bay City College is depicted as a charmless place without academic integrity. The campus is dominated by "featureless" steel and concrete buildings, and one of its more popular courses introduces students to the practice of spiritualism. Nor is the nearby neighborhood especially pleasant. At one point in the novel Lieutenant Brodsky is called away from his campus detection to deal with an ongoing holdup of a convenience store. After a uniformed policeman is killed a gunfight, the irate Brodsky kills several would-be robbers with an automatic rifle. The book includes an interesting vignette involving the school's president, Bryce Walton. Described as "a double-strength Hefty bag of wind," President Walton objects when Miss Melnick and her coeditor, Stan Webster, run a series of articles advising women on the campus how to take precautions against the murderer. Walton fears that negative publicity will diminish alumni donations. Many readers will revel in the blistering lecture delivered by Lieutenant Brodsky as he excoriates Walton for putting fiscal concerns above the safety of his female students.

Ed Naha was born in Elizabeth, New Jersey. He received a B.A. from Newark State College in 1972. Using his own name as well as several pseudonyms, Naha has written mysteries, science-fiction novels, and screenplays. A specialist in "novelizing" popular movies, Naha has produced book adaptations of motion pictures such as *Robocop* and *Ghostbusters II.*

315. PARKER, ROBERT B(ROWN) (B. 1932.). *PLAYMATES.* NEW YORK: PUTNAM'S, 1989.

Playmates stars Spenser, Robert B. Parker's popular series-character private detective. As the novel opens Spenser is hired to look into possible point-shaving by members of the nationally ranked basketball team at "Taft University" near Boston. Since his employer is the Taft board of trustees, the tough-but-tender Spenser has immediate access to some important information, but he also finds that many of the university people with whom he tries to talk are reluctant to be cooperative. For example, he has to punch basketball coach "Dixie" Dunham twice in the stomach before Dunham sees sufficient reason to help him with his inquiry. Although there are three deaths in the story, the primary mystery has to do with the whos, whys, and hows of the point-shaving incidents. A related question has to do with the illiteracy of Dwayne Woodcock, Taft's best player. Midway through the story Spenser discovers that Woodcock cannot read, and he sets out to learn how the six-foot, nine-inch, power forward has managed to become a senior with a C+ grade average. He interviews several of Woodcock's professors, and academic readers may be interested in the reasons those worthies offer for having awarding Mr. Woodcock better-than-passing grades.

The Godwulf Manuscript (177) and *Hush Money* (480), two other Robert B. Parker mysteries with Spenser as detective, appear in this bibliography.

316. SHUMAN, M. K. [M. S. KARL]. *THE MAYA STONE MURDERS.* NEW YORK: ST. MARTIN'S, 1989.

Tulane University is holding an exhibition of Mayan artifacts that have been excavated under its auspices, but someone is smuggling objects into (not out of) the show. Micah Dunn, an ex-marine who is now a New Orleans private detective, is asked to look into the matter. The person in charge of the exhibition is Gregory Thorpe, an arrogant Tulane professor of archaeology whose young wife, Cora, has a taste for copulating with members of a Tulane fraternity. When Gordon Leeds, a gay graduate student with whom the professor had argued, is the victim of a hit-and-run killing, Thorpe is arrested for murder, and Micah Dunn expands the scope of his sleuthing in an attempt to exonerate him. After Gordon Leeds's death, several more killings take place. Detective Dunn is himself jailed as a murder suspect, and he finds it necessary to escape to continue his investigations. The book has many scenes at Tulane and in nearby residential areas, and it includes many Tulane characters. It also contains a wealth of detail about the Maya civilization and its use of jade. At the end of the story the surviving members of the cast, including Micah Dunn, gather somewhere in Central America to inspect the Tulane excavation project, which is continuing to unearth Mayan treasures. Presumably, the trip also affords them opportunities to rest from their frenetic activities during the earlier parts of the book.

The Maya Stone Murders was the first in a four-novel series of mysteries featuring private detective Micah Dunn. At the time *The Maya Stone Murders* was published, M. S. Karl was a resident of Louisiana.

317. SKOM, EDITH. *THE MARK TWAIN MURDERS.* TULSA, OKLA.: COUNCIL OAKS BOOKS, 1989.

Marylou Peacock, a student of only modest intellectual abilities, is brutally murdered in a women's room in the architecturally futuristic library at "Midwestern University." The sleuths in the story are Beth Austin, a youngish, attractive professor of English, and Gil Bailey, a handsome FBI agent. Gil Bailey becomes involved in the case because the FBI is investigating the theft of rare books from the library. Professor Austin plunges into detection because she is obsessively curious about the sources for an obviously plagiarized term paper on Mark Twain submitted by the late Miss Peacock. Gil Bailey and Beth Austin are single, and a budding romance between them forms the basis for a subplot. The book is laden with literary references, and it includes a riveting scene in which Beth flees for her life through the bowels of the library after the murderer identifies himself to her. Most of the suspects in the case are Beth's English department colleagues. The author has a solid fix on the morals and manners of professors, and the book can be read not only as entertainment, but also as a cautionary tale about a particular form of professorial behavior that may well unleash murderous forces in anyone who practices it. Toward the beginning of the book, the villain of the piece is shown giving serious attention to the contents of undergraduate essays!

The Mark Twain Murders was the first in a continuing series of mysteries by Edith Skom to feature Professor Beth Austin as detective. Skom was a member of the English department at Northwestern University when the book was published. *The Charles Dickens Murders* (468), another Professor Beth Austin mystery by Edith Skom, appears later in this bibliography.

318. STORY, WILLIAM L. *FINAL THESIS.* NEW YORK: ST. MARTIN'S, 1989.

The narrator of this fast-moving mystery is Nick Toland, a professor of English at "Colton College," a high-status liberal arts institution in suburban Boston. Thanks to his army service as a military policeman, Toland has experience as a criminal investigator. As *Final Thesis* begins Toland refuses the request of Darlene Abbott, a Colton undergraduate, to look into the disappearance of her friend Kristin Williams, another Colton student, who has been writing a paper on prostitution and black-market adoptions in Boston's notorious "Combat Zone." However, when both Miss Abbott and Miss Williams are brutally murdered, and when the police begin to suspect Toland of the crimes, the professor drops his reluctance to engage in civilian sleuthing and he sets out to find the killer of the two young women. As the novel proceeds a Colton professor of journalism becomes the book's third victim, and the professor's murder is followed by that of a prominent Boston doctor. Meantime, with the help of Moira O'Shaughnessy, a beautiful departmental colleague whose area of professional specialization is Celtic literature, Professor Toland sets a trap for the book's villains. Some of this story takes place in the seamier sections of

Boston, but Toland finds plenty of reason to detect on the Colton campus as well. Lloyd Markham, Colton's suave president, plays a brief but crucial part in the tale, and readers who are fond of scrutinizing presidential behavior in college mysteries will take considerable interest in the nature of his extra-academic activities.

Final Thesis was William L. Story's second of two Professor Nick Toland mysteries. The first, *Cemeteries Are for Dying* (Garden City, N.Y.: Doubleday, 1982), is not a college mystery.

319. THOMAS, DICEY. *STATUTORY MURDER*. GREENSBORO, N.C.: TUDOR PUBLISHERS, 1989.

Bertha Barstow, an archaeological consultant in Cambridge, Massachusetts, finds the battered corpse of her friend, Harvard professor Aaron Hodgkins, in an elevator in Harvard's Widener Library. Only hours before his death Hodgkins had asked Barstow to examine a small, mysterious statue, and he had entrusted the statue to her care. The official investigator in this case is Lieutenant Anthony DeNovo of the Cambridge police. Bertha Barstow, who sometimes ruminates about a previous (and presumably unpublished) detection exploit having to do with a dead body she found in the British Museum, also sleuths, but because Barstow does not always tell DeNovo all she knows, her relationship with the policeman is sometimes strained. Indeed, at one point in the story Bertha hides by squeezing into a dryer at a laundromat to escape the lieutenant and his attempts to put a stop to her independent detection. The leading suspect in the case is Karl Svenson, a professor of archaeology at Memorial University in St. John's, Newfoundland. Long a strident opponent of some of Professor Hodgkins's theories about Vikings in America, Svenson happened to be in Cambridge to give a lecture the night Hodgkins was killed. Another set of possible killers is the "New England Druids," a cult of robed knife wielders who eviscerate animals and cadavers in response to astrological events. Some of this novel takes place at "Stone Hill," an archaeological site just outside of Cambridge, but there are many scenes at Harvard and at M.I.T. The first chapter, in which Bertha hurriedly searches for information in the Widener Library, and then finds Professor Hodgkins's corpse, will bring back memories to anyone who has ever been deep in the deserted stacks of a large university library just before closing time.

At the time this book was published Dicey Thomas lived in Durham, North Carolina. In addition to mysteries, Thomas has written historical novels and fiction for young adults. According to the very limited biographical information appended to *Statutory Murder*, Thomas is "a historian, librarian, and amateur archaeologist."

320. BABSON, MARIAN. *PAST REGRET.* LONDON: COLLINS, 1990; NEW YORK: ST. MARTIN'S, 1992.

The disappearance of her daughter brings Dee Sawyer from Connecticut to London. Daughter Connie has been participating in an overseas study program at an unidentified London college, and mother Dee's first stop is at the office of Professor Justin Standfast, the college's inimical acting dean. Professor Standfast lives up to his name and refuses adamantly to investigate, claiming that American students often disappear for weeks at a time to go on impromptu tours of Europe. With the help of a friendlier professor named Carson, a man with more sympathy for her fears about her daughter's safety, Dee Sawyer eventually rescues Connie from a very nasty situation. The novel includes only a few scenes on the college's campus, but as she pokes into various nooks and crannies in deepest London, Dee Sawyer meets several of the college's students, and she must deal with an especially noxious member of a faculty family.

Marian Babson was born in Salem, Massachusetts. A transplanted American, she lived in London when *Past Regret* was published. She is a former secretary of the British Crime Writers Association. *Past Regret* was her thirty-first mystery novel.

321. BRAEZNELL, GENE. *THE STAR OF SUTHERLAND.* NEW YORK: WALKER, 1990.

After his wife leaves him for a horse trainer, Jim Harrington resigns his position at an unidentified college in Saratoga Springs, New York, and takes a job teaching English at his alma mater, "Sutherland College," in the backwater town of "Sutherland," South Carolina. He rents a room in an inexpensive boardinghouse, and one night he finds Cowpens Martin, another resident, dying from a severe beating. Before he expires Martin directs Harrington to the location of "The Star of Sutherland," a huge uncut diamond that he found on a construction site. Down to his last $120, Harrington keeps the diamond, only to find that several parties in the town of Sutherland and at the college know of its existence and want it for themselves. John Hill, a geology professor, plays an important role in the story, as does meretricious

Yates Sutherland, the grandson of the college's founder and the school's current president. Neither Hill nor Sutherland are alive at the end of the novel. Jim Harrington, who comes under suspicion for Cowpens Martin's murder, narrates the tale in breezy fashion, and even while engaging in detection-for-survival, he offers readers many unflattering depictions of life at Sutherland. The town is home to a collection of unreconstructed rednecks, and the college is the kind of institution, if one is to believe Harrington, that requires constant alcoholic fortification for faculty survival. The college librarians ask "Why?" if a faculty member tries to see material outside his or her discipline, and the president lives in an ostentatious, redbrick French provincial mansion framed by huge gaslight torches that give the place the look of a "firehouse on fire."

According to dust-jacket information, Gene Breaznell attended a college in South Carolina that is "similar to that portrayed in this, his first novel." At the time *The Star of Sutherland* was published Breaznell lived in Garden City, New York.

322. CROSBY, VIRGINIA. *THE FAST DEATH FACTOR.* TULSA, OKLA.: COUNCIL OAKS BOOKS, 1990.

Julian Merton, the president of "Tipton College" in Southern California, dies in his office after drinking wine dosed with a fast-acting poison. An early suspect is Anne Parker-Brown, the tall, red-haired dean of the faculty, who is rumored to have had more than a bureaucratic relationship with her boss. When a lesbian assistant professor of psychology and then the school's director of buildings and grounds also become murder victims, the police are forced to look beyond President Merton's death toward the possibility that a serial killer is indiscriminately murdering people on the Tipton campus. The officer in charge of the case is Thaddeus Walker, chief of the Altamira, California, police. He is assisted by his disabled sister, Mary, who sleuths from a wheelchair. Mary is an assistant editor of the Tipton alumni magazine. During the course of this tale readers are introduced to many Tipton secretaries, faculty members, and administrators, and the plot of the novel twists and turns as the various Tipton characters come into play. The story, which involves art theft as well as faculty and administrative rivalries, contains much subtle satire and an unusual ending. It concludes with the surviving Tiptonites at a memorial service for Vince Riley, the late buildings and grounds director. Immediately following the service, Priscilla Merton, the murdered president's widow, stands alone and ignored outside the hall where the ceremony was held. She reflects on how, just two weeks earlier, as the president's wife she was a woman whose company was coveted by everyone on the campus.

Virginia Crosby wrote *The Fast Death Factor* after retiring from Pomona College in California as a professor emeritus of French. During her long career at Pomona, Ms. Crosby also served as dean, as director of public relations, and as secretary of the Pomona College Board of Trustees.

323. HILLMAN, DOROTHY ANN (B. 1933). *THE FALLEN NUN*. PORT WASHINGTON, N.Y.: ASHLEY BOOKS, 1990.

Sister Monica Celeste, an elderly, unpleasant teacher of medieval literature, falls to her death from the chapel tower at "St. Agatha's College." St. Agatha's is a Catholic school for women on the shores of Lake Champlain in "Pineport," Vermont. The local police believe Sister Monica was pushed, and Sister Corinne Cabot, St. Agatha's acting president, suspects that one or more of five undergraduate suitemates did the evil deed. The five young women in question all believe they were wronged in some way by Sister Monica. One of them, for example, will not be able to graduate with her class because Sister Monica gave her a failing grade. Another thinks that Sister Monica unjustly blackballed her and thus prevented her from winning St. Agatha's $10,000 Walbridge Prize, a award given to a graduating senior for scholarly achievement. There are several sleuths in the story, which eventually involves members of some of the five young women's extended families. Two policemen, Lieutenant Paganelli and Sergeant Schneider, handle the official detection, but President Sister Corinne and handsome Tim Bachmann, an undergraduate at nearby "Vermont State College," also investigate. Bachmann, who has already dated some of the five young ladies, is asked by Sister Corinne to renew his relationships with the quintet in order to learn about their movements on the night of Sister Monica's death. In the end it is Sister Corinne who identifies the villain in the piece, but not before that person almost replicates Sister Monica's death by trying to push Sister Corinne off the same tower. Readers who are interested in the ways in which college and university presidents are portrayed in fiction may find Sister Corinne an interesting character. The daughter of a former United States Supreme Court justice, Sister Corinne entered the religious life after spending a year at Harvard Law School. After taking her vows she obtained a doctorate in political science from the University of Vermont. Now in her early forties, she is an attractive woman who wears contemporary dress and who is openly pro-choice on the issue of abortion. The dean of English and history at St. Agatha's, she is serving as acting president while the actual head of the institution, Mother Hildegarde, is on a one-year sabbatical in Spain. Throughout the book Sister Corinne is romanced by Michael Bachmann, Tim Bachmann's uncle, who is a distinguished, pipe-smoking professor of political science at nearby Vermont State. Sister Corinne and Professor Bachmann were classmates at Harvard Law, where he fell in love with her. Though Sister Corinne does not yield to temptations of the flesh during this story, at the end of the book she hints that her days as a nun might be numbered.

According to information on the cover of this book, at the time the novel was published Dorothy Ann Hillman and her husband owned and operated a skiing lodge. Dorothy Hillman also was an associate editor of a college newsletter.

324. KLASS, DAVID (B. 1960). *NIGHT OF THE TYGER*. NEW YORK: ST. MARTIN'S, 1990.

A female Yale student is brutally murdered in the twelfth-floor stacks of the Sterling Library. The New Haven police consider the matter a self-contained incident, but Kevin Malloy Randall thinks otherwise. A professor of romance poetry, Randall associates the current killing with the death of his wife under similar circumstances two years before. In his wife's case, the police closed their investigation after the man they suspected of the crime died in an automobile accident. Now, thinks Randall, the real murderer of his wife has returned to strike again. As the story continues, Randall is proven correct, but the evildoer is not an easy person to identify. Only after another female Yale student is attacked in the Sterling stacks do the police begin to accept Randall's view that a serial killer is on the loose, and only after Randall takes it upon himself to make an investigatory trip to England does the identity of his wife's assailant become clear. Then, it takes a several-alarm fire in the Sterling Library and some inspired work with a saber on Randall's part before the guilty party is brought to justice. Those who are familiar with Yale will recognize many of the New Haven landmarks that are used as props in this story, and some may agree with Professor Randall when he muses that "no campus in America (is) as gloomy, as fortresslike, as shadowed, and as haunted as the Yale campus."

A native of Vermont, David Klass received a B.A. from Yale in 1982 and an M.A. from the University of Southern California School of Cinema-Television in 1989. He has taught English in a Japanese high school, created screenplays, and has written fiction for young adults. *Night of the Tyger* was his first novel for adults.

325. LAKE, M. D. [ALLEN SIMPSON]. *COLD COMFORT.* NEW YORK: AVON, 1990.

It is winter at a large institution of higher education that gives every appearance of being the University of Minnesota, and as she makes her campus rounds, hardworking security officer Peggy O'Neill seeks the solutions to several mysteries. Was the shooting death of Mike Parrish, a young, perfectly healthy computer expert in the biology department, really a suicide? Why would Jason Horn, an obscure professor of pharmacy, break into the office of Lucas Calder, the university's most celebrated scientist? And who would then stab Horn dead and throw his partially naked body into a campus snowbank? Before this fast-moving and subtly satirical novel ends O'Neill learns the answers to those questions. In the process, even as she survives two attempts on her life, she also learns about supercomputers, international business espionage, and the lust of some professors for money. On a less-lethal level, Officer O'Neill wonders about something else. Will kindly old Professor Hamilton, who taught her German during her days as a university student, ever finish his lifetime effort to write a book on Thomas Mann? Alas, that issue goes unresolved. At the conclusion of the story Professor Hamilton is still working on his decades-in-the-making manuscript.

Eight other Peggy O'Neill mysteries by James Allen Simpson are included in this bibliography. Those mysteries are *Amends for Murder* (313), *A Gift for Murder* (356), *Poisoned Ivy* (357), *Murder by Mail* (368), *Grave Choices* (411), *Once Upon a Crime* (412), *Flirting with Death* (431), and *Death Calls the Tune* (479).

326. LOGAN, MARGARET (B. 1936). *C.A.T. CAPER.* NEW YORK: WALKER, 1990.

The C.A.T (College Aptitude Test) is taken each year by those students who seek admission to high-status American colleges and universities. And each year, for five grueling days, nearly 150 teachers of English gather at the Beasley Center, a mansion north of Boston, to grade approximately 90,000 student essays written as part of the

C.A.T exam. Some of the teachers come from high schools; some come from colleges and universities. Reading student prose as fast and as furiously as they can, the graders experience severe numbing of the mind by day, but at night they unwind by socializing with each other and, on occasion, by entering into sexual relationships. The center is owned by Professor Prescott Beasley, a man of very advanced age, and the members of his family are increasingly worried about the disposition of the mansion after his death. The murder victim in the novel is Millicent Milledge, a feminist professor of English at "Mohawk College," who has been evaluating C.A.T. essays for many years. A woman with several enemies among the graders, Professor Milledge is found dead in her room with a severe injury to the base of her skull. Seen driving away from the center after the killing is Jason Armbruster, a born-again Christian high-school student with a police record, and Jason becomes the most likely suspect. The detection in the novel is handled by Dodge Hackett, a high-school teacher from Illinois, who suspects that an English teacher, not Jason Armbruster, did the evil deed. Although *C.A.T. Caper* does not take place on a college campus, it features many professor-graders as important characters. Furthermore, by way of justifying the inclusion of the book in this compendium of college mysteries, one must presume that it is thanks to these professors' heroic grading labors that many of the student villains and victims in the other mysteries in this bibliography were admitted to the schools of their choice.

Margaret Logan was born in China, the daughter of American missionaries. She has an undergraduate degree from the University of Richmond and an M.A. from Boston University. She is a travel writer as well as a writer of mysteries. At the time *C.A.T. Caper* was published Logan lived in Boston, where she was a teacher at the Harvard Extension School. *C.A.T. Caper* was her third mystery novel.

327. SMITH, ROSAMUND [JOYCE CAROL OATES (B. 1938)]. *NEMESIS.* NEW YORK: DUTTON, 1990.

Nemesis is an unremittingly grim suspense story set at the "Forest Park Conservatory of Music" in "Forest Park," Connecticut. Forest Park is a one-hour drive from New Haven. The conservatory awards degrees, and it possesses administrative and faculty-rank structures similar to those found in less specialized institutions of higher education. The event that fuels the tale is the homosexual rape of Brendan Bauer, a graduate student in composing, by Distinguished Professor of

Music and Composer-in-Residence Rolfe Christensen. When the arrogant Christensen subsequently dies after eating poisoned chocolates, Bauer becomes the prime suspect. Acting as detective is Maggie Blackburn, an accomplished concert pianist who is a Forest Park assistant professor. Blackburn refuses to believe that the shy, inoffensive Bauer killed Christensen, who was disliked by many people at the conservatory, and by wedging sleuthing between her classes and her concerts she looks for the professor's real killer. Several additional members of the Forest Park faculty appear in the novel. One of them becomes the book's second murder victim, and another disappears. Ex-marine Calvin Gould, the school's dean, also plays a prominent role. Upon hearing of the rape, Gould immediately starts the conservatory's judicial machinery in motion to deal with Professor Christensen. The result of the process will be of interest to many readers from academe. Although Christensen does not live to experience his "punishment," Forest Park permanently removes him from contact with students, but it allows him to retain his rank, his office, his faculty rights and privileges, and his considerable salary. The book contains some unusual twists of plot and more character development than is usually encountered in mystery novels. Both Maggie Blackburn and Brendan Bauer are portrayed as sexually repressed, and a prominent subtheme is their search for sexual identities.

Rosamund Smith is a pseudonym occasionally employed by Joyce Carol Oates, one of America's most prolific and most honored writers of fiction. Oates was born in Millersport, New York. She received a B.A. from Syracuse University in 1960 and an M.A. from the University of Wisconsin in 1961. She taught at the University of Detroit and the University of Windsor before becoming a writer-in-residence at Princeton in 1978. Oates subsequently became the Roger S. Berlind Distinguished Professor at Princeton. *Nemisis* was Oates's third mystery published under the Rosamund Smith pseudonym.

328. APPIAH, ANTHONY (B. 1954). *AVENGING ANGEL.* NEW YORK: ST. MARTIN'S, 1991.

The Apostles, an ancient scholarly organization at the University of Cambridge, suffers the sudden deaths of two of its members. David, Viscount Glen Tannock, a blue-blooded undergraduate with a severe intolerance for penicillin, expires after drinking a late-night cup of cocoa laced with the drug. Then Charles Phipps, a faculty member and one of the world's leading experts on brain chemistry, dies after consuming a Coca-Cola fortified with lethal neurotoxin. Shortly thereafter a third Apostle, mathematics professor Godfrey Stanley, almost meets his demise when he smokes a pipe sprinkled with more neurotoxin. Sir Patrick Scott, a distinguished London attorney and a one-time Apostle himself, is asked by Lord Glen Tannock's family to assist the police with their investigations. Along with a talent for sleuthing, Sir Patrick has the advantage of personal acquaintance with many of the Apostles, and by the end of the book he has trapped the guilty party into a confession. Because the Apostles have various university affiliations, Sir Patrick moves in and out of several Cambridge colleges as he detects. One of the lines of inquiry that Sir Patrick follows involves an event that occurred more than forty years earlier, during World War II. The characters in this story have none of the playfulness displayed by the performers in some on-campus whodunits, but *Avenging Angel* is nonetheless college mystery in virtually undiluted form.

Anthony Appiah was born in London. The son of a British diplomat, he spent much of his childhood in Africa. He received a B.A. from Clare College, Cambridge, in 1975 and a Ph.D. in philosophy from Cambridge in 1982. He has taught at the University of Ghana, Yale, Cornell, and Duke, and in 1991 he became a professor of Afro-American studies at Harvard. *Avenging Angel* was his first work of fiction.

329. BELFORT, SOPHIE [KATE AUSPITZ]. *THE MARVELL COLLEGE MURDERS.* NEW YORK: DONALD FINE, 1991.

This novel is set at the "Center for Participatory Politics" at "Marvell College," an institution that bears a striking resemblance to Harvard. The center is a think-tank in which professors, graduate students, politicians, and visiting activists study America's most pressing social problems. Two members of the center's staff are murdered. The first is Richard Llewellyn, a graduate student, who is stabbed dead in the Boston Public Library as he conducts research. The second is Jake Lawson, a United Auto Workers organizer who is at the center for a year on a "mid-career" fellowship. Jake Lawson meets his end when he is shot in his apartment after having sex with Margaret Donohue, a teachers' union officer who is another of the center's mid-career fellows. The detection is provided by Molly Rafferty, a professor of history at nearby "Scattergood College," and by her policeman boyfriend, Lieutenant Nick Hannibal. Hannibal asks Professor Rafferty for assistance because he reasons that her knowledge of academic folk far exceeds his own. The center is laced with personal and professional jealousies, and the two sleuths have an abundance of suspects. The book contains detailed descriptions of job interviews conducted by a center committee as it seeks to fill an assistant professorship for which the ill-fated Richard Llewellyn was a candidate. *The Marvell College Murders* is touted on the dust jacket as a "mordant satire," but the absurdities of the interviews may seem like only transcriptions of real-life dialogue to readers who have participated in actual candidate-vetting sessions. The character who is subject to the most telling satirical barbs is Norman Clausen, a professor of political and social statistics, who is the center's leading academic luminary. A small, fussy man, Professor Clausen has lost his favorite dictionary, and when writing his many books and articles, he avoids using words he cannot spell. At one point in the tale Clausen is accused by his wife of philandering while at a professional convention in Detroit. Clausen denies the accusation, claiming that he limited himself to "exchanging . . . hypotheses" with fellow attendees.

According to information on the cover of *The Marvell College Murders,* Sophie Belfort is a political historian who writes mystery novels "to keep me out of the slammer." At the time the book was published she lived in Somerville, Massachusetts. *The Marvell College Murders* was the second Sophie Belfort mystery to feature Professor Molly Rafferty and Lieutenant Nick Hannibal. The first, *The Lace Curtain Murders* (New York: Atheneum, 1986), is not a college mystery. Information on the cover of *The Lace Curtain Murders* tells us that Professor Rafferty and Lieutenant Hannibal detect "in the grand tradition of civilized lovers and witty sleuths such as Lord Peter Wimsey and Harriet Vane and Nick and Nora Charles."

330. CARLSON, P(ATRICIA) M(CELROY) (B. 1940). *MURDER MISREAD.* NEW YORK: DOUBLEDAY, 1991.

Did Talbott Chandler commit suicide, or was he murdered? A retired professor of educational psychology, Chandler is found shot dead on the campus of a large university in "Laconia," New York. A small pistol is clutched in his right hand. Curiously, Professor Chandler had just invited many of his friends to a luncheon to celebrate something he promised to reveal at the gathering. Furthermore, Chandler was left-handed. Helping the local and campus police look into Chandler's death is Maggie Ryan, a consultant from New York City. Ryan has come to Laconia to work as project statistician on a study of children's reading techniques. The director of the research is Charlie Fielding, an overworked associate professor of educational psychology. Since Ryan's doctorate is from the university, she already knows some of the many faculty and staff characters whom she encounters in this story, and benefiting from her head start in the learn-about-the-suspects department, she eventually uncovers the real facts about Professor Chandler's death. The story takes place in 1977, well before the promulgation of antismoking rules, and that explains why Professor of French Anne Chandler, the late Talbott Chandler's widow, can compulsively puff her "smelly" Gauloise cigarettes anywhere on the campus. However, the year in which the tale is set does not explain how Talbott Chandler, who seemed to have known some very disturbing things about members of the university's faculty, managed to survive a full four years into his retirement.

Murder Misread is the last of four Maggie Ryan exploits to appear in this bibliography. The first three Ryan college mysteries are *Audition for Murder* (248), *Murder Is Academic* (249), and *Murder Is Pathological* (262). In *Audition for Murder* Maggie Ryan meets actor Nick O'Connor, and in *Murder Is Pathological* O'Connor tries to entice Ryan to marry him. By the time *Murder Misread* takes place Ryan and O'Connor are, indeed, married and have two children.

331. FORREST, H. J. [PSEUD.]. *PUBLISH OR PERISH.* DUBLIN, IRELAND: GLENDALE PUBLISHING, 1991.

Set at an unidentified but high-status university in Dublin, Ireland, *Publish or Perish* deals with death and intrigue in the school's genetics department. Associate Professor Brian Berry expires in his office one evening of an apparently self-inflicted gunshot. However, when the police pathologist determines that Berry would not likely have been smoking his pipe with one hand while shooting himself with the other, Inspector Mitchell, the law-enforcement official in charge of the investigation, knows he has a murder case. A probable villain is the department head, Professor Bob Roche, whom Berry bitterly opposed for the department's top job some fifteen years earlier. The problem is that Roche was not on campus at the time of Berry's killing. Instead, he and most of the department were at a downtown hotel honoring Conor Dodd, another associate professor, who was receiving an award for his prodigious DNA research. Inspector Mitchell's gimlet eye then falls on attractive Catherine Gildea, a senior lecturer and Berry's one-time mistress, who, like Berry, had skipped the Dodd dinner and was working late in the genetics department's offices. But the inspector and Gildea soon have a steamy sexual liason, and rather than look for reasons to arrest a bedmate, Mitchell tries to come up with an alternate suspect. With a large cast of geneticists, most of whom have long-standing reasons for disliking each other, the book will find favor with those whose tastes run to college mysteries that focus on a single academic department. Adding to the flavoring for college-mystery fans, as Inspector Mitchell tries to find Brian Berry's killer, he (and readers along with him) learns a great deal about the structure, policies, and politics of higher education in Ireland.

According to information on the cover of this book, H. J. Forrest is the pseudonym of a senior lecturer at a Dublin university.

332. HADDAM, JANE [ORANIA PAPAZOGLOU (B. 1951)]. *QUOTH THE RAVEN.* NEW YORK: BANTAM, 1991.

The sleuth in this story is Gregor Demarkian, a retired FBI agent. Demarkian travels from his home in Philadelphia to "Independence College" in central Pennsylvania to give a Halloween-night lecture on the techniques used by the FBI to apprehend serial killers. No sooner is Demarkian on the Independence campus when two disturbing events occur. First, Professor Donegal Steele disappears. An obnoxious historian, Steele heads the college's interdisciplinary studies program. Then Maryanne Veer, Professor Steele's secretary, is horribly burned about her face and in her throat when she ingests lye in the college cafeteria. Demarkian, who is present when the Veer incident occurs, immediately notes that all the secretary had consumed was an untainted cup of tea. Thus, as he begins his detection, Demarkian's task with regard to the attempt on Miss Veer's life is not only to identify the culprit, but to discover how that person managed to administer the lye as well. Before Demarkian concludes the case, he is introduced to many, many Independence College faculty members and students, some of whom dislike each other, and all of whom despise the missing Professor Steele. He also learns that Halloween is a major event at Independence, that many folks at the college wear costumes on that day, and that the school's Halloween night bonfire can provide opportunity for a murderer. *Quoth the Raven* is slow moving. Many of the major characters, including Demarkian, are allowed lengthy internal monologues, and the novel is gorged with sly, satirical detail about Independence College and those who populate it. Students of college mysteries will appreciate the perspicacity of David Markham, chief of the local police. Chief Markham knows that many people in higher education disrespect policemen and believe they have inferior intellects. Markham is a graduate of both Swarthmore and Stanford Law School. To get members of the faculty at Independence College to drop their guards when talking with him, he consciously adopts a twang and otherwise behaves like, as he puts it, "an unspoiled primitive."

Orania Papazoglou was born in Bethel, Connecticut. She holds an A.B. from Vassar and an A.M. from the University of Connecticut. She did further graduate study at Michigan State. *Quoth the Raven* was the fourth in a continuing series of Gregor Demarkian novels written under Papazoglou's Jane Haddam pseudonym. A later Demarkian adventure, *Mother Superior* (New York: Bantam Books, 1993), takes the former FBI agent once again to a college campus. The institution is "St. Elizabeth College" in Radnor, Pennsylvania. At St. Elizabeth Demarkian solves the murder of Sister Joan Ester of the Sisters of Divine Grace. *Mother Superior* is not accorded an entry in this bibliography because the case is not "academic." The Sisters of Divine Grace are holding a convention at St. Elizabeth, and while the story takes place on higher-education turf, all of the major characters are nonacademic visitors to the St. Elizabeth campus.

333. HAYNES, CONRAD. *SACRIFICE PLAY.* NEW YORK: SEVERN HOUSE, 1991.

The sleuth in this humorous novel is Harry Bishop, a former army officer and CIA agent who is now a rumpled, freethinking professor of political science at "John Jacob Astor College" in Portland, Oregon. As part of an agreement regulating the timber trade between the United States and Japan, an exchange of students and faculty is proposed between John Jacob Astor and several Pacific Rim institutions of higher education. Professor Bishop and his lady friend, economics professor Kate Fairbain, become involved in the negotiations that take place in a downtown Portland hotel. The murder victims in the story are two men who, at first glance, seem to be American businessmen. However, as Professor Bishop discovers, the men had interests in matters more sinister, and more profitable, than timber sales. Much of this tale takes place at the negotiations hotel, but Bishop and Fairbain travel back to the nearby John Jacob Astor campus with enough frequency to qualify the book for admission to this bibliography. One on-campus episode will amuse readers who are familiar with the problematic operations of academic bureaucracies.

Thanks to one of John Jacob Astor's chronic administrative foul-ups, Professor Bishop receives a teaching schedule that takes him out of the classroom and assigns him to coach the men's basketball team. Instead of informing the administration of its error, Bishop gleefully packs away his syllabi, transports himself to the school's gymnasium, and prepares to assume his coaching duties.

Bishop's Gambit, Declined (280), and *Perpetual Check* (295), two other Conrad Haynes mysteries featuring Professor Harry Bishop, appear earlier in this bibliography.

334. HOLT, HAZEL (B. 1928). *THE CRUELLEST MONTH.* NEW YORK: ST. MARTIN'S, 1991.

Several bookshelves collapse in Room 45 of the New Bodleian Library in Oxford, and elderly part-time librarian Gwen Richmond is killed, apparently by a falling copy of the *Encyclopaedia Britannica.* The Thames Valley Police, who solve so many of the crimes found within the novels in this bibliography, make a wrong call on this one. They consider Gwen Richmond's death an accident. Fortunately for the cause of law and order, Sheila Malory suspects murder. An Oxford graduate, and now a modestly successful British literary critic, Mrs. Malory is in Oxford to do research on women writers of 1940s. She has a hunch that there was foul play in Gwen Richmond's death, and with the sporadic help of Chester Howard, a visiting professor from Harvard, she investigates. By the end of the novel Mrs. Malory has identified the villain, but not before she has attempted to bully a confession from an innocent man. The falsely accused individual, arrogant Oxford don Arthur Fitzgerald, denies murdering anyone, and in a scene in which most college-mystery fans will delight, Fitzgerald verbally demolishes Mrs. Malory's theory of the killing with all of the icy contempt for intellectual inferiors that one expects from Oxford faculty in fiction. *The Cruellest Month* offers a cast of engaging Oxford characters, a great deal of information about what is located where in the Bodleian Library, and several tours through the streets of Oxford. It also provides an intricate mystery that, as Sheila Malory discovers, has its roots in World War II.

Hazel Holt was born in Birmingham, England. She received a B.A. from Newnham College, Cambridge, in 1950. At the time *The Cruellest Month* was published Holt lived in Somerset, England, with her retired husband. *The Cruellest Month* was the second novel in Holt's popular Sheila Malory series. Another Sheila Malory mystery by

Holt, *Mrs. Malory, Detective in Residence* (390), appears later in this bibliography. Hazel Holt also is the author of *A Lot to Ask: A Life of Barbara Pym* (New York: Dutton, 1991). Holt and Pym were friends, and on Pym's death in 1980 Holt became her estate's literary executor.

335. KNIGHT, KATHRYN LASKY (B. 1944). *MORTAL WORDS.* NEW YORK: SUMMIT BOOKS, 1991.

The widow of a Harvard professor, Calista Jacobs is a resident of Cambridge, Massachusetts, an award-winning illustrator of children's books, and the mother of brilliant thirteen-year-old son. At a conference on children's literature in Boston Mrs. Jacobs is heckled by a religious fundamentalist, and that night another conference participant, children's author Norman Petrakis, is murdered in his room at the Sheraton Hotel. Petrakis's killing is so grisly that the Boston police refuse to release any details, saying only that the words "Monkey's Uncle" were scrawled in blood on a wall at the death scene. Even as Mrs. Jacobs tries to digest those unsettling events, someone breaks into her home and defaces one of the books she has illustrated. Chaffing at the inefficiency of the local law enforcement officials, young Charley Jacobs fires up his computer, illegally taps into several data bases, and comes to the conclusion that the source of the Boston-area incidents is to be found at the "Lorne Thornton College of Christian Heritage" near Dallas, Texas. Lorne Thornton College bears the name of the television evangelist who founded it and who acts as its president. Charley applies for admission to the school, and accompanied by his mother, he travels to Texas, takes a tour of the facilities, and meets many of Lorne Thornton College's staff, faculty, and students. As a result of Charley's inspired detection *Mortal Words* is the only mystery in this bibliography in which readers are taken inside an on-campus "Creation Science Center." The book contains scenes at two more institutions of higher learning as well. Calista Jacobs's significant other, Smithsonian archaeologist Archie Baldwin, is a member of the board of overseers for Harvard's Peabody Museum, and in one episode he attends a dinner at 17 Quincy Street, Cambridge, the ceremonial home of Harvard's president. For his part, Charley continues his detection in cyberspace after completing his examination of Lorne Thornton College, and toward the end of the story he makes heavy use of the computer facilities at a research institute associated with M.I.T.

Trace Elements (270), another Calista and Charley Jacobs mystery by Kathryn Lasky Knight, appears earlier in this bibliography.

336. MACKIN, EDWARD [RALPH MCINERNY (B. 1929)]. *THE NOMINATIVE CASE.* NEW YORK: WALKER, 1991.

Set at the "Lyndon Johnson" campus of the City University of New York, *The Nominative Case* is campus mystery at its most sardonic. Stanley Bledsoe, a full professor of English, has achieved rank and tenure through pedestrian professional writings, but he aspires to be a poet. He composes furiously and sends out a poem a week for possible publication. August Frye, his older and more playful office mate, submits a poem by Henry VIII to a prestigious journal under Bledsoe's name, and the poem is accepted. Unable to remember writing the accepted piece, Bledsoe celebrates, until the journal discovers the poem's source and Bledsoe is accused of plagiarism. Shortly after that Bledsoe is found asphyxiated in his locked automobile. Unable to believe that Bledsoe killed himself, and suffering pangs of guilt as well, August Frye enlists the help of Jim Cable, a former graduate student now a sergeant in the New York Police Department. From then on, events and related subplots pile onto each other. All of the surviving members of the English department (ten of them tenured) try desperately to avoid taking on the vacant department chairmanship, a post that Bledsoe had also shunned before his death. Dean Maggie Downs is murdered and an assistant dean falls to his death from the top of the arts and letters building. And an illiterate black student named Roy Hastings, one of the few students ever to flunk a course at Lyndon Johnson, continues to press his claim that Bledsoe had given him an unfair failing grade. Some of the flavor of this novel may be communicated by quoting one brief bit of dialogue. Before her death Dean Downs and a woman professor discuss August Frye as a possible department chairman. The professor doubts that Frye has the proper frame of mind for the job. "He despises (this college), its students, you, all of us," she says. "In short, he's a typical faculty member," replies the dean.

Ralph McInerny was born in Minneapolis, Minnesota. He received a B.A. from St. Paul Seminary in St. Paul, Minnesota, an M.A. from the University of Minnesota, and a Ph.D. from Laval University. He began a long and distinguished tenure as a faculty member at Notre Dame in 1955. McInerny's academic discipline is philosophy, and he is a recognized authority on St. Thomas Aquinas. Throughout his career McInerny has been a prolific author of mainstream and mystery fiction as well as professional articles and monographs. He has written more than forty mystery novels, including seventeen works in a continuing series featuring Father Roger Dowling as detective. Edward Mackin is one of several pseudonyms McInerny has sometimes employed on his fiction. *The Search Committee* (338), *On This Rockne* (446), and *Lack of the Irish* (465), three novels published under McInerny's real name, appear later in this bibliography.

337. MACLEOD, CHARLOTTE (B. 1922). *AN OWL TOO MANY.* NEW YORK: THE MYSTERIOUS PRESS, 1991.

The nocturnal owl count is one of the yearly highlights at "Balaclava Agricultural College" in Massachusetts. Led by rugged Thorkjeld Svenson, Balaclava's president, small teams of faculty members, accompanied by townspeople, fan out into the countryside to count and identify as many owls as possible. This year's event is ruined by a murder. The victim is Emory Emmerick, an engineer with the college's television station. As he looks for owls, Emmerick is caught in a net, lifted into a tree, and stabbed dead. The sleuth is Charlotte MacLeod's eccentric series-character detective, Professor Peter Shandy, who was in the same owling party as the ill-fated Emmerick. The faculty characters in the story include Winifred Banks, a professor of local flora who has just inherited a fortune so huge that it multiplies even while she tries to establish its size, and Professor Daniel Stott, the head of animal husbandry and the college's best owl watcher. The book includes a few scenes on the Balaclava campus but much of the action takes place at and near the school's out-of-town field station. Readers of this comic mystery will encounter part of the recipe (the other part is kept secret by the college faculty) for the "Balaclava Boomerang," a potent alcoholic drink invented by Belial Buggins, a nephew of the college's founder. The Boomerang is so powerful that President Svenson, a model of administrative restraint, limits himself to two at any single sitting.

An Owl Too Many was the seventh entry in Charlotte MacLeod's continuing, hugely successful Professor Peter Shandy series. Three other Shandy novels are sufficiently "academic" to have entries in this bibliography. They are *Rest You Merry* (198), *The Luck Runs Out* (201), and *Something the Cat Dragged In* (233).

338. MCINERNY, RALPH (B. 1929). *THE SEARCH COMMITTEE.* NEW YORK: ATHENEUM, 1991.

Herbert Laplace, chancellor of the "University of Ohio at Fort Elbow," is arrested for drunken driving while returning home from a massage parlor. Thoroughly disgraced, he resigns his office but agrees to stay on until a university search committee can agree on a successor. Peter Kessel, Laplace's young and aggressive assistant, and Valerie Kraft, Fort Elbow's vice provost, are the leading candidates, but both die after being poisoned. *The Search Committee* is as much a satirical "mainstream" academic novel as it is a whodunit, and there is no serious detection. The person who murdered Kessel and Kraft admits to those misdeeds three-quarters through the tale, and thereafter the question of who will become Fort Elbow's chancellor becomes the operative mystery. Matt Rogerson, an acerbic Fort Elbow professor of philosophy, plays a central role throughout the book. Rogerson, who is given to sour-but-witty pronouncements on topics ranging from religion to faculty politics, tries desperately to avoid consideration as Laplace's successor, and it is he to whom the murderer of Kessel and Kraft confesses. As for Herbert Laplace, he was willing to risk being discovered in the massage parlor because he reasoned that none of the women, even if they were moonlighting Fort Elbow students, would recognize a naked chancellor. During this witty story Laplace goes on a lecture tour giving self-flagellating speeches in which he remorsefully admits his sins. His talks bring him considerable public approbation and sizable fees. By the very end of the book he has so rehabilitated his image that he has become a viable candidate to succeed himself as chancellor.

Professor Matt Rogerson and many of the characters in *The Search Committee* can be found in two satirical mainstream novels by Ralph McInerny. Those novels are *Jolly Rogerson* (Garden City, N.Y.: Doubleday, 1967) and *Rogerson at Bay* (New York: Harper & Row, 1976). Three other mysteries by McInerny appear in this bibliography. One is *The Nominative Case* (336), written under the pseudonym Edward Mackin. The other two are *On This Rockne* (446) and *Lack of the Irish* (465) which was published under McInerny's real name.

339. MONNINGER, JOE (B. 1953). *INCIDENT AT POTTER'S BRIDGE.* NEW YORK: DONALD FINE, 1991.

The setting of this suspenseful will-he-do-it is "Colbin College" in "Coldstream," New Hampshire. George Denkin, a clerk in the college's admission's office, is a serial killer of young women. Although not all of those he has murdered were Colbin students, Denkin selects some of his prey by reading the files of female applicants, identifying targets, and then killing the women after they arrive on the campus. Some of *Incident at Potter's Bridge* deals with Denkin's bizarre homicidal history (he began his career by baking his mother under a hairdryer) but most of the book focuses on his efforts to kill Zelda Fitzgibbons, a Colbin student from New Jersey. Since Miss Fitzgibbons is unaware of her danger, she spends her pre-attack time in ordinary student pursuits, and readers are provided with extensive detail about undergraduate life at Colbin. Several Colbin College faculty members appear in the story, as does President Mathews, who provides one of the book's very few light moments. Recognizing the importance of positive presidential demeanor, Mathews is seen at one point struggling to train himself to smile rather than grimace in response to the stabbing pains produced by the onset of a lower back problem.

Joe Monninger was born in Baltimore. He received an A.B. from Temple University in 1975 and an M.A. from the University of New Hampshire in 1982. He was a member of the English department at Plymouth State College in New Hampshire when *Incident at Potter's Bridge* was published. *Incident at Potter's Bridge* was Monninger's sixth novel.

340. MORGAN, KATE [ANN WHITMAN]. *MURDER MOST FOWL.* NEW YORK: BERKLEY BOOKS, 1991.

"Evergreen" is an ornithological research station deep in the woods near the small American town of "Hamilton." It is supported by monies from nearby "Farrand State University," and the station's director, Jack Ridgfield, is a professor of ornithology at the university. Unhappily for the station and its small staff of scientists, Professor Otis Marion accedes to the chair of Farrand's ornithology department. Not a supporter of Evergreen, Professor Marion strongly hints that he will soon shut off the station's funding unless there is an immediate increase in the number of staff publications. When the unpopular Marion is found strangled dead in Evergreen's main building, Professor Ridgfield and several of his Evergreen associates come under immediate suspicion. The police detective in the story is Captain Fielding Brooker of the Hamilton police, but the sleuth who solves the mystery is Dewey James, a sixtyish widow who is both the director of the Hamilton Public Library and a Kate Morgan series-character sleuth. Mrs. James becomes involved in this story when she volunteers to help her friend Jack Ridgfield by bringing order to the chaos into which the book collection at Evergreen has fallen. *Murder Most Fowl* contains many scenes at the Evergreen research facility, and on one occasion Mrs. James visits Farrand State to discuss matters relevant to her detection with Luka Mihaly, the university's dean of arts and sciences. As a college mystery, *Murder Most Fowl* has, perhaps, two distinctions. First, it illustrates that even a university ornithological research station is not immune from campus politics. Second, it is the only mystery in this bibliography in which the sighting of a rare ivory-billed woodpecker ultimately leads to murder.

Ann Whitman graduated from the University of Pennsylvania. *Murder Most Fowl* was her second Dewey James novel.

341. PENN, JOHN [PALMA HARCOURT AND JACK H. TROTMAN]. *DEATH'S LONG SHADOW.* LONDON: HARPERCOLLINS, 1991.

Greg White, his wife, Jean, and Rosemary, their seventeen-year-old daughter, are held captive in their Oxford home by two masked intruders. Greg is a fellow in English literature at "St. Xavier's College." In return for a promise of his family's safe release White agrees to carry a bomb (hidden in a briefcase) into the college and place it in the master's study, where it is timed to explode just as a meeting of the college's administrative staff is scheduled to begin. White carries the bomb to St. Xavier's but puts it in a lavatory near the meeting room. When it goes off several people are badly injured, but no one is killed. The police official assigned to the case is Chief Inspector Richard Tansey of the Thames Valley Police. It is up to Inspector Tansey to discover a motive for the bombing and to identify the bombers. Before he does so a St. Xaviers' don is killed, an undergraduate commits suicide, and Jean White, freed as promised by her captors, is run down and murdered by a hit-and-run driver as she walks in front of her home. Almost all the characters in this book are connected in some way with St. Xavier's College, and the motive for all of the nastiness is rooted in the college's academic policies. Readers who lack a fondness for university administrators, committee meetings, or both may appreciate the scene, early in the book, where the author describes the havoc at the college's administrative gathering when the bomb planted by Greg White explodes. Those same readers may find satisfaction, too, when Sir Philip Pinel, St. Xavier's officious and unpopular master, resigns in disgrace at the end of the story to take up the presidency of a "minor university in Mid-West America."

John Penn is a pseudonym used by Palma Harcourt and Jack H. Trotman, a husband-and-wife team of mystery writers. Harcourt and Trotman live on the isle of Jersey, one of England's Channel Islands. Palma Harcourt received an M.A. from St. Anne's College, Oxford. She is a writer of mainstream novels as well as mysteries. Jack H. Trotman received a B.A. from Oxford. After leaving the British Army Intelligence Corps with the rank of lieutenant colonel, he served as an official with the British Foreign Office, with the Canadian Department of National Defence, and with NATO. He began writing mystery novels after taking early retirement in 1982. Both Harcourt and Trotman have published solo mysteries, some of which have been dramatized for radio by the BBC. *Death's Long Shadow* was their sixth collaboration as John Penn.

342. ROWLANDS, BETTY. *FINISHING TOUCH.* NEW YORK: WALKER, 1991.

Angelica Caroli is so beautiful she upsets the equilibrium wherever she goes. At London's "Ravenswood College of Art and Design" she refuses fellow art student Riccardo Lorenzo's marriage proposal, and she so angers him that he makes a public display of his unhappiness. At an awards ceremony Lorenzo takes top honors for a portrait he has painted of Miss Caroli, but after receiving his prize he stuns the audience by producing a knife and slashing the picture. The pulchritudinous Caroli's next stop is the "Mid-Cotswald College of Art and Technology," where she takes a secretarial job. At Mid-Cotswald several male students and faculty members fight for her attentions, and their girlfriends and wives seethe with jealousy. Thus, when Miss Caroli dies of stab wounds in her apartment, any one of a host of Mid-Cotswald people might have killed her. The sleuth in *Finishing Touch* is Melissa Craig, a Betty Rowlands series-character detective. Craig is a successful crime writer who has moved from London to the Cotswald town of "Upper Banbury" in search of a quieter life. Craig accepts an offer from Mid-Cotswald to teach a creative writing course, and she is just beginning her duties when Miss Caroli is murdered. A reluctant detective, Craig gets involved primarily because Barney Willard, a tutor in fine arts to whom she has become attracted, is high on the police list of suspects. As Melissa Craig tries to identify Angelica Caroli's killer, Sybil Bliss, an adult student in her creative writing class, becomes the book's second victim. The villain turns out to be a person no one in the novel thinks capable of murder, and Melissa Craig thereby gains inspiration for the plot of her next mystery. Because this leisurely novel sometimes deviates from Melissa Craig's detection to provide accounts of her everyday faculty activities at Mid-Cotswald, readers are exposed to a great deal about life in a nonelite British institution of higher education.

A language teacher, Betty Rowlands lived in Gloucestershire, England, when *Finishing Touch* was published. The book was the third in her continuing Melissa Craig series.

343. RUSSELL, E(NID) S(HERRY) (B. 1924). *DEATH OF A CLOUDWALKER*. NEW YORK: WALKER, 1991.

As a teenager Toby Frame had a near-fatal hiking accident in the North Carolina mountains, and his right leg was so damaged that it had to be amputated. While Frame lay writhing in pain a man appeared, but after chastising him for playing in the mountains while many local residents starved, the man disappeared without offering help. Now, with a doctorate from Harvard, Frame has just taken a position as an associate professor of psychology at a New England college. He is to work on a team of social scientists doing interdisciplinary research. He moves into an apartment in the home of professor Ault Allyn, the team's eccentric director, and in a closet he finds, to his amazement, a file containing newspaper clippings and other materials about all of the important events in his life. Shortly thereafter, Vincent James, a self-described teetotaler and a member of the history department, dies mysteriously after apparently binging on liquor. Then, Bill Hanrahan, a graduate student in history, physically attacks Frame without reason, smashing his $4,000 artificial limb in the assault. Most of this novel takes place at the New England college at which Frame is employed, but the book's climax occurs in the mountains of western North Carolina to which several members of the interdisciplinary team have come to inspect a remote mansion that Professor Allyn thinks he has inherited. During his revisit to North Carolina, Frame almost meets his death once again, but in the process he discovers the identity of the man who refused to help him fifteen years earlier, and he learns who has committed murder. Considering the life-threatening problems Professor Frame experiences both times he tries to enjoy mountain scenery, it might be argued that the moral of *Death of a Cloudwalker* is that academics should avoid rustic areas at high altitudes. On the other hand, Frame has his problems on the New England college campus as well, and it might also be contended that any self-respecting academic should avoid participating in a research project with goals that defy comprehension. The project on which Frame works is intended to test the proposition that "choices, whether consonant or not with an individual's psychology, are often at odds with his subculture as well as with the job opportunities open to him, and that the stress resulting from this collision can critically affect not only that individual but his community."

Enid Sherry Russell was born in Long Branch, New Jersey. She received a B.S.Ed. in 1946 from the University of Michigan and an M.Ed. from Boston University in 1971. She has worked as a schoolteacher, a school psychologist, and a clinical psychologist. *Death of a Cloudwalker* was her fourth mystery novel. At the time *Death of a Cloudwalker* was published Russell was a resident of Groton, Connecticut.

344. BARTH, RICHARD (B. 1943). *THE FINAL SHOT.* NEW YORK: ST. MARTIN'S, 1992.

The narrator of this breezy tale is Costas Agonomou, a suspended New York City policeman who has taken a job as a security guard at "St. Bartlett's college" in Brooklyn. The victim in the story is Vincent Pronzini, a popular professor of art. Pronzini dies when a heavy barbell falls on his face as he is exercising alone and late at night in the college's gymnasium. The police are inclined to write off Professor Pronzini's death as an accident, but Agonomou takes it upon himself to conduct an independent investigation, and he eventually learns that a murderer is loose on the St. Bartlett's campus. Agonomou's inquiries uncover feuds in the art department between the historians and the practicing artists, tensions between the college's teachers' union and its administration, and possible point-shaving by the star of the school's basketball team. The book provides considerable detail about life at a nonelite New York City college where many of the students require remedial work in reading and simple arithmetic. It also includes a scene, set at a basketball game, that may warm the hearts of some real-life professors. Before a crowd of thousands the villain holds a gun to the back of the head of St. Bartlett's pompous president, a man named Malloy, and threatens to execute him. As the crowd watches, the terrified Malloy is forced renounce his sins over the public address system.

Born in South Orange, New Jersey, Richard Barth received a B.A. from Amherst in 1964. In 1974 he received an M.F.A. from Pratt Institute. Barth has combined mystery writing with goldsmithing and jewelry design. As a mystery writer he is best known for his continuing series of novels featuring septuagenarian Margaret Binton in the role of detective. At the time *The Final Shot* was published Barth was an instructor at the Fashion Institute of Technology in Manhattan.

345. BUTLER, GWENDOLINE (WILLIAMS) (B. 1922). *CRACKING OPEN A COFFIN.* LONDON: HARPERCOLLINS, 1992; NEW YORK: ST. MARTIN'S, 1993.

Two undergraduates go missing from a new university in the Docklands area of London, and Gwendoline Butler's series-character sleuth John Coffin is the law-enforcement official charged with finding them. Coffin is a veteran of college mysteries. Then a police officer in Oxford, he served as the detective in Gwendoline Butler's *Death Lives Next Door* (119). Coffin is now chief commander of the socially and economically heterogeneous police district in which the new London university is located. One of the missing students is Amy Dean, the daughter of one of Coffin's former police associates. The other is Martin Blackhall, the son of Sir Thomas Blackhall, the rector of the university. Because Martin Blackhall was suspected a year earlier in the murder of a female student, Coffin fears that he has more than a routine missing-persons case on his hands. When Amy Dean's body is found buried in Essex, Coffin redefines Martin Blackhall's status from missing student to that of wanted man. *Cracking Open a Coffin* frequently takes its readers away from the university per se, but many of the book's central characters have connections with the school, and on several occasions Commander Coffin offers dour reflections on life in the world of higher education. Moreover, while many college mysteries reflect the "closed societies" of traditional colleges and universities, *Cracking Open a Coffin* offers an effective literary example of a new, urban institution that blends intentionally with its surrounding community.

In addition to *Death Lives Next Door,* another mystery by Gwendoline Butler appears in this bibliography. That mystery, published under the pseudonym Jennie Melville, is *A New Kind of Killer, An Old Kind of Death* (159). *Cracking Open a Coffin* was the twenty-first Gwendoline Butler mystery to feature Inspector John Coffin.

346. CLARK, MARY HIGGINS (B. 1929). *ALL AROUND THE TOWN.* NEW YORK: SIMON & SCHUSTER, 1992.

All Around the Town is a crisp psychological suspense novel that includes elements of conventional detective fiction. Laurie Kenyon, a student at "Clinton College" in New Jersey, is arrested for the stabbing death of Allan Grant, a Clinton professor of English. The victim of a traumatic abduction when she was four years old, Miss Kenyon seems to have multiple personalities, and the police have reason to believe that she was sending Grant letters that described assignations that never actually occurred. Sarah Kenyon, Laurie's sister, is an attorney, and she takes on her sister's legal defense. Sarah engages Brendon Moody, a retired police detective, to ferret out whatever information he can about the pre-murder lives of Laurie and Professor Grant. As Moody does his legwork, some of it on the Clinton College campus, he finds that Laurie Kenyon is not the only person in the case to have mental difficulties, and that several people possess important information that bears upon Professor Grant's murder. Much of the story takes place away from Clinton College, and there are nonacademic characters in major roles. However, the scenes at Clinton and in Professor Grant's home are strongly written, and in addition to Grant and Laurie Kenyon, several people connected with Clinton College make more-than-token appearances.

Mary Higgins Clark was born in New York City. She held a series of jobs after high school, including stewardess with Pan American Airlines. She was widowed with five children in 1975, entered college, and turned to writing thrillers and mysteries as a means of financial support. She received a B.A. from Fordham in 1979 and has become one of America's most commercially successful authors, specializing in suspense tales in which children and their parents find themselves in extreme peril. Clark is a past president of Mystery Writers of America. *All Around the Town* was her eleventh novel.

347. CLEARY, MELISSA. *A TAIL OF TWO MURDERS.* NEW YORK: DIAMOND BOOKS, 1992.

Recently divorced, Jackie Walsh has just taken up a new life as an instructor of film at "Rodgers University," an up-to-date institution of higher education in "Palmer," Ohio. Walsh also has acquired a dog, an Alsatian named Jake, that she hopes will be company for her young son, Peter. Walsh's entry into university teaching is not eased when she discovers Philip Barger, dean of the university's school of communications, laying dead of poison on the floor of a campus film-editing room. Nor do matters get easier when Danielle Sherman, a sophomore in one of Jackie's classes, is found dead of asphyxiation in a dumpster behind a local pizzeria. Reluctant to get involved, Walsh is asked to help in the detection by Lieutenant McGowan of the local police, in part because she and McGowan quickly become friends, and in part because Walsh has knowledge of a major film-making project that Professor Barger was attempting before his death. Many academic characters appear in this novel, and most of them, as well as academe itself, come in for tweaking by the author. For example, the university's dean of faculty, former classics professor B. Crowder Westfall, continually bores his listeners by referring to the great works of classical literature, none of which have been read at Rodgers for decades. At the end of the novel the villain invades Jackie's home and tries to kill her, but Jake, who is definitely more reliable in a crisis than any of the Rodgers faculty members or administrators in the story, saves her life.

A Tail of Two Murders was the first in what was to become a successful series of mysteries featuring Jackie Walsh and her dog, Jake. Two other novels from the series are sufficiently "academic" to be included in this bibliography. Those novels are *Dead and Buried* (381) and *First Pedigree Murder* (382). The bibliography's users might want to look, too, at *The Maltese Puppy* (New York: Berkley, 1995), yet another entry (the seventh) in the Walsh series. *The Maltese Puppy* centers on the murder of Dr. Linus Munch, a Nobel Prize winning physician and researcher, who comes to Rodgers University to give a series of lectures. Because almost all of the story takes place off campus, *The Maltese Puppy* does not qualify for inclusion in this bibliography, but it does offer interesting depictions of some Rodgers University characters. Furthermore, it carries forward the portraiture of Dean B. Crowder Westfall, whose initial appearance is in *A Tail of Two Murders*. Past sixty years of age, Dean Westfall is nearing retirement. A man whose academic success was based on teaching, Dean Westfall still yearns to be a recognized scholar. Over his career he has sent sixty-seven article manuscripts out for review. Only one was ever published, and it was edited to the point where Westfall barely recognized it as his own work. Furthermore, the journal spelled his name incorrectly.

348. CORY, DESMOND [SHAUN LLOYD MCCARTHY (B. 1928)]. *THE MASK OF ZEUS.* LONDON: MACMILLAN, 1992; NEW YORK: ST. MARTIN'S, 1993.

The sleuth in *The Mask of Zeus* is John Dobie, a cantankerous but brilliant professor of mathematics at a university in or near Cardiff, Wales. Dobie is a Desmond Cory series-character detective. In his first adventure, *The Strange Attractor* (London: Macmillan, 1991), the professor identifies the murderer of his estranged wife. While *The Strange Attractor* contains a few on-campus scenes, the story does not hinge on "academic" matters, and the book is not given a separate entry in this bibliography. In *The Mask of Zeus* Professor Dobie seeks to recover from the stresses he experienced in *The Strange Attractor*, and he takes leave from his home institution to accept a temporary post at the "University of Salamis" on the island of Cyprus. Upon his arrival he learns that murder has entered his life once again. The victim is Salamis faculty member Dr. Derya Tuner, one of the professor's former students, and Professor Dobie is not convinced that a confession her husband gave to the police was truthful. With long-distance advice and encouragement from Dr. Kate Coyle, a medical examiner in Cardiff with whom he is romantically entwined, Dobie detects and eventually discovers Dr. Tuner's real murderer. Written against the backdrop of Cyprus's political unrest, *The Mask of Zeus* contains many scenes at the University of Salamis, and the players in the story include a host of Salamis professors, some of them Cypriots and some of them British expatriates. Capable of witty, sardonic dialogue, as well as shrewd detective insights, Professor Dobie is clearly a worthy professor-detective. However, the honor for the most valorous character in the book clearly goes to Dr. Kate Coyle. She is the only person in college-mystery fiction who struggles to improve her grammar and syntax because, in the words of the book's author, "she is being laid by a university professor."

Shaun Lloyd McCarthy was born in Sussex, England. He is an Oxford graduate and former marine commando. The author of more than thirty books, McCarthy has written spy novels as well as detective tales. In addition to Desmond Cory he has employed the pseudonym Theo Callas. At the time *The Mask of Zeus* was published, McCarthy was a teacher of English at Eastern Mediterranean University on Cyprus.

349. FRANKOS, LAURA. *ST. OSWALD'S NICHE.* NEW YORK: BALLANTINE, 1992.

Jennet Walker, a graduate student in archaeology at UCLA, gets the ideal summer job! She is hired as a temporary secretary to Edwin Durrell, a retired British professor who happens to be the world's most distinguished medievalist. Durrell is participating in a dig at "St. Oswald's Abbey" in Northumbria, and Miss Walker takes up residence with the rest of the project staff at a nearby technical college in York. The central mystery in this murder-free story is the identity of the thief who steals a priceless medieval chalice that is uncovered during the St. Oswald excavation. All signs seem to point to Miss Walker, and with help from Matt Jonas, a fellow UCLA student, she must find the real culprit in order to avoid arrest. Dig mysteries ordinarily do not merit inclusion in this bibliography, but *St. Oswald's Niche* possesses several features that make it admissible. Much of the action takes place at the York technical college that serves as the project's headquarters. All of the major characters are graduate students or faculty members at institutions of higher learning, and much of their nondigging time is spent in academic shop talk. Furthermore, some of the motives for the misdeeds in the tale can be traced to the characters' desires to further their academic careers.

According to material on the cover of this book Laura Frankos attended UCLA, where she majored in history. She passed a Ph.D. exam in 1983 (in Roman history), but suspended progress on her doctorate to marry science-fiction writer Harry Turtledove and to have three children. *St. Oswald's Niche* was Frankos's first novel. At the time *St. Oswald's Niche* was published Frankos lived in the Los Angeles area.

350. GEORGE, ELIZABETH (B. 1949). *FOR THE SAKE OF ELENA.* NEW YORK: BANTAM, 1991.

The badly beaten corpse of Elena Weaver is found alongside the Fen Causeway in Cambridge. The profoundly deaf daughter of Anthony Weaver, a Cambridge professor of history, Miss Weaver was an undergraduate at "St. Stephen's College." Terrence Cuff, the master of St. Stephen's, asks that Scotland Yard, rather than the local police, investigate, and Inspector Thomas Lyndley and his assistant, Sergeant Barbara Havers, are assigned to the case. An autopsy shows that Miss Weaver was pregnant, and the two Elizabeth George series-character detectives also learn that she was well-known at the university for drunkenness and promiscuity. The case does not lack for suspects. Either of two university lecturers, one in English literature and the other in history, might have been the father of Miss Weaver's unborn child, and both are quickly placed on Lyndley and Havers's list of possible murderers. Gareth Randolph, another deaf undergraduate and a member of the university boxing team, might have killed Miss Weaver because she recently ended their romance. And then there is Professor Anthony Weaver, Miss Weaver's father. A finalist for Cambridge's prestigious "Penford Chair" in history, the professor fears that his candidacy may have been suffering because of his daughter's "spotty" behavior. Now, with his daughter murdered, Weaver stands to gain sympathy from the selection committee. *For the Sake of Elena* is considerably more novelistic than most of the mysteries in this bibliography. The author offers painterly descriptions of Cambridge, and she creates multidimensional portraits of her central characters, including her two detectives. Furthermore, by avoiding the murder-can-be-fun style of writing that characterizes many Oxbridge whodunits, she provides her readers with a serious look at the folkways and mores of contemporary Cambridge.

Elizabeth George was born in Warren, Ohio. She received a B.A. from the University of California at Riverside in 1970 and an M.S. from California State University in 1979. She has taught English at the high-school level and creative writing at several colleges and universities in California. *For the Sake of Elena* is the fifth novel in a very successful continuing series that features Inspector Thomas Lyndley and Sergeant Barbara Havers. At the time *For the Sake of Elena* was published George was a resident of Huntington Beach, California. All of the novels in the Lyndley-Havers series are so "British" that many readers have erroneously assumed that the author is a native of England.

351. HILL, DONNA (B. 1921). *MURDER UPTOWN.* NEW YORK: CARROLL & GRAF, 1992.

Murder Uptown is set at "Fuller College" of the City University of New York. Early one morning the body of Paul Raskin, a professor of sociology, is found in a garbage bag in an alley behind the school's fourteen-story, block-long building on New York's East Side. The professor has been dispatched by a blow to the skull. The New York City police work diligently to find the killer, but the most productive sleuthing in the story is done by Professor Melvina Trent, one of Professor Raskin's departmental colleagues. A "slender widow," the stylish Professor Trent is forty-six but, according to the text, she can pass for thirty-nine. Trent comes across a bloody paperweight in the office of Sterling Neu, another Fuller College sociologist, and not willing to believe Neu guilty of murder, she hides the weapon from the police and undertakes her own independent, and perilous, investigation. On three occasions she is attacked by the book's villain, but she manages to survive each encounter. Since the motive for Professor Raskin's killing is not immediately apparent, all the members of Fuller College's sociology department are suspects, as are several college basketball players with whom, Professor Trent finds to her amazement, Paul Raskin may have had drug dealings. Also on the suspect list is Belle Van Buren, a "bag lady" who actually lives in the college's old and cavernous building. The guilty party turns out to be a Fuller College faculty member who falls prey to a trap set in the college library by Trent and the police. When apprehended, the evildoer immediately admits all and, with true professorial loquaciousness, rambles on with so many details about the killing that Professor Trent and the police detectives have to ask for a halt to the confession.

Donna Hill was born in Salt Lake City, Utah. She earned an A.B. at George Washington University in 1948 and an M.L.S. at Columbia in 1952. Hill's extensive list of publications includes, novels, books for children, and a biography of Joseph Smith, the founder of the Mormon Church. She also is a widely exhibited painter. *Murder Uptown* was her first mystery. At the time *Murder Uptown* was published Hill was a resident of New York City and a professor emeritus at Hunter College, where, before her retirement, she was head of Hunter's education library.

352. JOHNSTON, J. M. *BITING THE WALL.* WESTMINSTER, MD.: ACME PRESS, 1992.

Set at "Wilbur Moody College" in the eastern United States, *Biting the Wall* is a comic mystery that focuses on the college's computer center. Llew McQuilla, the center's director, is suddenly removed from his position and reassigned, at significantly lower pay, to a lesser post as keeper of the center's archives. Then, the school's mainframe computer is replaced by another, and McQuilla finds that his personal files have been erased. There are no murders in the novel, but late in the book there is some derring-do in the computer center as McQuilla, trying to comprehend what is happening at Wilbur

Moody, confronts several villains who have perpetrated arson and espionage. Most academic readers probably will find the book's comedy at least as interesting as its mystery. President Horace ("Keep-'Em-Guessing") Crump is an advocate of extensive computer use by both students and faculty members because it "keeps 'em off the streets." The college's female physician tries to get Llew McQuilla to resume cigarette smoking. And the school's frosty vice president for business and financial affairs finds it useful to let people think that he carries a handgun in his coat pocket.

Biting the Wall was J. M. Johnston's third book-length work of fiction. Johnston also has written books about computers.

353. KEATING, H. R. F. [HENRY RAYMOND FITZWATER KEATING (B. 1926)]. *CHEATING DEATH.* LONDON: HUTCHINSON, 1992; NEW YORK: THE MYSTERIOUS PRESS, 1994.

Cheating Death is set in India at "Oceanic College," a division of the University of Bombay. A copy of an about-to-be-offered statistics exam is stolen from the locked office of the school's principal, Dr. Shambu S. Bembalker, and Inspector Ghote of the Criminal Branch of the Bombay Police is called to investigate. The most likely thief is a student, Bala Chambhar, but the unfortunate Mr. Chambhar, who sold the copy of the exam for fifty rupees, is now hospitalized and near death after ingesting an overdose of sleeping pills. Although university officials would like to believe that Mr. Chambhar tried to commit suicide, Inspector Ghote suspects that he was the victim of a murder attempt, and during much of the story Ghote concerns himself with finding the person responsible for Mr. Chambhar's condition. Most of the characters in the story are Indian faculty members, staff, or administrators at Oceanic, and the book often dwells upon the absurdities and inefficiencies of Indian higher education. A teacher of English, for example, delivers a formal lecture to the one student who attends his class, and the college's dean, forever influenced by his days as a student in England, insists upon wearing academic robes atop a tweed jacket even during the hottest days of summer. Academic dishonesty is depicted as a way of life in Indian universities, and at one point in the story the students at Oceanic disrupt Inspector Ghote's investigations with a near-violent protest demanding "the right to cheat."

Henry Raymond Fitzwater Keating was born in St. Leonards-on-the-Sea, Sussex, England. He received a B.A. in 1952 from Trinity College, Dublin. A one-time London journalist and reviewer of mystery novels for *The Times*, Keating has won many prizes for his own mystery fiction. In 1987 he was elected president of the Detection Club—an office held previously by G. K. Chesterton, Dorothy L. Sayers, and Agatha Christie. Inspector Ghote, a fallible but resourceful Indian police official, is a long running Keating series-character detective. *Cheating Death* was Inspector Ghote's twentieth published case. Although it is not sufficiently "academic" to make it into this bibliography, another Keating mystery (without Inspector Ghote) might be of interest to some readers of college-mystery novels. *The Dog It Was That Died* (London: Gollancz, 1962) features Professor William Bosenwite ("The Bosun") in a prominent role. A psychologist and director of the Institute for Human Relations at Leeds University in England, Bosenwite is first depicted receiving an award for academic achievement at Trinity College, Dublin. He is subsequently shown at various locales in Dublin engaging in strange-but-sinister activities that are explained only at the end of the novel.

354. KELLY, NORA [NORA HICKSON (B. 1945)]. *MY SISTER'S KEEPER*. NEW YORK: ST. MARTIN'S, 1992.

Although progressive in some respects, the "University of the Pacific Northwest" in British Columbia still retains considerable institutional sexism. One of those involved in the fight for women's equality on campus is Gillian Adams, a professor of history and the chairperson of her department. Adams is angered when Rita Gordon, an outstanding student and outspoken feminist, is denied a prestigious fellowship, and she is moved to detect when Ms. Gordon subsequently dies in an accident after someone tampers with the brakes on her motorcycle. During the story Adams experiences a series of indignities, some of them slights and insults because she is a woman, and some of them life-threatening events—including a beating outside her home—because she is getting close to finding Ms. Gordon's murderer. The harried Professor Adams copes, too, with the difficulties associated with giving up cigarettes. *My Sister's Keeper* offers much background information about the workings of Canadian universities and much foreground material about the changing roles of women in those universities.

Three other Nora Hickson mysteries, all of them with Professor Gillian Adams in the role of detective, appear in this bibliography.

Those mysteries are *In the Shadow of King's* (243), *Bad Chemistry* (367), and *Old Wounds* (463).

355. KEMELMAN, HARRY (1908–1996). *THE DAY THE RABBI RESIGNED.* NEW YORK: FAWCETT COLUMBINE, 1992.

Two assistant professors are contesting for one tenure opening in the English department of "Windemere Christian College" in Boston. One of the two, Mordecai Jacobs, has better qualifications. The other, Victor Joyce, is more inventive. He courts and marries Margaret Burke, the niece of Cyrus Merton, a powerful member of the Windemere Christian board of trustees. Merton begins to use his influence on Joyce's behalf, and it seems as though Joyce will win the continuing-appointment competition. However, Joyce dies after he is involved in an automobile accident near the Boston suburb of "Barnard's Crossing," and the police believe that it might not have been the car crash that killed him. The person who ultimately resolves the questions surrounding Victor Joyce's death is David Small, a Barnard's Crossing rabbi. The erudite Small is a Harry Kemelman series-character detective who once taught a course on Jewish thought at Windemere Christian. He gets involved when the local police chief asks him for help. Although Mordecai Jacobs is the obvious suspect, Small learns that the Joyce-Burke marriage was loveless, that Joyce was having an affair with Alice Saxon, a Windemere Christian associate professor of psychology, and that several people, in addition to Jacobs, might have wanted Joyce dead. Some of the book takes place in Barnard's Crossing, but there are many scenes on the Windemere Christian campus, and *The Day the Rabbi Resigned* is one of few entries in this bibliography that allows its readers to eavesdrop on meetings of college or university boards of trustees. In fact, readers of this novel can follow the arguments as the trustees decide to change the name of Windemere Christian College to Windemere College of Liberal Arts. The book takes its title from an event that occurs at the very end of the story. Donald Macomber, Windemere's president, offers Rabbi Small a full-time job creating a department of Judaic thought and philosophy at the college. Small accepts and, after twenty-five years at the head of his Barnard's Crossing congregation, he resigns his post as rabbi and signs on as a full-time toiler in the world of academe.

Tuesday the Rabbi Saw Red (169) and *That Day the Rabbi Left Town* (429), two other Rabbi Small novels by Harry Kemelman, have entries in this bibliography.

356. LAKE. M. D. [JAMES ALLEN SIMPSON] *A GIFT FOR MURDER.* NEW YORK: AVON, 1992.

Cameron Harris, a successful novelist and a visiting professor at a university in the Midwest, fails to keep a scheduled appearance to read from his latest work at the "Tower," a writer's cooperative near the university campus. Later that evening Harris is found dead upstairs at the Tower. His skull has been crushed by a poker that lies on the floor beside him. The police are baffled because there is no obvious motive for the murder, but Peggy O'Neill, a university security officer and a frequent Allen Simpson series-character sleuth, launches her own investigation. O'Neill eventually identifies Harris's killer, but not before Arthur Tique, an imperious professor of clinical psychology, is also bludgeoned to death, and not before the villain almost dispatches Officer O'Neill as well. Many faculty members and their spouses appear in the story, and as Peggy O'Neill discovers, some of them would have had much to lose had Cameron Harris's manuscript been finished and published. In addition to her regular nocturnal patrols of the university campus, O'Neill is depicted conducting lengthy investigations in the offices of both the English and the psychology departments. While visiting psychology she learns that Professor Tique, who until his death was the prime suspect in Cameron Harris's murder, had scheduled his classroom obligations to fall only on the fifteenth and the last days of each month. By some coincidence, the fifteenth and last days of the month are the very days on which the university distributes faculty paychecks.

A Gift for Murder is one of nine Peggy O'Neill mysteries by James Allen Simpson that appear in this bibliography. The others are *Amends for Murder* (313), *Cold Comfort* (325), *Poisoned Ivy* (357), *Murder by Mail* (368), *Grave Choices* (410), *Once Upon a Crime* (411), *Flirting with Death* (431), and *Death Calls the Tune* (479).

357. LAKE, M. D. [JAMES ALLEN SIMPSON]. *POISONED IVY.* NEW YORK: AVON, 1992.

The victim in this story is Donna Trask, the daughter of the attorney for a large Midwestern university that gives every appearance of being the University of Minnesota. A student at the university, Miss

Trask bites into an apple laced with cyanide at a dinner held in honor of Jeremiah Strauss, the institution's dean of the graduate school. Since Dean Strauss is universally unpopular, it is generally assumed that the apple was meant for him, and that poor Donna Trask was simply an innocent victim. Edith Silverman, a professor of humanities who has never hidden her loathing of Dean Strauss, is quickly arrested for murder. The detective in the tale is Peggy O'Neill, a cynical-but-determined campus policewoman who is an Allen Simpson series-character detective. Although O'Neill has no official role in the investigation, she takes it upon herself to get to the bottom of the affair because she believes Professor Silverman to be innocent. A quintessential campus mystery, *Poisoned Ivy* includes many university characters, and most of them emerge as suspects. The denouement takes place in the study of the university president's home. While Officer O'Neill is announcing the name of the murderer she also reveals past acts of chicanery on the part of several of the other academics gathered in the room.

Eight other Peggy O'Neill mysteries by James Allen Simpson appear in this bibliography. Those mysteries are *Amends for Murder* (313), *Cold Comfort* (325), *A Gift for Murder* (356), *Murder by Mail* (368), *Once Upon a Crime* (411), *Grave Choices* (410), *Flirting with Death* (431), and *Death Calls the Tune* (479).

358. MARIZ, LINDA. *BODY ENGLISH.* NEW YORK: BANTAM, 1992.

Laura Ireland is tall, beautiful, and studying for her doctorate in anthropology at UCLA. While getting her master's degree at "Western University" in Bellingham, Washington, Ireland was the bedmate of Professor Larry Todd, and she wrote him passionate letters. Ireland also helped Professor Todd illegally import Canadian Indian artifacts, and even though she now lives in Los Angeles and considers her former mentor to be an old rather than an active flame, the professor uses her letters to blackmail her into continued help with smuggling. When Ireland learns that Todd has been killed, she returns to Bellingham in hopes of retrieving her love messages, but she succeeds only in becoming a murder suspect and in receiving a superficial gunshot wound as she chases a person whom she thinks is Professor Todd's killer. Meantime, Ireland is a star volleyball player, a "spiker" with the "Gainesville Gatorades." During the brief period covered by this novel, the Gatorades are playing in a national tournament at the University of Washington, and Laura travels between Seattle and Bellingham as she juggles athletics with sleuthing. In addition to offering several play-by-play accounts of volleyball matches, *Body English* introduces its readers to many faculty members and administrators at Western University. One of those worthies, Dean Allessandro Siecetti, has just published a book on the nature of aesthetics. When Ireland wonders how a dean has the time to write a book, a Western faculty member responds by observing that Siecetti is not married. *Body English* also includes a police detective with the improbable name of Theopile Talbot. "Theo" and Laura Ireland fall in love during the story, and at one point Theo arouses Ireland's passion by handcuffing her to a bed so she will be unable to get into further trouble by detecting.

Linda Mariz was born in New Orleans. She holds a B.A. from the University of Missouri at Columbia and an M.A. from Western Washington University. During the 1970s Mariz taught at Whatcom Community College in Bellingham, Washington, and at Western Washington University. She has competed as a triathlete and swimmer. At the time *Body English* was published Mariz lived in Washington State. *Body English* was her first novel.

359. PETERSON, BERNARD [PSEUD.]. *THE CARAVAGGIO BOOKS.* NEW YORK: HARPERCOLLINS, 1992.

The Caravaggio Books is a police procedural set at elite "Kingsford University" in "Kingsford," New Jersey. The sleuths are Sam Dawson, the black chief of the Kingsford police, and Philip Costanza, the only detective in the small Kingsford police department. Dawson and Costanza investigate the murders of two members of the Kingsford faculty, both of whom are killed in the university library. The first victim is Hilda Robertson, an assistant professor of art who was trying desperately to finish her doctoral dissertation on "the role of secular and ecclesiastical patronage in Post-Renaissance art." Miss Robertson dies when someone enters her carrel and slashes her throat. A few days later Alardyce Stallings, a retired professor of English, is fatally beaten as he examines some rare Shakespeare folios in a deserted underground reading room. The detectives find most of their suspects in Kingsford's art department after they discover that Robertson was having an affair with Stanley Beecham, the department's chairperson, and after arrogant Stefan Lupescu, one of the world's leading art historians, walks out on Detective Costanza when he tries to ask him questions. In the end, the solution to the mystery centers on the circulation history of three books about Caravaggio that the unfortunate Miss Robertson had recently checked out of the library for her research. *The Caravaggio Books* is noteworthy for the detail it offers about the operation of university libraries and about academe in general. As Dawson and Costanza go about their sleuthing, university characters often provide them with explanations of matters such as library security systems, the meaning of tenure, and the nature of academic ranks. The book also contains one of the more protracted professorial death scenes in college-mystery fiction. After Professor Stallings's beating, he is taken to a hospital where he briefly lingers between life and death. Stallings is interviewed by Detective Costanza and, as he moves in and out of consciousness, the retired professor tells the detective about his appreciation of naked young women and his dislike of homosexuals.

The Caravaggio Books was the third mystery published by the person who employs Bernard Peterson as a pseudonym.

360. SUMNER, PENNY (B. 1955). *THE END OF APRIL.* TALLAHASSEE, FLA.: NAIAD PRESS, 1992.

The narrator of this unusual mystery is Victoria ("Tor") Cross, a young British private investigator. Although she is unmarried, Victoria takes offense when addressed as "Miss" and prefers "Ms." instead. Ms. Cross is hired by her aunt, an Oxford professor, to protect April Tate, a law-student protégé who has been receiving threatening letters. As cover for her assignment, Ms. Cross is also given a job as an archivist, examining materials that pertain to her aunt's study of nineteenth-century pornography. Ms. Cross's primary task takes on urgency when a visiting student from Germany is brutally murdered in April Tate's lodgings. Almost all of *The End of April* takes place in Oxford and its immediate environs, and there are many scenes in the aunt's college. All of the primary female characters in the story are lesbians, and while the mystery element carries the story forward, much of the text is devoted to same-sex romantic episodes involving Ms. Cross with April Tate and Ms. Cross's professor-aunt, a woman identified in the text only as "Rosemary," with "Eleanor," the dean of an Oxford college. Most of the male characters in the story are lechers, chauvinists, or worse, and the general image of the university that emerges from the novel is decidedly unflattering. Certainly, narrator Victoria Cross's view of Oxford is negative. Oxford, she observes, "is a bastion of racism, sexism, and class oppression."

Penny Sumner was born in Australia. She moved to England to do postgraduate studies at Oxford. At the time *The End of April* was published Ms. Sumner was a resident of Newcastle-upon-Tyne, a teacher of creative writing and contemporary literature at the University of Northumbria, and an editor of a feminist creative-writing magazine titled *Writing Women*. *The End of April* was her first novel and the first of a continuing series of Victoria Cross mysteries.

361. ALLEN, IRENE [ELSA KIRSTEN PETERS (B. 1960)]. *QUAKER WITNESS*. NEW YORK: VILLARD, 1993.

Paul Chadwick is a world-famous professor of paleontology at Harvard who is given to bullying and sexually molesting his female graduates students. Heretofore, the women under his tutelage have suffered in silence, but Janet Stevens, now his only female advisee, breaks tradition by lodging a formal complaint with the Harvard administration. The wheels of Harvard justice run slowly, and in frustration over the delays Stevens makes some intemperate public remarks about her loathing for Chadwick. Shortly after that someone tampers with a gas line in the professor's laboratory, and he dies after a burst of chlorine pentaflouride removes the oxygen from the laboratory's air. Familiar with the lab's mechanics, Stevens certainly has the technical knowledge to have done the deed, and when Chadwick's body is discovered, Stevens's status at Harvard immediately changes from that of whistle-blower to murder suspect. There are several sleuths in this story, but the primary detective is Elizabeth Elliot, a sympathetic widow who serves as the unpaid clerk of the Cambridge Quaker Meetinghouse. Ms. Elliot meets and befriends Janet, who attended a Friends school as a child, when Janet seeks a temporary respite from her problems by meditating in the Meetinghouse's worship room. Because the Cambridge police are busy coping with a series of killings near M.I.T., Ms. Elliot takes it upon herself to develop information that the police have no time to seek. Ms. Elliot's primary suspects come from among the many male Harvard deans, faculty members, and graduate students who are reluctantly drawn into the case. None of those Harvard males harasses women, but most are guilty of turning a blind eye toward sexism when it is displayed by others. Thus, the real villain in *Quaker Witness* is the widespread apathy toward misogyny that infects the author's version of Harvard.

Elsa Kirsten Peters was educated at Princeton and Harvard. Her field of academic specialization was geology. While at Harvard she was a member of Friends Meeting in Cambridge. At the time *Quaker Witness* was published Peters lived in Washington State. *Quaker Witness* was her second mystery with Elizabeth Elliot in the role of sleuth.

362. DEAVER, JEFFREY WILDS. *THE LESSON OF HER DEATH.* NEW YORK: DOUBLEDAY, 1993.

The protagonist of this long and polished novel is Bill Corde, a police lieutenant in "New Lebanon," a Midwestern community that houses "Auden University." When Jennie Golden, an Auden undergraduate, is found raped and murdered on the banks of a pond near the town, Corde assumes charge of the investigation. As he tries to find Miss Golden's killer, he learns that Auden University is rife with tension and suspicious characters. One suspicious individual is Randolph Rutherford Sayles, Auden's director of financial aid, who doubles as a professor of history. Dismissed from a former university because he was implicated in an assault on a female student, the chain-smoking Sayles spends most of his time desperately trying to raise money to pull Auden University out of a continuous financial crisis. Between out-of-town trips to visit potential donors, Sayles was having an affair with Jennie Golden. Then there is Brian Okun, a graduate student in psychology. The harassed research assistant of Leon Gilchrest, a professor who has raised obnoxiousness to new heights, Okun also was having sex with the busy Miss Golden. Meantime, evidence surfaces that Golden's killer may have been practicing some sort of occult ritual, and both the university folk and the townspeople fear that her killing may well be followed by others. Then, just to complicate matters, someone begins stalking Bill Corde's wife and two young children, and toward the end of the book Corde's daughter, Sarah, is kidnapped. College-mystery readers will find much to hold their attentions in this 418-page book, and although other novels in this bibliography make essentially the same point, *The Lesson of Her Death* offers compelling fictional evidence that lofty levels of intelligence and arrogance, when blended together in one person, can lead to a great deal of trouble for any university unlucky enough to have that individual on its payroll.

Jeffrey Wilds Deaver was a resident of New York City when this book was published. He holds a journalism degree from the University of Missouri and is a graduate of Fordham University School of Law. His work history includes stints as a journalist and as a Wall Street attorney. *The Lesson of Her Death* was his seventh novel.

363. FERRARS, E. X. [MORNA DORIS BROWN (1907–1995)]. *THY BROTHER DEATH.* NEW YORK: DOUBLEDAY, 1993.

The sleuth in this book is Patrick Carey, a middle-aged senior lecturer in biochemistry at England's "University of Knotlington." Carey receives a letter that falsely accuses him of bigamy. Before he can investigate his suspicion that the letter was the work of David, his black-sheep brother, the home of Professor Margaret Franks, Carey's immediate superior, is destroyed by fire, and the body of an unidentified young woman is found in the ruins. Then Professor Franks is killed by a blow to the back of her head, and her corpse is left in a gutter on a Knotlington street. Since Patrick Carey is the likely person to become the biochemistry department's professor after Margaret Franks's death, and because some significant evidence points to his involvement in her killing, the local police suspect that he may be behind the sudden spate of evil deeds. Afraid that the authorities will soon arrest him, Carey engages in sleuthing to bring the real culprit to justice. A great many University of Knotlington characters appear in this professionally written story, and some of them are hiding sordid secrets. American professors who have spent time in British universities may feel that Professor Franks's killing was not entirely without justification. Early in the book she is depicted rudely ordering a visiting professor from the University of California at Berkeley to leave the Knotlington biochemistry department's premises because, as she coldly informs him, her faculty and staff need to work on their research and not "gossip" with him.

A Murder Too Many (293), an earlier mystery written by Morna Doris Brown under her E. X. Ferrars pseudonym, appears in this bibliography. Like *Thy Brother Death, A Murder Too Many* is set at the "University of Knotlington," but the sleuth in *A Murder Too Many* is E. X. Ferrars's series-character detective, retired Professor of Botany Andrew Basnett.

364. GUR, BATYA. *LITERARY MURDER: A CRITICAL CASE.* NEW YORK: HARPERCOLLINS, 1993.

Iddo Dudai, a lecturer in the literature department of The Hebrew University of Jerusalem, drowns after an apparent accident while scuba diving. The next morning Adina Lipkin, the department secretary, is drawn by an unpleasant odor to the office of Saul Tirosh, a celebrated poet and the head of the literature department. There she discovers Tirosh's corpse. Tirosh has been beaten so badly that the police pathologist has difficulty establishing the precise cause of his death. *Literary Murder* is a more ambitious exercise in writing than most of the mysteries in this bibliography. Literary references are frequent, and at several points in the long (357-page) narrative some of the book's academic characters engage in serious discourse about poetry, literary theory, and ethics. The detective is long-suffering Police Superintendent Michael Ohayon. Armed only with a bachelor's degree in history, Ohayon survives several rarefied discussions of literary matters with Tuvia Shai, a surviving member of the literature department who, in intradepartmental squabbles, was Professor Tirosh's most reliable ally. Meantime, as he works to tie the possible murder of Iddo Dudai with the obvious murder of Saul Tirosh, Superintendent Ohayon finds himself dealing with plagiarism, chronic womanizing, and professional jealousies within the literature department. A dogged investigator, Ohayon actually reads an entire year's minutes of literature department meetings as part of his inquiry! Perhaps as reward for that titanic endeavor, toward the end of the story the author allows him to take his first trip to America, where he visits the University of North Carolina to interview a key informant.

Literary Murder: A Critical Case was Batya Gur's second Michael Ohayon mystery. At the time *Literary Murder: A Critical Case* was written, Gur was a teacher of literature in Jerusalem. *Literary Murder: A Critical Case* was originally published in Israel in 1971 by Keter Publishing. For its HarperCollins edition, the book was translated from Hebrew into English by Dalva Bilu.

365. HESS, JOAN (B. 1949). *POISONED PINS*. NEW YORK: DUTTON, 1993.

Things are not going well at the "Kappa Theta Eta" sorority of "Farber College" in the small American town of "Farberville." One sister reports having been attacked and beaten on the grounds of the sorority house, and another is killed when she is deliberately run over by an automobile. The narrator/sleuth in the story is Claire Malloy, who owns a bookshop near the college campus. The widowed, middle-aged Malloy is able to give invaluable assistance to Farberville Police Lieutenant Peter Rosen, her sometimes boyfriend, because she is acquainted with Martha Winklebury, Kappa Theta Eta's housemother. Malloy's exploits in this tale almost lead to her extinction at the hands of the villain, and they take her to a seedy local motel named "Hideaway Heaven," where she finds that some of Farber's female students are practicing an ancient form of entrepreneurship. The dean of Farber College's law school, John Vanderson, plays a role in the proceedings, as does his haughty wife, Esther. *Poisoned Pins* is a polished, light, commercial mystery. Readers will encounter few serious discussions of academic life, but they will learn the reason Esther Vanderson packs a "small and stylish" pistol in her handbag.

Poisoned Pins was Joan Hess's eighth Claire Malloy mystery novel. *Strangled Prose* (268), the first novel in the popular Claire Malloy series, also appears in this bibliography.

366. JONES, D. J. H. [PSEUD.]. *MURDER AT THE MLA*. ATHENS, GA.: UNIVERSITY OF GEORGIA PRESS, 1993.

Four senior professors, two of them men and two of them women, are murdered in Chicago at the annual meeting of the Modern Language Association. Since the four victims all come from different institutions, and since there is no common method of killing, there seems to be no thread to link the incidents. Boaz Dixon, the Chicago police official in charge of the case, is so confused that he asks for help from Nancy Cook, a strikingly attractive untenured assistant professor from Yale. After meeting Cook by chance in a hotel hallway, Dixon asks her to brief him on the operations of an MLA conference. The divorced Dixon, who bears a resemblance to a "craggy-faced Hoagy Carmichael," stirs some romantic fires in Cook, and it is not long before she decides to help the policeman by actively sleuthing. As readers of mystery fiction will immediately suspect, a connection does exist among the four murders, and as Dixon and Cook learn by the end of the story, the villain was motivated by a set of frustrations that many real-life attendees at large academic conventions have experienced. *Murder at the MLA* is written with biting wit, much of it directed at the process by which colleges and universities use professional meetings to recruit new faculty. In one scene Annette Lisordi, a job seeker from Emory University, appears by appointment at the hotel suite in which Wellesley College is conducting employment interviews. She appears just moments after Susan Engleton, the chair of the English department at Wellesley, expires from poison that has been added to a room-service pot of coffee. The four surviving members of the Wellesley recruiting team are paralyzed from shock and hysteria. Lisordi uses a telephone in the bedroom to call the police, but all the while she wonders whether Wellesley has staged the event as a bizarre test for evaluating prospective faculty.

Nancy Cook, D. J. H. Jones's sprightly professor-detective in *Murder at the MLA,* sleuths again in *Murder in the New Age* (Albuquerque, N.M.: University of New Mexico Press, 1997). Because *Murder in the New Age* is not a college mystery it is not given an entry in this bibliography. *Murder in the New Age* takes Professor Cook to Sante Fe, New Mexico, where, on sabbatical leave, she solves a mystery in a colony of New Age cultists.

367. KELLY, NORA [NORA HICKSON (B. 1945)]. *BAD CHEMISTRY.* LONDON: HARPERCOLLINS, 1993; NEW YORK: ST. MARTIN'S, 1994.

Wendy Fowler, the only woman in the chemistry department at the University of Cambridge, is found dead in the cold room of the department's laboratories. Although Fowler's demise seems to have been the result of an accidental fall, Detective Chief Inspector Edward Gisborne of Scotland Yard soon establishes that she was murdered. His suspects include two of Fowler's fellow researchers, Ron Bottomley and Alan Kennedy. A quarrelsome man, Bottomley had long-running professional feuds with several of his colleagues, and he feared that Fowler's research was eclipsing his own. Alan Kennedy was known to have scheduled an appointment with Fowler on the night of her death. The unmarried Fowler was pregnant at the time of her killing and Gisborne believes that the very married Kennedy may have been the father of her child. Gisborne is helped in his detection by Gillian Adams, his own lover. A professor of history at the "University of the Pacific Northwest," Adams is spending the summer at Cambridge, where she can be within easy traveling distance of Gisborne's flat in London. Before the novel concludes, the body of a seventeen-year-old girl turns up in a shallow grave, antiabortion zealots threaten the operation of a pregnancy clinic, Gisborne learns a great deal about the murderous uses of ether, and readers are taken into many academic and nonacademic corners of Cambridge.

Bad Chemistry is the third of four mysteries by Nora Kelly to appear in this bibliography. All four mysteries employ Professor Gillian Adams as sleuth. The first two Professor Adams novels are *In the Shadow of King's* (243) and *My Sister's Keeper* (354). The fourth is *Old Wounds* (463).

368. LAKE, M. D. [ALLEN SIMPSON]. *MURDER BY MAIL.* NEW YORK: AVON, 1993.

Paula Henderson and Lawrence Fitzpatrick are campus security officers at a large university in the upper Midwest. They also are an interracial couple, and they begin receiving anonymous hate letters in the mail. Meantime, Geoffrey Oates, a graduate student in psychology, is found shot dead in his automobile, and Harold Mullen, a wealthy man who has been giving sizable sums of money to the university, burns to death when his home is apparently torched by an arsonist. Tying together the various strands of this involved college mystery is Peggy O' Neill, another member of the university's security police and a veteran Allen Simpson series-character detective. Officer O'Neill finds Geoffrey Oates's body, and she becomes involved in the Mullen affair when her friend Paula Henderson emerges as a suspect in the man's death. Before the story ends O'Neill discovers that some professors are not fussy about the sources of their research money, and she learns, too, that studies involving human genetics can produce findings that may be interpreted in more than one way. The story features several psychology faculty members in significant roles, and readers also are introduced to a disheveled psychology research assistant named Bill Turner who literally lives in the laboratory in which he works.

Murder by Mail is one of nine Peggy O'Neill mysteries by Allen Simpson that have entries in this bibliography. The others are *Amends for Murder* (313), *Cold Comfort* (325), *A Gift for Murder* (356), *Poisoned Ivy* (357), *Grave Choices* (410), *Once Upon a Crime* (411), *Flirting with Death* (431), and *Death Calls the Tune* (479).

369. LORENS, M(ARGARET) K(EILSTRUP) (B. 1945). *SORROWHEART*. NEW YORK: DOUBLEDAY, 1993.

Four women have met their deaths from poison at "Dewitt Clinton College" in "Ainsley," New York. The police have dubbed the serial killer "The Heart Specialist," but they have no idea of the evildoer's identity. Meanwhile, the college's new president, James Temple Macauley, is spearheading a modernization program that is making him bitter enemies both on and off the campus. Macauley wants the city fathers to condemn "Sorrowheart," an old mansion near the college, so he can build a new dormitory in its place, and the mansion's octogenarian owner, Maxima Davenport Bergner, hates him with a passion. At the college itself Macauley has proposed a sweeping curricular reform, one that will deemphasize traditional liberal arts offerings in favor of more popular courses such as "The Soap Opera: An American Art Form," and he is despised by almost all of Dewitt Clinton's faculty. The sleuth in this very elaborate story, which occupies 387 pages of text in the original hardcover edition, is Shakespearean scholar Winston Marlowe Sherman, a Dewitt Clinton professor of English. Curmudgeon-like, witty, egotistical, and the writer of mystery novels under the pen name Henrietta Slocum, Sherman is an M. K. Lorens series-character professor-detective. Beyond retirement age, Sherman knows that President Macauley will soon force him out of the classroom, and when he gets information that suggests that Macauley may, in fact, be The Heart Specialist, he enthusiastically tries to prove the president guilty. Then President Macauley is assassinated in his campus office, and with the president's death Professor Sherman expands his detection to look for the killer of his archenemy as well as the murderer of the four female victims. Many academic characters appear in this novel, and some of them are developed in significant detail. More ambitiously written than most mystery novels, *Sorrowheart* mixes comedy with tragedy, and it tells several parallel stories. Some of the narratation is in third-person voice, but when Professor Sherman is on stage readers are allowed to hear what is happening directly from him.

Margaret Keilstrup Lorens received a B.A. from Midland Lutheran College in 1967 and a Ph.D. from the University of Nebraska in 1974. Before embarking on a full-time writing career she taught English at Fort Hays State University, Midland Lutheran College, and the University of Nebraska. *Sorrowheart* was the fifth M. K. Lorens novel to feature the detection of Professor Winston Marlowe Sherman, and the only book in the Professor Sherman series to have sufficient "academic" content to warrant inclusion in this bibliography. At the time *Sorrowheart* was published Lorens lived in Freemont, Nebraska, the site of Midland Lutheran College.

370. NEEL, JANET [JANET COHEN (B. 1940)]. *DEATH AMONG THE DONS.* LONDON: CONSTABLE, 1993; NEW YORK: ST. MARTIN'S, 1994.

Francesca Wilson, a British civil servant, has child-care problems, and she tries to reduce her out-of-the-home work hours by accepting a part-time job as bursar of "Gladstone College." Gladstone is a prestigious all-women's college in London located somewhere near

Heathrow Airport. Unhappily, Wilson's life does not improve with the job change. Gladstone is a school in trouble. Its finances are in a shambles, and a debate over whether to admit men rages through the institution. Moreover, as Wilson arrives to take on the bursar position, the warden of the college is found dead of mysterious causes in her apartment. Then two students and a woman professor are attacked on campus by a knife-wielding assailant. With assistance from her husband, London Police Superintendent John McLeish, Francesca Wilson finally brings order to the Gladstone chaos, but toward the end of the book, after a physical struggle with the villain of the piece, she finds herself in the hospital for her trouble. *Death among the Dons* is a solid British college mystery, incorporating wit, several subplots, and a large cast of academic characters, some of whom are engaging in extramarital affairs. It also contains an added attraction not found in other books in the subgenre. Because Francesca Wilson's official job at Gladstone is to handle the school's money, the novel offers readers an opportunity to learn a great deal about cost overruns in academe.

Janet Cohen was born in Oxford, England. She received an undergraduate degree from Newnham College, Cambridge, in 1962. Cohen has had a long career as a British civil servant and as a director of banking and business firms. She was made an associate fellow of Newnham College in 1988, and in 1994 she became a governor of the BBC. *Death among the Dons* was Cohen's fourth Francesca Wilson mystery novel.

371. SILVAS, RANDALL. *AN OCCASIONAL HELL.* SAG HARBOR, N.Y.: PERMANENT PRESS, 1993.

Alex Catanzaro is an associate professor of history at "Shenango College" in western Pennsylvania. Every Saturday after breakfast, so he tells his wife, Elizabeth, Catanzaro goes to the college library to do research for a book about the War of 1812. In fact, every Saturday morning Alex has a tryst with Jeri Gillen, a local waitress. One day Elizabeth learns the truth about how her husband spends his Saturday mornings, and she telephones rock musician Rodney Gillen, Jeri Gillen's husband, to inform him of their spouses' weekly arrangement. In short order Professor Catanzaro is found dead in a rural area outside of town, with an ancient musketball shot through his brain, and the police suspect that Elizabeth paid someone, perhaps Rodney Gillen, to do the evil deed. The sleuth in this story is Ernest DeWalt, a former private investigator and the author of a novel titled *Suffer No Fools*. After being wounded and almost killed on a previous case DeWalt has retired from the perils of detective work and he now teaches creative writing at Shenango College. Although reluctant to get involved, DeWalt finally succumbs to Elizabeth Catanzaro's pleas to prove her innocence. Some of this literate story is written in the present tense, and its unorthodox structure includes several flashbacks. A good deal of the action takes place nearby but not on the Shenango campus, but several of the college's students and faculty members appear in important roles. One of the more interesting faculty characters is Andrea Banks, an attractive professor of English who, according the book's author, is sexually aroused by words. "If books came with penises," notes the author, "she would have been a librarian." In any event, Professor Banks tries to seduce Ernest DeWalt, but he recognizes that any sex with her would bring trouble, and he discourages her advances by pretending to be a homosexual.

In a note at the beginning of this book Randall Silvas acknowledges the Thurber House in Columbus, Ohio, Mercyhurst College in Erie, Pennsylvania, and the National Endowment for the Arts for their support during the writing of *An Occasional Hell.* The book was his first mystery novel. Prior to *An Occasional Hell* Silvas was known primarily as a playwright, and he has been the recipient of several grants and fellowships in support of that endeavor.

372. SMITH, JOAN (B. 1953). *WHAT MEN SAY.* NEW YORK: FAWCETT COLUMBINE, 1993.

Oxford don Bridget Bennett and her American husband, Sam Becker, are holding a housewarming at an Oxfordshire farm to which they have just moved. The festivities come to a halt when children discover the decomposing body of a woman in a barn. A few days later the police tentatively identify the corpse as that of Paula Wolf, nineteen years old, of Oak Falls, Ohio, and they believe that she might have been wanted in the United States for bankrobbing. Although officers from the Thames Valley Police do most of the serious legwork in this case, the novel focuses on the attempts of series-character professor-detective Loretta Lawson to resolve the mystery of how and why Paula Wolf came to be in the English countryside. An ardent feminist, and one of Bridget Bennett's closest friends, Lawson is a part-time lecturer in English at London University. As she detects, Lawson becomes worried when Bennett, who is thirty-nine years old and pregnant, begins displaying signs of physical and emotional strain. She becomes even more concerned when she suspects that Bennett has not revealed, to her or to the police, all of the salient details of her personal life. The book features several academic characters in addition to Loretta Lawson and Bridget Bennett, and it contains many scenes in Oxford and its environs. Near the midpoint of the book alert readers are even allowed a quick glimpse of a faculty meeting at London University. At the end of the story the guilty party seems to have been identified, but matters have not worked out to Loretta Lawson's satisfaction. *What Men Say* may be the only college mystery in which a professor-detective breaks down in sobs as a villain is taken away by the police.

Joan Smith was born in London. She is a former reporter and theater critic for the *Sunday Times*. *What Men Say* was the fourth in a continuing series of Professor Loretta Lawson mysteries, and it is the only novel thus far in the series with enough "academic" content to merit inclusion in this bibliography.

373. WALSH, JILL PATON (B. 1937). *THE WYNDHAM CASE.* NEW YORK: ST. MARTIN'S, 1993.

Although this University of Cambridge mystery is set entirely in modern times, the story really begins in 1692, when a wealthy benefactor named Wyndham willed his sizable collection of books to "St. Agatha's College." To house his treasures, he also arranged for the construction of a vaulted building (now known as "The Wyndham Library") and had an immense, two-story bookcase ("The Wyndham Case") installed to hold the library's contents. Furthermore, he left the college the financial means to pay a librarian more than most professors, and among other curious codicils to his will, he stipulated that no books could be added or subtracted from the library's original holdings. If any changes were ever detected, the college would have to sell the books and deliver the proceeds to a local almshouse. Imagine, then, the consternation at St. Agatha's when, as the library is being opened one morning, Philip Skellow, a first-year student, is found dead on the floor after apparently falling from the top of the bookcase. The deceased, it seems, was trying to steal one or several of the Wyndham's ancient tomes. Enter Imogene Quy, the college's nurse, who is one of the first persons on the scene of Mr. Skellow's death. Nurse Quy is a thirty-something, unmarried dispenser of tranquilizers to administrators and faculty, as well as the giver of much reassurance to emotionally distraught students during exam periods. She finds it hard to believe that Mr. Skellow, whom she had known in her professional capacity, was a thief, and she adds detection to her college duties. As much a satire on special-collections libraries as it is of academe per se, this inventive novel features a feud between the overpaid Wyndham librarian and the underpaid, hardworking head of the main St. Agatha's library. It also includes the mysterious drowning death of another student and the abduction of a professor who discovers that one of his own rare books has been stolen.

Jill Paton Walsh was born in London and educated in St. Michael's Convent, North Finchley, and at St. Anne's College, Oxford. Until the publication of *The Wyndham Case,* Walsh was primarily a writer of children's literature. Her publications in that field won her many prizes, and she has lectured extensively about children's literature in both Great Britain and the United States. In 1966 she received the CBE for services to literature in Great Britain, and she was elected a Fellow of the Royal Society of Literature. *The Wyndham Case* was Walsh's first mystery novel. *A Piece of Justice* (414), her second mystery (also featuring Nurse Imogene Quy), has an entry later in this bibliography.

374. WEIR, CHARLENE (RAYE) (B. 1937). *CONSIDER THE CROWS.* NEW YORK: ST. MARTIN'S, 1993.

Susan Wren, the chief of police in "Hampstead," Kansas, has two murder investigations on her hands and both have to do with "Emerson College," the local emporium of higher education. One is the case of Lynelle Hames, a clerk-typist in Emerson's English department. Lynelle was found in a creek outside of town, drowned after receiving a blow to her head. The second murder was that of Audrey Kalazar, Emerson's vice chancellor. Thought to be away on a speaking trip, Dr. Kalazar was found dead in a local well, killed by a blow to the head before being dropped into the water. Curiously, the two murders seem to have occurred at almost the same time, and the prime suspect in both killings is Carena Egersund, a middle-aged woman who teaches statistics at Emerson. Lynelle Hames had recently begun harassing Egersund, claiming to be an illegitimate daughter she gave up for adoption. And Dr. Kalazar, described by one character in the novel as "never a woman to underestimate her own importance," had just threatened to fire Carena after Julie Kalazar, the vice chancellor's daughter, had received poor grades in one of Egersund's statistics classes. As Chief

Wren detects, the two investigations begin to blend, and by the end of this novel, in which all the academic principals are women, Lynette Hames and Audrey Kalazar are not the only people for whom Emerson College needs to find replacements.

Charlene Weir was born in Nortonville, Kansas. She attended the Fort Scott School of Nursing and the University of Oklahoma. *Consider the Crows* was her second mystery novel. Her first, *The Winter Widow* (New York: St. Martin's, 1992), was a nonacademic tale that also featured Susan Wren as detective. *The Winter Widow* won the St. Martin's Press's Best First Malice Domestic Mystery Contest in 1991. Weir's original intentions were to become a nurse. She turned to mystery writing after being diagnosed with multiple sclerosis.

375. WILSON, F(RANCIS) PAUL (B. 1946). *THE SELECT.* LONDON: HEADLINE, 1993. NEW YORK: MORROW, 1995.

The Select is a suspense novel, not a conventional murder-detection story. It is set at the "Ingraham College of Medicine" outside of "Laurel Hills," Maryland. Lavishly supported by the "Kleederman Foundation," whose money comes from the Kleederman pharmaceutical empire, the Ingraham represents elite education at its zenith. The Ingraham has America's best medical-school faculty and facilities, and in search of the most promising students, it admits only those who have top MCAT scores and who, in addition, pass its own entrance exam. Once admitted to the Ingraham, students pay no tuition, dormitory charges, or fees of any kind. *The Select* follows the adventures of Quinn Cleary, a University of Connecticut graduate, after her admission to the Ingraham. While Miss Cleary does not incur any student loans, she does almost lose her life after finding that the Ingraham includes some very dastardly people among its faculty and staff and that those people are doing very nasty things. The Ingraham's educational program includes such items as constant closed-circuit television monitoring of all students and the killing of students who break school rules. While some readers may consider those practices too severe, the fact remains that many of America's most prominent physicians are Ingraham graduates. Hence, those who think that medical education in America could be improved may get some ideas from reading this novel.

Francis Paul Wilson is a New Jersey medical doctor who has written many well-received science-fiction novels and medical thrillers. *The Select* was his fourteenth novel.

376. WRIGHT, ERIC (B. 1929). *DEATH BY DEGREES.* NEW YORK: SCRIBNER'S, 1993.

A search committee at Toronto's "Bathurst Community College" selects Maurice Lyall, a political scientist and professor of social studies, to be the next dean of the school's liberal arts division. Several members of the committee who were originally in favor of another candidate switched allegiances to Lyall in the final voting. Two weeks after assuming his new post, Lyall is shot dead in his home, the apparent victim of a robbery-murder. A Native American drifter, Henry Littledeer, is soon arrested for the crime after he pawns the professor's watch. Then the police begin to receive anonymous letters that tell them that the killer actually was someone from the college. The detective in this story is Inspector Charlie Salter of the Toronto police, an Eric Wright series-character. Salter's father is seriously ill, and he spends some of his time wrestling with that upsetting situation, but when he turns his attentions to the case of the dead professor he interviews many faculty members and administrators at Bathurst. By the end of this exemplary college novel, the writer of the anonymous letters proves to be correct, and Salter learns that the motives of those who cast votes on academic search committees are not always pure. Academic readers will especially appreciate the book's seven-page prologue, in which the dynamics of the search committee's deliberations are described.

Death by Degrees was the tenth entry in Eric Wright's Inspector Charlie Salter series. *The Night the Gods Smiled* (237), the first mystery in the Salter series, also appears in this bibliography.

377. ZUBRO, MARK RICHARD. *POLITICAL POISON.* NEW YORK: ST. MARTIN'S, 1993.

Gideon Giles, a professor of English at the University of Chicago, dies in his office after drinking a poisoned health-food drink. Recently elected a Chicago alderman, the ultraliberal Giles had many enemies, both at the university and in the world of Chicago politics. The sleuth in the novel is Detective Paul Turner, a gay Chicago policeman. Part of the story takes place away from the university, as Turner attempts to link the professor's murder to some Chicago politicians and their mobster associates, but the book contains many campus scenes and offers many academic suspects. One professor who might be the villain is pudgy Otto Kempe, whose interpretations of Chaucer had often been attacked viciously by the late Professor Giles. Then there is Lilac Ostergard, a black professor who is an extremely close friend of Laura Giles, the late professor's widow. Another potential faculty murderer is Atherton Sorenson, the suave head of the English department. Professor Sorenson admits that he considered Professor Giles's social activism to be troublemaking, and he objected, in particular, when Giles proposed that the English department be declared a nuclear-free zone. Professorial readers who think that their own campus offices are already free from nuclear weapons, and safe from all other kinds of death-dealing instruments as well, might be tempted to think again after reading *Political Poison*. Not only does Professor Giles consume his fatal potion and then expire within the confines of his office, shortly after his death Detective Turner and his partner are shot at from the hallway as they look for clues in the professor's office files.

At the time *Political Poison* was published, Mark Richard Zubro was a high-school English teacher and teachers' union president in Mokena, Illinois. He also was president of the Midwestern chapter of the Mystery Writers of America. Most of Zubro's mysteries have featured gay characters, and Paul Turner, the gay detective in *Political Poison*, is a Zubro series-character detective. *Political Poison* was the second in Zubro's continuing four-novel Paul Turner series.

378. ALBERT, SUSAN WITTIG. *HANGMAN'S ROOT*. NEW YORK: SCRIBNER'S, 1994.

Professor Dottie Riddle is a strident animal rights activist who rescues stray cats, and Professor Miles Harwick is a researcher who allows abysmal conditions for the animals in his laboratories. Riddle and Harwick hate each other, and since both are biologists at "Central Texas State University," their feud keeps the biology department in a constant uproar. Harwick is found hanging lifeless in his office one evening, and Dottie Riddle is charged with the killing. Riddle asks her friend China Bayles to represent her, but Bayles, who has given up her law practice and now runs a herb shop, refers her to another attorney. Instead of acting as Riddle's counsel, China Bayles detects, and thanks to her efforts Professor Riddle is exonerated by the end of the story and the real killer is identified. The book is crammed with academic characters, including Frank Castle, the biology department's powerful chairman, and Cynthia Leeds, his loyal, gun-toting secretary. For its part, Central Texas State University is crammed with people for whom malfeasance is routine behavior. As she sleuths on the Central State campus, China Bayles encounters embezzlement, falsification of university records, and insurance fraud as well as murder. According to Bayles, who narrates this tale and is an expert in matters concerning herbs, "hangman's root" is a tea-like drink made by brewing the leaves of catnip. When consumed it turns people into "mad dogs," and in the seventeenth century hangmen would drink the potion to get in the proper mood for their tasks. As Dottie Riddle notes, the biologists at Central State do not need hangman's root. "They're mad dogs without it," she observes.

Susan Wittig Albert earned a Ph.D. in English at the University of California at Berkeley, and for fifteen years taught and held administrative posts at the University of Texas at Austin, Newcomb College of Tulane University, and Southwest Texas State College at San Marcos. At the time *Hangman's Root* was published Albert was a full-time writer and lived near Austin, Texas. *Hangman's Root* was her third China Bayles mystery novel.

379. BABULA, WILLIAM (B. 1943). *ST. JOHN'S BESTIARY.* AURORA, COLO.: WRITE WAY PUBLISHING CO., 1994.

Eight cats are stolen from the laboratory of Professor Vernon Krift. A physiologist at a university in San Francisco, Krift was using the cats in his research on the effects of breathing disorders on sleep. A group calling itself CFAF ("Committee for Animal Freedom") leaves a note claiming responsibility, but because he suspects Claire, his own college-age daughter, of being the actual engineer of the catnapping, Professor Krift is reluctant to go to the police. Instead he consults Jeremiah St. John, a former lawyer who now heads a private-detective agency. Shortly after St. John accepts the case, he finds Claire Krift strangled dead in a San Francisco motel. Then, as he becomes involved in the search for Claire's killer, Olivia ("Ollie") Shimoda, an alluring research assistant in the university's Health Science Center, is discovered shot dead on the campus. Jeremiah St. John narrates this clue-stuffed tale in properly sardonic private-eye fashion. His adventures include an early-in-the-book sexual affair with the ill-fated Miss Shimoda and a life-or-death wrestling match with a member of the physiology department. Although St. John travels to several San Francisco locales during the story, much of the significant action takes place at the university, and most of the major characters are university connected. Readers of the book get to meet the only professor in college-mystery fiction who stars in, produces, and markets his own pornographic films, and they learn that evildoers at an institution of higher education can lurk in the unlikeliest of places.

William Babula was born in Stamford, Connecticut, and received an A.B. from Rutgers in 1965 and a Ph.D. from the University of California at Berkeley in 1969. He was a member of the English department at the University of Miami from 1969 until 1981, and in that year he became dean of the School of Humanities at Sonoma State University in Rohnert Park, California. He is a prizewinning playwright and prominent Shakespearean scholar. *St. John's Bestiary* was Babula's fourth Jeremiah St. John mystery.

380. BERLINSKI, DAVID (B. 1942). *LESS THAN MEETS THE EYE.* NEW YORK: ST. MARTIN'S, 1994.

Set at a large, unidentified university in Palo Alto, California, this novel is narrated by Aaron Asherfeld, a wisecracking private detective. Asherfeld is hired by the institution's dean of faculty to look into the mysterious death of philosophy professor Richard Montague. The local medical examiner will not release the results of the autopsy on Montague's body, and in the absence of official information rumors are circulating that Montague died in a sadomasochistic exercise that left him without a penis. The university is being blackmailed for $500,000 by someone who threatens to release pictures of Montague's mutilated corpse to the press. Of additional concern to the dean, Montague had a large research grant from the National Science Foundation, and millions of those dollars seem to have disappeared. During his investigations Asherfeld meets a host of unappealing students, faculty, staff, and administrators, many of whom are ferocious advocates of politically correct causes, and a few of whom are guilty of illegal activities. Some academic readers may take offense at the heavy-handed portraits of the campus radicals in the story, but others may be amused at the way Asherfeld, when confronted by hostile gays and militant blacks, deflates his antagonists with one-line put-downs.

David Berlinski combines academic scholarship with mystery writing. *Less Than Meets the Eye* was his second Aaron Asherfeld mystery. Berlinski is a professor at Stanford, and he has taught philosophy, mathematics, and English. He is best known in academic circles for his controversial book *A Tour of the Calculus* (New York:

Pantheon, 1995), a work that challenged many of the standard assumptions of modern science.

381. CLEARY, MELISSA. *DEAD AND BURIED.* NEW YORK: BERKLEY PRIME CRIME, 1994.

Several events occur in short order to shake "Rodgers University" in the Ohio town of "Palmer." Merida Green, a woman convicted of killing her lover and a former chairperson of Rodgers's communications department, is freed from prison after eighteen months when new evidence suggests her possible innocence. Walter Hopfelt, chief of campus security, dies mysteriously when he tumbles over a railing in a university building. Then, when the site of Hopfelt's fall is examined, a jacket belonging to Danielle Sherman is found near the scene. Miss Sherman, a Rodgers student, died the previous year, in what was officially ruled a suicide, when she drank a carrot soda dosed with poison. Fitting all the pieces of this puzzle together is Jackie Walsh, a thirtyish divorcée who teaches film in the Rodgers communications department. Ms. Walsh, who is assisted by Jake, her pet police dog, comes into the picture because, as a series-character detective, she has a reputation for solving crimes, and Algernon Foreman, Rodgers's acting president, asks her to investigate on behalf of the university. Some of Ms. Walsh's sleuthing takes place off campus, and some of the novel is taken up with her attempts to train Jake's son, Maury, a large and rambunctious puppy, but there are enough campus scenes and more than enough university characters in this light and sometimes satirical mystery to provide it with the credentials necessary for inclusion in this bibliography. Faculty readers may sympathize with the plight of President Algernon Foreman. When the previous president of Rodgers suddenly vacated his office Foreman, a professor of English, was dragooned into serving as his temporary replacement. Miserable in the job, he constantly bemoans the fact that the presidential search committee has not yet found a suitable candidate to replace him. Meantime, he is trying desperately to transfer Polly Merton, the overbearing and power-hungry secretary to the president, to some other unit of the university.

Dead and Buried was the sixth in a continuing series of Melissa Cleary mysteries starring Jackie Walsh as detective. *A Tail of Two Murders* (347) and *First Pedigree Murder* (382), two other Jackie

Walsh mysteries by Melissa Cleary, have entries in this bibliography.

382. CLEARY, MELISSA. *FIRST PEDIGREE MURDER.* NEW YORK: BERKLEY PRIME CRIME, 1994.

The Goodwillie brothers, Mannheim and Stuart, are rich men who have given millions to "Rodgers University" in "Palmer," Ohio. Despite their apparent generosity, they are not nice people, and along with the cash has come constant harassment and berating of Rodgers' administrators. As Mannheim Goodwillie is being interviewed on the college radio station he collapses and dies, and an autopsy reveals that a surge of microwaves was somehow aimed in his direction and his death was the result of a melted pacemaker. Keith Monohan, head of the Rodgers "radio studies" program, was one of the main victims of the Goodwillies' nastiness, and he is arrested and charged with Mannheim Goodwillie's murder. Believing their colleague innocent, some of the Rodgers faculty ask Jackie Walsh to conduct her own investigation. An instructor of film at Rodgers, the middle-aged Walsh is a Melissa Cleary series-character detective, and because she has several successful sleuthing efforts already under her belt, the faculty identify her as the person with the best chance to exonerate Monohan. As this breezy mystery goes on Walsh, along with her Alsatian dog Jake, looks for Mannheim's murderer both at the university and within the eccentric Goodwillie family. Toward the end of the book Jake helps his mistress escape an attack by the killer's own dog. President watchers will be interested in the portrait of Rodgers's president, Henry Obermaier, who has recently announced his intention to resign in order to take the presidency of a college in New England. In a candid conversation with Jackie Walsh he details his life history and tells of his as-yet-unsuccessful thirty-year battle to lose weight and stop smoking.

Two other Jackie Walsh mysteries by Melissa Cleary, *A Tail of Two Murders* (347) and *Dead and Buried* (381), are included in this bibliography.

383. CRIDER, BILL (B. 1941). . . . *A DANGEROUS THING.* NEW YORK: WALKER, 1994.

This sardonic mystery takes place at "Hartley Gorman College" in "Pecan City," Texas. With academically unprepared students, and with a dispirited faculty teaching five courses each semester, Hartley Gorman is one of the least appealing institutions of higher learning in college-mystery fiction. And matters have recently gotten worse! Gwendolyn Partridge, the newly hired academic dean, has turned out to be the queen of political correctness. Among other matters, she has banned smoking from all college buildings, and in order to save the energy needed to run a power mower she keeps two goats to graze the grass on her front lawn. In a sense, everyone at Hartley Gorman is a victim, but the person who dies in the story is Tom Henderson, a sociologist. Henderson plunges to his death from the window of a campus building. The book's detective is Carl Burns, the chairperson of Hartley Gorman's Department of English. A series-character sleuth with prior experience solving mysteries at the college, Burns is asked by "Boss" Napier, the local sheriff, to supplement the official inquiry into Professor Henderson's death. As Burns conducts his probe of Henderson's fall, the author of the book peppers the text with dialogue and incidents that display the perils of faculty life under a dean who is an "unreconstructed hippie." For example, the only covered place on the campus where faculty smokers dare to sneak cigarettes is the college boiler room, but the boiler itself is ancient and in imminent danger of exploding. The author also points out, through the roles he has assigned several of the novel's major characters, that those who appear to be the most virtuous on a college or university campus are sometimes only the most hypocritical.

Three other Bill Crider mysteries appear in this bibliography. Two of them, *One Dead Dean* (290) and *Dying Voices* (307), are set at Hartley Gorman College and have Professor Carl Burns as detective. The third, *Murder Is an Art* (473), is set at "Hughes Community College" in Texas and features Sally Good as sleuth.

384. CROSSMAN, D(AVID) A. *MURDER IN A MINOR KEY.* NEW YORK: CARROLL & GRAF, 1994.

The sleuth-protagonist of this sometimes-zany mystery is a reclusive professor of music known only as Albert. Consumed by his work, Albert leads a bachelor existence in which he chain-smokes cigarettes, lives on a diet of junk food, and has difficulty executing such everyday tasks as dialing a telephone. He has only one friend, a professor of archaeology named Andrew Tewksbury. Albert becomes a detective when Professor Tewksbury is arrested for the murder of Justin Glenly, an unpopular professor of classical languages. Believing Tewksbury to be innocent, Albert overlays logical deduction upon naiveté before eventually identifying the guilty party. The story includes a jailbreak, engineered by Albert, in which Tewksbury escapes from police custody, and it includes, as well, the fatal shooting of Melissa Bjork, Tewksbury's attorney. Miss Bjork's killing injects a note of tragedy into the otherwise largely comic proceedings because she and the socially isolated Albert fall in love just before her death. Several other professors at the unnamed American university appear in the novel, as do several students, and there are frequent on-campus scenes. The author provides many smile-provoking lines. For example, when a secondary character is committed to a mental asylum it is noted that she will not be released "until her madness (does) not exceed that of the public in general." Murder and detection give *Murder in a Minor Key* its movement, but the work is essentially a character study of the ultra-eccentric Albert.

According to information on the cover of this book, D. A. Crossman is an award-winning copywriter and graphic artist. He also is an accomplished composer. Crossman was born in Islesboro, Maine, and at the time *Murder in a Minor Key* was published he lived in Spruce Head, Maine. He has since written several regional mystery novels set in Maine.

385. DENTINGER, JANE (B. 1951). *THE QUEEN IS DEAD*. NEW YORK: VIKING, 1994.

Jocelyn "Josh" O'Roarke is a Jane Dentinger series-character sleuth. A professional actress, O'Roarke is a graduate of "Corinth College," an institution set high on a hill above "Lake Taconic" in upstate New York. When Tessa Grant, O'Roarke's former teacher, dies of an apparent heart attack, O'Roarke returns to the campus for her funeral and to refresh old acquaintances. Corinth, as one character in the novel describes it, is "a hotbed of intrigue and scandal," and at some personal peril to herself O'Roarke finds herself embroiled in yet another detection exploit. The cause of Tessa Grant's death, as O'Roarke discovers, was not natural, and there are murder suspects aplenty among the surviving members of the Corinth drama department and their spouses. O'Roarke is assisted in the case by her significant other, Lieutenant Phillip Gerrard, a homicide detective from New York City, and by Sheriff Calvin Kowaleski of the local police. As a campus mystery, *The Queen Is Dead* has several noteworthy ingredients. The language of the characters is somewhat more earthy than that found in most novels of the subgenre; one faculty suspect is a limnologist, a discipline rare in any branch of fiction; and the villain is so well-liked in the Corinth community that Sheriff Kowaleski offers his own money to hire that person a top-flight defense lawyer.

Jane Dentinger was born in Rochester, New York. She received a B.F.A. from Ithaca College in 1973. She has worked professionally in the theater as an actor and as a director. *The Queen Is Dead* was the fifth in Dentinger's continuing series of Jocelyn O'Roarke mysteries.

386. DEXTER, (NORMAN) COLIN (B. 1930). *THE DAUGHTERS OF CAIN.* NEW YORK: CROWN, 1994.

Inspector Morse of the Thames Valley Police is assigned to investigate the murder of a retired Oxford don. The victim is Felix McClure, a former tutor in ancient history at "Wolsey College." McClure was stabbed dead in his North Oxford apartment, but the weapon used to kill him cannot be found. The irritable Morse and his ever-patient assistant, Sergeant Lewis, probe McClure's background, and Edward Brooks emerges as the prime suspect. Until recently Brooks was a scout at Wolsey, and McClure had him dismissed because he augmented his regular duties by supplying drugs and women to several of the college's undergraduates. In Colin Dexter's reticular Inspector Morse novels the obvious solution to a mystery is seldom the correct one, and as this story progresses, a prostitute, a female schoolteacher, and Brenda Brooks, Edward Brooks's wife, all come under suspicion. Much of the novel takes place in areas of Oxford away from the university, but there are several scenes within Wolsey College, and at one point Inspector Morse finds himself looking for crucial information in the Pitt Rivers Museum of Ethnology and Prehistory. As an added point of interest to college-mystery readers, *The Daughters of Cain* offers its readers a rare in-depth look into the domestic life of a servant at an Oxford college.

The Daughters of Cain was the eleventh novel in Colin Dexter's continuing Inspector Morse series. Other Inspector Morse novels with entries in this bibliography are *The Silent World of Nicholas Quinn* (190), *The Riddle of the Third Mile* (228), and *Death Is Now My Neighbor* (422).

387. DOSS, JAMES D(ANIEL). (B. 1939). *THE SHAMAN SINGS.* NEW YORK: ST. MARTIN'S, 1994.

Late one night the sounds of an argument are heard coming from the physics laboratory at "Rocky Mountain Polytechnic" in "Granite City," Colorado. The police are called, and just as a deputy arrives on the scene Julio Pacheco, a campus maintenance man, runs from the building and eludes six shots fired at him by the overeager policeman. Then the badly beaten corpse of Priscilla Scott, a graduate student, is found in the lab. Open-and-shut case, with nothing remaining but to apprehend Mr. Pacheco? Not in the view of Scott Parris, Granite City's police chief. There are, you see, certain inconsistencies. For one thing, the twenty-something Priscilla Scott had the surprising forethought to leave a will. For another, no one can decipher the seven-letter word Scott left on her computer just before she was killed. *The Shaman Sings* has many threads. Julio Pacheco is chased through the deserts of the Southwest. Chief Parris, a widower who moved to Granite City from Chicago only three years before Priscilla's murder, finds romance with Anne Foster, a local newspaper reporter. An aged Native American shaman intervenes to help catch the guilty party. And three of Rocky Mountain Polytechnic's physics professors, two of whom employ firearms in the story, try to enhance their professional status. Some important portions of this novel take place off campus, but the zealous activities of the three ambitious professors, as well as the solid academic motive for Priscilla Scott's murder, render the book more than eligible for entry in this bibliography.

James D. Doss was born in Reading, Pennsylvania. He received a B.S. from Kentucky Wesleyan College and an M.A. from the University of New Mexico. At the time *The Shaman Sings* was written he was an electrical engineer at the University of California's Los Alamos National Laboratory in New Mexico. *The Shaman Sings* was the first in a continuing series of novels in which Scott Parris serves as detective.

388. DUDLEY EDWARDS, RUTH (B. 1944). *MATRICIDE AT ST. MARTHA'S.* NEW YORK: ST. MARTIN'S, 1994.

"St. Martha's College," one of the lesser segments of the University of Cambridge, is shredded by internal dissension. A down-at-the-heels college for women, St. Martha's has just received a large multimillion-pound bequest, and the fellows have split into three factions over how the money should be spent. One group, led by Dame Maud Buckbarrow, the college's mistress, wants to put the money into improving the school's programs in theology, palaeography, and medieval law, disciplines that are basic to the fossilized St. Martha curriculum. Another faction, dominated by a gaggle of aggressive, socially conscious lesbians, wants to establish a center for gender and ethnic studies. Still a third group would like to spend the money improving the college's shabby amenities, including the wine cellar and the food service. When Dame Buckbarrow and then Deborah Windlesham, the deputy mistress, are both murdered, the lesbians manage to elect one of their own to the college's top office, and it appears that the gender-and-ethnic center is about to become reality. But to Robert Amiss, a Ruth Dudley Edwards series-character detective, the lesbians also appear likely to have committed the murders. Amiss is a London-based British civil servant who, accompanied by his pet cat, is at St. Martha's on a one-year fellowship to improve the relationship between St. Martha's and the British government. The novel is populated by a multitude of St. Martha's characters, almost all of whom seem to have advanced degrees in outlandishness. The college's pertinacious bursar, for example, is a crusty old woman who goes by the name of Jack, smokes a pipe, and threatens total noncompliance with one of the lesbians' new dictates that bans smoking in college offices. Two police detectives share the sleuthing with Amiss. One of them, Inspector Robert Romford, is a confirmed male chauvinist who finds that he has walked into a den of lionesses. The other is Cambridge-educated Sergeant Ellis Pooley. *Matricide at St. Martha's* is a wildly comic novel but it has a serious undertone. Indeed, it is Sergeant Pooley who observes that the situation at St. Martha's, where some of its female fellows are struggling to uphold standards of scholarship, in this case against the forces of political correctness, contains echoes of Dorothy L. Sayers's *Gaudy Night* (30).

Ruth Dudley Edwards was born in Dublin, Ireland. She received a B.A. and an M.A. from University College, Dublin, and also did graduate work at Cambridge University. She is one of Great Britain's best-known and most-respected mystery writers. *Matricide at St. Martha's* was the fifth in an ongoing series of often-satirical mysteries that feature Robert Amiss as detective.

389. FROETSCHEL, SUSAN. *ALASKA GRAY*. NEW YORK: ST. MARTIN'S, 1994.

Jane McBride gives up her job in Boston and makes a midwinter move to Sitka, a town of approximately 8,000 people in the southern part of Alaska. McBride's intention is to take up a position as financial director for a land-management firm. Unfortunately, the firm's board of directors has suddenly decided to explore the construction of a ski resort, and it now wants a financial manager with different qualifications. The firm's vice president gives McBride $75,000 for her troubles and tells her she will not be joining the company. Alone in cold and snowy Sitka, with a financial windfall but without a job, McBride signs on to teach business courses at "Holmes Barrett College," a small outpost of higher education with a student body drawn almost entirely from Native peoples. McBride's sojourn in Sitka does not go smoothly. Her classes go badly. Moreover, she receives threatening phone calls, and a man attacks her in her home and ransacks her papers and computer files. Then Nancy Nelson, a Native student at the college, dies from what appears to be a massive self-inflicted overdose of vodka, even though her mother and her friends contend that she was a teetotaler. During the body of the novel, McBride tries to discover the source of the troubles in Sitka and at Holmes Barrett College. At the end of the story she and two friends engage the book's villain in a no-holds-barred physical battle that results in the evildoer's death. Several Holmes Barrett faculty members play important roles in the novel, as does the school's ambitious president, Henry Ellsley. The book contains some descriptive scenes in the college's museum of native culture, where McBride meets Daniel Greer, the museum's charming and handsome curator. Nancy Nelson, the student who dies in the tale, was at Holmes Barrett on a government scholarship, yet she had an IQ of only seventy-three. As McBride explores this anomaly, she gains insight into the ways in which Alaskan Native students are sometimes exploited by colleges like Holmes Barrett.

Alaska Gray was Susan Froetschel's first mystery novel.

390. HOLT, HAZEL (B. 1928). *MRS. MALORY: DETECTIVE IN RESIDENCE.* NEW YORK: DUTTON, 1994; PUBLISHED IN ENGLAND AS *MURDER ON CAMPUS.* LONDON: MACMILLAN, 1994.

Sheila Malory comes from England to spend a semester teaching at "Wilmot College," a small liberal arts school in eastern Pennsylvania. Although she has no affiliation with a British university, the recently widowed Mrs. Malory is well-known for her books and articles on lesser-known British women writers of the nineteenth century. Mrs. Malory quickly encounters two murders. The first is the shooting death of Max Loring, the head of research at the "Whittier Collection," a prestigious art museum located near the Wilmot campus. The second is the knifing of Carl Loring, Max's brother and a Wilmot professor of English. Max Loring is killed just before a reception at the museum, and Mrs. Malory finds his body. Carl Loring is dispatched in the English department's "common room" at Wilmot. Since both brothers were widely disliked, suspects exist in profusion both at the museum and at the college. Most professorial readers will also detest Carl Loring. One of his favorite activities is to coach students to complain about the teaching done by faculty rivals, thereby getting those rivals in trouble with Wilmot's administration and, when the subjects of his dirty tricks do not have tenure, sometimes getting them fired as well. Mrs. Malory becomes involved in detection when she develops a friendly relationship with local police detective Michael Landis, a man whose education ended with high school but who nonetheless has an extensive knowledge of Shakespeare's writings. Throughout this well-constructed story Malory displays a perceptive fascination with American culture and with American higher education in particular. As she attends faculty meetings and otherwise interacts with her colleagues, American academic readers have an opportunity to see themselves through British eyes.

Mrs. Sheila Malory is a Hazel Holt series-character detective. *Mrs. Malory: Detective in Residence* was Malory's fifth published adventure. *The Cruellest Month* (334), a Malory novel set at Oxford's Bodleian Library, appears earlier in this bibliography.

391. KUPFER, FERN (B. 1946). *LOVE LIES*. NEW YORK: SIMON & SCHUSTER, 1994.

A dark academic comedy overlaid upon a whodunit, *Love Lies* is set at "Stimpson College," a high-status liberal arts school somewhere in the American Midwest. Tyler Markham, a physical fitness fanatic who somehow teaches both poetry and philosophy at Stimpson, is killed in the college gymnasium when a barbell falls on his chest. At first, Detective Frank Rhodes of the local police writes the death off as an accident, but when G. P. Comstock, Stimpson's wrestling coach, tells him that Markham would never have used so much weight while working out alone, Rhodes begins to think that he may have something sinister on his hands. When he learns that Markham was a habitual philanderer, Rhodes begins to investigate his death as a murder. The protagonist of the novel is Fran Meltzer, a middle-aged divorced woman who is a Stimpson professor of English. Professor Meltzer is the best friend of Julia Markham, Tyler

Markham's widow. Julia Markham, too, teaches English at Stimpson. Meltzer takes up sleuthing when Detective Rhodes comes to suspect her pal Julia of murdering her own husband. Toward the end of the book Meltzer is kidnapped and almost killed by the book's villain. The novel contains heaps of witty dialogue, much of it supplied by the hyperarticulate Fran Meltzer, and the author of the tale often has her characters discuss the problems of women in the academic world. Readers concerned with women's issues may be interested in Stimpson's informal "Friday Club," a group of women from the college. Almost all of the club's members are divorced, and they meet in each other's homes for mutual support. Readers who are primarily interested in murder mysteries may want to take note of the Friday Club as well because several of its participants play crucial roles in the novel's whodunit component.

Fern Kupfer was born in New York City. She received a B.S. from the State University of New York College at Cortland in 1968 and an M.A. from Iowa State University in 1973. At the time *Love Lies* was published Kupfer was an associate professor of English and creative writing at Iowa State University. *Love Lies* was her third full-length work of fiction and her first mystery novel.

392. LITTELL, ROBERT (B. CIRCA 1935). *THE VISITING PROFESSOR*. NEW YORK: RANDOM HOUSE, 1994.

Lemuel Falk, winner of the Lenin Prize for his work on the nature of entropy, tries for twenty-three years to leave Russia. When his exit visa is finally approved, he accepts an invitation to become a visiting professor at the "Institute for Advanced Interdisciplinary Chaos-Related Studies" in upstate New York. The institute is a component of "Backwater University." During his stay at Backwater, Professor Falk employs his vast knowledge of randomness to identify a serial killer who has been murdering people in and near the university. Although his imperfect English often leads to miscommunications, Falk also finds time to meet a variety of often-odd people in the Backwater community. Among his contacts, he has a sexual fling with a politically active local hairdresser, who began smoking to protest the surgeon general's failure to deal with hazardous waste dumps. Although *The Visiting Professor* depicts Falk doing some detecting, the book is much less a mystery than it is a comic novel about American higher education. A school without academic standards, Backwater is one of the zanier universities in either mystery or mainstream fiction. Its faculty members apologize to their students for the fact that classes interrupt the students' orgies of drugs and sex. Seminars are held in the local jail for students whose incarceration makes it impossible for them to be on campus, and those seminars are taught by incarcerated faculty. And those of the university's professors who are attached to the institute spend their lives studying such matters as the chaos of snowflakes and the surface tension of teardrops.

The Visiting Professor was Robert Littell's eleventh novel. At the time the book was published, Littell lived in France. A one-time Eastern Europe and Soviet affairs editor for *Newsweek*, Littell probably is best known for a spy novel titled *The Defection of A. J. Lewinter* (Boston: Houghton Mifflin, 1973). Information on the cover of *The Visiting Professor* tell us that *The Defection of A. J. Lewinter* was eventually "turned into a dull feature film."

393. MANT, JANICE (MACDONALD) (B. 1959). *THE NEXT MARGARET*. BUFFALO, NEW YORK: MOSAIC PRESS, 1994.

The narrator of this brief (127-pages) but inventive mystery is Miranda ("Randy") Craig. Miss Craig gives up a modestly successful career as a freelance writer to work toward an M.A. in Canadian literature at the University of Alberta in Edmonton. She chooses Alberta because she wants to study with Associate Professor Hilary Quinn, academe's leading expert on Margaret Ahlers, a popular but reclusive Canadian writer whose three novels have recently brought her into literary prominence. Shortly after Miss Craig arrives at Alberta the press reports Margaret Ahlers's death. As Miss Craig learns more about Professor Quinn, and about the curious personal relationship she had with Margaret Ahlers, she begins to suspect that the professor may be a murderer. Some of this story takes place in the wilds of Northern Alberta, where Miss Craig surreptitiously examines Professor Quinn's summer cabin, but most of the tale takes place in Edmonton on or near the university campus. *The Next Margaret* is distinguished by crisp writing and by a verisimilar academic atmosphere. It also features a University of Alberta faculty member who employs an ingenious technique for obtaining tenure.

At the time *The Next Margaret* was published Janice MacDonald Mant was a resident of Edmonton, Alberta, Canada, where she taught courses on English literature and detective fiction at the University of Alberta. In an author's note Mant thanks the Alberta Foundation for the Arts for its support of the book.

394. MAXES, ANNA. *DEAD TO RIGHTS.* NEW YORK: ST. MARTIN'S, 1994.

"Burleigh College" in New England has long been known for its academic excellence, but it has never had any success in intercollegiate athletics. Yet in the last few years all of Burleigh's teams have suddenly become competitive, and as *Dead to Rights* begins Burleigh's women's softball team actually wins a national championship. Unhappily, even as the Burleigh players celebrate, Joanna Deering, the star player on the losing team, dies in the locker room of what a puzzled doctor attributes to "an acute allergic reaction to an unknown allergen." "Reggie" Lichtman, an investigator for the "College and University Athletic Association," is present at the softball tournament in San Diego, and she has strong suspicions that Miss Deering's death and Burleigh's almost-instantaneous rise to the top in athletics are both products of sinister forces. Throughout the rest of the book Lichtman travels across the United States, probing into the background of Pierce Nolan, the coach of the Burleigh women's softball team, and into the backgrounds of several Burleigh softball players as well. During her investigations she stops at several colleges, including Burleigh, and she meets a host of people connected with those colleges' athletic departments. Although most readers will correctly surmise early in the story that Burleigh's swift rise to athletic prominence was accompanied by corrupt recruiting practices, few will guess the very unusual reason for the school's new orientation toward athletics.

Dead to Rights was Anna Maxes' first novel. At the time the book was published Maxes was a resident of western Massachusetts.

395. MCSHEA, SUSANNA HOFMANN. *LADYBUG, LADYBUG.* NEW YORK: ST. MARTIN'S, 1994.

Kevin Cannivan, a seminary student at "St. Sebastian's College" in "Coldwater," Connecticut, is found dead in the Catholic college's chapel with a rope around his neck. The local police attribute his death to autoerotic asphyxia, but Kevin's mother, Louise, refuses to accept their diagnosis. The Cannivan family lives in "Raven's Wing," Connecticut, and when Louise Cannivan receives an anonymous phone call claiming that Kevin's death was not an accident, she enlists the aide of the "Hometown Heroes," four Raven's Wing senior citizens who enrich their golden years with amateur detection. Convinced that there has been foul play, Louise and the four elderly sleuths (two men and two women) transport themselves to St. Sebastian's for detection. St. Sebastian's proves to be an institution where some seminary students, as well as some of their priest-professors, wink at the notion of celibacy. In addition, it is a place where not all of the nuns are what they seem to be. By the end of the story several more murders take place, three of the Hometown Heroes are wounded (not fatally) by gunfire, and readers are led to wonder whether St. Sebastian's, an obscure and undistinguished school in the best of times, can survive all of the resulting negative publicity.

According to information on the book's cover, Susanna Hofmann McShea grew up in Ridgefield, Connecticut, the town upon which Raven's Wing is modeled. At the time *Ladybug, Ladybug,* was published McShea was a resident of New Jersey. *Ladybug, Ladybug,* was the third novel in McShea's continuing Hometown Heroes series.

396. MEYERDING, JANE (B. 1950). *EVERYWHERE HOUSE.* NORWICH, VT.: NEW VICTORIA PUBLISHERS, 1994.

Ted Simpson, an associate professor of philosophy, is found stabbed and dying on the campus of the University of Washington. The local police quickly arrest Barbara Randall, Simpson's ex-wife. Grossly overweight and overtly antagonistic in most of her personal relationships, Ms. Randall is now one of the more strident members of the "Furies," a radical lesbian organization given to violent activism. The police are led to Ms. Randall, in part, because fresh lesbian graffiti, including the Furies' labyris symbol (the two-headed axe of the Amazons), is found on a wall near Professor Simpson's body. The narrator-sleuth in this tale is Terry Barber, a first-year student at Washington. A resident of "Everywhere House," a lesbian collective, Barber is not convinced that Randall is Simpson's killer, and with the help of several other lesbian students she identifies Simpson's actual murderer. The story is set in 1977, against the backdrop of Patty Hearst's misadventures, and it is noteworthy for dealing, in some detail, with the ideological conflicts between different segments of the Seattle lesbian community. It is noteworthy, too, for the unusual way in which Professor Simpson, before his death, attempted to increase the number and quality of his publications. Prospective readers should also be alerted to a unique scene, early in the book, where the relatively thin, vegetarian Terry Barber, whose first teenage crush was on Gertrude Stein, ruminates about her attraction to "large-size" women while she attends a "Fat Oppression Workshop" at the Lesbian Resources Center near the University.

Jane Meyerding was born in Chicago. At the time *Everywhere House* was published she was employed as a secretary in Seattle, Washington. *Everywhere House* was her first novel.

397. MORSON, IAN (NAIME). *FALCONER'S CRUSADE.* LONDON: GOLLANCZ, 1994; NEW YORK: ST. MARTIN'S, 1995.

Falconer's Crusade is set in thirteenth-century Oxford. The detective is William Falconer, a teacher with the rank of master regent in the university's faculty of arts. Falconer turns from lecturing to sleuthing when Margaret Gebetz, a university servant girl, has her throat slit, and when Thomas Symon, one of his pupils, is thought incorrectly by many of Oxford's townsfolk to have committed the murder. As the story continues, Symon manages to escape harm, but several other Oxford students are beaten to death by angry townspeople, Master John Fyssh is killed in yet another throat slitting, and a student named Jack Moulcom is strangled dead and then eviscerated. *Falconer's Crusade* can certainly be read for its whodunit puzzle, but many academic readers probably will find themselves equally interested in the novel's heaps of historical detail. They can learn, for example, that Oxford students of the period paid four shillings a year for their instruction, and that an elite group of masters known as the Black Congregation made many of the university's rules. They can also learn that while some things have changed since the medieval period of higher learning, others have stayed the same. Thomas de Cantilupe, Oxford's ambitious chancellor, administers the university in ways that enhance his chances for high political office in London, and throughout the story Falconer is revolted by the "quibbling, disputatious nature" of many of his faculty colleagues.

Ian Morson was a resident of England's Cornwall region when *Falconer's Crusade* was published. The book was the first in a continuing series of William Falconer mysteries by Ian Morson.

398. OLEKSIW, SUSAN (B. 1945). *DOUBLE TAKE.* NEW YORK: SCRIBNER'S, 1994.

A murder occurs at the "Massasoit College of Art," a small, well-respected school in the coastal New England village of "Mellingham." The victim is Hank Vinnio, a poor but talented work-study student. Vinnio is found dead on the floor of a college painting studio, and his corpse is surrounded by a colorful mix of blood and paint. The detective in the novel is Joe Silva, Mellingham's perceptive chief of police. Chief Silva's first task is to learn the cause of Hank's death; then he must find the murderer. *Double Take* offers detail about life in an art college, and it features such a large cast of Massasoit College of Art characters that the author thoughtfully provides a page-long roster of the story's major players at the front of the book. Some of those college individuals conceal secrets from their pasts, and others, most notably Preston H. Mattson, the nattily dressed chairman of the Massasoit department of painting, hide their own creative mediocrity even as they unfairly disparage the work of their more talented pupils. In the end, the motive for the killing is not uniquely academic. Nevertheless, as Joe Silva searches for the guilty party *Double Take* becomes a polished whodunit that is set at a type of institution of higher education not often encountered in the college-mystery subgenre.

Susan Oleksiw was born in Southbury, Connecticut. She received a B.A. from St. Lawrence University in 1967 and a Ph.D. in Sanskrit from the University of Pennsylvania in 1977. She has taught courses in mystery fiction and in creative writing at several colleges in the Boston area, and she has been a regular contributor of reviews and essays to mystery-fiction magazines. Oleksiw is the author of *A Reader's Guide to the Classic British Mystery* (Boston: G. K. Hall, 1988). She also writes detective novels of her own, and *Double Take* was the second of her mysteries to feature Joe Silva as detective.

399. ORENSTEIN, FRANK (EVERITT) (B. 1919). *A VINTAGE YEAR FOR DYING.* NEW YORK: ST. MARTIN'S, 1994.

When unpopular Professor Al Beasley disappears, his wife seeks the aide of Hugh Morrison, a retired New York State policeman. Convinced her husband is dead, but not grieving about his presumed loss, Florene Beasley wants Morrison to find the professor's body so she can collect his insurance. Something of a gormand, Morrison has settled into a life of heavy-duty eating, and he is reluctant to get involved, but when Florene Beasley discovers hubby Al's corpse buried in the family backyard, the old trooper's detective juices begin flowing and he sets out to find the professor's killer. Al Beasley was a professor of English at a university near Kingston, New York, and one of several leads Morrison follows has to do with the grievances held against him by many of his departmental colleagues. Among other infractions of academic etiquette, Beasley had a habit of covertly studying his office mate's manuscripts and plagiarizing their best ideas. Hugh Morrison also delves into the student drug culture, since some of Professor Beasley's pupils were known to have frequented the Beasley home for parties in which the illegal use of controlled substances was the principal entertainment. *A Vintage Year for Dying* is not the purest example of a college mystery in this bibliography; some of Hugh Morrison's perambulations take him to nonacademic locales, including the back streets of New York City. Nonetheless, the book is well stocked with academic characters, and on the many occasions when his sleuthing takes him onto academic grounds ex-policeman Morrison, who narrates the story, offers many irreverent impressions of higher education and those who practice it.

Frank Orenstein was born in New York City. He received a B.A. from Dartmouth in 1940 and an M.A. from the University of Chicago in 1942. A former United States State Department official and a former vice president of the Newspaper Advertising Bureau in New York, Orenstein began writing mysteries after taking early retirement. Many of his mysteries have been set in the advertising world. *A Vintage Year for Dying* was the third in a continuing series of mysteries with Hugh Morrison as detective. At the time the book was published Orenstein lived in upstate New York.

400. SPRING, MICHELLE (B. 1947). *EVERY BREATH YOU TAKE.* NEW YORK: POCKET BOOKS, 1994.

Monica Harcourt, a painter and a teacher of art at England's "Eastern University," is invited to share a weekend-retreat cottage in Norfolk with Helen Cochrane and Laura Principal. Helen Cochrane is a librarian at Eastern, and Laura Principal is a London-based private detective. When Harcourt is brutally murdered in her Cambridge studio, even before she can begin to enjoy the cottage's restful environment, Laura Principal employs her occupational skills to investigate. Principal also narrates the story. Although much of this novel takes place in London and at "Wildfell," the Norfolk cottage at which Helen Cochrane and Laura Principal had hoped Harcourt would join them in a collective recharging of their batteries, it also contains lengthy scenes on the Eastern University campus and in the city of Cambridge. Several students and art instructors at Eastern are among the suspects in the story, as is Milton Bannister, Eastern's provost. Bannister has a properly engaging administrative smile. One of the more loathsome administrators in college-mystery fiction, he also has a shameful history of demanding sexual favors from the women faculty and staff who work under his authority.

Michelle Spring was born in Victoria, British Columbia. She earned a B.A. in Canada at the University of Victoria and an M.A. in England at the University of Essex. Until her retirement in 1997 to become a full-time writer, Spring was a professor of sociology at Anglia Polytechnic University in Cambridge. She also was an affiliated lecturer with the social and political sciences faculty at the University of Cambridge. Writing under the name Michelle Stanworth she produced many sociology books and articles and co-authored one of England's most widely used textbooks for introductory sociology courses. *Every Breath You Take* was the initial novel in what has become a continuing series of mysteries featuring Laura Principal as detective. An entry for Michelle Spring's *Nights in White Satin* (483), Laura Principal's fourth adventure, can be found later in this bibliography.

401. STALLWOOD, VERONICA. *OXFORD EXIT.* LONDON: MACMILLAN, 1994; NEW YORK: SCRIBNER, 1995.

Someone is stealing books from the libraries at Oxford, and to prevent the thefts from being detected, he or she is deleting the books' computer records as well. Meantime, Jenna Cates, a young woman training to be a library conservationist, is strangled dead shortly after a trip to California. And in a creative writing class being conducted by the Oxford extramural department, a student is producing essays containing information about both the book thefts and the murder. The sleuth in this story is Kate Ivory, a writer of historical romance novels. Ivory was once a cataloger at the Bodleian Library, and Andrew Grove, a senior assistant librarian at the Bodleian, asks her to look into the book thefts and computer deletions. Ivory eventually puts the several pieces of the novel's puzzle together, and her detection takes her to libraries at the Universities of California at Berkeley and "Santa Luisa," as well as to the Bodleian and several college libraries at Oxford. The book includes detailed information about the backstage operations of some of the libraries Ivory visits. Indeed, alert readers will learn to avoid the library at Oxford's "Leicester College" Wednesday afternoons, because they will not have access to the rare books kept on the library's locked gallery. Barbara, the clerk who ordinarily opens the gallery for visitors, takes Italian lessons that afternoon, and Kevin Newton, the college's singularly uncooperative librarian, and the only other person authorized to open the rare-books collection, refuses to leave his desk.

Veronica Stallwood was born in London. Before turning to mystery writing as a career, she worked at the Bodleian Library and the library at Oxford's Lincoln College. *Oxford Exit* was the second novel in a continuing series featuring Kate Ivory. The first Kate Ivory novel is *Death and the Oxford Box* (London: Macmillan, 1993; New York: Scribner, 1994). While some of *Death and the Oxford Box* takes place at "Leicester College" and in the Bodleian Library, the plot does not focus on academic issues, and the book does not have an entry in this bibliography. On the other hand, the third and fourth novels in the Kate Ivory series are, like *Oxford Exit*, solid college mysteries, and both books appear later in this bibliography. Those novels are *Oxford Mourning* (413) and *Oxford Fall* (438).

402. CROSS, AMANDA [CAROLYN GOLD HEILBRUN (B. 1926)]. *AN IMPERFECT SPY.* NEW YORK: BALLANTINE, 1995.

This novel is set at the "Schuyler Law School," an academically undistinguished institution in New York City. The protagonist is Kate Fansler, Amanda Cross's long-running series-character detective, who is a professor of English at a crosstown, high-prestige New York City university. Fansler comes to Schuyler for a semester to teach a course in law and literature with Blair Whitson, a young Schuyler law professor. Attorney Reed Amhearst, Fansler's husband, also comes to Schuyler, in his case to create a "clinic" through which students will work with convicted criminals who need legal representation. Through one of Schuyler's secretaries, a woman who calls herself Harriet Furst, Fansler becomes interested in the recent death of Nellie Rosenbusch, who was the only tenured woman member of the Schuyler faculty. Rosenbusch, who regularly provoked the ire of her male colleagues, fell in front of an oncoming truck while waiting to cross a New York City street, and there is a possibility she was pushed. As Fansler detects in the Rosenbusch affair, she also becomes involved in the case of Betty Osborne, who is incarcerated after being convicted of murdering her alcoholic and violent husband, a Schuyler professor. There is no doubt that Mrs. Osborne shot and killed her spouse, but Fansler and Amhearst believe that she failed to receive a proper "battered-woman defense," and they work to have her case reopened. Like many of the other books in the Kate Fansler series, *An Imperfect Spy* depicts Fansler challenging male authority and prerogatives in academe, and like many of the series' earlier entries, it speaks to the ways in which literature can bring meaning to people's lives. Fansler continues her habit of dropping quotations; Harriet Furst is a devoted reader of John Le Carre; and Betty Osborne, who once attended a class taught by Professor Fansler, is a fan of Thomas Hardy and devours all the works of literary criticism she can obtain while sitting in prison. The book also contains a scene, that certainly will get the attention of real-life professors, in which an unhappy male student physically attacks Fansler and Blair Whitson as they conduct their law-and-literature seminar.

An Imperfect Spy is the sixth of seven Professor Kate Fansler novels with entries in this bibliography. The others are *Poetic Justice* (156), *Death in a Tenured Position* (211), *Sweet Death, Kind Death* (238), *No Word from Winifred* (264), *A Trap for Fools* (308), and *The Puzzled Heart* (457).

403. CUTLER, JUDITH. *DYING FALL.* LONDON: PIATKUS, 1995.

Dying Fall takes place at and near "William Murdock College," an institution of "further-learning" in the center of the British city of Birmingham. Many of the college's students are members of disadvantaged immigrant families from India, Pakistan, and the Caribbean. The story begins when Sophie Rivers, a William Murdock teacher of English, finds the dead body of Wajid Achtar, a Muslim student, in an elevator. Achtar, whose expensive designer clothes do not match the claims of poverty he made to secure a large amount of financial aid, has been stabbed. Rivers is drawn into detection when other students begin furnishing her information about Achtar's death. Some of her sleuthing focuses on nonstudent members of Achtar's extended family, but there are many scenes at William Murdock, and the book offers some interesting views of faculty life at the nonelite school in England. Although she has ten years' seniority as a teacher at William Murdock, Rivers's "office" consists of a desk in a room she shares with thirteen colleagues. It is located on the fifteenth floor of a high-rise building, and while the police take several days to examine the elevator in which Achtar was killed, Rivers and her office mates must walk up fifteen flights of stairs to their quarters. Much of the instruction at the college is remedial, and property crime is so rampant that Rivers refuses to risk her car by parking it on the campus. As might be expected, faculty disillusionment is high. During the story one ambitious member of the faculty receives a doctorate in business. All of his associates assume that he will upgrade his academic status by taking a position at a British university.

Instead, he leaves William Murdock to begin a career with a firm of legal bookmakers.

Judith Cutler was born near Birmingham, England. Before becoming a full-time writer, she spent several years as a teacher in an inner-city education college. At the time *Dying Fall* was published Cutler lived in Birmingham, where she was a part-time lecturer at the University of Birmingham. *Dying Fall* was the first in a continuing series of mysteries starring Sophie Rivers as detective.

404. FOSS, JASON [JASON MONAHAN]. *SHADESMOOR.* NEW YORK: SEVERN HOUSE, 1995.

Jeffrey Flint, a junior member of the archaeology staff at "Central College" in London, takes a new job at the "University of North Yorkshire." Although North Yorkshire is a former polytechnic, and without academic prestige, the post means a promotion in both rank and salary. When Flint arrives at North Yorkshire he finds that he has been recruited to lead an excavation unit formerly headed by Tom Aiken, who has recently been bludgeoned to death with a Stone Age axe in his home. To make matters worse, he discovers that the excavation unit's current "dig" is at Shadesmoor, an ancient Yorkshire castle that is about to be transformed into a medieval theme park. The theme park is highly controversial, and many of the locals, from both town and gown, bitterly oppose it. Before this novel concludes Jeffrey Flint discovers who killed Tom Aiken, and he solves the mysteries surrounding a variety of other related crimes as well. There are many scenes on the cheerless North Yorkshire campus, and many members of the university's faculty play key roles in the story. Professor-readers may appreciate the scene, two-thirds through the book, in which Flint overwhelms his less-than-stellar North Yorkshire seminar students by dropping the names of Barthes, Marx, Foucault, and Derrida, in rapid-fire succession, into a classroom discussion. They may appreciate, too, the scene at the very end of the novel where the head of the North Yorkshire archaeology department, Professor Betty Vine, pleads with Flint to stay on at the university. After all of the unpleasantness he has experienced, it is Flint's natural inclination to resign and move to yet another situation. However, murders, arrests, and other resignations have so decimated the North Yorkshire archaeology ranks that if Flint leaves Professor Vine will be, in her own words, "a professor without a department."

Jason Monahan is an archaeologist. *Shadesmoor* was his third novel. At the time *Shadesmoor* was published, Monahan lived on Guernsey in the Channel Islands.

405. HERNDON, NANCY. *ACID BATH.* NEW YORK: BERKLEY PRIME CRIME, 1995.

Angus "Gus" McGlenlevie, a member of the English department at "Herbert Hobart University" in "Los Santos," Texas, calls the local police claiming that his ex-wife, Professor of Engineering Sarah Tolland, is trying to murder him. The responding officer is Elena Jarvis, a college-educated detective in the "Crimes against Persons" unit of the Los Santos Police. The womanizing McGlenlevie, who claims to have written a book of poetry titled *Erotica in Reeboks* (Casper, Wyo.: The Phallic Press), tells Jarvis an unlikely story. Professor Tolland, says McGlenlevie, somehow wired a snail that exploded in his face as he was eating it. After recording McGlenlevie's bizarre complaint Jarvis returns to her regular duties, but six weeks later university security calls her back to McGlenlevie's flat in a faculty apartment building on the Herbert Hobart campus. There she finds a skeleton in the bathtub, and she and the other investigating officers assume that the body belongs to McGlenlevie and that his body has been eaten away by some sort of acid. All of the above occurs in the first twenty pages of this novel, and the remainder of the book is devoted to Jarvis's sleuthing. Much of her detective work is conducted on the Herbert Hobart University campus and involves interviewing students, professors, and administrators. Recently divorced, Jarvis also finds time to start a romance with superhandsome Karl Bonnard, one of Sarah Tolland's colleagues in the engineering department. As for Professor Tolland, she is arrested for murder but is soon released on bail, and toward the end of the tale both she and Detective Jarvis are nearly killed by the real villain in the story.

Nancy Herndon is a former college English instructor. At the time *Acid Bath* was published she lived in El Paso, Texas. *Acid Bath* was the first in what was to become a series of mysteries featuring Elena Jarvis as detective. Two more Elena Jarvis adventures, *Lethal Statues* (426) and *Casanova Crimes* (476), appear in this bibliography. Still another Elena Jarvis adventure, *Time Bombs* (New York: Berkley Prime Crime, 1997), might interest the bibliography's users. *Time Bombs* is not a college mystery. It focuses on a dispute over water in draught-plagued Los Santos, but it begins with a scene at a Herbert

Hobart University ceremony at which Elena Jarvis is receiving an honorary degree for her sleuthing successes in previous cases. The ceremony is held outdoors under a tent. As it proceeds, trees suddenly begin exploding on the campus, and part of the tent collapses. The audience panics; Elena Jarvis pulls a pistol from beneath her academic robes and fires it as a method of crowd control; and President Sunnydale, a former television evangelist who fears the world is ending, falls to his knees and rededicates himself to God. After receiving her honorary doctorate in *Time Bombs*, in subsequent novels Detective Jarvis is often addressed as Dr. Jarvis by people who know of her degree.

406. HOLLAND, NORMAN (NORWOOD) (B. 1927). *DEATH IN A DELPHI SEMINAR*. ALBANY, N.Y.: STATE UNIVERSITY OF NEW YORK PRESS, 1995.

Patricia Hassler, a twenty-two-year-old graduate student in English, is attending a seminar at the State University of New York at Buffalo when she collapses and dies. An autopsy reveals that the cause of death was an exotic poison. The detective in the story is Buffalo Police Lieutenant Norman ("Justin") Rhodes. In addition to his work as a policeman Rhodes is a playwright. He also is the scion of a wealthy Buffalo family in whose ancestral mansion the university's English department is now located. Rhodes begins a long series of interviews with the six surviving seminar students and with Professor Norman Holland, the seminar instructor who, by some coincidence, bears the same name as the author of the book. The format of the seminar involved students criticizing each other's reading and writing styles, and considerable emotional heat had been generated before Ms. Hassler's death. Before Rhodes can identify the villain, another of the students in the seminar, Frank Kulper, is killed when he is struck in the head with a Scotch tape dispenser. All of the above may, or may not, accurately reflect the fundamental story line of this often-witty novel, because the book, subtitled "A Postmodern Mystery," is written from a variety of perspectives, each somewhat different from the other, and it often is up to the reader to interpret the "text." There is no usual narrative. The story is comprised of newspaper accounts, transcripts of interviews conducted by the Buffalo Police, English department memoranda, letters, and entries in personal journals. Since the book also incorporates much direct and indirect exposition of literary theories, *Death in a Delphi Seminar* can be read, by those who care to do so, as a monograph about contemporary literary criticism carried forward by a murder-mystery plot.

Norman Norwood Holland was born in New York City. He received a B.S. from M.I.T. in 1947, an LL.B. from Harvard in 1950, and a Ph.D. from Harvard in 1956. He joined the English department at the State University of New York at Buffalo in 1966 and was chair of the department from 1966 until 1968. In 1970 he was named director of the SUNY-Buffalo Center for the Psychological Study of the Arts. Holland has written many professional books and articles having to do with literary and film criticism and with literary theory. In particular, he is an expert in psychoanalytic literary criticism. At the time *Death in a Dephi Seminar* was published, Holland was Marston-Mibraruer Eminent Scholar at the University of Florida. *Death in a Delphi Seminar* was part of a series of books published by the State University of New York Press under the series title "The Margins of Literature."

407. HUNT, RICHARD (PATRICK) (B. 1938). *MURDER BENIGN.* LONDON: CONSTABLE, 1995; NEW YORK: ST. MARTIN'S, 1996.

An intruder breaks into the home of Sir Gordon Lignum and beats him dead with an iron bar. Before his sudden death, Sir Gordon was a well-known archaeologist at Cambridge University. His murder is investigated by Detective Chief Inspector Sidney Walsh of the Cambridgeshire Constabulary and the members of Walsh's special crimes unit. Sir Gordon had several enemies, including two undergraduates, Andrew MacGregor and Melissa Fairbrother. Sir Gordon was in the process of having Andrew and Melissa "sent down" from the university for having played practical jokes at a "dig" site. Another suspect is Ingrid, Sir Gordon's curvaceous, twenty-years-younger wife. Swedish by birth, and a former prostitute, Ingrid Lignum might have killed Sir Gordon to inherit his sizable estate. Chief Inspector Walsh's investigations take him many times to the university, where he and his team interview several of Sir Gordon's faculty colleagues, and the discussions with the dons lead Walsh to believe that the motive for Sir Gordon's killing may have had its origins in university politics. Because Inspector Walsh also follows leads having to do with members of Sir Gordon's extended family, *Murder Benign* is not an undiluted college mystery. However, it has a scene involving academicians that is unique in the college-mystery subgenre. Whereas most Oxbridge mysteries have their faculty participants eat in elegant college dining rooms, at one point in this story several of the book's academic characters can be found enjoying the cuisine at a Cambridge McDonalds.

Richard Patrick Hunt was born in Cambridge, England. He is an accountant and sometime violin maker who, at the time this book was published, lived in the East Anglia city of Norfolk. *Murder Benign* was the third in a continuing series of Inspector Walsh mysteries.

408. JEVONS, MARSHALL [WILLIAM BRIET (B. 1933) AND KENNETH G. ELZINGA (B. 1941)]. *A DEADLY INDIFFERENCE*. NEW YORK: CARROLL & GRAF, 1995.

A Chicago foundation wants to purchase the Cambridge, England, home of Alfred Marshall and use it as a center for the study of free enterprise. Marshall, who taught at Cambridge from 1885 until his retirement in 1908, is generally regarded as the father of modern economic theory. Henry Spearman, a Harvard economist and a Marshall Jevons series-character professor-detective, visits Cambridge to help arrange the purchase, but he learns that the owner intends to sell to Nigel Hart, the aging master of "Bishop's College," who covets the house as a place to live in retirement. Midway through the story Hart is stabbed dead outside the college dining hall as he is about to attend a meeting of the Jeremy Bentham Society, and a short while later Dolores Tanner, a young actress with family ties to Bishop's College, dies from a bullet to the brain. After considerable ratiocination, Professor Spearman apprehends the book's villain in St. Giles cemetery, as the latter attempts a nocturnal robbery of Alfred Marshall's grave. *A Deadly Indifference* is crisply written and highly entertaining, even if Professor Spearman sometimes seems to suffer from an advanced case of loquaciousness. Early in the story Pidge, Professor Spearman's wife, notes that her husband has a habit of giving lectures "whenever he thinks he has a student," and thanks to the professor's willingness to share his accumulated wisdom, the novel provides its readers with great amounts of information about, among other matters, the history of Cambridge University, the nature of modern economics, and the life history of Alfred Marshall. At one point Spearman even suggests to the Bishop's College head porter a revenue-producing plan that several real Oxford and Cambridge colleges have recently put into practice. He advises the porter to get maps of Cambridge and sell them to the many tourists who ask for directions at the porter's lodge.

Marshall Jevons is the pseudonym used by William Breit and Kenneth G. Elzinga, professors of economics at, respectively, Trinity University and the University of Virginia. *The Fatal Equilibrium*

(255), an earlier Marshall Jevons mystery with Professor Henry Spearman as sleuth, appears in this bibliography.

409. LACHNIT, CARROLL. *MURDER IN BRIEF.* NEW YORK: BERKLEY PRIME CRIME, 1995.

Hannah Barlow, a former policewoman, is a second-year student at the "William O. Douglas School of Law" in Orange County, California. Miss Barlow and Bradley Cogburn, her partner in a moot court exercise, come under suspicion of plagiarizing parts of a brief, and Cogburn, a brilliant young man of significant wealth, is soon found dead on a railroad track with his body mangled by a passing train. Although the police think that Cogburn's death was probably suicide, Miss Barlow is more inclined to think murder, and she draws on many of the skills of her previous profession to discover the truth. Some of the story takes Miss Barlow off campus to investigate the murky affairs of Bradley Cogburn's extended family, but the novel contains many scenes at William O. Douglas and many of the book's most important characters are connected with the school. Readers encounter a middle-aged dean who has both a passion for surfing and a wife who cannot hold her liquor, an attractive woman professor whose charms are some of the law school's most effective fund-raising assets, and an austere female student who has taken on the difficult task of saving a convicted murderer from the gas chamber.

A former court reporter, Carroll Lachnit spent nine years as a writer for the *Orange County Register. Murder in Brief* was her first Hannah Barlow mystery novel. Since appearing in *Murder in Brief,* Hannah Barlow has gone on to become a Carroll Lachnit series-character detective.

410. LAKE, M. D. [ALLEN SIMPSON]. *GRAVE CHOICES.* NEW YORK: AVON, 1995.

Late one December evening Peggy O'Neill, a campus security officer at a large Midwestern university, discovers the body of Russell Bell, a professor of art, inside the deserted studio arts building. Bell's head is almost entirely severed from his body. As she examines the bloody corpse, a figure dashes by and escapes into the night. O'Neill is able to identify the person as an Hispanic, and the police soon arrest Daniel Sanchez, a well-known local potter who once broke into an art department meeting and threatened Professor Bell's life. Sandra Carr, Sanchez's lover and an old friend of O'Neill, is convinced of her boyfriend's innocence, and she prevails upon the campus cop to spend her off-duty hours looking for Bell's real killer. Some of this novel takes place away from the university, but there is enough action on the campus (and more than enough academic characters) for the book to qualify for inclusion in this bibliography. Indeed, by the end of the tale Peggy O'Neill has not only learned the identity of Professor Bell's assassin, she has solved another, twenty-year-old murder in the art department as well. The book contains one of the better pieces of dialogue in college-mystery fiction. During her initial meeting with Officer O'Neill, Sandra Carr asks O'Neill if she is still regularly patrolling the campus, "acting as a bulwark between the academics and the hoodlums." After receiving an affirmative reply she asks, "How do you tell 'em apart?"

Eight other Peggy O'Neill mysteries by James Allen Simpson appear in this bibliography. Those mysteries are *Amends for Murder* (313), *Cold Comfort* (325), *A Gift for Murder* (356), *Poisoned Ivy* (357), *Murder by Mail* (368), *Once Upon a Crime* (411), *Flirting with Death* (431), and *Death Calls the Tune* (479).

411. LAKE, M. D. [JAMES ALLEN SIMPSON]. *ONCE UPON A CRIME.* NEW YORK: AVON, 1995.

An institution of higher education that resembles the University of Minnesota is holding a symposium on Hans Christian Andersen. One of the principal speakers is Jens Aage Lindemann, a professor from Denmark who is the world's leading Andersen scholar. Lindemann is found dead with his skull split open in the Andersen Room of the university library. The murder weapon is a statuette of the Little Mermaid. The detective in the tale is Peggy O'Neill, a campus policewoman who also serves as an M. D. Lake series-character sleuth. The cynical O'Neill is assigned to the case, despite being on medical leave, because she is already familiar with many people involved with the Andersen festivities. Indeed, she is playing the part of a police official in an American adaptation of Andersen's *Emperor's New Clothes* that is being staged in conjunction with the symposium. The participants in the story include Pia Austin, Professor Lindemann's daughter, and Christian Donnelly, Pia Austin's boyfriend. Miss Austin is a student at the university and Mr. Donnelly is the star quarterback on the university football team. Mr. Donnelly's parents, Clay and Denise, approve of Miss Austin, but before his death Lindemann makes clear that he hopes his daughter will marry someone with ambitions more lofty than professional football. At the end of the story Officer O'Neill identifies and confronts Lindemann's killer, but, for reasons that are revealed at the end of the book, the Danish professor's murder officially remains unsolved.

Eight other Peggy O'Neill mysteries by James Allen Simpson have entries in this bibliography. Those mysteries are *Amends for Murder* (313), *Cold Comfort* (325), *A Gift for Murder* (356), *Poisoned Ivy* (357), *Murder by Mail* (368), *Grave Choices* (410), *Flirting with Death* (431), and *Death Calls the Tune* (479).

412 LANGTON, JANE (B. 1922). *THE SHORTEST DAY: MURDER AT THE REVELS*. NEW YORK: VIKING, 1995.

Each year during the Christmas season a collection of Cambridge-town and Harvard-gown performers stages the "Revels," a program of lively ancient rites designed to challenge the cold and gloom of winter. This year's Revels is singularly ill-fated. Tom Cobb, the codirector, dies after eating a candy bar spiced with a lethal dose of lead. Henry Shandy, the featured folk singer, is run down by a Range Rover outside the show's venue, Harvard's Memorial Hall. And another of the large cast of onstage performers, Harvard Professor of Astronomy Arlo Field, nearly dies after his throat is cut by a sword during a Revels performance. Then, as if the Revels has not attracted enough misfortune, the surviving director of the show, Sarah Bailey, finds that her husband does not rejoice when he is told that she is pregnant. Meantime, even as more deaths and more almost-fatal incidents occur, a group of Cambridge homeless people demands that Harvard convert a classroom building into housing for the poor. The featured sleuth in the story is Jane Langton's series-character, Homer Kelly, a former police detective who now teaches American literature at Harvard. Mary Kelly, Homer's perceptive wife, is a member of the Revels' chorus, and Homer becomes involved in the case after Mary witnesses Henry Shandy's unfortunate death. A teacher of English at Harvard, Mary Kelly provides crucial insights as husband Homer detects. In addition to well-etched depictions of several real Harvard landmarks and many fictional Harvard characters, the book affords readers a rare opportunity to observe the curious consequences of a late-afternoon-in-December power blackout on the Harvard campus.

The Memorial Hall Murder (196), *Emily Dickinson Is Dead* (244), and *Dead as a Dodo* (432), all of which employ Homer Kelly as detective, are additional Jane Langton mysteries with entries in this bibliography.

413. STALLWOOD, VERONICA. *OXFORD MOURNING.* LONDON: MACMILLAN, 1995; NEW YORK: SCRIBNER, 1996.

The protagonist of this involved story is Kate Ivory, a romance novelist who lives near Oxford. Ivory is a Veronica Stallwood series-character detective. In this adventure Ivory is trying to complete a manuscript based on the life of Charles Dickens, and she learns that Dr. Olivia Blacket, of Oxford's "Leicester College," has some letters pertaining to Dickens's amours. She asks Dr. Blacket for access to the letters but is curtly refused. Not long afterward, Dr. Blacket is found dead in her college room, her head battered by an unknown instrument. In addition to the main mystery, *Oxford Mourning* has several subplots. A group of squatters, led by a cult leader called Ant, uses the vacant house of a junketing professor as its base for various antisocial activities. Kate Ivory tries to keep alive her romance with Liam Ross, another Leicester College faculty member who, as Ivory discovers, was a very good friend of the late Dr. Blacket. And Professor Brendan Adams, whom Ivory first meets in Dr. Blacket's home, promises to help obtain the letters Ivory needs, but he seems to require sexual favors in return. In addition to several plot threads, the novel also has more than its share of attention-getting incidents. Toward the end of the novel the strange man known as Ant threatens to throw Ivory off the roof of the Radcliffe Camera. And on the day of Dr. Bracket's death, Ivory tries unsuccessfully to break into Bracket's college room in order to view the denied letters. The "Mourning" in the book's title refers to an annual ceremony in memory of a student who, in 1527, was refused admittance to Leicester College as he was being pursued through Oxford by an angry mob. Each year, on October 20, Leicester College closes its doors to visitors as part of an atonement for that long-ago event. It is on October 20 that Kate stages her break-in attempt. Since no other visitors were in the college, she fears that she may have been noticed and may become a suspect in Dr. Blacket's murder.

Two other Kate Ivory mysteries by Veronica Stallwood also appear in this bibliography. Those mysteries are *Oxford Exit* (401) and *Oxford Fall* (438).

414. WALSH, JILL PATON (B. 1937). *A PIECE OF JUSTICE.* NEW YORK: ST. MARTIN'S PRESS, 1995.

The British publishing firm of Recktype and Diss desperately needs someone finish its biography of the recently deceased Gideon

Summerfield. A tutor of mathematics at Cambridge's "St. Agatha's College," Summerfield created an important mathematics formula late in his life. The biography already appears in the publisher's catalog, but the manuscript has never been completed because, in succession, two writers have disappeared and one has died. Leo Maverack, a Cambridge professor of biography, is asked to take up the task, but he is too busy, and he turns the project over to Frances Bullion, his top graduate student. When Miss Bullion begins work she finds that Janet Summerfield, Gideon's widow, is obstructing her progress, and that several of the mathematician's former Cambridge colleagues seem to know things about the late mathematician that are not suggested by his professional resume. Bullion lodges in the home of Imogene Quy, the nurse at St. Agatha's. Nurse Quy tries to help Bullion sort out her problems, and in doing so she uncovers murder, academic dishonesty, and a villain with an unlikely but noble motive for his crimes. She also takes time to testify at a disciplinary hearing for a student accused of cheating on an exam, and at one point in the book she travels to Wales in search of clues in the Summerfield affair. Portrayed as a compassionate, high-minded woman who detects in order to bring about justice, Imogene Quy is held in high regard by almost all of the characters in the novel. Nevertheless, considering how enthusiastically she embellishes her official nursing duties with unofficial sleuthing, some academic readers may agree with the book's evildoer, who, when caught, accuses her of being a "pestiferous, meddling person."

Nurse Imogene Quy is the sleuth in *The Wyndham Case* (373), an earlier Jill Paton Walsh mystery in this bibliography.

415. WILSON, DEREK (B. 1935). *THE HELLFIRE PAPERS.* LONDON: HEADLINE, 1995.

The detective in this professionally written, fast-paced mystery is Tim Lacy, a Derek Wilson series-character sleuth. Lacy operates a British security agency that specializes in protecting works of art. He is enlisted by Sir Evelyn Masquerier, the master of a financially struggling University of Cambridge college called "St. Mary's House," to bring back from Australia some sensitive papers that the college has recently been willed. The papers, so Sir Evelyn tells Lacy, are records of "The Hellfire Club," a group of highly placed eighteenth-century Englishmen who conducted satanic rituals in and around the town of High Wycombe. Sir Evelyn is concerned that the press might get hold of the papers, find well-known historical names among the Hellfire Club's participants, and write stories that could somehow hurt the college's ability to raise funds. As the book continues, the task that Sir Evelyn originally assigns to Tim Lacy quickly fades in importance because other, more pressing matters arise that demand the detective's attentions. Three members of St. Mary's House meet violent deaths, the Hellfire papers turn out to contain information about a very contemporary set of evildoers, and Tim Lacy's two children are kidnapped by one of the book's villains. Lacy's travels, including jaunts to Australia and New York City, on occasion take him far from Cambridge, but when the story stops at St. Mary's House it describes events such as chapel service and high table in great detail. Furthermore, a large number of academics appear in the story, including Princeton Professor of History Joseph N. Zangster, who visits St. Mary's House and is welcomed with an elaborate ceremonial dinner. At the very end of the book the authorities at St. Mary's House decide that possession of the Hellfire papers has brought the college too much pain and suffering. Seizing an opportunity to improve the college's finances, they arrange through the wined-and-dined Professor Zangster to sell the documents to Princeton.

Derek Wilson was born in Colchester, England, and received B.A. and M.A. degrees from Peterhouse College, Cambridge. He is a leading British writer of popular history, biography, and fiction. He is best known to historians for his several books about England's Tudor period. *The Hellfire Papers* was the third in a continuing series of Tim Lacy mysteries.

416. WILSON, ROBIN (SCOTT) (B. 1928). *DEATH BY DEGREES*. NEW YORK: ST. MARTIN'S, 1995.

The sleuth-narrator of this story is Peter Haas, an administrative assistant to President Harold ("Piggy") Piggott of "Monterery University" in California. Peter Haas and President Piggott once worked together as cold war CIA operatives in Germany. Piggott retired to the presidency of Monterey, and when the younger Haas became a victim of downsizing and was forced to leave the CIA, President Piggott hired him as his personal troubleshooter. At first, Haas's biggest problem was his unfortunate tendency to call the president "Piggy" in public, but now there is serious trouble at Monterey. Albert Steener, a data-entry coordinator in the office of the registrar, has been found murdered in a cheap "porno" motel, his body clad in women's underwear. President Piggott fears that any scandal will reduce alumni donations. He asks Haas to find the killer and, at the same time, minimize any public relations damage to the university. With assistance from his lover, campus security chief Hildy Barnes, Peter Haas eventually finds how, why, and by whom Mr. Steener was dispatched. In the process he learns how Steener, with his $27,000 annual salary, was able to deposit $2,000 per week in local banks. Toward the end of the story President Piggott joins in the detection effort, receives a nonfatal gunshot wound, and scores a public relations triumph when he is lionized in the press for his bravery. Peter Haas also comes face to face with death when a villain tries to assassinate him by smashing his skull with a desktop computer. The novel contains many pieces of inside information about Monterey University's operations, about the strained relationships between the school's faculty and its administrators, and about the various ways in which academic ideals at the school give way to academic necessities. In that context, readers from the real world of higher education may not be shocked to learn that the faculty at Monterey who teach in programs with low student demand refuse to support policies to end grade inflation. They believe that only by giving As and Bs can they attract enough students to hold their jobs.

Robin Scott Wilson was born in Columbus, Ohio. He holds a B.A. from Ohio State University and an M.A. and Ph.D. from the University of Illinois. He was president of California State University, Chico, from 1980 until his retirement in 1993. Earlier in his career Wilson was an intelligence officer with the Central Intelligence Agency and a professor of English at Clarion State College in Pennsylvania. *Death by Degrees* was his first mystery novel.

417. ASEN, DENNIS. *DEADLY IMPRESSION.* NEW YORK: BANTAM, 1996.

Lieutenant Seymour Pinchus is a veteran homicide cop in the eastern Pennsylvania town of "Hamilton." Known as "The Fox" for his sleuthing skills, Pinchus has one of his toughest cases when pretty Alice Schaeffer, a graduate student, is raped and brutally murdered in her apartment. Working toward a doctorate in biology at the local university, Alice had no enemies, and though Pinchus interrogates several of her professors and fellow students, he begins to conclude that the crime was, perhaps, random and not related to Alice's academic life. But, then, there is the matter of the bite marks that Alice's killer left on her body.

Thanks to Dr. Peter Roberts, a dentist who serves as a forensic consultant for the Hamilton police, Pinchus gets a new lead that eventually leads him to a motive and then to an evildoer. *Deadly Impression* has many campus scenes, including one in which Pinchus chases a suspect through the heating ducts of a dormitory. The book also contains several flashbacks that recount Pinchus's several cases at the university at earlier points in his twenty-five-year police career, and it is the only college mystery in which readers can learn about the differences in tooth structure between Caucasians, African Americans, and Asians.

Deadly Impression was Dennis Asen's first mystery novel.

418. BOWEN, GAIL (B. 1942). *A KILLING SPRING.* TORONTO, CANADA: MCCLELLAND & STEWART, 1996.

A Killing Spring is set at a university in the Canadian city of Regina. The sleuth-narrator is Joanne Kilbourn, a middle-aged, widowed teacher in the university's School of Journalism. During the course of the story the busy Kilbourn resolves not one, but five mysteries. What was behind the death of Reed Gallagher, the journalism school's head, who was found hanged, clad in women's lingerie, in a seedy roominghouse? Who trashed the school's offices, leaving homophobic graffiti behind? Why would anyone send obscene notes to Kellee Savage, an unattractive female student in one of Kilbourn's classes? Why was Miss Savage subsequently found dead in a field near the university, her blood filled with drugs and alcohol? And why would Val Massee, a handsome male student with a bright future, try to commit suicide? While dealing with those issues, Kilbourn must cope with the emotional fallout of racial slurs directed against her and her boyfriend, Police Inspector Alex Kequchtooway, a native Canadian Ojibway. In addition to Kilbourn, several members of the journalism faculty have significant parts in the proceedings. One is Tom Kelsoe, the school's most charasmatic professor, who is not above stealing words as well as ideas from his students. Another is Ed Mariani, who wants to succeed Reed Gallagher as head of the school. Professor Mariani worries that his habit of cruising the rougher sections of Regina in search of male companions will do damage to his career aspirations. The book has an unusual ending when Kilbourn confronts the villain of the piece as he is appearing on a television show. She chases him after he bolts from the studio and, in a bravura performance for a female professsor-detective, she subdues him with a perfectly aimed knee to his crotch.

Gail Bowen was born in Toronto. She received a B.A. from the University of Toronto in 1964, an M.A. from the University of Waterloo in 1975, and then did further graduate study at the University of Saskatchewan. *A Killing Spring* was the fifth Gail Bowen mystery to feature journalism teacher Joanne Kilbourn as detective. At the time the book was published Bowen was an assistant professor of English at the Saskatechewan Indian Federated College of the University of Regina.

419. BRADBERRY, JAMES. *RUINS OF CIVILITY*. NEW YORK: ST. MARTIN'S PRESS, 1996.

At a retirement celebration in his honor, Rainer Grass, the unpopular head of the architectural school at the University of Cambridge, shocks the assembled faculty and students by announcing that he has changed his mind and will not be retiring after all. A short while later he disappears from the party, and several days later his whereabouts are still unknown. Jamie Ramsgill, a Princeton professor of architecture on a two-week research trip to Cambridge, suspects foul play, and he alerts the local police. To his surprise, the detective chief inspector to whom he speaks turns out to be Lyndsay Hill, a Cambridge graduate and a teammate on a basketball team when Ramsgill, some twenty years earlier, was in Cambridge studying for his doctorate. From then on Ramsgill and Hill join forces to learn the truth behind Professor Grass's disappearance, and their attentions turn to many of the people who heard Grass make his unexpected announcement. Among the suspects are Dr. Iain Frontis, who was scheduled to succeed Grass in the architectural school's top job, and Amy Denster, Grass's current graduate-student paramour who is pregnant with his child. Much of the novel takes place in and around Queens College, and at the front of the book the author provides a college map as a guide for readers. Inventive and well constructed, *Ruins of Civility* melds two grisly murders and a kidnapping with the mannerly academic atmosphere of Cambridge. It also includes an element of romantic tragedy, as the married Professor Ramsgill, traveling without his wife, struggles to avoid rekindling an old flame with a British former girlfriend.

James Bradberry is a Philadelphia architect with master's degrees from the University of Cambridge and the University of Pennsylvania. He has taught at Pennsylvania, Yale, and Temple Universities. *Ruins of Civility* was Bradberry's second Professor Jamie Ramsgill mystery. The first, *The Seventh Sacrament* (New York: St. Martin's,

1994) is a nonacademic tale that has Professor Ramsgill solving a murder mystery at an architectural competition in Italy.

420. CHRAIBI, DRISS (B. 1926). *L'INSPECTEUR ALI À TRINITY COLLEGE*. PARIS: DENOËL, 1996.

Inspector Ali of the Morocco Police Force is sent to England to investigate the death of the beautiful Moroccan princess Yasmina, whose mortal remains were found in her room in Trinity College, Cambridge. Ali has never before been in England, and in keeping with his secondhand knowledge of British dress customs, he arrives from Casablanca wearing a bowler hat and patent leather shoes. Furthermore, equipped against the imponderabilities of the British weather, he carries an umbrella. Ali teams in his sleuthing with Sir Henry Westlake of Scotland Yard. Since the prime suspect is the princess's bodyguard, a member of the Moroccan Secret Service, Ali's work should be conducted with the utmost delicacy, but he actually exhibits such flagrantly tactless behavior that he proves to be a constant source of amazement to his British colleagues. He manages to offend virtually everyone with whom he comes into contact, including a female police inspector whom he startles with his crude sexual comments. He also alienates several members of the staid Cambridge academic community, and an Algerian guest lecturer at Trinity College learns that a rambling, long-winded speech is the perfect way to test the strictly limited boundaries of the inspector's patience. As the story unfolds, David Wembley, chairperson of philosophy at the university, is added to the suspect list when it is learned that he had been captivated by the unfortunate young princess's charms. With the help of MI5, Inspector Ali eventually traps the perpetrator and identifies that person in an unusual denouement. Students of college-mystery fiction who are competent in French (as of this writing the book has not been published in English) may take special interest in reading the Moroccan inspector's many penetrating comments about the ways of academic life in one of England's ancient seats of learning.

Driss Chraibi was born in Morocco but has spent most of his adult life in France. He studied in Casablanca and Paris. He is a much-honored mainstream novelist as well as a writer of mystery fiction. Inspector Ali is a series-character and *L'inspecteur Ali à Trinity College* was the third book in the continuing Ali series.

421. DAIN, CATHERINE [JUDITH GARWOOD]. *THE LUCK OF THE DRAW.* NEW YORK: BERKLEY PRIME CRIME, 1996.

The badly beaten body of Darla Hayden, a former graduate student in international finance at the University of Nevada-Reno, is found in the office of Professor Aaron Hiller, Nevada-Reno's ultra-eminent professor of business. Professor Hiller reluctantly admits to having had an affair with Hayden, but the police lack any conclusive proof that he is her murderer. Also on the suspect list is the business department's chairperson, Professor Randolph Thurman. Darla Hayden had incurred Thurman's animosity when she threatened to kill him because it was he who expelled her from the business program after she failed the comprehensive examination for her doctorate. The narrator of the story is "Freddie" O'Neal, a female private investigator who serves as a Catherine Dain series-character detective. O'Neal becomes involved in this case when a collections agency asks her to find Hayden—who had disappeared before her murder—and look into when, if at all, the young lady intended to pay a mountain of unpaid bills. The book includes many scenes on the Nevada-Reno campus, and in addition to Professors Hiller and Thurman several other university characters make appearances. One of them is Curtis Breckinridge, yet another Nevada-Reno professor of business, who is romancing Freddie O'Neal. The book contains a strong subtext that deals with the financial exploitation of graduate students by American universities. Some readers may want to ponder the fate of Professor Hiller. Although he is not the person who killed Darla Hayden, several other past and present student girlfriends come forward to reveal his chronic womanizing, and his reputation is forever damaged. Hoping to retain his professional luster, but wanting to minimize his contact with female students, the university agrees to continue him on the payroll if he does not teach classes.

Judith Garwood was raised in Reno, Nevada. She has an undergraduate degree from UCLA and a graduate degree from the University of Southern California. Before becoming a mystery writer she was a television newscaster and a writer and editor for the University of Southern California's Business Education and Research Center. *The Luck of the Draw* was the sixth novel in Garwood's continuing series of Freddie O'Neal mysteries.

422. DEXTER, (NORMAN) COLIN (B. 1930). *DEATH IS NOW MY NEIGHBOR*. NEW YORK: CROWN, 1996.

Sir Clixby Bream, the widowed master of Oxford's "Lonsdale College," is about to retire. Two of the college's senior dons, historian Denis Cornfield and anthropologist Julian Storrs, are vying to replace him. Meantime, in another part of Oxford, Rachel James is shot dead in her home. A physiotherapist, Miss James was an attractive young woman without any obvious enemies. James's murder is investigated by Colin Dexter's series-character detectives Chief Inspector Morse and Sergeant Lewis of the Thames Valley Police. As Morse and Lewis make their inquiries, newspaper reporter Geoffrey Owens, one of Miss James's neighbors, is also shot dead, and forensic tests show that both victims were assassinated with the same handgun. A complex tale with tentacles that reach into London as well as Oxford, *Death Is Now My Neighbor* has several twists of plot, and as the novel unfolds Morse and Lewis tie the James and Owens murders to the Cornfield-Storrs competition for the master's post at Lonsdale. There are many scenes at the college, and several more in the homes of Cornfield and Storrs. Sally Cornfield, Dennis Cornfield's young, American wife, and Angela Storrs, Julian Storrs's spouse, play important roles. Readers will want to pay close attention, as well, to Sir Clixby Bream, Lonsdale's manipulative master. Though he has reached the age of sixty-nine, his appetites for both power and sex remain strong, and at the end of the tale he agrees, without reluctance, to remain in office for an indefinite period.

Death Is Now My Neighbor was the twelfth novel in Colin Dexter's continuing Inspector Morse series. Three other Inspector Morse mysteries appear in this bibliography. Those mysteries are *The Silent World of Nicholas Quinn* (190), *The Riddle of the Third Mile* (228), and *The Daughters of Cain* (386).

423. GENTRY, ANITA. *NIGHT SUMMONS.* NEW YORK: ST. MARTIN'S, 1996.

The psychology department at "Westcott University," somewhere in the western United States, can match any department in college-mystery fiction for internal dissension. The faculty "old timers," oriented toward parapsychology, are doing battle with the "new bunch," made up principally of behavioralists, and even the graduate students and members of the department's office staff have taken sides. With the approval of their mentors, students heckle faculty of the opposing camp during lectures, unknown people destroy computer files, and obscene caricatures of professors are tacked on to department bulletin boards. And there has been violence as well! Steve Linstrom, a graduate student, has been killed in a road accident after someone tampered with his brakes, and a departmental typist named Suzie Frazier has been badly beaten in her home. Late in the story someone even sets fire to the building that houses the office of Professor Laszlo Honvagy, the leader of the parapsychologists. The sleuth in the novel is Althena Dawes, a young private investigator, who enters the case after the unfortunate Miss Frazier, a longtime friend, asks her to look for the person responsible for Mr. Linstrom's death. Dawes assumes the guise of temporary clerk in the department, and before her detection yields fruit she uses her position to search faculty offices and to "bug" the area around the department's mailboxes so she can listen to informal faculty conversations. Readers at the top of the professorial hierarchy may (or may not) want to file for future use the reaction of Professor Gerald Derring, the leader of the new bunch, when the campus police try to arrest him for arson. "You can't do this to me," he screams. "I'm a full professor. I have connections."

At the time this novel was published Anita Gentry lived in the Sacramento Valley in California. *Night Summons* was her first novel.

424. GRANT, LINDA [LINDA WILLIAMS (B. 1942)]. *LETHAL GENES.* NEW YORK: SCRIBNER, 1996.

Someone is sabotaging the genetic-engineering research being conducted in the maize laboratories at the University of California at Berkeley. Kendra Crawford, the busy plant biology professor who is in charge of the project, wants no heavy-handed police intrusion while she completes a crucial grant proposal, so she arranges for Catherine Saylor, a Linda Grant series-character private investigator, to look into the vandalism. Very quickly, things go from bad to worse. Raymond Zak, a lab technician is found dead in his home, and Chuck Nishimura, a graduate student, expires suddenly in one of the plant biology department's greenhouses. The exact causes of those deaths are unknown pending autopsies, but Catherine Saylor suspects that both of the deceased were murdered. Then Saylor barely escapes with her own life when a mysterious gas is allowed to flow into in a laboratory she is examining. On an acknowlegments page at the beginning of the book, the author thanks a Cal-Berkeley laboratory director and his staff for "generous help with research," and *Lethal Genes* includes much detail about the technical side of the plant biology department's research operations. The book also offers a relentlessly grim picture of the high-pressure lives led by those who conduct cutting-edge scientific explorations in the department's facilities. At the end of this tale the villain is identified and removed from the university, but the stressful organizational climate that produced the villainous behavior remains. Thus, readers may suspect that the Cal-Berkeley plant biology department depicted in this novel, while possibly free from additional murders in the immediate future, is not likely to become a fun place in which to work.

Linda Williams came to mystery writing after two years with the Peace Corps in Ethiopia and after a brief career as a high-school teacher. *Lethal Genes* was the fifth novel in her Catherine Saylor series. At the time the novel was published Williams was a resident of Berkeley, California.

425. GREGORY, SUSANNA [PSEUD.] (B. 1928). *A PLAQUE ON BOTH YOUR HOUSES.* LONDON: WARNER BOOKS, 1966; NEW YORK: ST. MARTIN'S, 1998.

It is 1348 and Michaelhouse College of the University of Cambridge is experiencing one calamity after another. Sir John Babington, the college's master, is found dead, impaled on the spokes of a waterwheel in the town. Augustus of Ely, an aged teacher of law, dies of apparent natural causes in his room, but his body soon disappears. Another older member of the Michaelhouse community, Brother Paul, is stabbed to death, and still another resident of the college, a man named Montfitchet, expires after being poisoned. Meantime, Thomas Wilson, the self-seeking new master of Michaelhouse, holds a lavish feast in honor of his ascendency to the mastership, and some townspeople, resentful of the riches that allow Michaelhouse to hold such an event, threaten to disrupt the proceedings. The sleuth in this tale is Matthew Bartholomew, a Susanna Gregory series-character who is a practicing physician and Michaelhouse's master of medicine. As Doctor Bartholomew begins his detection, one theory he hears and briefly entertains is that the murders are the work of the University of Oxford, which is trying to so disrupt the University of Cambridge so that the latter will be unable to attract students. Fortunately for Oxford's eternal reputation, Doctor Bartholomew learns that the actual reasons for Michaelhouse's murders lie elsewhere, and that the real culprit is a villain whose motive is more personal than institutional in nature. The book offers a large quantity of historical detail about Cambridge in the fourteenth century, and the author orients her readers by including both a medieval map of Cambridge and a floor plan of Michaelhouse College. Readers will be interested to learn that Michaelhouse was an actual medieval Cambridge college. Founded in 1324, it was absorbed into Trinity College when the latter was founded in 1546 by King Henry VIII.

Information on the cover of this book tells us that Susanna Gregory is the pseudonym of a woman who earned her Ph. D. at the University of Cambridge and later became a research fellow at one of the colleges. Before beginning her academic career, the woman was a police officer in Yorkshire. Matthew Bartholomew is a Susanna Gregory series-character detective, and *A Plague on Both Your Houses* was the first novel in the continuing Matthew Bartholomew series. The third novel in the series, *A Bone of Contention* (443) has an entry later in this bibliography. The foci of the second and fourth works in the series, *Unholy Alliance* (New York: St. Martin's, 1996) and *Deadly Brew* (London: Little, Brown, 1998), are away from the university and onto the town of Cambridge, but because both involve some characters from the university they might also be of interest to readers of college mysteries.

426. HERNDON, NANCY. *LETHAL STATUES.* NEW YORK: BERKLEY PRIME CRIME, 1996.

Analee Ribbon is the only African American student at "Herbert Hobart College," an academically undistinguished institution in "Los Santos," Texas, that caters to white and wealthy students with poor high-school records. One night, as Miss Ribbon works late in the college library, a villain attacks and kills her, and her body is found underneath a marble statue of a dancer that is part of the library's furnishings. The detective is Elena Jarvis, a Nancy Herndon series-character sleuth who is a member of the "Crimes against Persons" unit of the local police. The first mystery facing Jarvis is why Analee Ribbon, a brilliant student who could have been admitted to any college in the country, choose to attend low-status Herbert Hobart. The second mystery is who killed her. In pursuit of the answers to those puzzles, Jarvis seeks information from a wide-ranging set of academic characters both at Herbert Hobart and at the neighboring University of Texas at Los Santos. She also deals with an antiabortion organization known as the "Los Santonians against Rampant Immorality." In addition to its on-campus programs, Herbert Hobart College offers mail-order degrees for $20,000, and late in the story the school's president, a former television evangelist whose tax-exempt status was removed by the Internal Revenue Service after they caught him filing fraudulent returns, hosts a reception for the holders of the bogus degrees. After listening to the college's mail-order graduates engage in cocktail-party chit chat, one observer takes the uncharitable view that Herbert Hobart College seems to have "alumni who are dumber than its students."

Two other Elena Jarvis mysteries by Nancy Herndon, *Acid Bath* (405) and *Casanova Crimes* (476), appear in this bibliography.

427. HOLTZER, SUSAN. *BLEEDING MAIZE AND BLUE.* NEW YORK: ST. MARTIN'S, 1996.

The NCAA receives information that the University of Michigan is giving "illegal inducements" to its star athletes, and it sends an investigator named Alvin Greenaway to look into the matter. Greenaway has hardly arrived in Ann Arbor before he is found dead in empty Michigan Stadium, his stomach pieced by a pole onto which a Michigan banner is attached. There are several detectives in this story. One is Anneke Haagen, an Ann Arbor computer-whiz businesswoman. Another is Police Lieutenant Karl Genesko, a former Michigan all-American football player who is now Anneke Haagen's housemate. Additional sleuthing is done by Zoe Kaplan, a Michigan undergraduate who is a zealous reporter on the student-run *Michigan Daily* newspaper. A subplot has Miss Kaplan competing for stories about the university athletics scandal with Charlie Cassovoy, a Pulitzer Prize-winning sports columnist with *"The Detroit News."* The novel offers an abundance of information about the mechanics of "big-time" college football and about the ways in which some American institutions of higher education use and abuse their athletes. It also offers an interesting climax in which the six-foot-five, 250-pound Lieutenant Genesko chases the book's villain across the Michigan Stadium turf in front of 104,000 spectators who are there to watch Michigan defeat Wisconsin.

Susan Holtzer holds B.A. and M.A. degrees from the University of Michigan. She was a member of the staff of the *Michigan Daily* while an undergraduate. Before moving to San Francisco, where she lived when this novel was published, she was a longtime resident of Ann Arbor, Michigan. *Bleeding Maize and Blue* was the third

Holtzer novel to feature Anneke Haagen and Karl Genesko as detectives. *Black Diamond* (445) and *The Silly Season: An Entr'acte* (477), two later Haagen/Genesko mysteries, appear later in this bibliography.

428. KELLERMAN, JONATHAN (B. 1949). *THE CLINIC.* NEW YORK: BANTAM, 1996.

Hope Devane is found strangled dead on a street near the Los Angeles university where she was a professor of psychology. An ardent feminist, Professor Devane was also the author of a best-selling book titled *Wolves and Sheep: Why Men Inevitably Hurt Women and What Women Can Do to Avoid It.* The police detective is Milo Sturgis of the Los Angeles police department, but the real sleuthing in the story is carried out by Dr. Alex Delaware, a consulting psychologist. Dr. Delaware is a Jonathan Kellerman series-character to whom Detective Sturgis often turns for assistance. As Delaware probes into Professor Devane's past he turns up a plethora of unpleasant information. Academic readers probably will be most interested in the "Interpersonal Conduct Committee" that Professor Devane headed at the university. Though it had no official campus status, the committee investigated cases of alleged mistreatment of women, and it arranged for draconian punishments to be applied to those men whom it judged guilty of sexual wrongdoing. Not all of this fast-moving novel is set on academic terrain, but the story includes more than enough university students and faculty members to satisfy fans of college mysteries.

Born in New York City, Jonathan Kellerman received a B.A. from the University of California at Los Angeles in 1971 and a Ph.D. from the University of Southern California in 1974. A psychologist who has held faculty appointments at the University of Southern California, Kellerman became in the 1980s and 1990s one of America's most successful writers of psychological thrillers. *The Clinic* was the eleventh Kellerman novel to feature Dr. Alex Delaware as detective.

429. KEMELMAN, HARRY (1908-1996). *THAT DAY THE RABBI LEFT TOWN.* NEW YORK: FAWCETT COLUMBINE, 1996.

Professor of English Malcolm Kent, at seventy years of age the oldest member of the faculty at "Windemere College" in Boston, is found dead in a snowbank in the suburban town of "Barnard's Crossing," Massachusetts. At first glance the professor's death seems to have been caused by heart failure, but when the police discover a contusion on his forehead they suspect that foul play may have been involved. Helping the police with their investigations is Rabbi David Small, a veteran Harry Kemelman series-character sleuth. Small has recently resigned as rabbi in Barnard's Crossing and is now a professor at Windemere, where he is creating a new Department of Judaica. Thanks to some adroit ratiocination, the rabbi discovers that the reasons for Professor Kent's death are to be found on the Windemere campus. The often-satirical book offers many scenes at Windemere, a school that is trying to pull itself up from the bottom of the academic heap, and it includes many sardonic portraits of Windemere faculty members and administrators. For example, the school's pipe-smoking dean, a man named Cardleigh, was moved to his present job when, as a professor of classics, he had no students registered for his courses. Real-life professors who are accustomed to attending sleep-inducing official gatherings on their own campuses may want to skip the scene early in the story in which Dean Cardleigh conducts a faculty meeting at the beginning of the academic year. After passing out copies of Windemere's new catalog to the assembled teachers, Cardleigh goes on to take an entire morning reviewing each and every one of the changes from the previous year's edition.

Two other Rabbi Small novels by Harry Kemelman, *Tuesday the Rabbi Saw Red* (169) and *The Day the Rabbi Resigned* (355), appear in this bibliography.

430. KOEHLER, C. J. *MIND GAMES*. NEW YORK: CARROLL & GRAF, 1996.

Mind Games is a straightforward police procedural set at "Friar Close," an experimental residential community established with money from the "Grayson Foundation" and administered by a large, nearby American state university. A team of social scientists from the university uses the community as a laboratory to conduct research into matters having to do family living. The victim in the story is Dr. Issac Steiner, a sociologist member of the research team, who is stabbed dead with a butcher's knife in the community's administration building. Working the case for the police are Sergeant Ray Koepp, a former priest, and his assistant, Margaret Loftus. Koepp and Loftus discover that Dr. Steiner was using Friar Close as a base of operations for something even more nefarious than sociological research and that several people had good reason to murder him. Suspects include Karen Merrick, the seductive wife of another sociologist-researcher, and Neil Erickson, a young instructor of chemistry at the university who was receiving assistance from Dr. Steiner on a grant application. Although there are a few scenes at the university, most of story takes place at Friar Close. The book is included in this bibliography because Friar Close is university-administered property and because almost all of the principal players in the tale are professors or members of professors' families.

At the time this book was published C. J. Koehler lived in Fond du Lac, Wisconsin. Information on the book's cover tells us that he has had careers in journalism and public relations. *Mind Games* was Koehler's second mystery.

431. LAKE, M. D. [JAMES ALLEN SIMPSON]. *FLIRTING WITH DEATH.* NEW YORK: AVON, 1996.

This story centers on the happenings in and near a veterinary hospital at a large Midwestern university. The story is narrated by Peggy O'Neill, the experienced campus policewoman who has served as the detective in seven previous Allen Simpson college mysteries. Dana Michaels, a postdoctoral student in veterinary medicine, is bludgeoned dead one night on the hospital grounds. Although O'Neill has no official role in the investigation of Dr. Michaels's death, she sleuths nonetheless, and her primary suspect is a bearded young man, who calls himself Jason, who has been roaming the campus asking young women about their sex lives. Jason once tried to engage O'Neill in an improper conversation as she waited outside the veterinary hospital while a friend's dog was being examined, and on another occasion he stalked her while she walked her predawn campus beat. As the story unfolds several university faculty members join Jason on O'Neill's list of suspicious characters, and the financial practices of the veterinary hospital are called into question. In her earlier cases Peggy O'Neill is depicted as resourceful and aggressive. She displays those same qualities in *Flirting with Death,* but in this book she offers a new insight into her personal tastes that may endear her to professorial readers regardless of her other virtues. Justifying her preference for working the "dog watch" (from eleven P.M. to seven A.M.), she explains that during those hours "there are rarely any administrators around."

The seven earlier Peggy O'Neill mysteries in this bibliography are *Amends for Murder* (313), *Cold Comfort* (325), *A Gift for Murder* (356), *Poisoned Ivy* (357), *Grave Choices* (410), *Murder by Mail* (368) and *Once Upon a Crime* (411). A later Peggy O'Neill novel, *Death Calls the Tune* (479), also has an entry in the bibliography.

432. LANGTON, JANE (B. 1922). *DEAD AS A DODO.* NEW YORK: VIKING, 1996.

Accompanied by his wife, Mary, a fellow Harvard professor, Homer Kelly, a teacher of American literature at Harvard, is invited to spend a term at the University of Oxford. As a visiting scholar, Kelly is expected to give a series of lectures at the Oxford Museum. Shortly after his arrival a security guard plunges to his death from the museum's roof, the obnoxious husband of a museum research assistant dies after falling down a museum stairwell, and Oliver Clare, a young clergyman with romantic designs on "Freddy" Dubchick, the attractive daughter of the professor in charge of the museum's world-famous Darwin collection, is found dead of a slit throat in his Oxford flat. A veteran Jane Langton series-character sleuth, Kelly cannot resist giving assistance to Detective Inspector Gopel Mukerji of the local police. The book's characters include a coterie of ambitious Oxford dons, and in addition to Homer Kelly and his sagacious wife, Mary, several other visiting Americans play important roles in the story. Charles Darwin, Galileo, Joseph Priestley, and a talking iguanodon also have roles in the mystery. Late in the story Kelly imagines himself at a trial being conducted in the museum, and in the manner of *Alice's Adventures in Wonderland* the museum's statues and exhibits come to life to decide whether Darwin killed God. The author augments her ironic prose with many line drawings, some of them depicting displays inside the museum and some of them portraying Oxford scenes and landmarks. Although he is accustomed to teaching America's best and brightest students at Harvard, Kelly is unashamedly awed by Oxford, and most American readers who have spoken at the university will appreciate his "dithering" nervousness before his first visiting lecture.

Three other Homer Kelly mysteries by Jane Langton appear earlier in this bibliography. Those mysteries are *The Memorial Hall Murder* (196), *Emily Dickinson Is Dead* (244), and *The Shortest Day: Murder at the Revels* (412).

433. LEVINE, PETER (B. 1967). *SOMETHING TO HIDE.* NEW YORK: ST. MARTIN'S, 1996.

Why would anyone want to steal Zack Blumberg's almost-finished Yale doctoral thesis on the obscure French nihilistic philosopher Joseph de Maistre? And why would that person go to the trouble of stealing Blumberg's notes as well? The distraught Blumberg advertises for the return of his work and receives a message from Charles Wilson, a Princeton graduate student. Wilson tells Blumberg that his philosophy dissertation has been stolen as well. Wilson soon turns up dead, an apparent suicide, in an Arlington, Virginia, motel room, and Blumberg begins to play detective. Although Blumberg lives in New York City and teaches at an unidentified state college in the New York metropolitan area, there are several scenes at Yale, and Hannibal Davies, the powerful chairperson of the Yale philosophy department, plays an important role in the proceedings. Late in the novel Blumberg breaks into a Yale secret society and in doing so affords readers a glimpse of the innards of a secret-society building. Blumberg's investigations also take him to Princeton, where he meets Kate, the late Charles Wilson's girlfriend, who signs on as his sleuthing assistant, and to Cornell, where Professor of Philosophy Jules Hausman reluctantly offers assistance and is subsequently found hanged in his home. Indeed, Zack makes several trips to Cornell, one of them in handcuffs after being arrested in New Haven on suspicion of Professor Hausman's murder. Readers who believe that philosophy and philosophical ideas really matter will appreciate this book because the villains in the tale, some of them exceedingly important figures on the American political scene, clearly feel the same way.

Peter Levine graduated from Yale in 1989 and then received a doctorate in philosophy from Oxford, where he studied as a Rhodes Scholar. At the time *Something to Hide* was published Levine worked as a research scholar at the Institute for Philosophy and Public Policy at the University of Maryland. *Something to Hide* was Levine's first mystery novel.

434. RAPHAEL, LEV (B. 1954). *LET'S GET CRIMINAL*. NEW YORK: ST. MARTIN'S, 1996.

Perry Cross, a newly hired assistant professor at the "State University of Michigan," is found dead in a river that cuts through the heart of the campus. Did Cross accidentally fall from a nearby bridge, or was his death the consequence of something more sinister? The police soon have reason to suspect Stefan Borowski of murder. An out-of-the-closet homosexual, and one of Cross's colleagues in the Department of English, American Studies and Rhetoric ("EAR"), Borowski at first claims to have had only a casual acquaintance with the deceased, but when Cross's will is read Borowski is found to have inherited $150,000. In an attempt to discover the truth of the matter,

Nick Hoffman, Borowski's live-in lover and yet another member of the EAR faculty, takes on the role of sleuth. Before the novel is over Hoffman's detection not only reveals a murderer but leads to the unveiling of several other university malefactors as well. *Let's Get Criminal* contains some telling satire of academe, but it also incorporates some serious themes that are rarely encountered in the college-mystery subgenre. The novel explores with sensitivity the gay, sometimes-rocky relationship between Borowski and Hoffman, and because both men are Jewish the book also incorporates material about the fears and insecurities of Jews in a predominantly gentile academic setting.

Lev Raphael was born in New York City. He received a B.A. from Fordham in 1975 and a Ph.D. from Michigan State University in 1978. Before leaving the world of higher education in 1988 to become a full-time writer, Raphael was a university teacher. During most of his academic career Raphael was a member of the faculty of Michigan State. His academic specialty was the work of Edith Wharton. In addition to mystery novels, Raphael has published many short stories about Jewish life in America. *Let's Get Criminal* was Raphael's first mystery novel. *The Edith Wharton Murders* (449) and *Death of a Constant Lover* (481), two later Nick Hoffman mysteries by Lev Raphael, also appear in this bibliography.

435. SCHUMACHER, AILEEN. *ENGINEERED FOR MURDER*. AURORA, COLO.: WRITE WAY, 1996.

This unusual mystery is set at New Mexico State University at Las Cruces, and the book centers on corruption and murder surrounding the building of the school's new football stadium. The detective is Tory Travers, the young owner of an engineering consulting firm. Tory Travers is a faculty widow. Married for five years to Carl Travers, an entrepreneurial professor of engineering, she inherited the consulting company from her husband after his death from bone cancer. Hired to inspect the new football facility, Travers discovers many construction problems. Morevover, as she conducts her inspection, the son-in-law of a contractor disappears and a quality-control technician is killed. Travers shares the sleuthing in the novel with police Lieutenant David Alvarez, and at the end of the book the two have begun a romantic relationship. Although faculty members and students make only token appearances in this story, Charles Henderson, the university's director of facilities planning, takes part as a major suspect. Despite its lack of usual academic characters, the book offers many campus scenes, most of them at the stadium construction site. As to the fate of the disappearing son-in-law, after finishing *Engineered for Murder* academic readers may find themselves wondering what is inside the concrete columns at the football stadia on their own campuses.

Aileen Schumacher graduated from New Mexico State University. She is a registered professional engineer. When this book was published Schumacher and her husband owned and operated a consulting engineering firm. *Engineered for Murder* was the first novel in what has become a continuing series of mysteries featuring Tory Travers as detective.

436. SHAPIRO, BARBARA (B. 1951). *SEE NO EVIL.* NEW YORK: AVON, 1996.

Lauren Freeman is a graduate student in history at a world-famous (but unidentified) university in Cambridge, Massachusetts. She is in her mid-thirties, recently separated, and attempting to raise Drew, her seven-year-old son. Freeman is collaborating on a book with Jackie Pappas, a senior professor in the history department, about Rebeka Hibbens, a woman who was executed for witchcraft in Cambridge in 1692. Although Freeman sometimes has nightmares about Rebeka Hibbens and her torment, the writing project goes well until Professor Pappas dies in her home after a presumed fall from a step-stool. Then Freeman's life begins to change for the worse. She suffers a crisis in confidence when faced with finishing the Hibbens book on her own. She is arrested after trying to collect information at a gathering of modern-day witches. Her son is kidnapped. And, somehow, she cannot help but believe that Professor Pappas's death was not an accident. *See No Evil* is more a suspense novel than a conventional detective mystery, but Lauren Freeman nonetheless engages in a fair amount of sleuthing before the book reaches its conclusion. Although much of the tale transpires in downtown Cambridge, there are several campus scenes, and an important character in the story is Gabe Phipps, the prestigious chairperson of the university's history department. Phipps is so illustrious that he appears each week on television in a series about the Revolutionary War. Divorced, the attractive Professor Phipps courts the equally attractive Freeman during the story, and at one point in the narrative he meets young Drew. Some readers may empathize with Drew Freeman when he tells the professor that although he is aware that he is a television performer, he much prefers to watch Homer and Bart Simpson, who are on at the same time.

According to information on the cover of this book, Barbara Shapiro is a sociologist who has taught at Tufts University. *See No Evil* was Shapiro's third suspense novel. A member of several writers' organizations, Shapiro has served as president of the New England chapter of Sisters in Crime.

437. SIMONS, PAULLINA (B. 1963). *RED LEAVES*. NEW YORK: ST. MARTIN'S, 1996.

Kristina Kim, an undergraduate, is found dead in a snowbank at a remote part of the Dartmouth College campus. Except for boots, her body is naked. An autopsy reveals that she was suffocated but not sexually assaulted. Although Miss Kim was an active student with many friends, she had been buried in the snowbank for more than a week without anyone notifiying the authorities. A few days before her death Kim had a chance meeting with Spencer O'Malley of the Hanover, New Hampshire, police, and there had been a spark of romance. Now O'Malley is charged with finding Miss Kim's murderer. He begins by addressing the question of why her disappearance was never reported. At 354 pages, *Red Leaves* is a long, novelistic mystery with considerably more character development than most whodunits. Readers learn about the life histories, inner thoughts, and motivations of Detective O'Malley, Kristina Kim (her death does not occur until page 127), and several other students who play prominent roles in the story. "Red Leaves" is the name of a home for pregnant teenagers where Miss Kim worked as a volunteer. Those with real-life associations with Dartmouth may not appreciate the largely negative portraits of the wealthy and want-to-be-wealthy Dartmouth undergraduates whom Detective O'Malley investigates, but they will enjoy the extensive tour of Dartmouth College and the town of Hanover that the book provides as O'Malley pursues his inquiries.

According to information on the cover of *Red Leaves,* Paullina Simons was born in Leningrad and immigrated as a child to the United States. She has worked as a financial journalist and translator. At the time *Red Leaves* was published Simons lived in Texas.

438. STALLWOOD, VERONICA. *OXFORD FALL.* LONDON: MACMILLAN, 1996.

Christopher Townsend, development officer of the University of Oxford's "Bartlemas College," dies after an early-afternoon fall from the college's architecturally celebrated "Tower of Grace." Because he had imbibed several drinks at lunch, it is assumed that his plunge was the result of drunkenness. Before his fatal fall Townsend was organizing a two-week college conference on "gender and genre." After his death the college engages Kate Ivory to handle some of the conference arranging. A writer of historical novels, a resident of Oxford, and a Veronica Stallwood series-character sleuth, Ivory soon finds that many of the functionaries in the Bartlemas development office seem anxious and unfriendly, and she also discovers strange messages, apparently warning of danger, in Townsend's files. Before the novel concludes, Ivory discovers the real cause of Townsend's death, but not before she is stalked through the streets of Oxford and begins to fear that her own life may be in jeopardy. Readers who have experienced academic conferences in Oxford may agree with Emma Dolby, the Bartelmas tutor in charge of the academic side of the gender-and-genre gathering, who offers her view of the purpose of such events. They are held, she asserts, less for their intellectual value and more to augment the host colleges' budgets by attracting well-heeled people, primarily Americans, "who are willing to pay enormous sums of money to live in elegant discomfort."

Oxford Exit (401) and *Oxford Mourning* (413), two other Kate Ivory mysteries by Veronica Stallwood, appear in this bibliography.

439. ALCORN, ALFRED (B. 1941). *MURDER IN THE MUSEUM OF MAN.* CAMBRIDGE, MASS.: ZOLAND BOOKS, 1997.

The narrator of this novel is Norman A. deRatour, a mousy, inoffensive administrative employee of the "Museum of Man," an institution that nearby "Wainscott University" would like to absorb. DeRatour, who serves as the museum's recording secretary, tells the tale through a series of "unofficial" entries in the museum's log. His story begins with the death of Wainscott's Dean Cranston Fessing, who had been assigned by the university to examine the museum's operations and explore the feasibility of a takeover. Dean Fessing's corpse is found, elaborately cooked and partly eaten, in a dumpster behind the University's gender studies building. From then on, deRatour's log describes various events at the museum and at the university, several more deaths, and his own efforts to undertake detection. *Murder in the Museum of Man* is a mystery accompanied by a continuing series of satirical barbs aimed at academe and academics. Some of the satire is broad, but some of it is sufficiently subtle that it is probably best appreciated by readers who have spent their own adulthoods within the world of higher education. Among the more noteworthy aspects of the tale are a cannibal cult in the Wainscott anthropology department, an attack on deRatour by a group of vicious chimpanzees, and the response of a Wainscott professor when asked if it was he who killed and consumed the dean. As deRatour reports in his log, the professor replies that "he would never eat an old dean like Fessing, what with all that vitriol building up in him over the years."

Alfred Alcorn was born in England. He received a B.A. from Harvard in 1964. At the time this book was published Alcorn was director of the travel program at Harvard's Museum of Cultural and Natural History. Although Alcorn had already published several mainstream novels, *Murder in the Museum of Man* was his first mystery.

440. BREWER, STEVE. *SHAKY GROUND*. NEW YORK: ST. MARTIN'S, 1997.

David Field, a professor of biology at the University of New Mexico, disappears while doing research in the desert. Amber, his wife, asks irreverent private investigator Bubba Mabry to find him. By hiring a helicopter to fly above the area where David Field was supposed to have gone, private eye Mabry does, indeed, find the professor, but he has been shot dead. At this point Amber Field asks Mabry to find her husband's killer. Many of the suspects in *Shaky Ground* are University of New Mexico staff and faculty members, and Mabry spends much of his time on the New Mexico campus. One person who arouses his suspicion is Monica Gallegos, the attractive biology department secretary who wears "radioactive red" lipstick. Monica Gallegos gets Mabry's attention when she has a fistfight with a female undergraduate who reveals that the late professor had affairs with some of his female associates. Another possible murderer is department chairperson Anna Lipscomb. A "plain-looking woman who [is] trying for ugly," Professor Lipscomb attempts to get Mabry to stop his sleuthing because, as she explains it, she fears that adverse publicity might slow the flow of funds into her department. The book often digresses from the main story to follow Bubba Mabry's preparations for marriage to Felica Quattlebaum, a newspaper reporter, and among the important characters in the whodunit part of the plot are several people who are not connected with the university. Nonetheless, the weighting of this mystery is clearly on the academic side, and among other lessons related to higher education, readers can learn that not all biology professors are dedicated environmentalists.

Born in Arkansas, Steve Brewer began a long newspaper career by working ten years for the *Arkansas Gazette* in Little Rock. At the time *Shaky Ground* was published he was a reporter for the *Albuquerque Journal.* The book was his fourth Bubba Mabry mystery.

441. CROMBIE, DEBORAH. *DREAMING OF THE BONES.* NEW YORK: SCRIBNER'S, 1997.

Dr. Victoria McClellan is a fellow of "All Saints College" at Cambridge and a member of the university's English faculty. She is writing the biography of Lydia Brooke, a woman pioneer of confessional poetry, who was a student at Cambridge in the 1960s and who died by apparent suicide five years before the beginning of this story. As she conducts her research Dr. McClellan develops doubts about the cause of Lydia Brooke's death, and she calls on her former husband, Superintendent Duncan Kincaid of Scotland Yard, to assess the correctness of her suspicions. Accompanied by Sergeant Gemma Jones, his partner and lover, Kincaid ultimately must deal with contemporary murders as well as past ones before he brings the case to a conclusion. Many Cambridge characters, from both town and gown, appear in the story. *Dreaming of the Bones* is more novelistic than most mysteries. Each of the book's primary players, including Superintendent Kincaid, experiences difficult relationships within his or her personal orbit, and the book incorporates several subplots concerning romantic problems and family crises. Some of the text consists of lengthy letters written by Lydia Brooke while she was a Cambridge undergraduate; hence, in addition to many scenes of present-day Cambridge, readers are offered views of university life in the 1960s.

Deborah Crombie was born in Texas and earned a biology degree from Austin College. *Dreaming of the Bones* was her fifth Duncan Kincaid/Gemma Jones novel. Crombie has lived in England. At the time *Dreaming of the Bones* was published she made her home in Texas, but she was a regular traveler to England, in part to conduct field research for her mysteries.

442. DOBSON, JOANNE (B. 1942). *QUIETER THAN SLEEP.* NEW YORK: DOUBLEDAY, 1997.

Karen Pelletier, the divorced mother of an eighteen-year-old daughter, is an untenured assistant professor of English at exclusive "Enfield College" in rural Massachusetts. At a cocktail party in the home of Enfield's president she encounters Professor Randy

Astin-Berger, one of her department colleagues. Astin-Berger mentions something to her about an important letter, but because he is an obnoxious womanizer Pelletier wants to exit the conversation, and she pays little attention to what he is saying. A short time later she opens a coat closet and Randy Astin-Berger, now strangled dead, falls out and into her arms. The police investigator is Lieutenant Piotrowski of the Enfield police. On the chance that Astin-Berger's predeath comment to Pelletier might indicate that his murder was related to his research on Emily Dickinson, Piotrowski asks Pelletier to search through the late professor's files in search of clues, and in a rare stroke of good fortune for a fictional professor-detective, Piotrowski prevails upon his superiors to pay her $500 per day for her services! As the story proceeds, the scope of Professor Pelletier's sleuthing expands far beyond her original assignment, and toward the end of the story she earns her money and more when she is wounded by the book's pistol-packing villain. With a large cast of Enfield College characters, and with a surprise ending that will warm the heart of anyone who has ever faced the possible loss of valuable research material, *Quieter Than Sleep* is a solid college mystery. Students of literary anomalies will want to take particular note of the novel because it contains one of the few portraits of a "nice" college president in the college-mystery subgenre. Indeed, the young, divorced President Avery Claibourne Cabot Mitchell is so appealing that Karen Pelletier falls in love with him, and he falls in love with her. But *Quieter Than Sleep* is set in modern times. President Mitchell knows that a romance between Enfield's president and an untenured assistant professor would violate a campus policy that bars fraternization between persons of unequal status, and he reluctantly ends his politically incorrect relationship with Pelletier.

At the time *Quieter Than Sleep* was published Joanne Dobson was an associate professor of English at Fordham University. In academic circles Dobson is best known for her writings about Emily Dickinson. *Quieter Than Sleep* was the first of a continuing series of novels with Karen Pelletier as detective. Two other Professor Pelletier mysteries, *The Northbury Papers* (459) and *The Raven and the Nightingale* (474), appear later in this bibliography.

443. GREGORY, SUSANNA [PSEUD.] (B. 1958). *A BONE OF CONTENTION.* NEW YORK: ST. MARTIN'S, 1997.

This novel is set at the University of Cambridge in the mid-fourteenth century. The protagonist is Matthew Bartholomew, a physician and a fellow of Michaelhouse College. As a scholar, Bartholomew is trying to finish a ground-breaking treatise on fevers, but his research is often put aside because in his role as a man of healing he provides medical services not only to Michaelhouse College but to the university as a whole and to the town as well. Doctor Bartholomew also acts as Cambridge's resident forensic expert, and when the body of James Kenzie, a student, is found in a drainage ditch he determines that the cause of death was murder by heavy instrument applied to the top of the skull. As the book continues, the busy Bartholomew is drawn into the search for the student's killer, and as an added burden he must deal with whether a man, presumably murdered thirty years before, is still alive. The text is preceded by a street map of Cambridge as it was in 1348, and the book is rich with gritty, fourteenth-century Cambridge detail. In addition to the animosities between some of the fictional characters in the story, the story incorporates real intergroup conflicts of the period (among them, town versus gown, church versus crown, and Scots versus English). At one point in the tale a mob of townspeople tries to sack Michaelhouse College and take the silver plate, jewelry, and clothes of its "sniveling scholars." Doctor Bartholomew and the other denizens of Michaelhouse retreat behind the college's thick walls, and the mob is repulsed when its leader is killed by an arrow shot by a college marksman. Readers of this novel will be interested to learn that Michaelhouse was an actual medieval Cambridge college. Founded in 1324, it was absorbed into Trinity College when the latter was founded in 1546 by King Henry VIII.

A Bone of Contention was the third novel in the continuing Matthew Bartholomew series by Susanna Gregory. The first novel in the series, *A Plague on Both Your Houses* (425), appears earlier in this bibliography.

444. HART, CAROLYN G(IMPEL). (B. 1936). *DEATH IN LOVERS' LANE*. NEW YORK: AVON, 1997.

Recently widowed and on the far side of sixty, Henrietta ("Henrie O") Collins decides on a life change. A renowned newspaper reporter, she leaves the busy world of deadlines and editors to teach journalism at "Thorndyke University" in "Derry Hills," Missouri. Maggie Winslow, one of Henrie O's students, chooses as a class project to write a series of articles about three unsolved Derry Hills murder cases. Not long afterward Maggie is found strangled dead at the remote site where, in one of the cases, two university-student lovers were killed a decade before. The local police arrest a nonacademic suspect, but Henrietta soon comes to believe that the actual culprit is a member of the university community, and she embarks on detection. By the end of the story Henrie O has demonstrated conclusively that her investigative talents exceed those of the police. Of the many Thorndyke University people who appear in the book, professorial readers may be especially interested in Tom Arnold, a professor of English who has prospered through publishing to become Derry Hills' wealthiest citizen. Literary critics sometimes grade college mysteries according to the degree to which their characters display the thought processes found in the real world of higher learning. On at least one count *Death in Lovers' Lane* gets an A+. Early in the book Thorndyke's oily president, David Tucker, tries to pressure Henrietta to stop Maggie Winslow's research. He reasons that investigating forgotten murders can only reopen old wounds on the campus. The famous Henrietta, who has a Pulitzer Prize among her many honors, can probably get any job she desires, inside or outside of academe. Yet the weapon that President Tucker uses, in a vain attempt to get Henrietta to comply with his wishes, is a threat to prevent her from getting tenure.

Death in Lovers' Lane was the third Carolyn G. Hart mystery to feature Henrietta Collins as detective. *A Little Class on Murder* (309), a Carolyn G. Hart mystery with series-character Annie Laurance Darling as detective, appears earlier in this bibliography.

445. HOLTZER, SUSAN. *BLACK DIAMOND*. NEW YORK: ST. MARTIN'S, 1997.

Clare Swann, a University of Michigan undergraduate, inherits some papers from her aunt. Before she can examine them, her dormitory room is trashed and her long-lost father, once a distinguished professor of anthropology, is found dead of a knife wound amid the litter. The primary detecting in *Black Diamond* is done by local businesswoman Anneke Haagen and her boyfriend, Ann Arbor Police Lieutenant Karl Genesko. Haagen and Genesko are joined in their labors by Zoe Kaplan, a Michigan undergraduate who often skips class to work as a reporter for the university's daily newspaper. Haagen, Genesko, and Kaplan are all Susan Holtzer series-characters. Some of the investigation in this story is literary. By examining hundred-year-old letters Miss Swan received as part of her aunt's estate, the sleuths are able to tie events that occurred in northern Michigan at the turn of the twentieth century to the killing of Professor Swann. Much of the tale takes place on the Michigan campus, and the motive for Professor Swann's killing turns out to be one that prompts many villains in college mysteries to commit murder. Professor Swann's nephew Patrick, a graduate student in economics, appears in the book's cast of characters. As for Clare Swann, the late professor's daughter, she is not a person with a passion for neatness. The book offers graphic descriptions of the disarray in her dormitory room that, as several characters observe, looked almost the same before it was trashed as it did afterward.

Black Diamond was the fourth novel in Susan Holtzer's Anneke Haagen/Karl Genesko series. Two other Haagen/Genesko mysteries by Susan Holtzer, *Bleeding Maize and Blue* (427) and *The Silly Season: An Entr'acte* (477), have entries in this bibliography.

446. MCINERNY, RALPH (B. 1929). *ON THIS ROCKNE.* NEW YORK: ST. MARTIN'S, 1997.

Marcus Bramble, of the class of 1957, announces his intention of giving a large donation (perhaps as much as ten million dollars) to his alma mater, the University of Notre Dame. Bramble wants his money to be used for a proper monument to legendary football coach Knute Rockne. Debates begin on the campus about just what sort of monument to Rockne would be appropriate. Some, including university trustee Madeline Rune, have the nerve to hint that the money might best be spent on academic matters rather than on a new stadium or some other athletics-oriented project. Madeline Rune is soon found dead in her home, the victim of a smashed skull. The likely suspect is Madeline's husband, Stanley, a former Notre Dame halfback, who claims to have been in Chicago at the time of his wife's death but who is found to have been staying at a local motel instead. Stanley Rune stands to inherit Madeline's estate, which includes the valuable papers of her father, a famous sports historian. Stanley Rune soon disappears, and a few days later his body is found in the St. Joseph River. There is official police detection in this novel, but the sleuths who eventually resolve matters are the Knight brothers, Philip and Roger. Philip Knight is a private investigator of average size. Roger Knight is an exceedingly fat Notre Dame professor who fully occupies an endowed chair of Catholic studies. Professor Knight is so rotund that he sometimes needs assistance squeezing through the door to the university archives. In addition to Roger Knight, several other members of the Notre Dame faculty and administration appear in the story, including Henry Hadley, a young teacher of English. Hadley becomes a suspect when it is found that he had an unrequited crush on the two-decades-older Madeline Rune. Another interesting character is Sebastian Quirk, an aged priest who was an undergraduate while Rockne was coaching football. Father Quirk is a font of information about Rockne and his players. Almost all readers of this book will be surprised to learn, just as are almost all the characters in the story, that Knute Rockne once wrote a novel. Titled *The Four Winners* (New York: Devon-Adair, 1925), the famed coach's only published work of fiction figures significantly in the plot of *On This Rockne.*

Three other mysteries by Ralph McInerny appear in this bibliography. One of them, *The Nominative Case* (336), was published under the pseudonym Edward Mackin. The others, *The Search Committee* (338) and *Lack of the Irish*, were published under McInerny's real name. *Lack of the Irish* follows the further detection exploits of the Knight Brothers of Notre Dame.

447. MINICHINO, CAMILLE. *THE HYDROGEN MURDER*. NEW YORK: AVALON BOOKS, 1997.

What does an unmarried woman in her mid-fifties do after taking early retirement as a professor of physics at the University of California at Berkeley? If she is Gloria Lamerino she returns to her hometown of Revere Beach, Massachusetts, and volunteers to act as a consultant to the local police department. Revere Beach is not burdened with many crimes that call for the retired professor's scientific expertise, hence the introspective Lamerino, who narrates this story, ordinarily has abundant time to ponder her uncertain future. In *The Hydrogen Murder,* a killing at a "Massachusetts University" physics laboratory in Revere gives her a chance to test her sleuthing talents. Eric Bensen, a graduate student who is working alone in the lab, is shot dead in the small hours of the morning. Bensen, who was one of a team of scientists working on a project to produce metallic hydrogen, had just discovered that important research data had been fabricated. Acting in concert with Revere Police Sergeant Matt Gennaro, Professor Lamerino looks first at Bensen's research associates, any one of whom might have committed the murder to prevent him from revealing his finding. Then she turns to the matter of the graduate student's convoluted romantic life. Although it is Lamerino's knowledge of scientific formulae that allows her to develop leads in the case, she must resort to hand-to-hand combat at the end of the tale to bring the villain to justice. The book's academic suspects include Dr. Ralph Leder (the womanizing head of the laboratory), Connie Provenza (an ambitious postdoctoral member of the hydrogen project who plans to get an M.B.A. and demolish all glass ceilings in the world of business), and Janice Bensen (Eric's Bensen's whining wife, who made her husband's life miserable by constantly complaining about the delays in completing his Ph.D.). Dr. Leder does not survive to the end of the tale. Sleuth Lamerino, on the other hand, not only survives but also begins to think that Sergeant Matt Gennaro, a Boston College graduate who is approximately her own age, might make a good marriage partner.

Camille Minichino was raised in Revere Beach, Massachusetts. She earned a Ph.D. in physics from Fordham University in 1968. According to information on the cover of this book, she has "had a long career in research and teaching." At the time *The Hydrogen Murder* was published she was retired and lived in San Francisco, where she continued to teach in adult education programs. Among the courses Minichino offered her adult students were The History and Philosophy of Science, Science for Non-Scientists, and Mystery Writing. *The Hydrogen Murder* was the first in what has become a continuing series of mysteries featuring former professor Gloria Lamerino.

448. PEARS, IAIN (GEORGE) (B. 1955). *AN INSTANCE OF THE FINGERPOST.* LONDON: CAPE, 1997; NEW YORK: RIVERHEAD BOOKS, 1998.

An Instance of the Fingerpost is a more ambitious literary work than any of the other novels in this bibliography. Almost 700 pages long, the book is set in seventeenth-century Oxford, just after the restoration of the British monarchy. It centers on the murder of Robert Grove, an unpleasant and widely disliked fellow of New College, and the subsequent execution by hanging of an innocent girl named Sarah Blundy. By turns, four narrators who claim to have firsthand knowledge relate tales of the murder and its aftermath, and each one offers a selective view, based on his particular perspective and on his special motives for telling what he claims to know. Thus, as the book's readers try to learn who actually killed Dr. Grove, they receive sometimes-contradictory information, and they must decide what elements of each narrative to believe and what to discard. The tellers of the tale place the murder in its fuller political context, and by the end of the book readers have been given an enormous amount of information about the intrigues surrounding the overthrow of Charles I and the subsequent recall to the throne of Charles II. The first narrator is a visiting Italian physician who has pretensions to immortality as a pioneer of medical science. The second is a mentally disturbed Oxford student whose main interest is to prove that his Royalist father was innocent of treason. The third is an Oxford professor of mathematics who, somehow, managed to work as a cryptographer both for the forces of Oliver Cromwell and for their Royalist enemies. The fourth is an antiquarian whose main concern seems to be that history remembers him as a decent and pious man. Luminaries such as John Locke and Christopher Wren appear in the story, and almost all of the participants are based on real people of the period. The author provides an appendix in which he outlines the actual life histories of his characters. Because of their exposure to four unreliable accounts, readers of the novel may never feel that they have fully solved the book's whodunit, but readers who are interested in British history will learn much about the turmoil in Oxford and in England during the Restoration.

Iain Pears was born in Coventry, England. He received a B.A. from Wadham College, Oxford, in 1977 and a D.Phil. from Wolfson College, Oxford, in 1982. He also did graduate study at Yale. Before becoming a full-time writer Pears worked as a journalist for Reuters News Agency. *An Instance of the Fingerpost* was his seventh novel. Prior to writing *An Instance of the Fingerpost*, Pears created a six-novel series of mysteries in which British art dealer Jonathan Argyil serves as detective.

449. RAPHAEL, LEV (B. 1954). *THE EDITH WHARTON MURDERS.* NEW YORK: ST. MARTIN'S, 1997.

Two murders occur during a conference on Edith Wharton that is being held at the "State University of Michigan." The first victim is Chloe DeVore, a famous novelist with a penchant for writing acidic book reviews that destroy the reputations of rival novelists. DeVore, who is present at the gathering even though she is not known to have any scholarly interest in Edith Wharton, dies outside the conference auditorium when someone bashes her skull. The second victim is Priscilla Davidoff, an associate professor in the university's Department of English, American Studies, and

Rhetoric ("EAR"). Professor Davidoff expires after being shot in her car in a campus parking lot. Doing the lion's share of sleuthing is Nick Hoffman, a junior member of the EAR faculty, who is the conference organizer. Assistant Professor Hoffman, who is openly homosexual, is assisted by Stefan Borowski, his live-in significant other, and by Angie Sandoval, an undergraduate criminal justice major who is a whiz at detection through the internet. A consummatory college mystery, *The Edith Wharton Murders* incorporates many academic characters from the State University of Michigan ("SUM") and it provides glimpses of faculty conference attendees from many other institutions of higher learning as well. Sharply written, and abounding with witticisms, the book offers a compelling mystery that hinges on the tangled, often gay or bisexual, mating lives of the central players. At the same time it pokes barbed fun at the political correctness, the petty jealousies, and the status insecurities that can be found in the world of academe.

Two other Nick Hoffman mysteries by Lev Raphael can be found in this bibliography. Those mysteries are *Let's Get Criminal* (434) and *Death of a Constant Lover* (448).

450. SHABER, SARAH R. *SIMON SAID*. NEW YORK: ST. MARTIN'S, 1997.

The detective/protagonist of this thoroughly academic mystery is Simon Shaw, a professor of history at "Kenan College," a high-status liberal arts institution located in a suburb of Raleigh, North Carolina. An expert in local history, Shaw is asked by the police to help in the investigation of a seventy-year-old murder. The victim was a socially prominent young woman whose body is found, with a bullet hole through her skull, during an archaeological dig outside "Bloodsworth House," an 1826 Greek Revival structure on the Kenan campus. In search of clues, Shaw visits libraries and interviews elderly people who knew the deceased and her family. All the while he is imperiled by a present-day villain who tries three times to end his life. Professor Shaw also feuds with a nasty departmental colleague over a C-grade he gave to the colleague's favorite student. *Simon Said* is noteworthy both for its focus on sleuthing through historical evidence and for its attention to the details of academic life. Many professor-readers will experience déjà vu when they encounter the scene, midway through the story, in which a history department meeting degenerates into vitriolic argument. The book is noteworthy, as well, for its in-depth, multidimensional portrait of Professor Shaw. A Pulitzer Prize-winning writer, and the youngest person ever promoted to full professor at Kenan College, the part-Jewish and part-Irish Shaw is separated from his wife. He is a constant guzzler of Coca-Cola and a depressive whose medicine cabinet is stocked with a variety of prescription tranquilizers.

According to material on the cover of *Simon Said,* Sarah R. Shaber was a resident of Raleigh, North Carolina, when this book was published. She was employed in the world of advertising and public relations. *Simon Said* was Shaber's first mystery novel.

451. SMITH, TAYLOR. *THE BEST OF ENEMIES.* DON MILLS, ONTARIO, CANADA: MIRA BOOKS, 1997.

The protagonist of this incident-laden novel is Leya Nash, an assistant professor of English at "Mount Abbey College." Mount Abbey is a high-status institution for women in Winslow, Massachusetts. Leya is the daughter of Carter Nash, who was once a brilliant CIA operative but who is now badly disabled by a stroke. Carter, who lives in Winslow to be near Leya, once worked in Washington with Arthur Stroud, now the United States' ambassador to Israel. Holly Stroud, Arthur's daughter, is a Mount Abbey undergraduate. Holly Stroud disappears from the campus, and Ambassador Stroud, calling from Tel Aviv, asks Leya Nash to help look for her. A short time later a huge bomb destroys an industrial site near Winslow, killing several people, and the authorities begin to suspect that the missing Holly may be part of an international terrorist group. At this point Leya Nash, a rejuvenated Carter Nash, and a host of local and federal law enforcement officers begin work, on the Mount Abbey campus and elsewhere, to discover Holly's whereabouts and to find out who is guilty of the bombing. Meantime, more explosions occur and several romantic subplots develop. *The Best of Enemies* is certainly not the most subtle novel in this bibliography, but in between its explosions and its matings it offers detailed descriptions of the scenic Mount Abbey campus, and it introduces its readers to many Mount Abbey students and faculty members.

Taylor Smith, a native of Winnipeg, Canada, served in Canada's foreign service before launching a full-time career as a writer. *The Best of Enemies* was her third novel. At the time *The Best of Enemies* was published Smith lived in Southern California.

452. STRONG, TONY (B. 1962). *THE POISON TREE.* NEW YORK: DELACORTE, 1997.

Recently divorced, Terry Williams moves from London to Oxford to resume her graduate studies in English at "St. Mary's College." Her specialty within English is the study of detective fiction. She rents a house in which the last tenant, a young man named Hugh Scott, was brutally murdered. The crime is still unsolved. As Williams explores her new quarters, she encounters a cat that shows evidence of having been tortured. Williams brings her finding to the attention of Inspector Richard Girdler of the Thames Valley Police, and before long the attractive Williams and the strong-but-sensitive inspector are not only sleuthing together but sleeping together as well. Many Oxford students, faculty, and townspeople, most of them with strong (and sometimes kinky) sexual appetites, appear in this novel, and there are many scenes at the university. At one noteworthy juncture, the author explains why the food at some college high tables is barely edible. *The Poison Tree* offers a compelling mystery and heaps of detail about Oxford in the 1990s, but prospective readers should be alert that it also contains vivid accounts of homosexual rape, sadism, mutilation, and other unpleasant activities.

Tony Strong was educated at Oxford. *The Poison Tree* was his first novel. At the time the book was published, Strong lived in Oxfordshire and was employed as an advertising copywriter.

453. WRIGHT, SALLY S. *PUBLISH & PERISH.* SISTERS, ORE.: MULTNOMAH BOOKS, 1997.

The protagonist of this engaging mystery is Ben Reese, an archivist at "Alderton University" in "Hinsdale," Ohio. The time is late November of 1960. While conducting research in Oxford, Reese receives a late-night, transatlantic telephone call from his good friend Richard West, the chairman of Alderton's English department. West tells him that he has uncovered an act of "treachery," but because the "culprit" has just entered his office he will explain more in a subsequent call. The next day Reese receives a telegram informing him that Richard West has died of a heart attack. He returns immediately to Alderton, suspects that Professor West's death was, somehow, the result of foul play, and begins to detect. Before he can apprehend the villain, a professor of French becomes the killer's second victim, and Reese almost freezes to death when stranded on a lonely road in the midst of a raging blizzard. As Reese struggles to unmask the murderer, *Publish & Perish* deals with some of the moral dilemmas encountered by those who make careers in the academic world, and all of the primary players in the story are drawn with considerable flesh on their bones. Ben Reese, for example, is a former World War II commando who was badly wounded in action. He is also a widower, and he has recurrent dreams both of his late wife and of military combat. At the beginning of the book the author provides a roster of the twenty-one major characters in the tale, and all of them except Chester Hansen, Hinsdale's chief of police, are connected with the world of higher education. Amateur detective Ben Reese eventually captures Alderton University's resident murderer, but his independent sleuthing endangers himself and others. Although Chief Hansen is the only nonacademic with a significant role in the novel, he is allotted one of the book's better bursts of dialogue when he gets to do what many other police officials in college mysteries only dream of doing. At the end of the story Chief Hansen gives Ben Reese a protracted tongue lashing for operating outside of the law.

Sally Wright has an undergraduate degree from Northwestern University and has done graduate work at the University of Washington. *Publish & Perish* was her first novel.

454. BICKHAM, JACK (MILES) (1930–1997). *MURDER AT OKLAHOMA*. NEW YORK: BERKLEY PRIME CRIME, 1998.

The murder of Lilith Weilman shocks the University of Oklahoma. A professor of English and a successful novelist, Weilman is stabbed dead in the bedroom of her home. Professor Weilman had the usual complement of academic enemies, but as far as anyone knows no one had a motive to kill her. Then, to add complexity to the proceedings, when the Norman police begin to investigate the professor's death they discover that someone has wiped clean the hard drive of her computer. The primary detective in the story is Phyllis ("Flip") Ryan, a doctoral candidate in electrical engineering who has supplemented her engineering studies by taking writing courses in the English department. Blonde, "leggy," and divorced, Ryan enters the case when one of her former English professors, John Milton Thrush, becomes a suspect, and she gets unofficial status as a helper-to-the-police when they learn that her expertise with computers can be useful in their investigations. The book takes its readers to many places in Norman and on the Oklahoma campus, and most of its characters are faculty members, students, or administrators at the university. Indeed, former United States Senator David Boren, the actual president of Oklahoma when the book was written, has a significant, but not especially flattering, part in the story. Concerned with the public-relations risks associated with the negative information about the English department that Ryan is uncovering through her sleuthing, President Boring asks her to report all of her findings directly to him so that they can be "evaluated and passed on to the authorities in the way most likely to reflect well on the institution."

Jack Bickham received a B.A. from Ohio State in 1952 and an M.A. from the University of Oklahoma in 1952. He began his working life as a writer and editor for newspapers in Oklahoma City. In 1969 he joined the journalism faculty at the University of Oklahoma and eventually became a professor of journalism. Sometimes employing the pseudonyms Jeff Clinton, John Miles, and George Shaw, Bickham produced over fifty works of fiction, many of them mystery novels.

455. BLOCK, BARBARA. *VANISHING ACT.* NEW YORK: KENSINGTON BOOKS, 1998.

Melissa Hayes disappears from the campus of a large but unidentified university located on the side of a hill in Syracuse, New York. A sophomore, Miss Hayes was having boyfriend problems as well as academic difficulties. The police suspect that she has simply gone on a brief hiatus to reassess her life, but Brian, Miss Hayes's brother, fears foul play. He engages Robin Light to discover what happened to his sister. The owner of a Syracuse pet shop, Light doubles as a private investigator, and during this novel she pokes into various of the university's nooks and crannies in search of information about the missing Melissa. Light narrates the story with proper private-eye flippancy, but frustrations arise when, as a cigarette smoker, she finds places to puff almost as scarce as clues on the university campus. As she detects, Light meets a male undergraduate who keeps a twelve-foot snake in his fraternity-house room and a corpulent professor of psychology. The latter, a man who resembles a "befuddled, fatter version of Albert Einstein," bakes large batches of chocolate chip cookies at night for consumption the next day in his office.

At the time this mystery was published Barbara Block lived in Syracuse, New York. Robin Light is a Barbara Block series-character sleuth. *Vanishing Act* was Block's fifth Robin Light mystery.

456. CONNOR, BEVERLY (B. 1948). *DRESSED TO DIE.* NASHVILLE, TENN.: CUMBERLAND HOUSE, 1998.

The skeleton of Shirley Foster, a professor of art and history at the University of Georgia, is found buried on her husband's rural property four years after her disappearance. Another skeleton, this one dressed in a shirt and tie, tumbles from a crate of valuable artifacts delivered to the university, and the artifacts themselves then begin disappearing. A female undergraduate is killed when she is run over by a bus, and a police detective who is investigating the missing artifacts is stabbed dead. Involved in the simultaneous investigations of all of the above is Lindsay Chamberlain, an untenured, female archaeologist at Georgia who also acts as a Beverly Connor series-character detective. In fact, nasty associate dean Ellis Einer believes that Professor Chamberlain may be a little too interested in criminal activity. Wondering how an untenured assistant professor can afford to own a $50,000 Land Rover and a $100,000 Arabian horse, he deduces that Chamberlain herself may be a thief, if not a murderer as well, and he tells the police of his suspicions. By the end of this involved tale a great many University of Georgia characters have made appearances, and Professor Chamberlain's inquiries have taken her to many places on the Georgia campus. Much of Chamberlain's sleuthing has to do with the forensic examination of human remains, and the book contains several scenes in university laboratories. No matter what professor-readers may think of the body of this story, many will agree that the ending is a gem of imaginative academic fiction. Still angry that Dean Einer pointed the gaze of the police in her direction, Professor Chamberlain consults an experienced attorney who advises her to sue the university for $5,000,000 in damages. There seems to be a strong probability that Chamberlain can win her case and achieve a lifetime of financial independence. However, when the university offers her tenure if she will drop her suit, Chamberlain immediately accepts the school's offer.

Beverly Connor was raised in Oak Ridge, Tennessee, majored in anthropology at East Tennessee State University, and earned an M.A. from the University of Georgia. At the time *Dressed to Die* was published, Connor lived in Oglethorpe County, Georgia. *Dressed to Die* was her third Lindsay Chamberlain mystery.

457. CROSS, AMANDA [CAROLYN GOLD HEILBRUN (B. 1926)]. *THE PUZZLED HEART.* NEW YORK: BALLANTINE, 1998.

Reed Amhearst is kidnapped as he leaves his office at a large, prestigious university in New York City. Amhearst is a professor of law. He also is the husband of Kate Fansler, a professor of English at the university. Professor Fansler, in turn, is Amanda Cross's well-known series-character sleuth, and as might be expected she sets out immediately to locate Amhearst and free him. She enlists the help of Harriet Furst, an old acquaintance who is now a private investigator, and before the story reaches its halfway point Fansler, Furst, and Tori Giamotti, Furst's employer, rescue Amhearst from his captors. Amhearst was being held in a university apartment by four young women, but the quartet of "nymphs" (as Amhearst calls them) clearly was following the orders of someone else. Hence, as the novel proceeds the several detectives, now joined by Amhearst, look for the person or persons behind the kidnapping. When Amhearst is kidnapped Fansler receives a note demanding that she renounce her "insane" feminist views if she wants her husband released, and thus her initial suspects in the case are people and organizations, most of them with university connections, that advocate right-wing, antifeminist positions. By the end of the novel the liberal Professor Fansler learns that political incorrectness, while it certainly causes her displeasure, may only be a red herring when it comes to detecting.

The Puzzled Heart is the seventh Professor Kate Fansler mystery to appear in this bibliography. The others are *Poetic Justice* (156), *Death in a Tenured Position* (211), *Sweet Death, Kind Death* (238), *No Word from Winifred* (264), *A Trap for Fools* (308), and *An Imperfect Spy* (402).

458. DELFFS, D(UDLEY) J. (B. 1964) *THE MARTYR'S CHAPEL.* MINNEAPOLIS: BETHANY HOUSE, 1998.

Griffin Reed, the Episcopal rector at prestigous "Avenell College" in "Avenell," Tennessee, gets a distressing telephone call from Gentry Truman, the college's Pulitzer Prize winning writer-in-residence. Truman says that his own death is imminent and asks Reed for help. Then the line goes dead. Attempts to locate Truman prove fruitless until, several days later, Reed finds the writer's bloody corpse in a little-used, auxillary campus church known as the Martyr's Chapel. In part because the police think he may be the murderer, and in part because he wants to find the person who violated the Martyr's Chapel, Reed turns detective. He is assisted by his busybody sister, Bea, with whom he lives, and by Caroline Barr, an attractive assistant professor of English who is seen by Bea as a possible wife for her recently widowed brother. "Father Grif," as Reed is addressed by nearly everyone, is helped, too, by the willingness of so many people in Avenell to confide in him. Some of Reed's sleuthing focuses on members of the Truman family. In particular, he takes a long look at Marcia Truman, Gentry Truman's wife, who was a famous actress before moving to Avenell. He learns that Marcia has had difficulties adjusting to life in a small college town and to her husband's philandering. Despite the frequent focus on the Truman clan, there are many campus scenes in the crisply written story, and before the book reaches its surprising conclusion Reed finds that several members of the Avenell College community are hiding guilty secrets. Because Reed narrates the tale, and sometimes wanders from reporting upon his murder investigation to address the sensitive nature of the everyday activities associated with his campus position, the book is the only mystery in this bibliography that offers serious insight into the frustrations and rewards of a college rector.

Dudley J. Delffs holds a B.A. and an M.A. in English from the University of Tennessee. At the time this book was published he was an assistant professor of English at Colorado Christian University. Delffs has published religiously oriented non-fiction, as well as poetry and short stories. *The Martyr's Chapel* was his second novel.

459. DOBSON, JOANNE (B. 1942). *THE NORTHBURY PAPERS.* NEW YORK: DOUBLEDAY, 1998.

The Northbury Papers features the detection of Karen Pelletier, an untenured assistant professor in the English department at "Enfield College" in Massachusetts. When the book begins Pelletier is just starting work on a biography of Serena Northbury, a long-forgotten nineteenth-century novelist whose estate, "Meadowbrook," is near the Enfield campus. As part of her research, Pelletier interviews Dr. Edith Hart, Mrs. Northbury's medical-doctor granddaughter, who is Meadowbrook's current resident. Soon after the interview Dr. Hart dies in her sleep, and the local police define her death as suspicious. Professor Pelletier is drawn into the investigation of her death when, thanks to Dr. Hart's will, she becomes a suspect. Dr. Hart left Meadowbrook, along with $10,000,000, to Enfield College on the condition that the school use the bequest to establish the Northbury Center for the Study of American Women Writers. The will also specifies that Enfield is to employ none other than Karen Pelletier as the center's director for as long as she might care to serve. Although some of this story takes place off campus, while Professor Pelletier delves into the adumbrated history of the sometimes-malevolent Northbury family, there are many scenes at Enfield and many Enfield characters grace the book's pages. Readers get the opportunity, for example, to observe the behavior of stodgy Miles Jewell, the veteran chairperson of Enfield's English department, who vehemently opposes queer studies, multicultural studies, and senior seminars on Emily Dickinson. They also get entry to a faculty party, held by Enfield sociologist Jill Greenberg, at which the unmarried Greenberg joyously announces that she is four months pregnant but adamantly refuses to identify the father of her child. And readers get to watch the divorced Karen Pelletier and the divorced Avery Mitchell, Enfield's young president, fight valiantly against their politically incorrect romantic attraction for each other.

The Northbury Papers was Joanne Dobson's second Karen Pelletier mystery. The first Pelletier novel, *Quieter Than Sleep* (441), appears earlier in this bibliography. The Pelletier-Mitchell romance begins in *Quieter Than Sleep.* In that book readers learn that a relationship between an assistant professor and the school's president is forbidden at Enfield College because it violates a rule against fraternization between employees of unequal status. The third entry in the continuous Professor Pelletier series, *The Raven and the Nightingale* (474), also appears in this bibliography.

460. DOHERTY, P(AUL) C. *THE DEVIL'S HUNT.* NEW YORK: ST. MARTIN'S, 1998.

It is the summer of 1303 and things are not going at all well in Oxford. Several beggars have been killed and then decapitated. A shadowy figure known as the "Bell Man" is posting messages on church doors that call for treason against the crown and threaten the king's agents. At the university Robert Ascham, the archivist of Sparrow Hall, has been murdered with a crossbow in the college's locked library. And John Copsale, Sparrow Hall's regent, has mysteriously died in his sleep in what may or may not have been a natural death. Disturbed by these events, King Edward asks Sir Hugh Corbett, his longtime friend and ally, to go to Oxford to bring order out of the chaos. Before completing his royal detection assignment, Corbett finds that Sparrow Hall is a cauldron of treachery and intrigue, and he learns that fourteenth-century Oxford colleges, though walled off from their immediate environs, are not divorced from the broader political battles being waged around them. According to an author's note at the end of the novel, *Sparrow Hall,* though it has long ceased to exist, was once an actual Oxford college. Readers of *The Devil's Hunt* have the opportunity to observe many of the institution's medieval faculty, staff, and students and to learn about the often-raucous nature of academic life during the reign of Edward I.

Paul C. Doherty holds a doctorate in history from Oxford. *The Devil's Hunt* was his tenth Hugh Corbett mystery novel. At the time the book was published Doherty was the headmaster of a school in Essex, England. In addition to his Hugh Corbett series, Doherty has produced six other historical mystery series (using pseudonyms Michael Clynes, Ann Dukthas, C. I Grace, and Paul Harding), and his total output now exceeds thirty novels.

461. FOSTER, ROBERT. *MURDER GOES TO COLLEGE.* ELGIN, ILL.: TENTH MUSE PRESS, 1998.

Rare books are being stolen from the library of "Carlton-Stokes College," in "Walton," Missouri. As the investigation of the thefts begins, a security guard, apparently killed by a collapsing bookcase, is found dead in the library's stacks. Then Professor Jack Zinecor, visiting Carlton-Stokes from "Goodman College," in Quincy, Illinois, is shot dead in a deserted classroom building. The sleuth in the story is John Badger Smith, a Carlton-Stokes professor of English. He is helped by his elderly aunts, Bernadine and Blanche Badger, both former librarians, and by Doug Borto, the college's chief of buildings and grounds. Several Carlton-Stokes faculty members are suspects in the story, as is Dennis Marlin, a local gentleman farmer. Dennis Marlin is thought to be the possible book thief and murderer because he is a Harvard graduate, and the assembled detectives have difficulty thinking of any legitimate reason for an Ivy Leaguer to live near Walton, Missouri. Professor Smith, who is known to everyone in Walton as "Badger," has a terrible memory for the names of people he meets. On the other hand, he seems to have total recall of every book he has ever read, and much of his sleuthing consists of looking for parallels between the facts of the case and the plots of classic novels. In the end, Professor Smith solves the mystery when events at Carlton-Stokes turn out to mirror the plot of Nathaniel Hawthorne's *The Scarlet Letter.* Although churlish users of this bibliography might complain that *Murder Goes to College* is not the most polished of college mysteries, no one can contend that the book lacks literary references and allusions. Each chapter is prefaced by a passage from a poem or classic work of prose, and John Badger Smith, as he detects, constantly mentions literary characters and plot shards from classic novels.

Robert Foster received degrees from Culver-Stockton College, the University of Iowa, and Northern Illinois University. According to information on the cover of this book, Foster has spent most of his life teaching English "from grade school to graduate school." *Murder Goes to College* was Foster's second Professor Badger Smith mystery. At the time the book was published Robert Foster lived in Elgin, Illinois.

462. HARRISON, RAY(MOND) (VINCENT) (B. 1928). *DRAUGHT OF DEATH.* LONDON: CONSTABLE, 1998.

Edward Dawson, a science professor at University College, London, experiences what some might interpret as an enviable exit from worldly cares. While conducting field research on wort-spoiling bacteria at Tyrrell's Brewery, he falls into a vat of beer and drowns. Although the professor's death might have been the result of an accident, Detective Sergeant Joseph Bragg of the City of London police treats it as murder, and his investigations take him to University College, where he finds several people who had reason to end Dawson's life. His prime suspect is Roger Turnbury, a junior lecturer, whom Dawson had recently caught fudging research data. However, when Turnbury is battered dead with an iron bar in his University College rooms, the working-class Sergeant Bragg must delve deeper into the unfamiliar motives and manners of academics. The story is set in the 1890s. Along with his inquiries at University College, Sergeant Bragg looks at the internal rivalries at Tyrrell's Brewery, a relatively small, struggling firm that is facing increased competition from the giant Whitbread organization. In one interesting segment of the book Professor Dawson's death forces Tyrrell's management to engage in some hygienically questionable cost savings. Sergeant Bragg warns Tyrrell's chief brewer, a man named Lubbock, that Dawson, while drowning, probably voided into the two thousand gallons of beer in which he expired. Rationalizing that some religious sects in India routinely drink their own urine, Lubbock decides that Tyrrell's cannot afford to waste such a large quantity of its product, and he tells Bragg that the tainted suds will be sold as part of the firm's regular output.

Ray Harrison holds B.A. and M.A. degrees from the University of Cambridge. He became a full-time writer in 1983 after a thirty-year nonliterary career, first as an inspector of taxes with the British Department of Inland Revenue, and later as an executive with an insurance firm. At the time *Draught of Death* was published Harrison lived in County Cork, Ireland. *Draught of Death* was the sixteenth in a continuing series of Harrison turn-of-the-century mysteries to feature Detective Sergeant Joseph Bragg in the role of sleuth.

463. KELLY, NORA [NORA HICKSON (B. 1945)]. *OLD WOUNDS*. LONDON: HARPERCOLLINS, 1998.

This quiet, smoothly written mystery is set at and near "Stanton College." Located north of New York City on the banks of the Hudson River, Stanton is a school for women. The victim is Nicole Bishop, a Stanton undergraduate, who is found stabbed dead in a woods near the campus. Eli Pink, the local police chief, thinks that Arnold Mitchell, a strange, hermitlike man who lives near the college, may be the killer, but he lacks conclusive proof. The case becomes more complex when Pink investigates Nicole Bishop's background and finds that she was financing her higher education by working as a high-priced prostitute in Manhattan. Despite Eli Pink's efforts, the principal sleuth in the book is Gillian Adams, a professor of history at the "University of the Pacific Northwest." A Nora Kelly series-character detective, Professor Adams has taken leave from the university to stay with her ill mother, who lives in the Adams family homestead near Stanton College. Adams has arranged to teach an upper-level seminar at Stanton, and Margaret Bristol, the college's president, asks her to put her sleuthing experience to work by looking into Miss Bishop's death. Although there are many campus scenes in the book, *Old Wounds* is not the most "academic" mystery in this bibliography because some of the story's major participants are townspeople. Furthermore, Professor Adams spends some of her time using the telephone and e-mail to maintain her romantic relationship with Edward Gisborne, a Scotland Yard Inspector who appears in earlier Gillian Adams tales. Gisborne makes a brief visit to Stanton College during this story, and he offers some detecting advice. Readers who have admired Professor Adams's sleuthing in earlier adventures have an opportunity in *Old Wounds* to trace her detection talents to their source. When Adams arrives home to nurse her mother, she is pleased to find that her childhood collection of Nancy Drew novels is still in her old bedroom.

Three other Professor Gillian Adams mysteries by Nora Kelly appear in this bibliography. Those mysteries are *In the Shadow of King's* (243), *My Sister's Keeper* (354), and *Bad Chemistry* (367).

464. MANESS, LARRY. *STRANGLER.* NOVATO, CALIF.: LYFORD BOOKS, 1998.

When Albert DeSalvo was apprehended in 1962 and accused of being the "Boston Strangler," there were some who thought the police had arrested the wrong man. DeSalvo was eventually convicted of murdering thirteen women, and he was later killed in prison. As *Strangler* begins it is the 1990s and another spate of murders, reminiscent of those of the Strangler, is taking place in the Boston area. This time the victims are women connected with Harvard University's psychology department, and, more specifically, the women are all associated with a research project about serial killers. Lori Churchwell, a student interviewer, is the first to die. Then Ruth Hill, a secretary, is killed. And then Jan Rybicki, the roommate of Vicki Shaw, the project's principal investigator, is dispatched. The sleuth in this grim story is Jake Eaton, a Larry Maness series-character private detective. Eaton is asked by Bruce Drummond, a Boston newspaperman, to investigate because Drummond and Vicki Shaw are collaborating on a book. Bruce Drummond soon becomes yet another murder victim, as does Ellison Kitter, a Harvard professor of psychology, who experiences one of the most brutal professorial deaths in college-mystery fiction. Much of this corpse-filled tale takes place away from the Harvard campus, but most of the major participants have Harvard connections and Harvard faculty politics figures prominently in the story. Detective Eaton eventually ties the current murders to the original Strangler case, and readers learn how a deadly feud between two illustrious psychology professors has severely reduced the Harvard psychology department's status in the world of higher education.

At the time *Strangler* was published Larry Maness lived in Somerville, Massachusetts, where he worked as a novelist, playwright, and television writer. *Strangler* was his third Jake Eaton mystery novel.

465. MCINERNY, RALPH (B. 1929). *LACK OF THE IRISH.* NEW YORK: ST. MARTIN'S, 1998.

Notre Dame schedules Baylor University in football for the first time in the schools' long histories. The game, to be played at Notre Dame, is preceded by a conference on theology attended by faculty members from both institutions. Edwina Marciniak, the illiberal pastor of a small, "independent" Protestant congregation in South Bend, vehemently objects to Baylor, a Baptist university, meeting Catholic Notre Dame. To make matters worse in Pastor Marciniak's view, the game is to be held on Reformation Day, and she sets out to disrupt the event by whatever means might occur to her. A few days before the game Hazel Nootin, a Notre Dame office employee who is helping to organize the theology conference, is found bludgeoned dead in a campus parking lot. Then Elijah Phipps, a black Baptist from rural Texas who is Notre Dame's starting quarterback, mysteriously leaves the team and disappears. The detectives in the story are Philip Knight, a South Bend private investigator, and his corpulent brother, Roger, a Notre Dame professor of Catholic studies. Before the story ends the Knight brothers identify Mrs. Nootin's murderer and, of far more interest to the fans of Fighting Irish football, they also locate the missing Elijah Phipps. *Lack of the Irish* contains Notre Dame and South Bend characters in abundance and it takes its readers to many places on the Notre Dame campus. It also offers an extended account of the Baylor-Notre Dame gridiron contest. Pastor Marciniak, whose distaste for Catholicism is on display throughout the narrative, serves as a negative benchmark against which the ecumenicalism of all of the book's other major actors can be measured. As for Professor Roger Knight, a man with many interests, he proves to have a level of influence with the Notre Dame administration that real-life faculty readers will envy. Learning that one of his classes has been scheduled for Monday evenings, he arranges to have it moved to Thursday afternoon so that he can watch Monday Night Football.

Lack of the Irish was the second Ralph McInerny mystery to feature Philip and Roger Knight as detectives. The first Knight brothers novel, *On This Rockne* (445), is also set at Notre Dame. In addition to the two Knight brothers mysteries, two other novels by Ralph McInerny appear in this bibliography. They are *The Nominative Case* (336) and *The Search Committee* (338). *The Nominative Case* was published under the pseudonym Edward Mackin.

466. MURPHY, MARGARET. *CAGING THE TIGER*. LONDON: MACMILLAN, 1998.

The School of Life Sciences at a university in Chester, England, is in a state of extreme stress. It has made a poor showing in the national Research Assessment Exercise, and as a result academic departments are to be combined within the school, and many people with lose their jobs. Although the firings and the forced early retirements will be processed formally through all of the proper university committees, the real decision-maker will be Professor Edward Wilkinson. Until, that is, Professor Wilkinson is stabbed dead in his home. Wilkinson, whom one character in the story describes as "a walking phallus," had a history of philandering as well as a history of enjoying the exercise of power, and Inspector Jack Nelson and Detective Sergeant Terry Hackett of the Cheshire CID find that everyone in the School of Life Sciences, and many of their spouses, wanted him dead. The many suspects in the case include Helen Wilkinson (the professor's faculty-member wife), Ruth Marks (Helen Wilkinson's best faculty friend), Valerie Roberts (Edward Wilkinson's middle-aged secretary who was about to be sacked in favor of the professor's latest mistress), and John Ellis (a graduate student with a guilty secret). The book provides detail about the generally dismal domestic lives of most of its participants, including the two police investigators, and it offers some extended interior monologues. In a dramatic scene at the end of the tale Professor Wilkinson's murderer is identified, but many academic readers may feel that the human culprit in the story must share the role of villian with the Research Assessment Exercise. Developed in the mid-1990s, the scheme directs finanical resources to British academic departments according to their relative rankings of research productivity. In short, the more productive a department has been (or is seen to have been), the more money it gets in the future. Although real-life British academics probably are only too familiar with this program, *Caging the Tiger* contains some nuts-and-bolts information about the plan that may be instructive for Americans.

A resident of England, Margaret Murphy has worked as a schoolteacher. Her specialty is the teaching of children with dyslexia. *Caging the Tiger* was her third mystery novel.

467. ROBINSON, LILLIAN S. *MURDER MOST PUZZLING*. GREEN FARMS, CONN.: WILDCAT PUBLISHING, 1998.

The narrator of this story, Margaret ("Jamie") Jameson, takes her first full-time academic position. It is a temporary, one-year appointment as a teacher of poetry at "Ebbing College," a school located in the remote Pennsylvania town of "Jaegersville." Part of Jameson's assignment is to examine the recently unsealed papers of Elizabeth Ebbing Brock, a minor turn-of-the-century poet and a relative of the college's founder. In a journal Jameson finds that Mrs. Brock, in her youth, had a lesbian relationship. The journal is soon stolen, and a short while later Sharon Reilly, a professor of history, is found dead of a bashed skull in Jameson's office. Because the local police suspect that Jameson is the guilty party, she detects in order to find the real killer. Although Jameson is heterosexual (she has an affair early in the book with Preston Walters, Epping's dean of the faculty), the book features several lesbian characters in major roles, and the villain of the piece is guilty of homophobia as well as murder. The book contains an interesting scene late in the story in which Jameson and two women undergraduates emerge victorious after engaging in physical combat with the knife-wielding killer. It also contains a great deal of thoughtful discussion about faculty life in a small, nonelite college with a four-course-per-term teaching load. Jameson, whose doctorate is from the University of California at Berkeley, has produced several publications even before taking her initial teaching job, and her precocious productivity is the subject of considerable resentment at Ebbing College, where even senior professors have few, if any, publication credits.

Lillian S. Robinson received A.B. and M. A. degrees from Brown and a Ph.D. from Columbia. She has taught English at M.I.T., SUNY-Buffalo, and the University of Paris. At the time *Murder Most Puzzling* was published, she was a professor of English at East Carolina University in Greenville, North Carolina. *Murder Most Puzzling* was her first novel.

468. SKOM, EDITH. *THE CHARLES DICKENS MURDERS.* NEW YORK: DELACORTE, 1998.

At the University of Chicago in the late 1940s Jill Jansen, an undergraduate, was shot dead in her room in a women's residence hall. Her killer was never found. Fifty years later one of Miss Jansen's fellow students at Chicago tells her daughter about the unsolved crime. The daughter is Beth Austin, a professor of English at "Midwestern University." Her mother's tale spurs Professor Austin to seek out Miss Jansen's other surviving friends and acquaintances from Chicago in hopes of identifying the murderer. The professor eventually brings about some long-delayed justice, but not before the guilty party is responsible for another, contemporary murder. The book contains some modern-day scenes at Midwestern as well as many extensive flashbacks to Chicago. Except for Beth Austin, the primary academic characters in the story are 1940s Chicago undergraduates who, by the time the professor interrogates them, are well into late middle age. One of college-mystery fiction's more compulsively literate professor-detectives, Austin finds that several of the Chicago people she interviews resemble characters from Charles Dickens's novels. By recalling information about the Dickens characters she is able to gain insight into the actions and motives of her Chicago suspects.

The Charles Dickens Murders was the third in a continuing series of Edith Skom mysteries employing Professor Beth Austin as detective. It is the second Professor Austin adventure to qualify as a college mystery. The first, *The Mark Twain Murders* (317), appears earlier in this bibliography.

469. SODERQUIST, LARRY (B. 1944). *THE LABCOAT.* FRANKLIN, TENN.: HILLBORO PRESS, 1998.

The Labcoat is set at "Mellon University," a high-status institution located somewhere in the American South. The body of Professor Frank Willard is found in a stairwell of the chemistry building. He appears to have died of a heart attack, but before an autopsy can be conducted there is an administrative snafu and his corpse is cremated. The police then examine the lab coat Willard was wearing at the time of his death, find that it holds traces of cyanide, and deduce that they have a murder on their hands. The detective in the story is Eric Berg, a distinguished Mellon University professor of theology who somehow manages to hold a joint appointment as assistant chief of the Mellon University campus security force. A former military policeman, Berg packs a concealed .38-caliber Smith and Wesson pistol. He mounts an aggressive investigation of Professor Willard's death and finds a legion of suspects. Willard's wife, Doris, was known to have been unhappy about her husband's philandering. Madilyn Harris, a chemistry department secretary, was angry because Willard was trying to get her fired after she inadvertently deleted several chapters of his new book manuscript from an office computer. Several of Willard's chemistry-faculty colleagues saw him as a threat to their academic ambitions. And chemistry graduate student Janet Miller, the campus nymphomaniac, was displeased when Willard ended their affair. Miss Miller seems ready to move on to new couplings, however, and tries to seduce Professor Berg. He does not object, but Miller aborts the proceeding in surprise when her roaming hands detect the gun he carries on his right hip. Berg is helped in his sleuthing by Kate Michaelman, a beautiful police detective, one of several women in the story toward whom the married theologian feels a strong sexual attraction. Professor Berg finally brings *The Labcoat* to a successful conclusion when he shoots the villain of the piece dead with three hollowpoint slugs from his trusty sidearm.

Larry Soderquist was a professor at Vanderbuilt Law School and a counsel to a Nashville law firm when *The Labcoat* was published. Before becoming a professor he was a captain in the United States Army, practiced law on Wall Street, and at one point lived and worked in Moscow. Soderquist has published extensively in the area of securities law.

470. THOMAS, SCARLETT. *DEAD CLEVER*. LONDON: HODDER & STOUGHTON, 1998.

When Lily Pascale, a twenty-five-year-old aspiring actress, tires of an unsatisfactory romance in London, she returns to her home in Devon. Pascale holds an M.A. in literature, and she quickly finds a job teaching courses in creative writing and crime-and-horror literature at a local university. As she meets her first class, Pascale learns that Stephanie Duncan, one of the students on her attendance list, has just been brutally murdered. A few nights later Jason Davies, another of her students, dies after apparently taking an overdose of drugs. Then handsome Fenn Baker, a teaching colleague to whom Pascale finds herself becoming romantically attracted, suddenly disappears. After Pascale is visited by the police, who suspect that Baker may be involved in the Duncan murder, she begins to detect. By the end of the story, Pascale has experienced some serious personal peril but, thanks to her efforts, the university is cleansed of several miscreants. The novel contains an especially notable academic character—Professor Charles Valentine. The often-rude head of literature at the university, Professor Valentine is ordinarily too busy to engage in pleasantries with his staff and faculty, but he can find time to have affairs with his female students. Moreover, he is often too busy to consult with his faculty about day-to-day departmental matters. Readers who are classroom teachers will sympathize with the shocked Lily Pascale when a television news crew, sent by Professor Valentine without either her knowledge or her permission, suddenly bursts into her class to film a story about the grief felt by Stephanie Duncan's classmates. Professor Valentine is noteworthy as well for his curious relationship with Freddie Future, the charismatic leader of a local drug-taking cult. Thanks to his association with Mr. Future, Valentine is the only lecherous professor in college-mystery fiction who truly values the brains of his female conquests as much as he covets their bodies.

Scarlett Thomas was born in London. She has worked as a writer for several British magazines and for *The Guardian*. *Dead Clever* was her first novel and the first in a continuing series of Lily Pascale mysteries.

471. THOMAS-GRAHAM, PAMELA. *A DARKER SHADE OF CRIMSON*. NEW YORK: SIMON & SCHUSTER, 1998.

A Darker Shade of Crimson is a well-constructed college mystery that delves into some of the unsettling racial issues affecting contemporary academe. The book is narrated by Assistant Professor Veronica ("Nikki") Chase, the only African American in Harvard's economics department. Late one night, during a power blackout following a committee meeting in a Harvard classroom building, Professor Chase discovers Dean Rosezella ("Ella") Fisher lying face down and unconscious on a darkened staircase. The dean, who also is African American, is suffering from a bloody wound on the back of her head. An ambulance is called, but Dean Fisher dies on the way to the hospital. The police seem inclined to attribute Dean Fisher's death to an accidental fall, but Professor Chase, who considered the dean both a good friend and an African American role model, thinks that her death may have been murder, and she begins to add sleuthing to her already-crowded schedule of activities. *A Darker Shade of Crimson* includes several classroom scenes and almost bursts its seams with Harvard characters, of whom the most prominent is certainly Leo Barrett, the university's president. Barrett becomes a suspect when Professor Chase learns that he and Dean Fisher may have been having an affair. Other possible killers include two African American professors, whom the often-outspoken Dean Fisher was fond of criticizing for their pomposity and status climbing, and Christian Chung, the university comptroller, who may have been involved in an embezzlement scheme that Dean Fisher had recently uncovered. *A Darker Shade of Crimson* presents a well-crafted whodunit, but some academic readers may find Ella Fisher's unusual route to a deanship as fascinating as anything concerning the investigation of her murder. With only a Mississippi high-school education and a diploma from the "Letter Perfect Secretarial

School," Fisher was able to rise through the ranks of office workers at Harvard to become dean of students at the Law School.

Pamela Thomas-Graham graduated Phi Beta Kappa from Harvard and then followed that achievement by graduating from the Harvard Business School and Harvard Law School. At Harvard Law School she was an editor of the *Harvard Law Review.* At age thirty-two Thomas-Graham became the first black woman partner at McKinsey & Company, the world's largest management consulting firm. She has served on several boards of directors, including that of the New York City Opera. *A Darker Shade of Crimson* was her first mystery novel. In a lengthy acknowledgments section at the front of the book Thomas-Graham thanks over one hundred people, many of then connected with Harvard, for various forms of help and encouragement. Thomas-Graham's second mystery, a Yale whodunit titled *Blue Blood* (484), appears later in this bibliography.

472. WYLE, DIRK [PSEUD] (B. 1945). *PHARMACOLOGY IS MURDER.* HIGHLAND CITY, FLA.: RAINBOW BOOKS, 1998.

Dr. Geoffrey Westley, the medical examiner for Dade County, Florida, has a baffling case. Charles Cooper, chairperson of the pharmacology department at the "Bryan Medical School," has died suddenly from unknown causes, and Dr. Westley believes that one of the twelve surviving members of the pharmacology department may have administered an impossible-to-detect poison. Hoping to learn who had both the motive and method to kill Cooper, Dr. Westley asks Ben Candidi, a bright young laboratory technician in his office, to enroll for a Ph.D. in pharmacology at Bryan. Candidi, whose undergraduate degree is from Swarthmore, is to provide Dr. Westley information about the pharmacology faculty. In return, Westley will furnish financial assistance and, whatever happens in terms of his sleuthing, Candidi will be supported in the program until he obtains his doctorate. The long (384-page) story is narrated by Candidi, and through his words readers learn a great deal about pharmacology, about the education of pharmacologists, and about the vicious faculty infighting that characterizes Bryan Medical School's pharmacology department. They learn, too, that Bryan's unpleasant chief administrators, who do not take kindly to graduate students who double as snoops, are willing to employ physical as well as academic intimidation to protect their institution. The book contains many in-depth seminar and laboratory scenes, including one laboratory episode in which Candidi grinds the brains of a mouse into small particles. There is also a noteworthy off-campus scene at a Mensa Society meeting, and readers get to observe Candidi, a member of the society's Dade County chapter, competing with other attendees to see who can produce the wittiest and most brilliant conversation.

The person who employs Dirk Wyle as a pseudonym is a resident of Miami, Florida, who has spent thirty years in the field of biomedical science. *Pharmacology Is Murder* was the first mystery by Dirk Wyle.

473. CRIDER, BILL (B. 1941). *MURDER IS AN ART.* NEW YORK: ST. MARTIN'S, 1999.

This mystery is set at "Hughes Community College." The school is located near Houston at the intersection of Texas Highways 6 and 288. Val Hurley, a bachelor professor of art, is bludgeoned dead in his office with a statuette of *Winged Victory.* Hurley had recently been accused of sexually harassing Tammi Thompson, a married undergraduate. Shortly after Hurley's murder, Mrs. Thompson is found murdered as well. The principal police detective in the case is Eric Desmond, Hughes Community College's chief of security, but the person who solves the mystery is Sally Good, chair of the college's Division of Arts and Humanities. Many of the college's faculty members appear in this sharply satirical story. All of them, except Sally Good, are eccentric, and most of them are, at one point or another, suspects. There is, for example, Jack Neville, a professor of English, who helps Sally Good with her detecting when he can tear himself away from *Minesweeper*, a computer game to which he has become addicted. Then there is Perry ("A.B.D.") Johnson, another member of the English faculty, who has acquired his nickname after seventeen years of trying (and failing) to finish his doctoral dissertation. Johnson has perfected whining to a high art. He constantly complains about his treatment at Hughes Community College, and for a brief period he is a suspect because, just before Val Hurley's death, he had protested to Sally Good that Hurley had a better office chair. There are many appearances by Harold Fieldstone, Hughes Community College's excitable president, who tries to intimidate his faculty by wearing $900 suits, and *Murder Is an Art* is the only college mystery that features an academic "prison coordinator" in a prominent role. Jorge "Rooster" Rodriquez, a convicted murderer who has served his time, directs Hughes Community College's extensive program of in-prison classes for convicts.

Three other mysteries by Bill Crider appear in this bibliography. Those mysteries are *One Dead Dean* (290), *Dying Voices* (307), and . . . *A Dangerous Thing* (383). All three of those mysteries are set at "Hartley Gorman College" and feature Professor Carl Burns as sleuth.

474. DOBSON, JOANNE (B. 1942). *THE RAVEN AND THE NIGHTINGALE.* NEW YORK: DOUBLEDAY, 1999.

The victim in this involved-but engrossing mystery is Elliot Corbin, a nasty, pompous professor of English at "Enfield College." Enfield is a high-status private institution in western New England. An expert in the writings of Edgar Allen Poe, and the author of that classic work of scholarship titled *"The Transvestite Poe,"* Corbin is stabbed dead in his home on Thanksgiving Day. The protagonist-narrator of the story is Karen Pelletier, an untenured Enfield assistant professor of English. Professor Pelletier also functions as a Joanne Dobson series-character sleuth. A woman from a working-class background, Pelletier came to academe in mid-life after a divorce and after raising a daughter who is now a student at Georgetown. Shortly before Professor Corwin's murder she received an unsolicited package of documents pertaining to the relationship between Poe and Emmeline Foster, a nineteenth-century poet who killed herself when her love for Poe was not returned. Thanks to Pelletier's own professional interest in Poe, and because she already has been instrumental in solving two previous murder mysteries involving the Enfield English department, Lieutenant Piotrowski of the local police asks her to help sort through Professor Corbin's files and identify any leads that might arise from them. Soon someone breaks into Pelletier's office and steals some of the Emmeline Foster papers, and it appears that the Poe connection is, indeed, at the core of the matter. Almost all of *The Raven and the Nightingale* takes place on the Enfield campus and in the homes of faculty members. The book incorporates as much material about college politics, faculty gossipmongering, and the travails of teaching as any novel in this bibliography. It includes lengthy classroom scenes, deliberations about who will fill the prestigious "Palavar Chair" of Literature Studies at Enfield, scenes in which Professor Pelletier tries to advise students who are sometimes beyond advice, and an attempt by Pelletier to track down the sources in a case of undergraduate plagiarism. Among the Enfield College players in the tale, in addition to Professors Corbin and Pelletier, are Monica Cassale (the English department's chronically unhappy secretary who had a longstanding personal "arrangement" with Professor Corbin), Amber Nichols (an ambitious young instructor of English who aspires, among other things, to a job at Duke), Jane Birdwort (a fiftyish visiting poet), and Mike Vitale (an undergraduate whose propensity for irreverent argument enlivens Karen Pelletier's classes).

The Raven and the Nightingale was the third in a continuing series of Professor Karen Pelletier mysteries by Joanne Dobson. The first two novels in the series are *Quieter Than Sleep* (442) and *The Northbury Papers* (459). By the end of the *The Raven and the Nightingale* readers may wonder about the mental health of those Enfield College personnel who have survived three murder mysteries in three years (the time span covered by the series' first three novels). For Professor Pelletier the psychological stress has been at least partially offset by material rewards. In both *Quieter Than Sleep* and *The Raven and the Nightingale* she receives $500 per day for her services to the Enfield police.

475. GOLDEN, CHRISTOPHER. *BODY BAGS.* NEW YORK: ARCHWAY, 1999.

The protagonist of this gory story is Jenna Blake, a first-year student at "Somerset University" in "Somerset," Massachusetts. The daughter of a Somerset professor of criminology, Miss Blake hopes to become a doctor, and she takes a part-time position in the Somerset Medical School as a pathology assistant in the office of Dr. Walter Slikowski, Somerset's medical examiner. Her first day on the job she helps with the autopsy of a man who has died of a mysterious illness. Before his death the man had suddenly been transformed into a homicidal maniac, and he had killed three people, one of them for violating antismoking rules, in the lobby of the local courthouse. A few days later, while attending an international relations class taught by mild-mannered Professor Jose Mattei, Miss Blake witnesses Professor Mattei's death from the same disease. Before he falls dead, Mattei grows increasingly irritable, begins to bleed from his eyes, punches Miss Blake in the face, and among other acts of violence throws a male student through the window of his third-floor classroom. Soon Miss Blake's professor-father nearly contracts the same malady when a Central American insect that carries the disease is found in his ear. Eventually the medical mystery becomes a human one when a knife-wielding man chases Miss Blake across the Somerset campus and, after she narrowly escapes that attempt on her life, tries to shoot her in the medical school's autopsy room. Local police detective Danny Mariano and an FBI agent named

Jeffries handle some of the book's detection, but it is Jenna Blake whose plucky sleuthing breaks the case. *Body Bags* is not among the most elegant of college mysteries, but it describes autopsy procedures in relentless detail, and some professorial readers may consider the episode in which Professor Mattei physically assaults his own students a classic college-mystery scene.

Christopher Golden is a native of Massachusetts and a graduate of Tufts University. He is a commercially successful writer of dark-fantasy novels and comic books. Many of his novels have included vampires in their casts of characters.

476. HERNDON, NANCY. *CASANOVA CRIMES*. NEW YORK: BERKLEY PRIME CRIME, 1999.

Casanova Crimes is set at "Herbert Hobart University" in "Los Santos," Texas. The sleuth is Elena Jarvis, a detective with the Los Santos Police. A Nancy Herndon series-character, Jarvis has a long history of solving crimes at Herbert Hobart, and she has even been awarded an honorary doctorate by the university for her efforts on its behalf. In this tale Jarvis investigates the murder of Graham Fullerton, a Herbert Hobart undergraduate, who expires in his dorm room after ingesting cyanide. The poison was placed inside capsules that Fullerton thought held AZT, a drug he was taking to keep his early-stage case of AIDS from progressing. Despite having AIDS, Fullerton was one of the more sexually active students in college-mystery fiction, and he left behind a little black book with the names of thirty-one sexual contacts. Jarvis and her police associates suspect that one of the thirty-one women may be Fullerton's killer and, as the novel proceeds, they set out to interview the entire list. Meanwhile, Angus McGlenlevie, a professor of English who has recently impregnated one of his students, is wounded by a campus sniper, and Wayne Quarles Jr., a Herbert Hobart undergraduate who is about to be arrested for date rape, disappears from the university. Then, just to keep the Herbert Hobart administration from thinking that matters cannot get worse, the school's cleaning staff threatens to go on strike. *Casanova Crimes* incorporates wit and humor, and many of the Herbert Hobart characters are properly eccentric. Yet the book has a serious subtext. As Detective Jarvis tries to find out who killed young Mr. Fullerton (and as she tries to warn his sexual contacts of their danger), her efforts are seriously hindered by confidentiality laws and policies, and she is frustrated by widespread ignorance of AIDS, its causes, and its perils.

Two earlier Elena Jarvis mysteries by Nancy Herndon have entries in this bibliography. Those mysteries are *Acid Bath* (405) and *Lethal Statues* (426).

477. HOLTZER, SUSAN. *THE SILLY SEASON: AN ENTR'ACTE.* NEW YORK: ST. MARTIN'S, 1999.

When mysterious lights are seen in the sky over the University of Michigan campus, Professor T. Edison Stempel rushes to investigate. Although his academic discipline is history, Stempel has become a recognized authority on UFOs. One night, after the lights make another appearance, Stempel is found dead of apparent electrocution in an open area on the university's North Campus. A murder weapon cannot be located, and there is speculation that he was killed by aliens. The primary investigator in the story is Lieutenant Karl Genesko of the Ann Arbor police, but he does not lack for assistants. Police Sergeant Wes Kramer lends a hand; Zoe Kaplan, a student reporter for the *Michigan Daily*, does much of the important investigation; and Anneke Haagen, Genesko's fiancée, provides crucial support as well. Because the lights have attracted a gaggle of bizarre UFO followers to Ann Arbor, Genesko has many suspects among the visitors, but Conrad deLeeuw, a member of the Michigan faculty, comes under suspicion as well. Professor deLeeuw, a biochemist, had feuded for years with Stempel. A disbeliever in extraterrestrials, deLeeuw considered Stempel a charlatan and an opportunist for building a career around the study of a nonexistent phenomenon. Then there is Professor Ledyard, the chair of the university's history department. He admits to the police that he wanted to kill Stempel because he was tired of going to professional meetings and being "razzed" for harboring a "nutcase" in his department. The book offers its readers insight into a variety of explanations for UFOs, and it contains an unusual scene, before Professor Stempel's death, when Stempel and deLeeuw get so angry with each other that they engage in an impromptu wrestling match. In a preface the author credits the "famous Ann Arbor Sightings of 1966" for inspiring this story.

Two other mysteries by Susan Holtzer, *Bleeding Maize and Blue* (427) and *Black Diamond* (445) have entries in this bibliography. Like *The Silly Season*, *Bleeding Maize and Blue* and *Black Diamond* are set at the University of Michigan and feature Lieutenant Karl Genesko, Anneke Haagen, and Zoe Kaplan as sleuths.

478. ISENBERG, JANE. *THE "M" WORD*. NEW YORK: AVON, 1999.

Thanks to Dr. Altagracia Garcia, its new, aggressive president, "River Edge Community College" in Jersey City, New Jersey, is beginning to acquire academic respectability. President Garcia is upgrading the faculty, staff, and curriculum, and she is trying to improve the school's rundown physical facilities as well. As she brings changes to River Edge, Dr. Garcia develops strong supporters and strong enemies. One night, at an off-campus college fund-raiser, Dr. Garcia falls dead of cyanide poisoning after eating food prepared by Oscar Beckman, a student in the River Edge culinary arts program. The police arrest Beckman, but Sybil "Bel" Barrett, a River Edge professor of English who once taught Beckman in a children's literature class, thinks her former student is innocent. She enlists the help of Betty Ramsey, President Garcia's administrative assistant, and Illuminada Gutierriez, a professional private detective who moonlights by teaching criminal justice courses at the college, and the three middle-aged women begin to look for President Garcia's real killer. After some life-threatening detection, the sleuths identify the villain, who proves to have had an unusual motive for the murder. The tale is narrated by Bel Barrett, who takes every opportunity to inform her readers, and many of the female characters in the story, of her personal problems. Divorced with two grown children, Professor Barrett finds herself breaking out in an embarrasing blush when she meets attractive men such as Hudson County politician Thomas Koladnar. She worries that she has not yet become a grandmother; she experiments with techniques to ward off bladder problems; and she suffers from the stresses often associated with menopause. Several of the book's chapters are prefaced by e-mail messages to and from a menopause support group. Fortunately for readers interested in faculty life in an inner-city community college, the chatty Professor Barrett provides extensive reflection about that as well. Readers are told, for example, that while weekend grading of student essays can be time consuming, the process is similar to having hundreds of "pen pals." No matter how poorly composed the papers may be, each offers insight into how the writers, many of them "nontraditional" students, are trying to achieve the American dream.

Jane Isenberg was born in Passaic, New Jersey. Information on the cover of this book tells us that she has been teaching English to urban community college students since the 1960s. It also tells us that Isenberg is a resident of Hoboken, New Jersey. *The "M" Word* was Isenberg's first novel.

479. LAKE, M. D. [JAMES ALLEN SIMPSON]. *DEATH CALLS THE TUNE.* NEW YORK: AVON, 1999.

Professor Evan Turner dies in a fall from a cliff overlooking Lake Superior. Before his plunge Turner was a professor of music at a large Midwestern university that bears a remarkable likeness to the University of Minnesota. The professor was teaching in a university summer program being held at the school's lakefront conference center. The police write Turner's death off as an accident, but his mother, a wealthy university benefactor, is skeptical, and she asks campus security officer Peggy O'Neill to investigate. Officer O'Neill narrates the story, and as she conducts her inquiries she finds herself probing music department politics and looking back twenty years into another mysterious death. She also must deal with a gang of thieves, one of whom takes two separate opportunities to do her physical harm. Many members of the university's music faculty appear in the lively tale, as do several music-faculty spouses, and there are scenes on the university's main campus and at its conference center. Through it all, series-character Peggy O'Neill conducts herself with her usual mix of cynicism, guts, and good sense. She also reveals herself as the only campus security officer in fiction (or probably in real life) whose idea of leisure-time amusement is to read Oscar Wilde.

Campus security officer Peggy O'Neill appears as the detective in eight other M. D. Lake mysteries that appear in this bibliography. Those mysteries are *Amends for Murder* (313), *Cold Comfort* (325), *A Gift for Murder* (356), *Poisoned Ivy* (357), *Murder by Mail* (368), *Grave Choices* (410), *Once Upon a Crime* (411), *and Flirting with Death* (431).

480. PARKER, ROBERT B(ROWN) (B. 1932). *HUSH MONEY.* NEW YORK: PUTNAM'S, 1999.

Robinson Nevins, an African American, is an accomplished junior member of the English department at a large, Boston-area institution that is identified in this book only as "the university." Politically and academically conservative, Nevins is denied tenure by a departmental committee. Aware that incorrect rumors have circulated linking him with the apparent suicide of Prentice Lamont, a homosexual graduate student, he asks Spenser, Robert B. Parker's veteran series-character detective, to find the source of the false accusations and, if possible, to discredit them so that he might have his tenure decision reversed. Along with Hawk, his African American sidekick, Spenser goes to the university and finds that several members of Nevins's tenure committee entered into their deliberations with considerably less than open minds. For example, there is Amir Abdullah, once known as Dennis Caldwell, who fears that Nevins may soon supplant him as the university's most visible African American professor. And there is Lillian Temple, a dedicated feminist, who resents the fact that Nevins insists on teaching the works of "dead, white men" in his classes. Eventually, Spenser's sleuthing uncovers blackmail and murder. *Hush Money* contains a nonacademic subplot—in which Spenser is stalked by a seductive female client—and not all of Spenser's detecting in the Nevins affair takes place on university grounds. Nevertheless, the book more than qualifies as a college mystery. Displaying his customary iconoclasm, Spenser peppers his tale with jaundiced observations about academe and about the academic characters he meets during his inquiries, and the book is enlivened by a rousing fistfight in the university's African American Center, when Spenser and Hawk do physical battle with Professor Amir Abdullah and four of his "teaching-fellow" bodyguards.

Hush Money is the third of Robert B. Parker's Spenser mysteries to appear in this bibliography. The first two are *The Godwulf Manuscript* (177) and *Playmates* (315).

481. RAPHAEL, LEV (B. 1954). *THE DEATH OF A CONSTANT LOVER.* NEW YORK: WALKER, 1999.

The narrator of this engrossing college mystery is Nick Hoffman, an assistant professor of English at the "State University of Michigan." While picnicking on the campus with Angie Sandoval, an undergraduate, Hoffman witnesses a violent altercation between a group of religious zealots and a harassing gang of fraternity types. When the disturbance ends, one of the "preachers," undergraduate Jesse Benevento, lies dead of a stab wound. The son of a history professor at the university, young Mr. Benevento had a habit of threatening to denounce his professors (including Nick Hoffman) for "immoral" classroom remarks. As Detective Valley of the university police is launching the official investigation of Mr. Benevento's death, Lucille Mochtar, Hoffman's office mate, begins receiving hate mail, and someone throws a brick through a window in her home. Angie Sandoval soon disappears, and as Hoffman looks for clues through which to solve all of the above mysteries, he discovers Delaney Kildare, a Uriah Heep-like graduate student, dead of a bashed skull in the men's room of the building that houses the Department of English, American Studies, and Rhetoric ("EAR"). This skillfully written book offers a sensitive treatment of the relationship between Hoffman and Stefan Borowski, his writer-in-residence lover, and through the witty Hoffman's often-cynical narration it illuminates some of academe's more grotesque absurdities. Many readers will appreciate the opportunity, toward the middle of the book, to eavesdrop on an especially acrimonious EAR faculty meeting, and all real-life academics will recognize elements of themselves and their colleagues in the parade of faculty and graduate-student characters that crosses the story's pages.

Death of a Constant Lover was the third in a series of three Nick Hoffman novels by Lev Raphael. The first two novels in the series, both of which have entries in this bibliography, are *Lets Get Criminal* (434) and *The Edith Wharton Murders* (449).

482. ROBERTS, LES (B. 1937). *THE BEST-KEPT SECRET.* NEW YORK: ST. MARTIN'S, 1999.

Jason Crowell is a seemingly inoffensive first-year student at "Sherman College," a high-tuition school in the suburbs of Cleveland, Ohio. He also appears to be a young man whom someone is out to destroy. First, a circular goes up all over campus identifying him as the college's "rapist of the month." Although the flyer does not identify Crowell's victim or the source of the accusation (other than to claim that it is the work of a previously unknown organization calling itself the "Women Warriors"), Dean Arthur Lilly and Dorothy Strassky, the Sherman official in charge of investigating sexual harassment, are eager to believe its veracity. Then Ms. Strassky is bludgeoned dead in her home, and the police tag the unfortunate Mr. Crowell as their prime suspect. Hoping to minimize any publicity damage to Sherman, Dean Lilly suspends Crowell from the college, and shortly thereafter he is ejected from his apartment near the campus. After Crowell's rapid eviction, a stash of heroin is found concealed in his bathroom, and he is arrested as a drug dealer. The sleuth in this story is Milan Jacovich, a hardworking, down-to-earth Cleveland private investigator. Jacovich comes on the case after the rape accusation in response to a request for help from Reginald Parker, Crowell's high-school principal. Parker believes his former student is the victim of some horrible mistake. As Jacovich deals eventually with Crowell's whole collection of problems, he meets a variety of decidedly unlikeable Sherman College characters. Dorothy Strassky's idea of investigating sexual harassment is to treat all male suspects as guilty until proven innocent. Dean Lilly is a man so impressed with himself that he looks as if "he is waiting for someone to paint his full-length portrait." Mel Dunwoodie, the chief of Sherman's security police, is a nasty, ignorant bully. And Schuyler Dotson III, the young political scientist who is Jason Crowell's faculty advisor, proves to be far more interested in his own problems than in those of his advisees. In addition to the book's many scenes at Sherman College, it offers a brief excursion to another institution of higher education when Milan Jacovich takes time from his Sherman caper to visit his undergraduate, football-player son at Kent State.

Les Roberts was born in Chicago. He attended the University of Illinois and Roosevelt University. He has been a screenwriter, a jazz musician, an actor, and a television producer as well as a writer of mysteries. Roberts also has taught creative writing at Notre Dame College of Ohio and at Case Western Reserve. *The Best-Kept Secret* was Roberts's eleventh Milan Jacovich novel. At the time the book was written, Roberts lived in Cleveland Heights, Ohio.

483. SPRING, MICHELLE (B. 1947). *NIGHTS IN WHITE SATIN.* NEW YORK: BALLANTINE, 1999.

Katie Arkwright, a first-year student at Anglia Polytechnic University in Cambridge, disappears while attending a May Ball at St. John's College at the University of Cambridge. Anglia University is a lower-status school that coexists in Cambridge with the ancient university. Hoping to ward off negative publicity, Philip Patterson, the master of St. John's, hires private investigator Laura Principal to find the missing woman. A Michelle Spring series-character detective, Principal soon finds herself involved in a murder case when the corpse of Stephen Fox, a senior tutor at "St. Bartholomew's" College, turns up in the college's stately "Echo Room." Dr. Fox, who was dispatched by heavy blows to the skull, had recently informed Principal about a sexual attack on Miss Arkwright that occurred while she was serving as a waitress at a dinner of a St. Bartholomew's drinking club. During this artfully constructed novel Principal comes into contact, some of it life-threatening, with several University of Cambridge students, and her sleuthing leads her to spend time with the operator of a London escort agency and with the staff of a London brothel. Principal also learns about faculty rivalries at St. Bartholomew's and about the turbulent life of the Arkwright family. There are many scenes at the university, and in one cautionary episode readers discover that it may not be a good idea to explore for hidden spaces under the floors of Cambridge college rooms. Readers find, too, that virulent male chauvinism is alive and well in modern-day Cambridge, that upper-class arrogance can still be encountered among the university's undergraduates, and that even the most opulent surroundings do not insulate an academic institution from internal violence.

Nights in White Satin was the fourth novel in Michelle Spring's continuing Laura Principal series. Spring's first Laura Principal mystery, *Every Breath You Take* (400), appears earlier in this bibliography.

484. THOMAS-GRAHAM, PAMELA. *BLUE BLOOD.* NEW YORK: SIMON & SCHUSTER, 1999.

The sleuth in this brisk and twist-filled mystery is Veronica ("Nikki") Chase, an assistant professor of economics at Harvard. Professor Chase, who is the only African American in Harvard's economics department, travels to New Haven to comfort old friend Gary Fox, a Yale dean, whose wife, Amanda, has just been murdered. Amanda Fox, a professor at the Yale Law School, was found stabbed dead, with her left hand nearly severed from her body, in an inner-city New Haven neighborhood. Professor Chase becomes involved in detecting when she has strong doubts that Marcellus Tyler, an African American Yale undergraduate who is arrested for the crime, did the evil deed. As Chase works to find the real killer, she encounters several suspicious Yale students and professors, and she meets two New Haven African American ministers, one of whom provokes a violent racial disturbance on the Yale Old Campus. Chase also manages to enter most of Yale's outstanding landmarks, including the Beinecke Rare Books Library, the Chapel Street Art Gallery, the Yale Bowl, Mory's, and the Yale Co-Op. The book's climax comes at the top of Harkness Tower, where Chase and the villain engage in physical combat. Throughout the story the author raises issues associated with modern-day race relations in academe, and she touches, as well, on the ways wealth and poverty coexist side-by-side in New Haven. Many academic readers will admire Professor Chase's spirited detection, but some may wonder about Harvard's faculty-attendance policies. To sleuth in New Haven, right in the middle of the fall semester, Chase turns her classes in Cambridge over to teaching assistants. The head of her department, while not happy about her absence, does not insist on a firm deadline for her return.

Blue Blood was the second in a continuing series of Pamela Thomas-Graham "Ivy League" mysteries featuring Nikki Chase as detective. A Harvard mystery titled *A Darker Shade of Crimson* (470), the first novel in the series, has an entry earlier in this bibliography.

485. WELK, MARY. *SOMETHING WICKED IN THE AIR.* CHICAGO: KLEWORKS PUBLISHING CO., 1999.

A rock resembling a rune stone is found on the campus of "Bruck University" in "Rhineberg," Illinois. Sensing an opportunity for professional fame, Professor of English Andrew Littlewort tries to prove that the stone is legitimate and that the Vikings penetrated as far into central North America as Rhineberg. As Littlewort's investigations are proceeding, Emma Reiser, the Rhineberg postmistress, dies after mysteriously tumbling down a staircase in the post office, and the professor comes under suspicion of murder because he was seen running from the building shortly after Ms. Reiser's fall. The detection in this sometimes-comic tale is handled by Caroline Rhodes, a middle-aged registered nurse at a Rhineberg hospital. A Mary Welk series-character detective, Rhodes already has solved one mystery in Rhineberg, and she is asked by Garrison Hurst, Bruck's president, to look into the Reiser matter because Hurst fears that the police and FBI are convinced of Professor Littlewort's guilt. Rhodes is assisted in her sleuthing by Carl Atwater, a septuagenarian professor of history, whose girth and beard give him a marked resemblance to Santa Claus. Atwater also is part owner of a local watering hole known as the Blue Cat Lounge. Although some of this tale takes place in off-campus parts of Rhineberg, there are many campus episodes, and many Bruck University characters have important roles. In fact, *Something Wicked in the Air* is one of very few college mysteries to feature a campus gardener among its major players, and academic readers may be interested in learning what motivates that individual, improbably named Charlie Branch, to take such loving care of the university's colorful flower displays.

Mary Welk graduated from St. Anne's Hospital School of Nursing in Chicago, and for thirty years she worked as a registered nurse. During her nursing career she found time to appear as a guitarist with folk music groups and to write songs, plays, and short stories. *Something Wicked in the Air* was her second novel. Her first, *A Deadly Little Christmas* (Chicago: Kleworks Publishing Co, 1998), also employs

Caroline Rhodes as detective. In *A Deadly Little Christmas* Rhodes discovers the identity of the person responsible for a fatal bombing at the Rhineberg hospital that employs her. Although *A Deadly Little Christmas* lacks sufficient "academic" content to qualify as a college mystery, on several occasions the book takes its readers onto the Bruck University campus, and some denizens of Bruck, most notably Professor of History Carl Atwater, have significant parts in the story.

486. WOLZIEN, VALERIE. *THE STUDENT BODY.* NEW YORK: FAWCETT GOLD MEDAL, 1999.

The sleuth in this cozy mystery is Susan Henshaw, a middle-aged, happily married woman who returns to college after twenty-five years of child rearing. The school Henshaw attends is not identified, but it is in a suburban town within easy driving distance of her home in the wealthy community of "Hancock," Connecticut. One day, in an astronomy laboratory, Mrs. Henshaw inadvertently exchanges backpacks with Meredith Kenny, her much younger lab partner, and a short while later Miss Kenny is found dead in her off-campus apartment. She has been strangled with the straps from Henshaw's backpack. Henshaw quickly becomes a suspect in the killing, and she embarks on detection after it appears that Michael O'Reilly, the investigating police officer, is about to arrest her. Henshaw is assisted by "Jinx" McCulley, another older, returning student whom she meets early in the book. Most of Henshaw's inquiries focus on Meredith Kenny's college-related activities, which included an affair with a corpulent, married professor of psychology, mysterious meetings in an expensive Greenwich, Connecticut, restaurant with an aging professor of creative writing, and (though she had never been married) regular attendance at the gatherings of a campus support group for divorced women. Henshaw also looks into Miss Kenny's relationship with Rick Dawson, a handsome graduate-student teaching assistant. Unhappily for Mr. Dawson, he is abruptly erased from Henshaw's list of suspects when he is shot dead in his sociology department office. The leisurely story includes many classroom scenes and student-professor conferences, and it provides painstaking detail about the problems faced by women who reenter college after years of domestic life.

Valerie Wolzien was born in Ohio, raised in New Jersey, and attended colleges in Colorado and Alaska. *The Student Body* was the twelfth Valerie Wolzien mystery to feature suburban housewife Susan Henshaw as detective.

Bibliography of Articles, Books, and Journals About College-Mystery Novels

Auden, W. H., "The Guilty Vicarage," *The Dyer's Hand and Other Essays.* New York: Random House, 1948, 146–158.

In this essay the celebrated poet and devoted mystery reader W. H. Auden offers a general analysis of detective fiction and, in the process, creates the classic statement about college mysteries. Fundamentally, Auden argues that an institution of higher learning in detective fiction is often portrayed as a "Great Good Place," a closed and innocent environment. Thus, detective novels with college or university settings are rendered effective as literature because of their inherent irony; crimes occur where crime would be least expected. The same novels also conclude with optimistic fantasies. The unexpected crimes violate and disrupt the institutions, but thanks to the books' detectives the criminals are apprehended, expunged from the scene, and the institutions are restored to their original states of grace.

Blythe, Hal & Charlie Sweet. "The Case of the Academic Mystery Writer." *Clues* 8, no. 1, (spring/summer 1987): 59–66.

Two academicians, who are themselves mystery writers, suggest eight hypotheses, any or all of which might explain why so many members of college and university faculties write mystery fiction. The article does not concentrate on why so many academicians write college mysteries per se, but readers who are concerned with that issue might find hypothesis 6 ("The Vengeance Is Mine Theory") especially heuristic.

Carter, Ian. *Ancient Cultures of Conceit: British University Fiction in the Post-War Years.* London & New York: Routledge, 1990.

This book is a sweeping review of post–World War II British fiction that is set at universities. The book offers many discussions of college mystery novels, and for purposes of establishing historical background, the author often refers to British college mysteries of the 1930s and 1940s.

Charney, Hanna. *The Detective Novel of Manners.* Rutherford, N.J.: Fairleigh Dickinson University Press, 1981

The author argues that the modern detective novel has many of the features of the English novel of manners, in particular the creation of a fictional world that only seems to mirror real life. The text includes discussions of many college mysteries.

Cook, Wister. "Crime and Comedy on Campus" in *Comic Crime*, ed. Earl F. Bargainnier. Bowling Green, Ohio: Bowling Green State University Press, 1987.

This essay looks at comedy in college mysteries, largely in terms of the ultimate intentions of the mysteries' authors. The writer of the essay concludes that college mysteries contain a wide range of comedy. At one end of the scale are college mysteries that celebrate higher learning. At the other extreme are college mysteries that satirize and pass "ironic judgement" on academe. The essay includes references to many of the wittiest novels in the college-mystery subgenre.

Cook, Wister. "Death by Administration: Presidents, Deans, and Department Heads in Academic Detective Novels." *Clues* 9, no. 1 (Spring/Summer 1988): 95–105.

The author contends that administrative characters in college mysteries tend to be "pretenders." In particular, they only pretend to be committed to one of the central missions of higher learning—the search for the truth. The article is based on a survey of twenty-five college mysteries.

DePaulo, Rosemary. "Scholastic Skullduggery." *The Armchair Detective* 21, no. 3 (Summer 1988): 280–284.

With reference to several exemplars of the college-mystery subgenre, the author raises and offers answers to a series of questions. Why are institutions of higher learning so often the settings for whodunits? What motivates fictional academics to commit crimes? Why do fictional academics make good detectives? And why are professors so often the authors of college mysteries?

Gottschalk, Jane. "Mystery, Murder, and Academe." *The Armchair Detective*, April 1978, 159–169.

A survey of college mysteries and sleuthing professors (some of whom detect on campus and some of whom do not). With regard to college mysteries, the author concludes that "there is no formula; there are multiple approaches."

Kramer, John. "How to Become a Series-Character Professor-Detective." *Clues: A Journal of Detection* 9, no. 2 (Fall/Winter 1988): 75–94.

With his tongue well into his cheek the author offers a series of guidelines (for example, "Cultivate Your Eccentricities") for real-life professors who might want to become series-character professor-detectives. He supports his prescriptions by referring to fifty-one series-character professor-detectives in mystery fiction, some of whom sleuth in on-campus college mysteries.

Krouse, Agate Nesaule & Margot Peters. "Murder in Academe." *Southwest Review* (Autumn 1977): 371–378.

After reviewing some early college-mystery novels and finding that those mysteries seem consistent with W. H. Auden's "Great Good Place" formulation, the authors contend that many college mysteries of the 1960s and 1970s depict academic environments that are so flawed that a "return to grace" seems to be impossible.

Marchino, Lois. "The Female Sleuth in Academe." *Journal of Popular Culture* 23, no. 3 (Winter 1989): 88–100.

This article deals with female detectives, most of them professors, who sleuth in college-mystery novels. Special attention is paid to Amanda Cross's Professor Kate Fansler. The author contends that many modern-day creators of female sleuths in college mysteries write their novels as critiques of sexism and other ills in academe.

The Journal of Mystery Readers International 4, no. 3. (Fall, 1988).

Each issue of this popular journal has a specific theme, and this issue is devoted to "academic" mysteries. It contains twenty-three short essays and collections of reviews, some of them written by mystery-fiction authors. Although a few of the entries deal with high-school mysteries, most deal with mysteries set at colleges or universities. College-mystery authors with pieces in the issue are Robert Barnard, Charlotte MacLeod, Margaret Maron, and Herbert Resnicow.

The Journal of Mystery Readers International 12, no. 4 (Winter 1996–1997).

This is the second issue of *The Journal of Mystery Readers International* to have "academic" mysteries as its theme. It offers thirty brief essays, columns, and collections of reviews by a variety of people, most of whom write about mysteries set at institutions of higher education. Authors of college mysteries who have contributions in the issue are Catherine Aird, Robert Barnard, P. M. Carlson, Susan Holtzer, Jane Langton, Jessica Mann, Janet Neel, Betty Rowlands, Edith Skom, and Guy Townsend.

Nover, Peter. *The Great Good Place? A Collection of Essays on American and British College Mystery Novels.* Frankfort/M & New York: Peter Lang, 1999.

This is first book-length publication to focus exclusively on college mysteries. The anthology includes fourteen essays that cover, among many topics, crime and comedy on the campus (Uwe Baumann), Oxbridge mysteries (Andrew Taylor), the professoriat and the police force (Barrie Hayne), and the history of the American college mystery (John Kramer).

Rockett, Will, "Tension at the Verberant Core: Academic Subcultures and Their Effects in British and Americana College Fiction." *Clues* 12, no. 2 (Fall/Winter 1991): 91–113.

The author explores the attraction of college mysteries for academic readers, and he ranges through the subgenre for many examples to illustrate his discussions.

Scheper, George L. *Michael Innes.* New York: Ungar, 1986.

This book is a review of the life and works of John Innes Mackintosh Stewart, the Oxford don and prolific writer who often employed the pseudonym Michael Innes. Innes is the author of *Death at the President's Lodging* (34), first published in 1936 and now generally considered an archetypical novel in the college-mystery subgenre. Chapter 4 of Scheper's book, a chapter titled "Bodley Harm: Murder in the Great Good Place," looks at Innes's several college and prep-school mysteries in the context of W. H. Auden's seminal formulation about detective stories with academic settings. The chapter also contains discussions of non-Innes college mysteries, especially Dorothy L. Sayers's *Gaudy Night* (30).

Title Index

Author Index

Character Index

This index refers only to characters mentioned in the annotations of the mysteries. The annotations mention most of the major participants in the stories, but the mysteries contain many unindexed minor characters. The annotations do not identify villains. Hence, while many villains appear in the annotations (and in the index) because they play important parts as the stories proceed, other villains emerge as noteworthy characters only at the ends of the tales, and those villains appear neither in the annotations nor in the index.

Index of Colleges and Universities

** indicates that the institution that appears in the novel is unnamed or bears a name other than that of the actual college or university it greatly resembles.*

About the Author

John E. Kramer Jr. is Professor Emeritus of Sociology at the State University of New York College at Brockport. He holds an A.B. from Dartmouth College, an M.A. from George Washington University, and M.A. and Ph.D degrees from Yale. After three years at the University of Missouri at St. Louis, Professor Kramer taught at SUNY-Brockport from 1968 until his retirement in 1997. During the 1974–1975 academic year, he was a visiting professor at the University of Kent at Canterbury in Great Britain. Professor Kramer has published extensively in urban sociology, political sociology, and the sociology of literature. In the latter area most of his publications have focused on works of fiction that are set in the world of higher education. Academe in Mystery and Detective Fiction is Professor Kramer's fifth book. His other books are North American Suburbs (Glendessary, 1972), Strategy and Conflict in Metropolitan Housing: Suburbia Versus the Greater London Council, 1965–1975 (Heinemann, 1978) with Ken Young, The American College Novel: An Annotated Bibliography (Garland, 1981), and College Mystery Novels: An Annotated Bibliography Including a Guide to Professorial Series-Character Sleuths (Garland, 1983) with John E. Kramer, III.